# The Meeting that Changed the World

*The Council of Jerusalem,* AD *49*

— MICHAEL KNOWLES —

Sacristy
Press

**Sacristy Press**
PO Box 612, Durham, DH1 9HT

www.sacristy.co.uk

First published in 2019 by Sacristy Press, Durham

Sacristy Limited, registered in England & Wales, number 7565667

**British Library Cataloguing-in-Publication Data**
A catalogue record for the book is available from the British Library

ISBN 978-1-78959-026-5

*I dedicate this work to my wife Jane without whose support and patience it would never have been written; and to our three children Helen, Anna and Paul and his wife Kimie, and the grandchildren.*

# Acknowledgements

There are three people whose assistance and input I must acknowledge. David Allan, my brother-in-law, a biochemist and a convinced and argumentative atheist, took a most active, helpful and challenging interest in the subject matter that the book addresses. I would not say that he has made a comment on absolutely everything in it, but certainly on many matters, including the fundamental issues. Time and again his comments forced me to show the evidence for and defend my conclusions. David Roffe is an English medieval historian who specializes in the study of Domesday Book, about which he has published major works. He has a very extensive experience in the interpretation and use of medieval manuscripts, and his research interests include the Danelaw, landscape history, the Church at that time and insanity in the Middle Ages. He has helped me in various ways. One was how to read an historical document. That input has provided the most useful of insights; it influenced how to read Luke's texts. He also brought what I might call a Church-of-England agnosticism to bear upon the theological contents and conclusions of the research this book contains. He is also a self-taught computer wizard. His help in that regard just cannot be over-estimated. He has put what I have written into the shape publishers require. I am also most grateful to Natalie Watson, commissioning editor. Her perspective on and suggestions about many issues in this book have been most helpful and incisive, indeed invaluable and indispensable. Needless to say, any errors of fact or interpretation are mine. I also wish to acknowledge, with equal gratitude, the contribution made by two cultures which have shaped my Christian outlook, that of the missionary Society of the Divine Word and that of the Catholicism I was born into and brought up with in Salford and Manchester.

# Contents

# A Note on the Cover

The book's cover picture, an icon of the twelve apostles, shows four Christian men from a very early period in Church history. There is no woman in it. No piece of art of any form portraying a woman from those early years of the Church has been found. Given the immense contribution made by women to the origin, the life and the spread of Christianity in the years leading up to the Council of Jerusalem, their absence from the cover is a matter of great regret to the author and the publishers of this book.

The presence and the contribution of women to Christianity in its very origins are attested to both in the four Gospels and the Acts. Mary gave birth to and brought up Jesus to manhood. Luke and Matthew provide details enough. No other person, no apostle, did more than her. Her presence in his ministry, and that of other women such as Mary Magdalene and the sisters Martha and Mary, is recorded. Three women stood with Jesus beneath his cross when all except one man had fled. The significance of that is beyond adequate description. So is the astonishing fact that it was women who discovered the resurrection and told the apostles. That was the very first, and the greatest, gospel/good news action. Women shared in the meetings held by the apostles after the Ascension and before Pentecost Sunday, as Luke tells us. They didn't just share in prayers and meetings however. As Luke informs us, they shared also in the harsh and savage opposition of the Jewish Council to the Church, to being seized and sent into prisons and to "the murderous threats" of Saul and being forced by him all the way from Samaria and Judea to Jerusalem.

We cannot be sure but it is likely that the Council of Jerusalem itself was held in the house of Mary, the sister of Barnabas. Her house was able to hold, again as Luke tells us, a large number of people and women would definitely have been among them. The apostles inclusive of both

Peter and Paul were accompanied on their missionary journeys by their wives; and Philip called the evangelist had three daughters, all of them recognized and called prophets. In a word, women were very active in the foundation years and work of the Church.

For all these many reasons, and just by using plain eyesight and common-sense experience to recognize the obvious, we know that women were part and parcel of the whole Christian venture in the first century, inclusive of the Council of Jerusalem. It is unfortunate that no suitable artwork could be found for the cover of this book that testifies to their role.

# Introduction

The Council of Jerusalem, held in the year 49, some fifteen or more years after Christ's death, has been called the most important meeting ever in the history of Christianity.[1] That is some statement. It is, however, a correct one to make, because if the Council hadn't been convened and hadn't taken the decisions it took on what constituted Christian belief, Christianity would not have survived more than two or three more decades. It would have been no more than just another sect within Judaism and more likely than not would have disappeared with the destruction of the Temple in the year 70, or at best lingered and limped along a little bit longer. That did not happen. The Council enabled Christianity not just to survive but to grow and expand by establishing it as a religion distinct from the Judaism that had given it birth. This was brought about by clarifying what its distinct and essential beliefs were about Jesus and his role in God's eternal plan to save humanity from the consequences of sin and bring about reconciliation with himself. The Council established Christianity as a religion distinct and separate from all others, and, by reason of the decisions it made, made it possible that Christian beliefs could be placed before all humanity with genuine confidence that they might be accepted. Christian beliefs have an understanding and a perspective on the nature of God and on humanity which are different from those of all other religions, cultures and philosophies of life. With that achievement the Council changed the world.

Yet, for all its importance the Council has been consistently overlooked, and it is a safe bet that most Christians, even some who have some knowledge of Church history, if asked to give the names of its councils, will mention such as Nicaea (325), Ephesus (431), Chalcedon (451), Trent (1545–63), Vatican I (1869–70), Vatican II (1962–5), but not Jerusalem. The reason may well be that the issue the Council addressed and the significance of what it achieved have never in fact been adequately studied

1

and appreciated, let alone taught, because, superficially considered, it seems a matter which is now taken for granted. Regrettably its importance has neither been sufficiently perceived nor understood.

The Council dealt with a disagreement between members of the Church at its foundation, particularly in Jerusalem and Judea, over what is the most fundamental doctrine of Christianity, namely its understanding of Jesus Christ and what constitutes salvation. There was a powerful faction within Jerusalem, initially the headquarters of the Church, which was challenging the understanding of the role of Christ in the saving plan of God which Peter and his fellow apostles had come to over the previous 15 years. The challenge came to a head in the year 49 and was addressed at the Council. In the statements made by Peter it formulated and established that identity of Christian belief about the nature of God's salvation of humankind and the role of Jesus in it. The issue is no longer in contention. However, its outcome at the time had consequences, one of which was a refusal by some members to accept and apply what the Council had decided, just as happened after later Church councils, even in our own lifetime.

At first glance, the issue in the year 49 might appear to be one just about religious practices and rituals. The faction, which might be called the Judaic faction, wanted the new Church and all who converted to it, inclusive of Gentiles, to hold to the religious practices and rituals of Judaism. After all, first Christians such as the apostles themselves had been brought up and had lived as Jews all their lives. Luke refers to it as the Law of Moses. The faction insisted (Acts 15:1) that the performance of practices such as regulations about food and particularly circumcision was necessary for salvation, and, consequently, if Gentiles wished to be admitted to Church membership and be saved, they had to live by those practices. What it amounted to was that the members of the faction were claiming that it was not "the grace of the Lord Jesus" (Acts 15:11) that brought about our salvation but the performance of these Jewish rituals. The doctrinal implications were immense. Their claim would have made the Church a Jewish sect, and that would then have made it extremely difficult, in practice impossible, to preach the Christian gospel with any real hope of success to people who were not Jewish. That is what the first 15 chapters of the Acts are about.

"Go into all the world and preach the gospel to all creation" (Mark 16:15) was the instruction Jesus gave to the apostles after his resurrection and before his departure into heaven. That is of course difficult to do in many places today where other religions, as in the Middle East, and their governments, as in the Far East, erect barriers against it. However, we need to look carefully at ourselves in the Western world, by which I mean Europe, the Americas, the Philippines, Australia and New Zealand, where Christianity is strongest and has the bulk of its membership, and consider with honesty and insight if the Church can successfully carry out Christ's instruction while it continues to conduct itself in ways which are unacceptable within Western culture and which are incompatible with what our culture firmly regards as positively good. Within the Catholic Church, which has over 50 per cent of the total Christian population, two examples of widespread unacceptable attitude and behaviour are its male–female relationships and the way it governs itself. It is an attitude and behaviour which is deeply antagonistic to modern Western culture. It offends, and it alienates. We have to consider if the Church is itself thereby maintaining and "manning" barriers to the preaching of the gospel of Jesus.

My contention is that it is now the time when the leadership of today's Church, with insight and discernment, with courage and honesty, must take a fresh look at the Christianity it has created over the past two millennia, a Christianity in which we have been brought up and lived all our lives up to this second decade of the first century of the third millennium and consider what needs to be changed, and then change it. Living things that do not change die. Acceptance by the apostles and first disciples in council in the year 49 of the necessity of fundamental change saved the Church from being just a small sect within Judaism and dying out. That gave it its own identity and independent existence, and at that time and until recently it enabled it to take the gospel to almost every nation.

One of the two main issues before the Council in the year 49 was about how human beings are saved from the consequences of sin, about how humanity in God's plan is to be reconciled to him. Is it by the free gift of God in the person of Jesus Christ, or is it by continuing with and carrying out the Law? Peter's reply was a firm pronouncement:

"We believe that it is by the grace of the Lord Jesus that we are saved" (Acts 15:11). The issue the Council addressed was solidly Christological. What the apostles and elders stated in their letter to the three churches of Antioch, Syria and Cilicia, who had asked the apostles to resolve the issue, was that the version of Christianity proposed by the Judea/Jerusalem faction within the Church would have "hollowed out/plundered your souls" (15:24), robbed them of a true understanding of what was the essence of Christianity. The achievement therefore of the Council was to define Christianity. It was as important as that. It had to be convened to resolve the conflict between two versions or understandings of what Christianity was and what it was for. Nothing in Church history has been more important. The decision the Council came to, the choice it made, liberated Christianity from Judaism and enabled the Church to take the gospel into the Gentile world. If the Apostolic Church had demanded of the non-Jews, the Gentiles, when it preached the gospel to them, that they adopt the Jewish way of life, it would not have been possible for the Church to spread throughout the world, which was the command of Christ.

Today, in the second decade of the twenty-first century, that issue has returned, though in a different way. The Catholic Church is now two thousand years old. In that long period of time it has made many decisions, about faith and morality, about what is to be believed and how its members should behave; and it has had to do that within the human cultures which it has inhabited. There are grounds to say that the four most important cultural blocs in today's world are those of the West, of the Middle East, of India and of China. Christianity has had a massive influence on the whole culture of the West, on its legal systems, its moral codes, its art, its politics, its educational and scientific outcomes and, as a result, the day-to-day behaviour of its peoples and the relationships of men and women. As a result of Christianity women in the cultural West enjoy a level—by no means a perfect level but a level nonetheless—of education, freedom and equality with men which is actively opposed in Islamic countries and as yet not achieved in India and China. Nor within the Catholic Church. That situation will be explored in various places in this work. Western culture in many important ways is proving attractive to the populations of those other cultures, if there is the political and religious freedom to make it achievable and for people to choose.

That same Western culture is now pulling away in a number of important moral and scientific matters from its ancient Christian roots, which are by no means its only roots of course. It is important to realize that the Western world and Western culture have radically changed in certain most important ways which are benefiting humanity greatly. Over time, be it since the Enlightenment or later throughout the Industrial Revolution or both, a monumentally huge and powerful intellectual bloc or movement or establishment has built up which now owes no allegiance to Christianity whatsoever, which repudiates religious faith in the interests of what it considers evidence. It rejects creationism and most aspects of religion in favour of either evolution or agnosticism and, of course, atheism; and in many ways, and often openly, it is hostile to religion. This is the case in countries the culture of which has Christian roots, because in those countries there is the freedom for such a bloc to exist and to expand. Intellectual as well as political and religious freedom is a major aspect of the philosophy of the Western world.

It is not the case in all cultures of course. In some Islamic countries, for example, such intellectual freedom is not permitted, and atheism, even agnosticism, if made public, can be dangerous for its adherents. However, in the West it is what the Church has to deal with. Firmly and squarely in the public market place of debate, of proof and evidence, it has to argue its corner like any other movement, it cannot appeal to anything other than its arguments and how its members behave; and even with its own membership, living and operating actively in societies which are secular, it has to provide evidence of its worth. Its history, its standing, its past achievements are no final argument. They help but they are not decisive. What matters is the content of its gospel, how its gospel is presented and the arguments for it, how the Church governs itself, the social relationships it promotes, and how its membership behaves. The Western world has changed. Religion is no longer an object of reverence, it has to prove itself. Christianity has achieved many good things in and for the lives of people, but so have modern science, healthcare and technology. The Church has got to look carefully at what the achievements of all three are, and with all the positivity and support it can muster, and where applicable, take them into its own life. That is the least the church leadership must do. Otherwise it will not retain the adherence of its membership or exercise influence within the societies where it exists.

To an extent Pope Francis is pointing the Catholic Church in a direction which might open it to the changes that are required or at least to a serious consideration of them. He represents a beginning of a long term process of reform which has to happen. The Church cannot stay where and how it is. If it does not change, it will continue to shed membership in great numbers; it will attract few new members; and its priesthood will be reduced to a trickle. That prospect, however, does not put off the opponents to change within it. The situation has been reached where some cardinals and bishops, some members of the Vatican curia and some theologians are openly challenging the direction in which Pope Francis is pointing the Church to go. They are a faction that wants the Church to hold to the version of moral and sacramental teaching which they have inherited and believe should be enforced without any change, universally across the world and forever. In certain most important areas they live in the past and want the Church to remain there with them.

Pope Francis, the successor of Peter, who took the infant Church through the immense changes endorsed at the Council of Jerusalem, is proposing to the Church that there are reasons for re-consideration. The disagreement which we are witnessing between Pope Francis and a powerful faction is about what sort of church will be on offer to the world of the twenty-first century, and indeed to its membership. What consideration is the Church giving to the radical changes that have happened in human society over the last two to three hundred years and are happening now with great speed and immense force? What sort of church, what changes in it, are required to enable it, with a reasonable prospect of success, to offer the gospel of the Lord Jesus both to its present membership and to the three quarters of humanity who are not Christian?

The evangelist, to whom by tradition we give the name Luke, wrote two of the books which are in the canon of the New Testament, his Gospel and the Acts of the Apostles, somewhere between the years 80 and 90, very likely in Syria. Fifty-two chapters in all, 24 for the Gospel, 28 in Acts. Of those 52, 15 are about what led up to the Council and what happened at it, as much as 29 per cent of the whole. That is some indication of how important he held the Council to be. It wasn't as if he was short of material and needed the odd filler. Quite the opposite. As we will see, he had too much, far more than he could deal with. He had to select from "the account of the things that had been fulfilled among us" from "eye-witnesses and servants of the word", who had been present and had been part of it all "from the very start" (Luke 1:2ff.). Luke's selection of material was not haphazard; for both books he chose material with great care in order to execute the purpose he had in mind in writing them. He will emerge as a writer with a clear focus.

The general opinion among scholars is that Luke was a Greek-speaking Gentile who first had converted to Judaism. Both aspects most certainly would be enough to explain the immense interest he had in what led up to and happened at the Council. At some point, he became a Christian. Regrettably, we know nothing of how that happened or, also, how he then became a companion of Paul; but meet him he did, and obviously they were kindred souls; not just fellow Christians but also close friends. He accompanied Paul on his second and third missionary journeys. He was witness to him writing possibly all of his letters. He may even have been his scribe for one of them, namely Galatians. He was with him on his disastrous and ill-advised visit to Jerusalem, stayed with him in the two years of his imprisonment there and in Caesarea, and was with him on his ship-wrecked voyage to Malta, and then in Rome. We do not know if he was still with him when Paul was martyred, beheaded under Nero. Among his companions on those missionary journeys there was Silas who had played a prominent role in the Council of Jerusalem, and Titus, who had attended it too. Luke had met with some, probably all, the apostles, spoken with them, listened to them and prayed with them.

In a word, his sources were immense, and he had every credential needed to write both his books. In addition, in my opinion, he had met with Mary. Two statements about her in his Gospel justify that assertion: "Mary treasured up all these things and pondered them in her heart" (Luke 2:19) and "His mother treasured up all these things in her heart" (2:51). How else could anyone say that about her unless he had met with her and spoken with her? He would have listened to her talking about the conception, birth, circumcision, infancy and boyhood of her son. Other than in conversation with Mary, how could Luke have come to know, not just the bare facts of the Presentation in the Temple and the time Jesus stayed behind in Jerusalem and left Mary and Joseph searching for him, but also the intimacy of her feelings about what was happening and what was being said, as when Simeon told her that a sword will pierce her soul when her son gets rejected by his people (v. 35)? Only her husband Joseph was present when Simeon said it to her, and, as far as we can make out, he had died before Jesus began his ministry. Likewise, I have little or no doubt that it had to be Mary who told Luke about what had happened to Zechariah and Elizabeth, who was her kinswoman (1:36). The Magnificat (1:46–55) is her meditation upon everything that had happened to her, when he visited her and spoke with her about it all, and possibly he assisted her in its composition.

As he wrote his Gospel, he had both the *Quelle* text and Mark's Gospel in front of him, possibly Matthew's too. To all that we can add the singular fact that for years, day in, day out, he had been in the company of the "eye-witnesses and servants of the word" (Luke 1:2). He had witnessed no end of things that had happened within the infant Church, mixed with and prayed with the apostles, talked with any number of others who made up the first of the church members. Luke just had a mountain of varied sources to write from. His problem was he had too many, oral and written. If only someone had collected all his sources together, kept a note of all the conversations he had with those witnesses and all the "traditions" he makes reference to (v. 2) as he prepared his text, then had put everything into crates and stored them away and kept the versions and the rejects he put into his waste-paper baskets, and we had it all now. He had so much, he just had to select out the material he decided was pertinent and useful to the purpose he was writing his two books for. He must have made draft after draft and thrown away reams. If only someone had gathered them all up and preserved them.

In the end he tells the story, which we call the Acts, without, as will become clear, a word being wasted. Of the 12 apostles he focused almost entirely on what Peter did and said. It is Peter who produced the theology which took the Church forward, defeating the circumcision or Mosaic faction within the infant Church. It was Peter who provided Paul with those basic themes which have come to be called Pauline theology. We have no idea what contribution the other apostles made, because Luke reports on none of them. Their next-to-total exclusion from his account of the foundation years of the Church is little short of mind-boggling. He must have had any amount of reports and stories of what they did, what their contributions were. He must have talked with them. They undoubtedly gave him an immense amount of salient information; together with Peter they were after all the most important of all "the eye-witnesses and servants of the gospel" (Luke 1:2), but he just cut them right out. He even cut out most of what Peter had to say at the Council, even most of what he said in Jerusalem on the day of Pentecost itself. Luke informs us that his record of what Peter said on that day was only a small selection of what he had in front of him. He concludes Peter's Pentecost speech with the words: "And with many other words he (Peter) testified and exhorted them" (Acts 2:40). As J. Rawson Lumby writes: "There is no attempt made by the writer of the Acts to produce more than the substance and character of what was here said, and we may be sure that he uses the same rule always."[2]

However, wherever somebody suited the theme he was pursuing, he had no hesitation in incorporating him or her into his narrative. Stephen, a Greek-speaking convert like himself, receives maximum attention. The theological interpretation of God's dealings with both humanity in general and the Jews in particular that Stephen preached to the Jews is constructed by Luke into the longest single speech in the entire Acts; and the missionary activities of Philip, like Stephen a Greek-speaking Jew, are described in detail, because what he both did and said represented essential and necessary steps on the road to the crucial decision to be taken by the Council in Jerusalem. It is the same with Barnabas, although Luke does not provide us with a single word he spoke, only with what he did.

In the opening paragraph of his Gospel, Luke tells Theophilus (Luke 1:1ff.) that he "had traced the course of all the things accurately which had happened among us in order to draw up a narrative of what had been handed down from the beginning by the eyewitnesses and servants of the word". He didn't tell him that, when it came to describing how the Church progressed after the Ascension, he had one specific thing in mind, and that all the rest, doubtless at least 90 per cent of events, would not get a mention.

In Acts, Luke is exceptionally single-minded and focused. As a former Gentile himself he first concentrates almost totally on how the Church was liberated through the activities and theological insights of Peter from the narrow one-nation theological outlook of Judaism. It was that that then set the Church free to take the gospel and the grace of Jesus, "the new covenant" of which Jesus is "the mediator" (Hebrews 12:24), to all of humanity, to every nation, to the ends of the earth, as Jesus had commanded. Once he had shown that that had been achieved, Luke devotes all the remainder of his history to an account of the activities and preaching of Paul in non-Jewish lands and cultures (Acts 15:36–28:31). However, it must be said that Paul, who called himself "the apostle to the Gentiles" (Romans 11:13), went first to the local synagogue, almost invariably wherever he was, made it his base, preached first to his fellow Jews and only then to the Gentiles.

Luke had this development of doctrine and evangelism at the forefront of his mind from start to finish. For that reason his "connected narrative" (Luke 1:4) of two books concludes with Paul saying to the leaders of the Jews: "Take notice that the salvation of God had been sent to the Gentiles, and the Gentiles will listen" (Acts 28:28). Paul then "stayed there (under house arrest in Rome) two full years . . . proclaiming the kingdom of God and teaching the facts about the Lord Jesus Christ quite openly and without hindrance" (v. 31). In a number of different ways, Paul's preaching of the gospel of Jesus as related by Luke was always to both Jew and Gentile.

Acts 1—15 are the sole source of what we know about the Council of Jerusalem. However, they do of course tell us about much more than just the Council. We learn about the Ascension, about the descent of the Holy Spirit on Pentecost Sunday, about the first steps the Church took, about the first preaching in the Church by Peter, how radically the apostles' understanding of Jesus developed, how the Church spread, how it was treated by the Council of the Jews, about the seven Greek-speaking Christians we call deacons, about Stephen and his martyrdom, about Philip and his ground-breaking missionary work, about Paul, about Peter in Joppa and Caesarea and his seminal and radical theology of salvation, and about the first Gentiles who were converted and Paul's first missionary journey. They are developments, people and events of immense significance which stand by themselves. Yet, it is fascinating to observe how, incident by incident, person by person, Luke weaves them into a "connected narrative" which leads directly to the event and the decisions of the Council of Jerusalem.

What that Council decided was put into a letter to be taken to the churches in Antioch, Syria and Cilicia. It was a mere 149 (Greek) words, just seven verses. We might compare that with the immense length of the conciliar documents of, for example, the Second Vatican Council which amounted to a quarter of a million words, and that excludes thousands of words expended in copious notes and references. The Second Vatican Council was also attended by scores upon scores of *periti* (experts), assisting both bishops individually and the Council as a body in matters theological, pastoral, liturgical and governmental. It takes little effort to imagine the volume of what they produced separately. Those 149 words of the Council of Jerusalem must be by far the shortest pronouncement any church council, synod or congress ever made, yet it was the most important meeting in the history of the Church. Diamonds are carried in small packets.

What is it then about the Council of Jerusalem that makes it so important and historic? For one thing, if it hadn't taken place and hadn't promulgated the conclusion it came to, there certainly wouldn't be Christianity as we now encounter it. Instead, Christianity would have been no more than just a sect of the Jewish religion; and it may well have been scattered within a matter of a mere few years along with the Jewish people after the destruction of Jerusalem by the Romans. The Jewish religion survived that catastrophe, the Christian Church as a sect within Judaism might not have done. The Council of Jerusalem, however, was the moment when the Church, expressly claiming to be acting under the declared and explicit guidance of the Holy Spirit (Acts 15:28), declared what God's saving plan for all of humanity (v. 11) was, and in and by whom it was achieved, namely "the Lord Jesus" (v. 11). It declared that God had first made a covenant with one nation only; and then in Christ had extended that covenant, a covenant of salvation, to include all people, all nations, the whole of humanity, equally, irrespective of race. That belongs to the essence of Christianity.

That is what the author of the letter to the Colossians calls "God's mystery/secret which is Christ in whom are hidden all the treasures of wisdom and knowledge" (Colossians 2:2). In Christ, says the author of the epistle, "all the fullness of the Godhead lives in bodily form" (2:9). To know him is to know God's "secret purpose", kept hidden now in Jesus Christ; and knowing Jesus Christ is the gift of God to everyone. "There is no question here of Greek and Jew, circumcised and uncircumcised, barbarian, Scythian, freeman, slave; but Christ is all and is in all" (3:11).

It is that crucial understanding of who Jesus Christ was, his role or mission, and that God's choice of the Jewish people as his chosen people had now been extended to embrace all humanity that constituted the break with Judaism. The Jews of course could have embraced Christ as the Messiah, and Paul in his letter to the Romans expresses in the most heartfelt way possible his sadness that they did not and looks forward with intense longing and ardour to the time when they will. But that did not happen; and in its way that is what the first 15 chapters of Acts are also about. The Christian Church, however, retained its connection with its Jewish origins through its Scriptures and its liturgy, which both contribute in an essential manner to the theology and the prayer and sacramental life of the Church. God's supernatural revelation of himself is first to the Jewish people. God's revelation in Christ is the fulfilment of precisely that revelation. Revelation is one, it has the oneness of God himself. Christianity is massively Jewish, not as some accident of history or geography but of its very essence. That is the plan of God, it is salvation history. God's saving plan is through the Jews. Jesus wasn't Jewish just by birth or blood or culturally. He was Jewish because salvation comes through the Jews. That is the point of Matthew's Gospel (Matthew 1:1–17) and Luke's (Luke 3:23–38). Those passages aren't just giving us a genealogy, essential though that is. They are telling us of God's saving purpose. For that reason Luke concludes his genealogy with "son of Adam, son of God". God is the origin, and Christ is the goal. He is God's secret, he is God's mystery and "in him lie hidden all God's treasures of wisdom and knowledge" (Colossians 2:3).

From being no more than a tiny group of men and women, as obscure as it gets, living in a little province of a mighty empire, Christianity expanded exponentially so that within four hundred years not only had its membership spread and multiplied throughout the Middle East and the Mediterranean basin, but it had been declared the official religion of the very empire an officer of which had put its founder to death; and today Christianity is spread throughout the whole world. The significance of the Council of Jerusalem is that it put the stamp of Church approval authoritatively and definitively upon that understanding of what Christianity was about that would make that achievement possible. That is why it is the most important Christian Council and one of the most significant events in human history.

As from the day of the Resurrection (cf. Luke 24:21) and that of the Ascension (Luke 1:6), two understandings of the mission of Jesus and of the nature of the Church he founded clashed. One won out, the one which the Council in the year 49 authoritatively endorsed. I use the word "authoritatively" purposely. The Council explicitly declared itself to have the God-given authority to make that decision: "ἔδοξεν γὰρ τῷ πνεύματι τῷ ἁγίῳ καὶ ἡμῖν." "It is the decision of the Holy Spirit and our decision," wrote the apostles and elders in the letter they sent out promulgating the outcome of the Council (Acts 15:28). Significantly, the verb ἔδοξεν, which is used three times in this letter, is one often used in the official announcements of public resolutions or decrees made by an authority.

The decision was not easily arrived at. Most definitely not. It was preceded by years of hard argumentation accompanied by some bitter disagreements between two opposing camps of Christians, indeed disagreement of such a kind that the author of the Acts wrote: "There arose fierce dissension and controversy" (15:2). Out of that controversy, as Luke informs us as he develops his narration of the issue, there emerged a deepening understanding of the Christian faith, developing progressively out of the experiences of one Christian community after another right across the eastern Mediterranean world, starting with two disciples walking the seven miles from Jerusalem to the little village of Emmaus on Easter Day itself (Luke 24:12–35) and expressing the limited understanding they then had of Jesus by telling him "We had been hoping that he was the man to liberate Israel" (v. 21).

Luke takes us on a theological journey to Christian communities of towns and villages across Judea, Samaria and Gaza such as Joppa and Caesarea, above all Jerusalem itself; then much further north to the city of Antioch, which was then in Syria and is now in Turkey and called Antakya, a city of immense significance in Christian history; to the island of Cyprus and to the districts of Cilicia, Pamphylia and Pisidia in the Roman province of Asia Minor, now Turkey. The journey returns by sea to Antioch where the controversy reached such a boiling point that it just had to be settled. It was settled at the gathering at Jerusalem in the year 49 which was convened by apostles and leaders of the church in Jerusalem at the request of the church in Antioch. The Antioch delegation to it included Paul and Barnabas.

That gathering and its outcome constitute the Council of Jerusalem. It settled an issue of defining importance in the faith and the history of Christianity. However, the journey did not quite end there. The decision the Council had made was brought back to Antioch where it was warmly welcomed. However, elements in the Jerusalem church itself remained deeply unhappy with it. Their discontent festered and a mere five to eight years later some of them travelled all the way to the district of Galatia in Asia Minor to persuade new converts made by Paul to disregard it; and Paul had to deal with them. His letter to the Galatians settled the issue definitively. From Emmaus to Galatia it is a tale of a development in theological understanding which Luke decided he would set out, and in fact set out for all Christian posterity. It is as important indeed in our own day as it was in the year 49, though we now take it for granted, so taken for granted by us that we ignore the important struggle that gave it its birth.

The immediate post-resurrection understanding of the apostles and other disciples of the person and mission of Jesus and of the membership of his Church was that it was to be restricted to the Jewish people. It was in fact only with immense difficulty that Peter himself eventually came to understand that all races could receive the Holy Spirit through baptism and become members of the Church, that there was no longer any one chosen people but that, as the writer of the letter to the Ephesians tells us with immense emphasis and eloquence, God had intended from eternity to make all of humankind his chosen people:

> Therein lies the richness of God's free grace lavished upon us, imparting full wisdom and insight. He has made known to us his hidden purpose – such was his will and pleasure determined beforehand in Christ, to be put into effect when the time was ripe: namely that the universe, all in heaven and on earth, might be brought into a unity in Christ. (Ephesians 1:7–10)

So animated and concerned was the writer to tell this to "God's people in Ephesus" that he repeated it two chapters on. Assuming the name of Paul he wrote:

> To me, who am less than the least of all God's people, he has granted his grace of proclaiming to the Gentiles the good news of the unfathomable riches of Christ, and of bringing to light how this hidden purpose was to be put into effect. It was hidden for long ages in God the creator of the universe in order that now, through the church (a three-word phrase of great theological significance), the wisdom of God in all its varied forms might be made known to the rulers and authorities in the realms of heaven. This is in accord with his age-old purpose, which he achieved in Christ Jesus our Lord. (Ephesians 3:8–11)

What should not be overlooked in this foundational statement of God's eternal purpose for humankind is the role it ascribes to the Church.

Whoever wrote this epistle, it is a statement of the Christian faith, because the Church in due course declared it to be such by putting it in the canon of Holy Scripture, the foremost written statement of its faith. It is a truly cosmic vision, it is cosmic understanding. The hands and arms of Jesus were stretched out on the cross to embrace all men and women irrespective of race, time and place. The Council of Jerusalem, when convened, laid the foundations of the endorsement of this understanding of its founder and his Church as Christian belief. If it is a short journey in terms of years that is being described in this paper, in terms of profundity of meaning and understanding it is one that the Christian world will spend forever meditating upon. Additionally, let it be noted that these statements and the declaration of Peter (Acts 10:34) represent humankind's first repudiation of racism in all its forms. They radically changed the course of human history. Judaism did not come to terms with it, but in the prediction of Paul that will happen. It was in part for that reason that Christianity departed from Judaism, as it had to. The stretched-out arms and hands of Christ upon the cross embraced "the universe, all in heaven and on earth" (Ephesians 1:10).

The prophet Hosea tells us what God felt for the Jewish nation:

> When Israel was a boy, I loved him. I called my son out of Egypt
> . . . It was I who taught Ephraim to walk. I who had taken them
> in my arms, and they did not know that I harnessed them to
> leading-strings and led them with bonds of love, that I lifted them
> up like a little child to my cheek and that I had bent down to feed
> them (11:1–4) . . . I will be as dew to Israel that Israel may flower
> like a lily, strike root like the poplar and put out fresh shoots,
> that it may be as fair as the olive and fragrant as Lebanon. Israel
> shall again dwell in my shadow and grow corn in abundance
> and flourish like the vine and be famous as the wine of Lebanon.
> I am the pine tree that shelters you, to me you owe your fruit.
> (Hosea 14:3–4)

Are there in all of Scripture verses so tender? They are inexpressibly moving and loving.

However, what the Council of Jerusalem declared, using the significant formula "the decision of the Holy Spirit and ourselves", was that the meaning of "the chosen people" no longer was directed at any one race or nation, and indeed, as Ephesians tells us, ultimately never had been so intended, but in the eternal plan of the Triune God had embraced all humanity. Not that God has rejected his people (Romans 11:1). Anything but, as Paul tells us. Their offence, as he puts it, "has meant the enrichment of the Gentiles" (v. 12). They will return, and how. "If their transgression enriched the world and if their defeat enriched the Gentiles, how much the more will their return achieve!" (ibid.). We therefore look forward to the time when Israel will understand that God will indeed fulfil his promises to them within, but only within, the shared commonwealth of all nations, who are the object of God's love as much as they are. The tender love of God for Israel as described by Hosea always was, is now and always will embrace all humankind, every person, every nation. It is for the Jewish people to surrender what possibly is their most cherished belief that they alone are still God's chosen people and instead happily accept that everything Hosea said about them is now revealed, with the coming of Jesus, to be how God regards all men and women whatever their race.

"I do not wish you to be ignorant of this mystery, my brothers," Paul wrote in his letter to the Romans (11:25). He wrote even more, of course, in that chapter, not just the incredible doxology (vv. 33–6) but also his wondrous assurance that in God's good time "all Israel shall be saved . . . for God's gracious gifts and his call are irrevocable" (vv. 26,29). If this book helps somehow towards making the designs of God a little better known, it will have been well worth the effort.

# CHAPTER 1

# Luke's Account of the Resurrection

There were two fundamental issues which the Council of Jerusalem dealt with. One was salvation, how and by whom it was achieved; the other was its universality. Peter's statement, his pronouncement, in the speech he made at the Council, set out what the faith of the Church was on both matters: "διὰ τῆς χάριτος τοῦ κυρίου Ἰησοῦ πιστεύομεν σωθῆναι καθ' ὃν τρόπον κἀκεῖνοι" "We believe that it is by the grace of the Lord Jesus that we are saved, and so are they" (Acts 15:11). They are Peter's last recorded words. What he was doing was putting a meaning to the notion of Messiah which was fundamentally different from the then current understanding of it which he and all his fellow Jewish Christians at the Council had been brought up with. The "we" in "we are saved" were his fellow Jews who made up the overwhelming majority of the Christians at the Council. They were the Jews both at the Council and those in Jerusalem and Judea and throughout the diaspora who had accepted Jesus as their saviour, as the Messiah. The "they" in "so are they" were the Gentiles, non-Jews, some of whom might well have been in the room, having accompanied Paul and Barnabas in the Antioch delegation. Such an understanding of salvation is no news to us today. On the day of the Resurrection, however, it was not how the first disciples of Jesus had understood it; and because we today are not where they were on that day, we can easily fail to appreciate and feel for their situation, we just do not stand in their shoes, we do not share their background and upbringing, we do not share their certainties and their uncertainties, and their confusion.

What Luke describes to us in Acts 1—15 is the journey of understanding Jesus which the Church of the first disciples found itself on. In the course of it there were events of the highest importance and each had its own significance. There was the Resurrection and the Ascension. There was then the confrontation between the apostles and the Jewish leadership, the imprisonment the apostles suffered, their defiance of the Jewish authorities, the conversion of diaspora Jews, the trial, speech and martyrdom of Stephen, the missionary work of Philip among Samaritan Jews, the vision and revelation Peter experienced in Joppa, the conversion of Cornelius the Roman centurion, his fellow officers and his family, the conversion of Paul, and his first missionary journey which was into Gentile country. Each of them is of great significance in itself. Liturgically we celebrate them, thinking we know all about them. But we do not experience them, we do not feel them, as the first Christians felt them and experienced them. For us, the Christian catechism of belief has long been written; we have our doctors of the Church like Chrysostom and Augustine; we have Aquinas' *Summa Theologica*; we have our Liturgical Year; we have our seven sacraments to take us from the cradle to the grave; we pretty well know it all, or at least we think we do. Not so the first Christians. They were learners, they felt the full shock of the new, they had to make something of it; and Luke describes to us how they stumbled through event after event, events that were the building blocks of the Church and of their growing understanding of Jesus and his mission.

To understand it all to whatever extent we can we must start where Luke starts, with the apostles as they were at the Resurrection and then at the Ascension. That is crucial if a reading of the Acts is to be fruitful. Above everything else, the Council of Jerusalem was the settlement of a massive, a most fundamental, difference within the Church between two irreconcilable understandings of what the messiahship of Jesus of Nazareth the son of Mary consisted in. Luke started out by informing us that the understanding the apostles and their fellow disciples had of Jesus as at the time of his resurrection and ascension and even after the descent of the Holy Spirit, was that Jesus was human, and his messiahship was that of a human being, of "a prophet powerful in speech and action before God and the whole people" (Luke 24:19). Nothing more. And that makes perfect sense. There was no way the apostles and the other disciples could have had an awareness of the divinity of Jesus when he was with them. Such an awareness would have been too much to live with. The apostles just couldn't have coped with being in the company of someone they believed was their creator, the creator of the universe, almighty, eternal, omniscient and all the rest. No one could. They saw in a glass darkly, to put it mildly. There was the incident (Mark 8:33) when Peter, astounded and almost beside himself with disappointment at Jesus prophesying his death, grabbed him by the arm to get him to withdraw what he had said. It was a gesture which informs us that for Peter Jesus was just a human being. It is common sense that during the ministry of Jesus and well after his ascension the apostles could not have perceived that Jesus was divine. They didn't even after the descent of the Holy Spirit on Whit Sunday and for some time after it, and only then after stumbles and arguments and with the guidance of the Holy Spirit, as will become apparent. It was to take a lot of reflection and discussion on their part aided by the insight-giving of the Holy Spirit before they fully understood whose company they had been in for the years of his ministry, his death and his resurrection. The details provided in the first 15 chapters of Acts makes all that clear. There is, most interestingly, no statement in Acts by any of the apostles or other disciples that Jesus was divine. However, within no less than seven years after the Council of Jerusalem, and some thirty years before Luke wrote Acts, we have Paul asserting the divinity of Jesus, in Philippians 2:5ff. Cardinal Newman's articulation of the development of doctrine is no abstract theory. It is hard fact.

The apostles, and indeed all the first disciples, were Jews. That simple fact is one of immense significance. They stood in an immeasurable spiritual and cultural tradition. For that reason their Christianity when they became Christians was rooted in Judaism and could not be anything else. When Peter, Andrew, Nathaniel, John and his brother James first encountered Jesus, they had already been ardent seekers after the Messiah who they believed would one day liberate the Jewish people and re-establish the sovereignty of Israel. That is why when we first meet with them they are disciples of John the Baptist. They had gone to John hoping he was the Messiah. It is the Baptist who then directs them to Jesus, saying "Behold the Lamb of God", and when, after spending a whole afternoon with Jesus at the Baptist's suggestion, Andrew rushes to his brother Peter at his house and shouts to him "We have found the Messiah" (John 1:41), we get an excellent insight into what Peter and Andrew and co really were into. That one shout tells us so much about them. Andrew and his unnamed colleague were convinced they'd struck gold. They just couldn't contain themselves, they ran like greyhounds in their excitement to Peter, Andrew's older brother, their group leader, and barged through the door of his house shouting: "We have found the Messiah".

Peter, Andrew and the rest weren't just simple fishermen whom Jesus met on the beach of the Sea of Galilee and whom Jesus out of nowhere told to follow him and become fishers of men. Nothing of the sort. He did that only after meeting and getting to know them first. They were committed believers. They had formed a group; they didn't just go fishing as a living together; they were also comrades in a passionate search for the Messiah. One of them, Simon, was even called a Zealot. The Zealots were Jews who were especially strict in the observance of Mosaic ritual. Peter, Andrew and the others had become followers of the Baptist, they had joined up with him thinking he might be the Messiah. Peter, who had his own fishing business and a boat that could take seven fishermen, as we know from John 21:2, might well have had some of them in his employment or they paid him for their use of it. This group of them had obviously got together, united by a common passion for their Jewish religion, probably attended the local synagogue together, studied the Scriptures together and were united in trying to find the promised Messiah. That was why they were with the Baptist, they thought he might be the Messiah. Given the close bond between Mary the mother of Jesus and Elizabeth the mother of John, mentioned by Luke in the first chapter of his Gospel, Jesus and John may have been cousins, and, if not, then friends. Some of the apostles might therefore have met with Jesus while being in the company of John. It was the Baptist who then pointed them in the direction of Jesus as John the Evangelist tells us (1:29). Their concept of the messiahship of Jesus was that of the Judaism of their time. It could hardly have been anything else. There was no notion that he was divine. Such a notion would have been impossible for them, it would even have deeply offended them. They were Jews, and for the Jews the concept of God was one of profound reverence and awe. Understandably, throughout the ministry of Jesus they did not recognize his divinity. Not only is this easily demonstrable but it is the clue to a proper understanding of the quite crucial developments narrated in the first 15 chapters of the Acts.

So, we start with the last chapter of Luke's Gospel, his story of the two disciples on their way to a village called Emmaus some seven miles from Jerusalem. It was the day of the Resurrection itself. Verse 33 of the chapter tells us some things about them. Neither of them were apostles, rather they were members of the company gathered round Jesus and the apostles. From what Luke tells us we have grounds to conclude that in walking away from Jerusalem, from the Eleven, and indeed from Mary and his relations, they had given up on Jesus, they had decided his arrest and crucifixion between two thieves had put an end to all messianic aspirations about him. Despite everything Jesus hadn't lived up to the expectations the two men had had of him. Instead, he had turned out to be a complete failure, in fact worse than a failure, he had been eliminated, zeroed, executed along with common criminals. So the two of them decided to cut their losses and look elsewhere. They resigned themselves and their dreams to defeat, they gave up and they walked out of Jerusalem and took the road to Emmaus some seven miles away.

One of them was called Cleopas (Luke 24:18). They must have belonged to a more intimate circle of the followers of Jesus, as they were close enough to the apostles to know the location of the house where the apostles were assembled, possibly hiding (v. 33); and it was they whom Jesus chose to appear to, to tell them what his real mission was and to convey that to the apostles. Furthermore, as verse 30 informs us, they recognized Jesus by the way he blessed the bread they gave him to eat, then breaking it and offering it back to them. In other words, they had been at meals with Jesus. We know from John's Gospel that "the disciple whom Jesus loved" was at the Last Supper, and it is the opinion of the scholars that that disciple was not one of the apostles. It is therefore possible that these two men had been at the Last Supper as well.

The reason for focusing on these details is to make it clear that these two men were significant members of the company following Jesus believing him to be the Messiah. They were on the inside track. Yet, for all that, they had gravely misread him, gravely misunderstood him, and, all things considered, maybe they cannot be blamed for it. When Jesus asked them why they were so sad and what they were talking about, they replied it was because of "Jesus of Nazareth, a prophet powerful in speech and action before God and the whole people" and "We had been hoping he was the man to liberate Israel" (Luke 24:19–21). Being close followers of Jesus and close to the apostles and obviously well-acquainted with what Jesus did and said, what they now had to say about him can be held to provide us with a reliable idea of what they and their fellow believers at that moment understood him and his mission to be. Their reply clearly informs us that they regarded Jesus as just human. A powerful prophet, yes indeed, but human. There is nothing in how they described him which indicated anything more than that. Simply nothing. And that of course would apply equally to the apostles who were their companions.

Furthermore, they understood his messiahship to have a political purpose. They doubtless understood his prophetic status as more than just that, but it was that aspect of it which was clearly foremost and uppermost in their minds, because that was what they mentioned. And, additionally, it was only about Israel, there was nothing for non-Jews in it. That is how it reads; and again it should be stressed that we are not talking here of men on the fringe of the Jesus group. Far from it. Jesus valued the two of them so much he appeared to them, and so close were they to the apostles, they doubled back on their journey to return at once to Jerusalem and tell them what had happened to them. Their understanding of Jesus, as we have it in this Lucan account, can for the reasons given be taken as a reliable indicator of what his followers generally understood him to be, and that certainly up the moment when they and the apostles and the whole company of believers were made aware he had risen from the dead.

They returned to Jerusalem. What sort of state of mind they were in having just met with the living resurrected Jesus, who had even spoken with them and had a meal with them, we can hardly imagine. I doubt their feet touched the ground at all the seven miles of the journey back to Jerusalem, and then they found that the apostles and the other disciples with them already knew about the resurrection. In the same instant, Jesus appears to them all again, convincing them he had risen physically and was not a ghost by asking them to touch him, even by eating a piece of fish in front of them. God alone knows how they all, both individually and collectively, dealt with what was happening before their eyes. How would anyone deal with it, being confronted by the person who they knew to have been killed some two days earlier and then put in a tomb and a stone rolled up to it to close it, and then have him appearing from nowhere and standing in front of them, and then to top it all see him eat a piece of fish before their very eyes? We take the Resurrection for granted. We shouldn't. If we've never felt, sometime or other, a tremor of astonishment, of awe, even of doubt, even of disbelief, we've never really given it enough thought.

If I might digress somewhat by looking at the John Gospel, we will see that its author (or school) around the year 100 was tackling exactly the same objection to Christianity that Luke was tackling twenty or so years earlier, namely incredulity when it came to the issue of Christ's resurrection. The apostle Thomas surely represents all humanity when he expressed doubt about what his companions were telling him. He demanded proof: "Unless I see the mark of the nails on his hands, unless I put my finger into the place where the nails were and my hand into his side, I will not believe it" (John 20:25). That was sound common sense. He wanted, literally, tangible proof; he knew exactly what he was asking for. For all his adherence and love and admiration for Jesus, he was being knowingly hard-headed. He wanted ultimate proof. He wanted proof that his companions weren't kidding themselves with some sort of self-induced belief in a ghost or some figment of a group-created imagination. If Jesus has risen, then Jesus had to show himself to be physical like they were, with a real body that could be touched and held like anyone else's. Thomas was saying to himself, and to his companions: "Don't think for a minute I'll just go by the reports I've heard. It might all be just wishful thinking and nothing more. I want proof." He understood the power of self-suggestion, and he wasn't going to fall for it. Thomas undoubtedly understood the possibility that the raging waves of disappointment his companions felt when their whole world, all their hopes, were collapsing in front of their very eyes, could have induced a powerful group delusion. He was doing us all a favour; he was asking for evidence.

It was precisely with what he asked for that Jesus answered him. Jesus showed real respect for his demands, though of course it was either that or nothing. The demands of Thomas had to be met; they just could not be ignored; they were sensible and reasonable; and met they were: "A week later the disciples were again in the room and Thomas was with them. Although the doors were locked, Jesus came and stood among them saying: 'Peace be with you!' Then he said to Thomas: 'Reach your finger here, see my hands. Reach your hand here and put it into my side. Be unbelieving no longer but believe" (John 20:26f.).

There is deliberate defiance of all sensible expectation in this statement. John is making it clear that it was not just a case of a dead person coming back to life, which is incredible enough, but it is also a case of a bodily object occupying space already occupied by another one, in this case a locked door, while retaining the physical quality of touchability. It clashes totally with normality. And it was all deliberate on the part of John. He was presenting his readership with a miracle. He was confronting head-on any doubters among his readership or anywhere else. It wasn't a ghost that was appearing to the apostles, it was not some sort of vision, not an apparition. It was the real deal. It was the physical Jesus back from the dead, whose body Thomas could touch and whose hands he could take hold of. Really physical, yet able to pass through another physical object, a pair of doors, without opening or damaging them. "This is what happened," the John author is saying, "and there is proof it happened. It had witnesses. This Jesus who rose from the dead is therefore really something special and worth listening to."

On that belief of the apostles and disciples, of women as well as men, as Luke in his account of the Resurrection makes clear (Luke 24:10f.), on their acceptance that Jesus had risen from the dead, everything depended. Everything. Their belief in the Resurrection was their reason for the transmission of the gospel, for their establishment of Christianity, for their communication of the message of salvation to the whole world. "He was the one who was not abandoned to Hades and whose body did not experience corruption," said Peter to the crowd on the day of Pentecost. "God raised this man Jesus to life and all of us are witnesses to that" (Acts 2:31f.). God worked his plan of salvation through these people, these followers of Jesus. They began with what they had witnessed, and in their own witness to it to both Jews and Gentiles they themselves came to understand more and more the reality that Jesus was. The exclamation of Thomas was the author's way of giving to his Gospel a conclusion that was in line with how he started it, namely his prologue. Thomas of course did not make that declaration on that occasion but sometime later when they had all come to realize that Jesus was God. Not, however, at that moment. John knew about Thomas's confession of faith whenever Thomas made it, and having begun his Gospel with the declaration that Jesus was both the Word of God and God (John 1:1)—it was a most suitable way to end it. It was a statement of the faith that the Church had arrived at.

Similarly like John, Luke, when writing his Gospel, puts into the mouth of Elizabeth, the kinswoman of Mary, the understanding of Jesus the Church had arrived at by the time he wrote his Gospel: "Who am I that the mother of my Lord should visit me?" (Luke 1:43). Elizabeth didn't have, and couldn't have had, knowledge of the divinity of Jesus when Mary arrived on her doorstep. The John school was most likely writing its Gospel some twenty years after Luke, and by that time an even deeper understanding had been achieved. The letters of Ignatius of Antioch (c.108) contain more evidence of this development. "There is," he writes to the church in Ephesus, "only one physician of flesh and of spirit, generate and ingenerate, God in man, true life in death, son of Mary and Son of God, first passible and then impassible, Jesus Christ our Lord" (v. 7); and in para 18 of that letter he speaks of Jesus as "our God, Jesus the Christ, borne in the womb of Mary."[3]

We return to the two disciples hurrying back from Emmaus to Jerusalem. The text needs to be re-read. On getting there, they told "the Eleven and the rest of the company" what had happened to them; and then suddenly, "as they were talking about all this, there he was, standing among them. Startled and terrified they thought they were seeing a ghost. But he said: 'Why are you so perturbed? Why do questionings arise in your minds? Look at my hands and my feet. It is I myself. Touch me and see. No ghost has flesh and bones as you can see that I have.'" They were still unconvinced, still wondering, for it seemed too good to be true. So he asked them: "Have you anything here to eat? They offered him a piece of fish they had cooked which he took and ate right in front of them" (Luke 24:36). Doubtless their eyes were almost out of their sockets, watching every mouthful as he ate it.

What Jesus was doing was addressing, and giving an answer to, the bewilderment, the confusion, the bitter disappointment they all had felt when they saw that the man whom they had followed believing him to be the Messiah had been killed. For them he was going to be the long-awaited liberator of their nation, but he had actually shown himself powerless before both the Roman governor and the leaders of the Jewish people, so powerless he had been arrested, tried, condemned to death and crucified like a common criminal, indeed in the company of other criminals (Luke 23:32) and even mocked by one of them with the one jibe which must have struck home more than any other: "One of the criminals who hung there with him taunted him: 'Aren't you the Messiah? Save yourself and us'" (v. 39). That taunt alone explains how bitter and disappointed the two disciples on the road to Emmaus were feeling. Jesus addressed their confusion and their disappointment by reminding them what the Scriptures—the Law, the prophets and the psalms—had in fact all foretold about what sort of Messiah they should have been expecting, if only they had looked properly at them: not as a liberator of Israel from foreign domination but a liberator from sin; and to achieve that he had to suffer and die. "This is what is written," he said to them: 'The Messiah is to suffer death, and to rise from the dead on the third day'" (v. 46). He tells them: "Yes indeed, I am the Messiah, but not the sort you have in mind."

What sort then? He tells them, and Luke gives us a summary of what he said to them: "This," he said, "is what is written: that the Messiah is to suffer death and to rise from the dead on the third day, and that in his name repentance bringing the forgiveness of sins is to be proclaimed to all nations. Begin from Jerusalem: it is for you who are witnesses to all this" (Luke 24:46–8). One would have thought Jesus couldn't have made it clearer than that. His messiahship was one of suffering and death, not one where he triumphs over any foreign rulers of Israel; his resurrection from the death which he suffered at the hands of the Romans had nothing to do with any national triumph over enemies. It was diametrically different. It wasn't political in any way at all, and it wasn't racial or one nation either. It just was of a totally different order, its purpose was about repentance and forgiveness, and that not just for the people of Israel. That he had risen from the dead, as he told "the Eleven and the rest of the company" was to enable the message of repentance and forgiveness "to be proclaimed to all the nations" (v. 47) in his name. His messiahship was for all humanity. It was universal, forgiveness from sin was open to all people in every nation under heaven, and "in his name", that is, because of him and through him.

Now, one might think that with that "the Eleven and the rest of the company" could do nothing else but get the message. But they didn't and Luke tells us they didn't. He begins his second book, the Acts, with a short account of the Ascension (Acts 1:1–11); and what is it that they ask Jesus? "Lord, is this the time when you are to establish once again the sovereignty of Israel?" (v. 6). It is difficult to understand the reply which, Luke tells us, Jesus gave to their question. However, what Jesus says to them a couple of verses later does amount to his repudiation of the mentality it represented and his affirmation that in due course, when the Holy Spirit had come down upon them, not only will they understand that his messiahship is a universal one but also that they will devote themselves to telling the whole world about it: "You will receive power when the Holy Spirit comes upon you; and you will bear witness for me in Jerusalem and all over Judea and Samaria and away to the ends of the earth" (v. 8). J. R. Lumby writes: "The change from the spirit which dictated the question in this verse (1:6) to that in which St Peter (Acts 2:38f.) preached repentance and forgiveness to all whom the Lord should call, is one of the greatest evidences of the miracle of Pentecost. Such changes are only wrought from above."[4] This is a most perceptive comment. It is scriptural insight second to none. It directs us back to the promises made by Jesus to the apostles in both Luke and John: "I am sending upon you what my father promised" (Luke 24:49), and "When he comes who is the Spirit of truth, he will guide you in all truth" (John 16:13).

Luke gives us no explanation at all about how the apostles progressed from that moment before the Ascension when they showed themselves still thinking that the messiahship of Jesus consisted in establishing an independent Israel to realizing that it consisted in bringing about repentance and forgiveness. For Luke it was obvious and needed no explanation. God was fulfilling his promise.

# CHAPTER 2

# Ascension Thursday to Pentecost Sunday

Luke is the Evangelist of the Holy Spirit. His description of its dwelling and its activities in the life of Jesus and in the founding and growth of the early Church is relentless. In his Gospel and the Acts, there is a keen awareness of the Spirit of God dwelling in the Church and being alive, active and vigorous in it and through it. It is Luke who relates to us how Mary, Simeon, Elizabeth, Zacharias and the Baptist received the Holy Spirit to carry out their roles in the life of Jesus. What he tells Mary: "The Holy Spirit will come upon you and the power of the Most High will overshadow you" (Luke 1:35), is something that he describes happening time and again to members of the Church, each in their own way, at different moments, though not of course as significantly as to Mary. Mary after all was the mother of Jesus, mother of God.

In the final narrative in his Gospel, as we have just seen, he relates the assurance the risen Jesus gave to "the Eleven and those who were with them" (Luke 24:33), that he would send them what his Father had promised. That phrase "the Eleven and those who were with them" might well have greater significance than just its literal meaning. What the Father was promising to give to the apostles was not just for them but for all fellow believers, then and throughout all the ages; and that, as we will see almost immediately, is what happens when the Spirit descends, on the apostles on Pentecost Sunday and then also on Samaritans (8:17) and Gentiles (10:44).

Throughout the Acts he describes the instances, relentlessly, one after the other, when the Holy Spirit is sent to inspire, instruct, direct and empower. First there is the descent of the Spirit on Whit Sunday, again not just on the twelve apostles but on the whole group, numbering "about one hundred and twenty" (Acts 1:15), "all together in one place", and "all of them were filled with the Holy Spirit" (2:4). Then significantly, in the first speech the Church in the person of Peter makes to the world, there is in the prophecy of Joel that same assertion that the Holy Spirit will descend on all believers: "God says: 'I will pour out my Spirit on all people'" (2:17). Jesus himself has received the Holy Spirit from the Father (v. 33); it is through believing in Jesus as Lord and Messiah (v. 36) and being baptized in his name that that prophecy is fulfilled and men and women receive the gift of the Holy Spirit (v. 38).

Peter is "filled with the Holy Spirit" when he replies to the hostile questions from the Council of the Jews (Acts 4:8). When he and his colleagues return to the house of their friends where they were staying, they say a prayer of thanks, and the whole house "rocked and all were filled with the Holy Spirit and they spoke the word of God with boldness" (4:31). The Spirit is present in how Stephen preaches (6:10), and he is "full of the Holy Spirit" at the moment of his martyrdom (7:55). It is the Holy Spirit that the Samaritans receive when Peter and John lay their hands on them, after they had accepted the word of God preached by Philip. It is the Spirit, recorded as speaking himself for the first time, that tells Philip to go and speak to the eunuch returning to the court of the Queen of Ethiopia, and when the eunuch had been baptized, it is the Spirit that takes Philip away to preach the gospel in all the towns en route to his home town of Caesarea. It is the Spirit himself that tells Peter to go with the delegation of Roman soldiers to Caesarea. It is "the gift of the Holy Spirit" that is poured out on the Gentiles who made up the household of Cornelius the Roman soldier (10:45), to the total astonishment of those believers "who had been circumcised", namely the Jewish Christians who had accompanied Peter to Caesarea (10:46). Barnabas, chosen by the church leadership in Jerusalem to deal with the problems that had arisen in Antioch, is described as a man "full of the Holy Spirit and faith" (11:24), as is Paul when confronting Elymas the sorcerer in Cyprus (13:9).

It is the Holy Spirit that tells the church in Antioch to set Paul and Barnabas apart for him for what was to be the first of Paul's missionary journeys. The Holy Spirit speaks to the members of the church in his own person. "There were at Antioch, in the congregation/church prophets and teachers, Barnabas, Simeon, Lucius, Manaen and Saul. While they were offering worship to the Lord and fasting, the Holy Spirit said: 'Set

Barnabas and Saul apart for me to do the work to which I have called them'" (Acts 13:2). According to Lumby, the verb Luke uses here has a "middle force" and should be translated "I have called them for myself".[5] The Holy Spirit, the third person of the Trinity, himself is speaking. They are his words. He is, he is telling us, personally concerned, directly involved. The preaching of the gospel to all nations is his work, and he is calling Barnabas and Saul to do it on his behalf. The Holy Spirit isn't just the inspirer, he is above all else the doer. The work of these two missionaries is his work. They are set apart "for me", he says.

The Holy Spirit is a living and active guide within the heart and mind of the Church. The Church, as he began it on Pentecost Sunday, is both his creation and his partner, his voice, in the work of salvation. In their letter to the churches in Antioch, Syria and Cilicia the elders and apostles write that the Holy Spirit directed and guided them and as their partner in reaching the decision they took at the Council of Jerusalem. That decision, they said, was "the decision of the Holy Spirit and ourselves" (Acts 15:28). There is a defining finality of importance both in how the statement described how the decision was reached and in the implication it contains that the presence, the power and the intervention of the Holy Spirit in the Church are integral to its existence and mission.

In Luke's exposition of this active presence of the Spirit within the life of the Church corporately in its individual members, there is that one ever-recurring theme, that one thing he keeps bringing to our notice. It is that the presence of the Spirit produces visible, indeed startling, effects. "The apostles in Jerusalem now heard that Samaria had accepted the word of God and they sent Peter and John, who went there and prayed for them (the converts) that they might receive the Holy Spirit . . . So Peter and John laid their hands on them, and they received the Holy Spirit" (Acts 8:14–17). In the early Church as Luke narrates the story, they virtually saw his presence, they felt it, it was real, even physical, to them. So much so that Simon the magician, "when he saw that the Spirit was bestowed through the laying-on of the apostles' hands, he offered them money and said: 'Give me the same power too so that when I lay my hands on anyone, he will receive the Holy Spirit'" (vv. 18f.).

On the day of Pentecost "they were all filled with the Holy Spirit and began to talk in other tongues", giving the impression that they were wildly drunk, with Peter having to shout it wasn't intoxication caused by alcohol. While Peter was still speaking to the Gentiles that made up the household of Cornelius, "the Holy Spirit came upon all who were listening", and the Jewish Christians present "heard them speaking in tongues of ecstasy and acclaiming the greatness of God" (Acts 10:46). The outpouring of the Holy Spirit in these first days of the life of the Church was effectively visible and tangible; one could almost reach out and touch it.

By no means was it just enthusiasm and charismatic behaviour. It was that but it had another purpose, as Peter understood. No sooner had he got back to Jerusalem from Caesarea than he was confronted by "those who were of the circumcision" (Acts 11:2), namely the Judaic faction. Of course, all the first believers in Jesus were Jewish, but this faction wanted Gentile converts to adopt Jewish religious practices in the belief that this was necessary to achieve salvation. As will be seen in great detail in due course, Peter's refutation of their position would consist in saying that the undeniable fact that they had received the Holy Spirit without adopting Jewish practices proved that adoption of Jewish practices and the Law was in no way a requirement for church membership and for salvation but that faith in Jesus as saviour alone mattered. That was the fundamental issue that the Council of Jerusalem was about. From this we can see, as we must, that Luke's constant mention and description of the Holy Spirit in the life of the Church in all sorts of ways is not due to some personal spiritual orientation on his part, it is no private personal devotion. It is the Christian faith, it is Christian theology; it is what Christianity is, it is what salvation is, it is what the Church is, it is Luke's unerring perception of the salvific partnership between Spirit and Church which manifested itself in the foundational Church history he himself witnessed and has kept manifesting itself in various ways ever since.

However, if we want to appreciate fully the significance of that decision, we need to pause a moment to reflect awhile on the mind and mentality, the feelings of identity and loyalty, of each and every one of the small band of believers in Jesus as they were on the day of the Ascension. All of them were Jews, and their sense of identity as belonging to God's chosen people was their lifeblood. Mary the mother of Jesus felt it; the apostles felt it; they all felt it. Mary gave expression to it in her great hymn of praise, the Magnificat: "He has given help to his servant Israel in remembrance of his mercy, as he spake to our fathers, to Abraham and to his seed forever" (Luke 1:55). They all knew what they belonged to, they all felt it in their blood and bones. God's love and care for the people of Israel, as shown to us already in the prophecy of Hosea, was, and is, indescribably tender.

The prophet Hosea had told them: "When Israel was a boy, I loved him . . . It was I who taught Ephraim to walk, I who took them in my arms and bound them to leading-strings and led them with bonds of love. I lifted them up like a little child to my cheek and I bent down to feed them . . . I will be as dew to Israel that Israel may flower like a lily, strike root like the poplar and put out fresh shoots, that it may be as fair as the olive and fragrant as Lebanon. Israel shall again dwell in my shadow and grow corn in abundance and flourish like the vine and be famous as the wine of Lebanon. I have spoken and I affirm it. I am the pine tree that shelters you, to me you owe your fruit" (from chapters 11–14).

Paul had those same feelings of intense belonging and pride too, though regrettably they drove him, as passionate feelings can, to persecute Christians as enemies of the Jewish people till Jesus appeared to him. He gave wonderful expression to the feeling he had for his people; and nothing else in all the New Testament better describes the mind, the emotions and the sentiments of the first followers of Jesus, a tiny group standing hesitatingly between two worlds, their loyalties about to be tried and torn: "They are Israelites," wrote Paul. "They were made God's sons; theirs is the splendour of the divine presence, theirs the covenants, the Law, the temple worship and the promises. Theirs are the patriarchs, and from them, in natural descent, sprang the Messiah" (Romans 9:4f). What was being asked of them by belief in Jesus was an almost impossible transformation of themselves, and to Paul's unutterable dismay there were only a few of his fellow Jews who were managing to make it: "In my heart there is great grief and unceasing sorrow" (v. 2). With intense longing he wanted Christ to be received in faith by his fellow Jews as the Saviour not just of their own people but of all peoples. And it is not just universalism that they are being asked to accept. In his letter to the Romans he is even telling them that "God's way of righteousness" (v. 2) was this Jesus of Nazareth, a single human being, a man who had been crucified; and that this person "ends the Law and brings righteousness to everyone

who has faith" (10:4) in him. How could the Jewish people be expected
to believe all that about a mere human being? They had been told from
time immemorial that the observances of the Law were their way to God
and God's way to them, and now they are being asked to repudiate that
faith, their faith, and believe instead that faith in this man was "God's way
of righteousness" (v. 2). It was a lot to ask, a mountain to climb.

Paul told the Roman Christians that he was prepared to suffer what
would have been for him the greatest loss imaginable if it would enable
them to do it. "I could even pray to be outcast—ἀνάθεμα—from Christ
myself for the sake of my brothers, my kinsfolk according to the flesh"
(Romans 9:3). He loved and honoured his fellow Jews intensely: Their
salvation is his "deepest desire and prayer" (10:1), but "their zeal is an
ill-informed zeal. For they ignore God's way of righteousness and try
to set up their own" (vv. 2f). God's way of righteousness is Christ. It is
Christ that "brings righteousness" (v. 4). Christ is God's righteousness
"for everyone who has faith" (ibid.). "If on your lips there is the confession
'Jesus is Lord' and in your heart the faith that God raised him from
the dead, then you will find salvation" (v. 9). What caused Paul intense
sadness then was the repudiation by his kinsfolk of what, and who, truly
constituted righteousness before God, and with it salvation. It wasn't
salvation for the Jewish nation alone. Because righteousness before God
was through faith in Jesus, and in nothing else, it was for all humanity.
"Do you suppose God is the God of the Jews only? Is he not the God of
Gentiles too? Certainly, of Gentiles too, if it be true that God is one. He
will therefore justify both the circumcised in virtue of their faith, and the
uncircumcised through their faith" (9:30). It is not race, nor observance
of a law, nor any ritual, it is faith in Jesus that saves. That represents the
immensely difficult emotional, cultural, spiritual and religious, indeed
theological, journey the first Christians, all Jews, had to make and it
would involve "no small amount of dissension and controversy" (15:2)
and the rise of a divisive faction (cf. v. 5) within their community before
there was resolution of the matter. The issue was as fundamental as it gets.
It was a journey in understanding what the essence of their Christian
faith was.

The traditional picture we have in our heads of the events of the feast
of Pentecost, our Whit Sunday, is of the Holy Spirit descending visibly in

tongues of fire on the apostles, imbuing them with shafts of enlightenment and courage, galvanizing them to bound out of the house like greyhounds from the traps, leap into the huge crowd of Jewish pilgrims from all parts of the Middle East, the Mediterranean, Egypt and North Africa, speak to them in their own languages, and there and then start making converts. Such an idea, commonplace though it is, is not just inaccurate, it also paints a misleading picture of the apostles and first disciples themselves and of how the Holy Spirit actually brought the apostles and disciples to the right understanding of Jesus. It was not achieved in a flash. There certainly was a descent of the Holy Spirit upon them, there was an infusion of courage and power (cf. Acts 1:8) into them by the Holy Spirit (cf. 2:4). However, the evidence is that moment was the conclusion of one process and the start of another, not an instant transformation. There was a period of gestation beginning with their calling at the start of Jesus's ministry, a gradual process by which human intellect on the one hand and grace in the form of divine guidance on the other worked together to achieve in the Church a correct understanding of the nature and the purpose of the messiahship of Christ. That in turn brought about a radical change in the Church in its relationship to Judaism. Painfully—no less—and slowly they came to understand that the Judaism they had been brought up in was incompatible with the Christian gospel. It must be stressed that it was the Judaism represented by what, as will be shown, was the Judaic faction within the infant Church that was not compatible with Christianity. There is a wide variety of different traditions within Judaism. Any religion that can have, on the one hand, Leviticus and Numbers as two of its sacred books, and on the other the Song of Songs and the book of Job surpasses categorization. It is wild beyond description. It had to be to take humanity to the Incarnation, to God becoming human, an event, an intervention which is beyond thought.

All three synoptic Gospels provide evidence of the immense problem the apostles and disciples had with what Jesus told them about what his messiahship would really consist in. Mark graphically illustrates through the reaction of Peter what a huge disillusionment it was, what a rude awakening, what a violent change of understanding, was being asked of them:

> Jesus and his disciples set out for the villages of Caesarea Philippi. On the way he asked his disciples: 'Who do men say I am?' They answered, 'Some say John the Baptist, others Elijah, others one of the prophets.' 'And you?' he asked them, 'Who do you say I am?' Peter replied 'You are the Messiah.' Then he gave them strict orders not to tell anyone about him; and he began to teach them that the Son of Man had to undergo great sufferings, and to be rejected by the elders, chief priests and doctors of the Law; to be put to death, and to rise again three days afterwards. He spoke about it plainly. (Mark 8:27–33)

That is how their re-education began. How hard it was for them to cope with it, how much it threw them and challenged them is shown by Peter's immediate reaction: "At this Peter took him by the arm and began to rebuke him." Peter reacts quite violently and shouts at him. The apostles' idea of the Messiah had been fundamentally challenged, indeed violated. Jesus, however, is adamant. He makes no concessions to the alarm and confusion he has caused them. "Jesus turned around." One can see Jesus shaking off Peter's hand, pulling himself away and facing up to him eyeball to eyeball. "Looking at his disciples, he rebuked Peter. 'Away with you, Satan.'" There were no holds barred. "You think in a human way, not as God thinks." The Incarnation is beyond human thinking in more ways than one. It is incomprehensible and beyond any possible anticipation. And as we will see, with that last statement, as brief and as succinct as it gets, Jesus anticipated the conclusion the Church at the Council of Jerusalem would come to when it rejected the position that the Judaic faction within the Jerusalem church had taken, anticipating also the statement of Paul in his letter to the Romans some twenty years later: "Their zeal is an ill-informed zeal. For they ignore God's way of righteousness and try to set up their own" (Romans 10:2f.). Therein lay the reason for the parting of the ways. "God's way of righteousness" was, and is, simply unanticipatable, incomprehensible. It is a pure gift, the gift of his Son, we cannot either earn it or grasp it. He who is mighty has done great things for us.

Matthew, taking his text from Mark's Gospel, recounts the same event with some differences which are highly significant. It was an event and an exchange of views between Jesus and the apostles which doubtless lasted far longer and contained a lot more than the account that Mark has given us. In Matthew's account Jesus tells the apostles that it will be the religious leaders of the Jewish nation themselves who will bring about his death; and worse than that, will even conspire with their foreign rulers to achieve it.

> Jesus was journeying towards Jerusalem and on the way he took the Twelve aside and said to them: 'We are going to Jerusalem and the Son of Man will be given up to the chief priests and the doctors of the Law; they will condemn him to death and hand him over to the Gentiles to be mocked and flogged and crucified, and on the third day he will be raised to life again.' (Matthew 20:17–19)

The Jewish leadership, not recognizing Jesus for what he was, wasn't just bringing about the rejection, even the execution, of the Messiah whom God has sent to his people, but was even doing it by getting the foreign power ruling over them to do it, when liberation from foreign rule was what, in their understanding, the Messiah was sent by God to achieve. But of course they did not see Jesus as the Messiah. Little wonder Jesus on their behalf prayed the prayer: "Father forgive them for they know not what they do" (Luke 23:34).

Matthew took those words of Jesus from Mark (Mark 10:32–4). Mark wrote his Gospel for a purpose and in circumstances different from those of Matthew. He wrote it to provide guidance, solace and encouragement to the Christian community in Rome, which was struggling to come to terms with the horrendous persecution under Nero and the dire impact it had had on them. The Christians of Rome had hardly signed up to become Christians in anticipation of what Nero did to those who were arrested and killed in a most horrible manner. Tacitus will describe it as 'quaestissima poena', "most exquisite torture". It was for the survivors of that persecution that Mark wrote his Gospel, and he chose to tell the story of Jesus in such a way as to enable them to understand that what they had been through Jesus himself had been through. For that reason Mark recounted to them one statement of Jesus which had direct relevance to their experience and at the same time gave expression to the sort of Messiah he was: "The Son of Man did not come to be served but to serve and to surrender his life as a ransom for many" (Mark 10:45).

Luke also reproduces Mark's detailed prediction by Jesus to the apostles and disciples of the sufferings, mockery and death he will endure, and of his resurrection, though with some slight variations; and he makes a very significant comment on it: "But they—the Twelve—understood nothing of all this; they did not grasp what he was talking about; its meaning was concealed from them" (Luke 18:34). Luke is being more than factual about the Twelve, he is being blunt and possibly critical of them. We know why. Even when Jesus had risen from the dead and had given the apostles convincing evidence of his resurrection (vv. 38–43) and had told them again that, as per the Scriptures—Moses, prophets and psalms—the Messiah had to suffer death (v. 46). He had done his best to open their minds to understand (v. 46); they still did not comprehend and were still asking him: "Lord, is this the time when you are to establish once again the kingdom of Israel" (Acts 1:8).

There are crucial issues here. Firstly, that question put to Jesus by the apostles, despite everything he had said to them and everything that had happened, tells us where the apostles were at in their understanding of his messiahship, of its nature and its purpose, as up to the day of the Ascension itself. Yet a mere ten days later, on Whit Sunday, the day of Pentecost, Peter was presenting Jesus to the people of Jerusalem as "both Lord and Messiah" (Acts 2:36) with no mention at all, not even the slightest indication, of anything about him as a liberator or anything about the establishment of the kingdom of Israel. Instead Peter was urging them to "repent and be baptized, every one of you, in the name of Jesus the Messiah for the forgiveness of your sins, and you will receive the Holy Spirit" (Acts 2:38-9). And anything in any way relating to their old and inherited notion of messiahship was never mentioned again by them.

How did that change of understanding come about? How could it possibly come about within no more than a little over a week? When it did, it radically altered the relationship of the new Christian messianic community to their parent body, the people of Israel, to which racially, culturally and spiritually they all belonged. What God had from the beginning intended with his promise of a Messiah, which was realized in Jesus, was incompatible with the inherited and prevalent Judaism of the day. The new and different understanding of the Messiah announced by Peter on Pentecost Sunday, to be developed as we have seen by Paul in Romans 10, was the cause of the decisive parting of the ways between Christianity and Judaism. It was an educational process that had been begun by Jesus himself during his ministry, as we have seen. There are two accounts of it happening in the post-resurrection period. One is in Luke 24:27, when he tells us about the two disciples travelling to Emmaus and what Jesus says to them.

The second is Acts 1:44ff.. This time the risen Jesus speaks to "the Eleven and the rest of the company" (Luke 24:33). The number of them in the assembly could have been as many as one hundred and twenty (Acts 1:15) "with a group of women including Mary the mother of Jesus and his brethren" (v. 14) among them. It is next to impossible to comprehend how Mary, the family of Jesus and the disciples coped with being in a room looking at and listening to someone who had been killed and put into a tomb, now alive and well, in front of their very eyes. How his mother especially coped is quite beyond comprehension, what ideas about him were racing through her head we can only guess at. It must have been incredibly eerie as well as a moment of astonishing happiness. Luke describes another side of the experience: "Startled and terrified they thought they were seeing a ghost" (Luke 24:36), and anyone anywhere can sympathize with that. However, Mary, the apostles and the disciples, up to at least five hundred of them as Paul tells us, were able to see the Risen Christ with their own eyes, while no other Christians were to have that experience. Yet, belief that Jesus rose from the dead is what is required of us: It is the "word of faith" which the Church proclaims (Romans 10:8); and if "you confess with your lips Jesus is Lord and believe in your heart that God raised him from the dead, you will be saved" (v. 9). Blessed indeed are those who unlike Thomas have not seen but have believed (John 20:29).

Jesus set out to try to correct the understanding the disciples had of him: "And he said to them, 'This is what I meant by saying while I was still with you, that everything written about me in the Law and in the prophets and psalms was bound to be fulfilled'. Then he opened their minds to understand the scriptures. 'This', he said, 'is what is written:

that the Messiah is to suffer death and to rise from the dead on the third day, and that in his name repentance bringing the forgiveness of sins is to be proclaimed to all nations. Begin from Jerusalem. It is you who are the witnesses of these things. And mark this: I am sending upon you my Father's promise. So stay in this city until you are clothed with the power from above'" (Luke 24:44–49). Luke does not tell us how Jesus "opened their mind(s) to understand the Scriptures", but it is reasonable to assume that he took the apostles through the relevant Old Testament texts, in the same way as he had dealt with the two Emmaus disciples, namely "beginning with Moses and all the prophets and explaining to them the passages which referred to him in every part of the Scriptures" (v. 27). It must have been a long session, a spell-binding session.

This was a defining moment in the history of Christianity. There must have been a series of meetings between the risen Jesus and his disciples. There would have been discussion. It could have lasted days, we just do not know. They are all looking at and listening to and talking with a man who had died, died cruelly and horribly, bloodstained, nailed to a cross, pierced in his side with a sword and now alive, standing in front of them, presentable, washed clean of the bloodstains. Their initial reaction had been the only one humanly possible: "Startled and terrified they thought they were seeing a ghost" (Luke 24:37). What then followed is given to us only by Luke, it is not in John or the other two Synoptics. Luke had his own sources for this, it could have been any one of the apostles whom he had met and conversed with in his years with Paul, or with Mary herself. At first Jesus expresses surprise at their reaction: "Why are you so perturbed? Why do questionings arise in your hearts?" (v. 38). It would seem he was expecting they just might have paid some attention to the clear predictions he had made to them during his lifetime. The strong words he used to rebuke the two men journeying to Emmaus (v. 25) he could well have used again here. However, he then shows consideration for their state of mind, as well he might. He offers proof it's really him: "Look at my hands and my feet", doubtless showing them the scars of his crucifixion. He invites them to approach him and touch him, probably holding out his hands for them to take and hold: "See that it is I myself. No ghost has flesh and bones as you can see I have" (vv. 39f.).

What he is saying defies every law of physics that there is, and of course common sense. He is saying that his appearance is really physical, it is a real flesh-blood-and-bone body that they are looking at, that they can touch, the real physical himself. The way Luke describes their state of mind is a little gem. He says "they were still disbelieving out of sheer joy" (Luke 24:41) in other words "because it seemed too good to be true", as the New English Translation translates it. So Jesus goes one massive step further, he asks for something he might eat and before their eyes he eats a piece of fish. Then once more he turns to the Old Testament, beginning with Moses and going through the prophets and psalms, to drive it home that "the Messiah is to suffer death and to rise from the dead on the third day, and that in his name repentance bringing the forgiveness of sins is to be proclaimed to all nations" (v. 46).

He ate with them. If the teaching session went on for more than a day, they would have had to sleep somewhere. Did he? Or just come and go? Did they cook for him? And to ask one profoundly theological question, did he help out with the washing-up? We must not make any mistake about it, it was the strangest of strange situations and one might wonder how the apostles and the whole company dealt with it. How did they cope? How can anyone cope when in the presence of a person whose death and burial they had witnessed? In its way, to any non-Christian looking at it, the whole situation must seem strange. Christians too should definitely feel unsettled; it is not at all easy to get one's head round it.

However, it was not an instance of blind faith. It is helpful to stand back and look at the book of the Acts of the Apostles in its entirety. It is the story of how the apostles and others responded to what they had experienced. From being, first, desolate and defeated, then being simultaneously perturbed, confused and thunderstruck when confronted by what they saw in front of them to be the Risen Jesus, in a word going from incredulity and doubt to total assurance on the basis of the evidence before them, they went on to devote their lives to preaching faith in Jesus. They would never have done that, and done it with such astonishing success, if they had not been totally convinced of the reality of the resurrection of Jesus back to life based on what they themselves had witnessed of him. They were convinced by the evidence; and that evidence is not just in what the four evangelists have recorded but also in the fact that those who witnessed and experienced the Risen Jesus responded to it by devoting their whole lives to preaching it to everyone they could; and as we have seen over the past 2,000 years, with immense success.

Luke's narrative method of sticking to the evidence finds a most interesting corroboration from another early source. In due course the faith of the Church progressed even further, to recognition of Jesus as the incarnate Word of God. "In the beginning was the Word and the Word was with God . . . and the Word became flesh, the Son . . . " (John 1:1,14). The author of John's Gospel wrote those lines sometime in the last two decades of the first century or even later, but if before the year 90, which really is unlikely, it could just have been when Luke was writing his Gospel and the Acts.

The Fourth Gospel is a different document about Christ and Christianity from Luke's. The contrast on this specific point between the two authors is highly significant. Luke informs Theophilus, for whom he is writing both documents, that his account adheres to "the traditions handed down to us by the original eyewitnesses and servants of the Word". Luke is keenly aware of the necessity of authenticity. For that reason, as he assures Theophilus, he first went "over the whole course of these events in detail", narrating them in chronological order, so that he can provide him with "authentic knowledge about the matters of which you have been informed" (Luke 1:1–3).

That this is Luke's purpose and attitude is supported by the fact that, unlike John, neither in his Gospel nor in the Acts, does he attribute to the apostles any assertions of the divinity of Jesus even though well before the year 80 that was the faith of the Church. The first letter to the Thessalonians, written by Paul as early as the year 50/52, is decidedly Trinitarian; and when in about the year 56 he writes to the Philippians, he makes his well-known assertion of the divinity of Jesus (Philippians 2:6). Luke, however, while well aware at the time of his writing the Acts of this development, is careful to be factually accurate in what he reports about the assertions and the actions of the apostles and their companions, and for that reason he does not ascribe any declarations of Christ's divinity to them. His Gospel and the Acts are what he said in the first six verses of his Gospel, a narrative based on the evidence of the original eyewitnesses. They are not like the Gospel of John, which in addition to being a narrative is a meditation. Luke is the first narrator of the history of Christian theology. He was acutely aware of its development. He presents the apostles and their fellow believers and the nascent Church to us factually, namely, as they were at the time of his narrative. He made clear to his readers that he knew where the Church was at at the time of the Ascension, and in the first 15 chapters of the Acts he traced its progress, focusing on the arguments for and the achievements of its break with Judaism.

The Council of Jerusalem is about what and who Christ is. Peter's speech at the Council, which Luke records, and which briefly, too briefly, is summarized by him, is the first Christology. It is foundational. Paul in his letters then went so much further, as did the John school. Between the three of them they have provided us with more than any one person can possibly deal with.

The faith of Luke was that Jesus was God. Yet, he has him in a room, talking with human beings, reading out loud to them, turning over pages, explaining things to them, eating with them. It is all beyond comprehension, you couldn't make it up, It's wild. Christianity is wild, totally and utterly wild. There are people, earnest, well intentioned and erudite, who for good interfaith reasons say that the God of Christianity and of Judaism and of Islam is the same God. How true in one way. How very incorrect in others. God is one and in that respect the God believed in by Muslims is the one God. God, however, is as he has revealed himself to us, God as Triune, God as incarnate, God as a human being, God the Son the son of a woman is almost anything but the God of Islam. Mohammad saw that and said so. The religion of Mohammad at his birth and throughout his upbringing was polytheism. However, he converted to monotheism in his middle age in the course of meetings and conversations with Jews and Christians during his 25 years of merchant life up and down the coast from Aden to Egypt and to Syria. His concern was then to eliminate the polytheism of his fellow Arabs, for whom the Kaaba in Mecca was central to worship. It could not be dislodged from their religious mentality, so tactfully he retained it. He preached a very simple notion of God, an idea of God which conforms to human intellect. His God is one God with no complications, a God who is great above all else, and that for Muslims is what matters and it colours all their religious practice. Very simple, very straightforward. For Mohammad the Christian belief in a Son of God, and God as Triune, was polytheism.

In Judaism, on the other hand, whose Scriptures wonderfully present immense subtleties about God, God is indeed one, but he is a God who also loves passionately and jealously and intervenes. The prophet Malachi has to be read and re-read to see and feel the intensity of it, even, if it might be said, to a point that is almost absurd. He has God fretting and getting furious over silly things like the food being brought to the altar going off and turning stale. The object of the Old Testament God is the nation of Israel, Israel is his love, his passion, his concern, and for that reason his interventions are represented as for the one nation of the Jews. When the God of the Old Testament, the God of Judaism, revealed himself in Jesus, all that understanding of God, all that love, all that passion, all that concern, all those interventions, are understood to be directed at all humankind and what Jesus explained to the apostles and disciples was staggeringly different from what they had been brought up to believe. The Messiah was a person "who was to suffer death and to rise from the dead" in order to achieve "repentance" in the hearts of men and women, "bringing the forgiveness of sins to be proclaimed to all nations" (Luke 24:46f.).

With those elements the notion the Jews had of the Messiah was repudiated by the Messiah himself. Their understanding of the Messiah was one tied to their concept of themselves as a distinct and separate people whom the one God had chosen as the sole object of his love and concern, and it was tied to their notion of the land they lived in as uniquely holy and uniquely theirs. It was tied to the idea that when the Messiah came, he would be their liberator from foreign rule. What Jesus taught his disciples constituted a decisive break with all of that, a repudiation of it. The importance of that break cannot be stressed too much; Jesus himself taught it them "beginning with Moses and all the prophets and explaining to them the passages which referred to him in every part of the Scriptures" (Luke 24:27).

The evidence from Luke's account of the activities of the apostles and fellow believers during the ten-day interval between the Ascension and Whit Sunday is that Peter's declaration on that Sunday was not just the result of some sudden, massive one-off act of enlightenment by the Holy

Spirit represented as coming down on each one of them in a tongue of fire. Rather in that period leading up to Whit Sunday they all applied their minds themselves to understanding the experience of Jesus, his life, his preaching, his miracles, his suffering and death, his resurrection and his ascension. There were no robots in any of it, no puppets on strings, no taking-over of minds by God in any way. The Church was being built on men and women, not robots and puppets. The apostles weren't rude uneducated fishermen chosen on a beach of the Sea of Galilee, they weren't what the Council of the Jews was to call them, ἰδιῶται. They were keen followers of the Jewish religion and students of its scriptures. The enlightenment given by the Holy Spirit to the apostles did not consist in a sudden wipe-out of the beliefs and attitudes they had imbibed in their upbringing followed by a dramatic substitution of other beliefs; it was an educational and enlightenment process with conscious and active intellectual input from the apostles themselves.

Luke describes the first reaction of the apostles to the Ascension. In its way it was a crazy situation. Jesus, whom they believed was the Messiah, had gone; he'd taken himself away; he just wasn't there. He'd vanished before their very eyes. They suddenly found they were believing in someone who wasn't there. He wasn't there to do what they believed a Messiah should do, which was to lead the people of Israel. They were leaderless; and they themselves couldn't do what they'd been expecting him to do. They had his promises all right (Acts 1:8) that they would receive power when the Holy Spirit came upon them. But how? And when? And for what? In his absence what sense did it all make? He'd said they were to bear witness to him "in Jerusalem, all over Judea and Samaria and to the ends of the earth". To the ends of the earth? Whose leg was he pulling? They were just a tiny group of fishermen and others, most of them from a province in Israel, as obscure as it gets, mere "men of Galilee" (v. 11). Who anyway would believe in someone who wasn't to be seen or heard? Luke chose a quite brilliant way, a telling metaphor, to describe how at first they felt lost and abandoned, as well they might (vv. 1:9–11). He described them as staring up into the sky, into an empty space. However, it was a totally different situation they were then in from the immediate aftermath of the crucifixion. Jesus might have left them and disappeared but as Luke said, "he had shown himself to these men after his death and given ample proof to them that he was still alive" (v. 3). Furthermore, they had his promise: "Be assured, I am with you always to the end of time" (Matthew 28:20). He had told them "You must wait for the promise made by my Father, and within a few days you will be baptized with the Holy Spirit" (Luke 1:8). So they held on, they gave encouragement to each other, they stood there on the hillside for a while, they talked it all through among themselves and then they decided what they would do. They "returned to Jerusalem from the hill called Olivet, which is near Jerusalem, no further than a Sabbath day's journey, where on entering the city they went to the room upstairs where they were lodging" (v. 12f.).

Luke records for us only the gist of the discussion the apostles had and the decision they made, a momentous one if ever there was one. He knew an important moment when he saw it, he appreciated the significance, the fundamental importance, of the decision they took. For that reason he highlights it with an embellishment which we will find him using again in the Acts (for example in 10:1–8 and 12:6–10). To highlight the importance of certain major moments in the development of the infant Church, to put it crudely, he brings on a sort-of supernatural being, "two men in white clothes", a literary device to demonstrate the huge significance of how the apostles responded to the departure of Jesus from them.

It's not at all difficult to relive what the apostles said to each other on that hillside once they had got over the shock of Jesus's disappearance. It would have been something like them saying to each other: "Look, we're men of Galilee, aren't we? We don't give up that easily. We're made of sterner stuff, aren't we? We're not just going to stand here and do nothing except look up at where he's disappeared to. That's a complete waste of time. He's told us he'll be back. He came back from the dead, didn't he? We're all witnesses to that, aren't we? Now, wherever heaven is and whatever it is, that's where he's gone and returning from there will be a lot easier for him than returning from the dead, that's for sure. He hasn't told us when, but he's told us he will, and we rely on him to keep that promise. And he's told us what we're to do in the meantime. We're to bear witness to him in Jerusalem, and by that he must have meant in the temple first and foremost; and in the rest of Judea, even—you heard him—to the Samaritans; and what's more to the ends of the earth. We can do that. Our fellow Jews have synagogues everywhere throughout the world. Wherever they are we'll go to them and preach Jesus as the Messiah to them. No, not as a liberator from the Romans or from anyone else for that matter. That sort of thing is precisely what he told us to keep clear of. We know what his message is, to get our people wherever they are to repent of their sins by believing in him as the Messiah. And he's proved he's the real Messiah because God raised him from the dead and we witnessed it. We saw him, we spoke with him, he ate meals with us, he took us through the Scriptures to understand them properly. Only God can raise anyone from the dead, that means he had God supporting him, he had God's backing. So if we preach faith in him as the Messiah, we will have God backing us. We just cannot lose. We've just got to do it. And we know now what sort of Messiah he is. Faith in him liberates us all from sin. That's the sort of Messiah he is, that is what the prophets foretold. And that, brothers, is what we are going to preach. But not immediately. He's told us to wait till the Holy Spirit comes upon us. Now what he means by that we don't know yet either but whatever it is, we have to wait and see. So now let's get back to Jerusalem."

And that is what they did "with great joy" (Luke 24:53). The city was no more than a day's journey from the hill Olivet, and when they got there all eleven of them "went to the room upstairs where they were lodging" (Acts 1:13). Annoyingly Luke does not tell us whose house the room was in. It must have been some house to cater for at least eleven grown men as lodgers. It could well have been in the house where the Last Supper took place, which in Mark 14:15 is described as "a large room upstairs" (and in Luke too, 22:12, lifting the phrase straight from Mark). It's what Luke tells us next that matters. After giving the names of the Eleven, for which he doubtless had a purpose, he says "All these were constantly at prayer together with the women and Mary the mother of Jesus and his brethren" (Acts 1:14); and in the next verse he tells us there were as many as 120. In the final line of his Gospel he also tells us that they had returned from the scene of the Ascension "in great joy and spent all their time in the temple praising God".

In a word, in the nine or ten days between the Ascension and Whit Sunday they didn't hide, they didn't stay behind closed doors and shutters, they didn't keep their heads down, they didn't creep around in fear of the Jewish authorities, waiting for the Holy Spirit to descend on them and transform them from being petrified and ignorant and fill them instead with courage and enlightenment, at which moment, full of illumination, they would pitch into the crowds and preach about Jesus. In no way. Instead, they returned to Jerusalem from the hill of the Ascension "full of great joy", they prayed publicly in the temple, and in the temple they told fellow Jewish worshippers about Jesus as the Messiah when people asked them what they were about, doing the same at the shops and in the market place and the streets wherever people talked to them. As a group of one hundred and twenty people, minimum, in great spirits, praying openly, they could not hide, and definitely did not want to. The trial and crucifixion of Jesus had taken place only just over a month earlier, and people would naturally have taken every opportunity to talk to his followers about it, and about all the reports and the rumours of him rising from the dead.

Also, in those nine or ten days after the Ascension the apostles and disciples, just as naturally, talked to each other about Jesus as the Messiah, reading and re-reading the texts he had brought to their attention, thinking about and discussing what his death and his resurrection really meant for them and for all the people of Israel, answering the questions people put to them, and arguing with them. In this way they prepared themselves, got themselves ready, for the descent of the Holy Spirit. We can see this in Luke's account of the election of Matthias as the twelfth apostle. "During this time Peter stood up before the assembled brotherhood, about one hundred and twenty in all" (Acts 1:15). In other words, and this is an interesting thought, in the nine-day interval, and indeed later, they were holding general meetings, probably all invited, and going by 1:14 and 5:7 open to women too. Infuriatingly as usual, Luke tells us about only one item they discussed, namely getting a replacement for Judas Iscariot, but common sense dictates there must have been others. If we look carefully into the reasons Peter brings forward for replacing Judas, it becomes clear that the whole group of them had been hard at work talking this matter through and searching the scriptures for guidance. They doubtless discussed many other matters as well. No reason is given why Peter and his fellow apostles wanted to bring their number back up to twelve. However, it could be that during his ministry Jesus had told them that they constituted the new Israel and that their number represented the twelve tribes that had made up the old Israel.

But really, it is difficult to understand why Luke singled out this specific item for mention when the number has no obvious relevance for the theme and reason of the history that he wrote; and in the rest of the Acts he tells us next to nothing about what any of them did except for Peter.

Whoever was chosen would serve as a "witness to the resurrection of Jesus" (Acts 1:22). This tells us that the apostles had really understood the foundational position the Resurrection held in establishing the veracity of their claim that Jesus was the Messiah; they had realized that when it came to preaching about it, actually having seen and spoken with the risen Jesus face to face, ate food with him, gone about with him and witnessed his Ascension could not be rated highly enough, that there was nothing more compelling in the work of conversion than that reason for believing in him. Quite possibly this was the reason why Luke made mention of only this one thing that the apostles did prior to Whit Sunday, the day of Pentecost. That Jesus had risen from the dead was both ultimate proof and display of his transcendent significance. It also meant everything to Paul personally. He felt that his experience of the risen Jesus through how Jesus had revealed himself to him was as valid and direct as any experience the Twelve had had. "Am I not an apostle? Have I not seen the Lord Jesus?" (1 Corinthians 9:1). It definitely seems that for Paul to have seen the Lord face to face was what made him an apostle; and it might be said that the intensity of his faith in and his overwhelming concern for the veracity of our resurrection, as he speaks about it in 1 Corinthians 15:12–57, must have come out of that shattering moment when he met with Jesus on the road to Damascus, saw him and spoke with him, face to face, living person to living person.

By their praying both in their lodgings and in the temple, by their joint study of the Scriptures, and by their discussions among themselves about Jesus and about what their mission was, and by their preaching to Jews in the temple and elsewhere, they prepared the ground for the descent of the Holy Spirit upon them at Pentecost. It wasn't on puppets or robots that the Spirit of God descended nor was it into empty heads and hearts that he entered. By Whit Sunday the members of the nascent Church had energetically prepared themselves for the promised coming of the Holy Spirit, they had made themselves all ready to go. The grace of God works with nature, it does not substitute itself for it.

# CHAPTER 3

# Pentecost, the Descent of the Spirit, the Day of the Lord

Whit Sunday, the Feast of Pentecost, the Descent of the Holy Spirit, the great, the resplendent Day of the Lord (Joel 6:31 and Acts 2:20).

"And when the day of Pentecost arrived, they were all together in one place" (2:1). Words matter. Writers choose them carefully. Luke chose the word ὁμοῦ with a purpose. Its customary translation into English is "together" which does not do justice to what he had in mind. J. R. Lumby makes this comment: "This word, and that which takes its place in the Text recept. i.e. ὁμοθυμαδόν, occur frequently in this part of the Acts and mark very strongly the unity which existed in the new society but which was so soon destined to be broken."[6] That was the story Luke wanted to tell in Acts 1—15. Luke presents a Church that was united, and ready to receive the inspiration of the Holy Spirit. But in a short time divisions arose. To one such division Luke devotes the opening verses of Acts 6. He then plots the course of another one, the far more significant one, up to when it is dealt with at the Council of Jerusalem by Peter, the rest of the apostles and the elders (Acts 15). A faction within the Church, mainly in Jerusalem and Judea, had put forward a version of the messiahship of Jesus and of how men and women can be saved which would radically distort or "hollow out" (ἀνασκευάζοντες) (v. 24) what constituted Christianity, and in such a way as to make any acceptance of it by the non-Jewish or Gentile world impossible. But despite that, as was to happen to many future councils of the Church such as Nicaea and Vatican I and II, the Council of Jerusalem was then followed by attempts to undermine its decrees. In this case some members of the Judaic faction travelled to Galatia to persuade Paul's recent converts to repudiate what the Council had decided and adopt what it had expressly denounced. Paul in his epistle to the Galatians dealt with them decisively.

Peter in Acts 2:14 says about the moment when he and his fellow apostles went among the crowd and preached to them that it was in "the third hour of the day", which in the way the Jews at that time calculated the time of day was about nine in the morning. The descent of the Holy Spirit upon the apostles and disciples preceded it. As devout Jews, they would have joined in various ways in the services which followed the feast of the Passover. They knew from the promise Jesus had made that they would be visited by the Holy Spirit. Their anticipation of it must have produced a strange feeling in all of them, immense curiosity at the least about what would happen and what form it would take.

> There came from the sky a sound like that of the rushing of a mighty wind which filled the whole house where they were sitting. And there appeared to them tongues like flames of fire, dispersed among them and resting on each one. And they were all filled with the Holy Spirit and began to talk in other tongues as the Spirit gave them power of utterance. (Acts 2:1–4)

We can speculate forever about what exactly happened, exactly how "they were all filled with the Holy Spirit", but they were, and in a way that was somehow palpable and in its effect upon them even visible. The apostles, and indeed everyone else in the house, experienced something tangible and intimate, something that shot right through them with all the violence of a mighty wind. Peter made mention of it time and again, as in Acts 10:47 and 15:8. Luke, as we will see when discussing Acts 10:3 and 12:7, always had his own distinct way of presenting these moments of divine intervention, he does not hesitate to give them a dramatic description which need not be taken literally. The image of a tongue of fire over the head of all present in the room could well be his choice of imagery to describe the dramatic descent into their hearts and minds of the Holy Spirit. Wind and fire are powerful, and indeed in this case appropriate, metaphors. To say that everyone in the room was "fired up" might sound banal, yet it might well be a good way of describing the event; and fire loves a mighty wind.

Something happened inside each one of them, the Holy Spirit worked in them; but about what form it took, what changed in them intellectually, what new thoughts they had, what new vision of things, it is all speculation except for two things. One is what it was that Peter, and with him of course the other apostles, then began to preach openly as recorded by Luke. The other was the way Peter kept referring to the experience and the moment in his dealings, both with Gentiles and with what was going to be a hostile Judaic faction, who in due course would be disagreeing with him about what to demand of Gentile converts. How that moment affected Peter, which thanks to Luke we know something about, was the same with the other apostles, though about what the other apostles did and said on that great and resplendent day and in the years that followed we know next to nothing, except for a minimum of mentions of John, and even then only when he was with Peter.

"Now there were living in Jerusalem devout Jews drawn from every nation under heaven; and at this sound the crowd gathered, all bewildered, because each one heard the apostles talking in his own language" (Acts 2:1f.). Though Luke uses a different word for the "sound" that got the attention of the crowd from the one he used to describe the descent of the Holy Spirit, we might presume they are referring to the same thing. The traditional Pentecost picture we have in our heads is that of the apostles immediately going out and preaching to a great crowd of Jewish pilgrims. However, it could well have been a much smaller crowd, just a section of it. It could well have been the case that the apostles and company had got together that morning for the purpose of getting out into the crowd early and had organized their activity in advance, having decided who went where and having made sure they would all be singing from the same hymn sheet. We do not know but that is likely. All we do know for sure is what Luke tells us, and about that he had his own specific purposes in mind.

There must have been a number of things about the crowd that Luke could have written about but he carefully focuses on one aspect, namely he lists the countries the pilgrims who were in Jerusalem for the feast of Pentecost had come from. He tells us nothing else about them except that they were "devout Jewish men" (Acts 2:5). That was his focus, the different parts of the world they originally came from, be they resident in

Jerusalem or there just for the feast day of Pentecost. The list is evocative: Mesopotamia, Judea, Cappadocia, the region of the Pontus, Asia, Phrygia, Pamphylia, Egypt, Cyrenia in Libya and Rome. What's more, he doesn't just call them Jews, he speaks of them as well as "Parthians, Medes, Elamites, Cretans and Arabs" (Acts 2:8–11). Why this detail? It can hardly be the case that the variety of places the Jewish pilgrims had come from mattered to the apostles on the day. What mattered to Peter, when he addressed them, was that they were of the House of Israel (Acts 2:36), be they from Jerusalem and Judea or from "far away" (Acts 2:39), all those scattered in the varied and distant diaspora. Luke, however, had something else in his sights. He was presenting a reading of the event that wasn't in the heads of Peter and his fellow apostles. He was using the Pentecost event to describe the situation the Church had already arrived at, had already achieved, by the time he began to write his Gospel and the Acts. The Church had by then achieved an international membership. "Our Church," he is saying, "has Parthians, Medes, Elamites, Cretans and Arabs in it as well as Jews in Judea and Jerusalem. It is to be found in Mesopotamia, Judea and Cappadocia, in far-away Pontus on the shores of the Black Sea, across all of Asia Minor, in Phrygia, Pamphylia, in North Africa in Egypt and the Cyrene district of Libya, where Simon who helped Jesus carry his cross (Luke 23:26) and his two sons Alexander and Rufus (Mark 15:21) came from, and there are people living in Rome who are Christian, and there are Cretans and Arabs who are Christian." Luke is saying something that just was not in the head of Peter at that great and resplendent moment, he was saying that Jesus is not saviour just for one nation, neither was the Church a one-nation church.

Luke was himself a Gentile and in this passage he was celebrating the most fundamental transformation of the Church ethnically and racially from what it was on the day of its foundation. Of that transformation he had not just been a witness, he had himself actively participated in achieving it. His list of nations and countries, recited ever since throughout the world, year in year out at Whitsuntide, was his celebration of the progress towards the universality of the Christian Church achieved in his own lifetime. What he is saying and what he is positively glorying in, is that the Christian Church was now no narrow one-nation body; rather its membership was from all races across the whole wide world, open to "every nation under heaven" (Acts 2:5), and that is what he wanted Theophilus and all his readership to realize and appreciate. That was one reason why he was writing the history of the Church and one determinant of what he put into it and what he left out.

As I have said, that wasn't of course the way Peter and his fellow apostles were seeing it at that moment. At that moment that wasn't Peter's understanding of the nature of the messiahship of Jesus. His appeal that day was to Jews only: "Let all the house of Israel accept as certain that God has made this Jesus whom you crucified, both Lord and Messiah" (Acts 2:36). It would not be till some years later, not until Joppa where he had his vision of the sheet full of non-kosher food, not until Caesarea where he met with Cornelius the Gentile Roman centurion, that Peter would understand fully the universality of the mission of Jesus; and when he did, defying a vocal, and in its way well thought-out, opposition, he authoritatively set out the basics of the redemption theology of the Church, which Paul, who will witness what Peter will be saying, was influenced by and was later to develop.

Luke writes: "Each person (in the crowd) heard the apostles talking in his own language. They were amazed and in their astonishment exclaimed: 'How is it that we hear them, each of them in our own language in which we were born?'" (2:6–8). In Parthian, in Arabic, in the old Persian languages of the Medes, in Aramaic, in Latin, in Greek, in the Pharaonic/Coptic language of Egypt, in all the languages of the Mediterranean basin, the Middle East and beyond. In recording this event what Luke was also doing quite consciously was celebrating what might be called the cultural universality of the Church as it had been achieved by the time he sat down to write the Acts. For him, the universality of Christianity was displaying itself in this way too, as home to the languages of all nations, all were welcome. One wonders if what Luke was also thinking about, when he described this event the way he did, was the story of the Tower of Babel, in which the Old Testament narrator had portrayed the total confusion caused by the existence of any number of different languages as God's punishment for human pride and arrogance (Genesis 11:1–9). Is Luke saying that in Christ, the universal saviour, the diverse languages of humanity and the cultures they represented had been taken into the redemption that he had wrought and were now to be regarded as celebrating the wonderful variety of God's creation? And when he spoke of each pilgrim hearing their own language being spoken by the apostles and their fellow Christians, was he actually celebrating the fact that by the time he was writing his account of how the Church had developed, every language was being spoken by its members and in its liturgy?

Some eight years later Paul was in the port of Troas in Greek-speaking Asia Minor on the edge of Asia, facing across to Europe. It was towards the end of his third missionary journey. Luke and Silas were with him, and so were some others whose different nationalities he placed before his readership. Sopater was from Beroea in Macedonia, Aristarchus and Secundus were from Thessalonica, Gaius from Derbe in Galatia, Timothy, Tychicus and Trophimus from different parts of Asia Minor. I doubt Luke was just getting geographical, rather he was celebrating the multi-national state of the membership Christianity had achieved. Then, "on the first day of the week", together with the local Troas Christian community, they all assembled for the liturgy of "the breaking of the bread" (Acts 20:7). The language they had in common was Greek. So the eucharistic liturgy, the Christian transformation of the Jewish Passover meal, was in Greek, not in Hebrew and not in Aramaic, the language of Christ and his mother, the language Christ had used at the Last Supper, the first Eucharist. That Troas eucharistic service was in the language of the place where they were, in the language common to the participants. Luke, looking back at the events of that first Whit Sunday, could have been recognizing them as, among other things, the beginning of the development of the Church's cultural universality which complemented the universality of the salvation wrought by Christ. The journey of the Christian religion to becoming culturally "catholic", καθολική, universal, had begun.

What a contrast this presents to the mentality and efforts of some members of the Roman Curia. Ten years ago or so a committee of them had responsibility for the recent translation of the Latin Rite into the vernaculars of those Catholics who are within that rite and who constitute the majority of Catholics today. The committee was set up either in the final years of Pope John Paul II or in the pontificate of his successor, Benedict XVI. Both men were very conservative. Whichever of them set it up instructed the committee members to come up with vernacular translations which would conform to and express as rigidly as possible the ancient Latin text. However, in 1998 the eleven English-speaking conferences of bishops across the world had already accepted the translation of the new Latin missal prepared by the International Commission on English in the Liturgy (ICEL). This translation was in very attractive, modern and excellent idiomatic English, whilst being true to the Latin original. When it was submitted to the Vatican for acceptance, a certain Cardinal Jorge Medina Estevez, then Prefect of the Congregation for Divine Worship and the Discipline of the Sacraments, intervened. He rejected this translation. He had been born in Chile in 1926. He was 76, his own language was Chilean Spanish. He set up a new ICEL which imposed the version known as *Liturgiam authenticam* with guidelines for translators described by Professor Peter Jeffery of the University of Notre Dame as "the most ignorant statement on liturgy ever issued by a modern Vatican congregation". On the one hand, here in the Acts, which is the word of God, there is celebration of linguistic diversity as we saw in Luke's description of the events on the first Whit Sunday in Jerusalem, and on the other we now live under the dead hand of bleak uniformity. A great pity. It is hard to imagine any other mentality as well equipped both to alienate all the church membership and to frustrate the achievement of Christian unity.

CHAPTER 4

# The Proclamation of the Gospel Begins

The crowd that had assembled around Peter and his fellow apostles would have heard a lot about Jesus already; many of them must have seen him and listened to him, met him and knew him, and knew about, had even witnessed, his miracles. Peter was about to remind them of it all: "Men of Israel, listen to me. I speak of Jesus of Nazareth, a man singled out by God and made known to you through miracles, portents and signs, which God worked among you through him, as you well know" (Acts 2:22). Some of them as well would have witnessed his crucifixion. Any number of them might have been among the people welcoming him into the city on Palm Sunday; it had happened only a few weeks earlier, as had the crucifixion. The talking about it among the Jerusalem population must have been in every street, every shop, every synagogue. Jesus was someone with a huge reputation and so popular with the people that the chief priests and doctors of the Law had at first been afraid to take action against him (Luke 22:2). The manner of his death, how he was condemned, his trial before the High Priest and the whole Jewish Council, how he had been paraded under guard across the city to be arraigned before both Pilate and King Herod, how he was set against Barabbas by Pilate and how the Jewish leaders had worked the crowd to get them to shout for Barabbas, and then of course the crucifixion itself—all that would have been one of the hottest topics of conversation for weeks. For Peter to speak to such a crowd as this, in which all sorts of opinions about Jesus must have been raging, let alone remind those among them who, in whatever way they did it, had lent support to the crucifixion of Jesus, some even shouting out for him to be crucified, took some nerve.

And then of course there was the talk of Jesus's resurrection from the dead. The apostles most definitely had been talking about that on every occasion possible. Luke tells us (Luke 24:53) that once Jesus had given them his final instructions and had blessed them before "departing from them", they then "spent all their time in the temple praising God". The obvious thing they praised God for was the Resurrection, and they would have told everyone they met around the city and prayed within the temple about it. Inevitably and naturally as people do, they would have been asked about it; and doubtless most people in the city regarded the very idea of a resurrection from the dead as sheer nonsense. It was, however, the thing that more than anything else inspired the apostles and disciples, filling them with confidence and faith in Jesus as the Messiah. The buzz among the Jerusalem people must have been huge and one can easily imagine how agitated and insecure (cf. Acts 4:1; 5:26) the Jewish leaders were becoming because of it all. The Romans had actually crucified Jesus, but it was the Jewish leaders who had publicly conspired to bring it about; and now the outcome wasn't turning out to be what they had hoped for. In other words, when Peter and his fellow apostles and disciples, inspired by the descent of the Holy Spirit, emerged from the house they had been using since the Ascension, they could hit the ground running. The people in the crowd weren't at all ignorant of who they were and what they were about. It had been talked about for weeks. The coming of a Messiah was a perennial and persistent issue, and here was one group putting forward a candidate for it, who, if the evidence for his claim that his followers were putting forward were true, namely his resurrection from the dead, could hardly be ignored.

Peter's task that day was a difficult one, but he and his fellow apostles and disciples had carefully prepared for it. He was going to tell the crowd that the man whom they had put to death by nailing him to the cross was in fact the Messiah; and they had done this "with the help of lawless men" (Acts 2:23), namely the Romans, by which he meant a people who weren't Jewish and did not live by God's Law. That man was "Jesus of Nazareth, a man approved by God through mighty works, wonders and signs, which through him, as you well know, God had worked among you" (v. 22). There was double condemnation in what Peter was saying to his listeners. Not only was he including some of them in the crucifixion and killing of Jesus, he was also accusing them of using non-Jews, heathens, their foreign rulers and oppressors, to do it. Using that word "lawless" was a killer of a way to describe the degree of betrayal the Jewish leaders had sunk to. They had employed the Gentiles, who lived outside what was most sacred to the Jewish nation, namely the Mosaic Law, godless people, people whom no Jew should ever associate with, to kill the man approved by God. That, Peter was implying, was betrayal of both God and of Israel itself. He was taking a huge risk, it was a delicate and brittle moment. Yet, it was hardly likely that he was saying this to the crowd on the spur of the moment. It comes across as a prepared speech, it had begun with words that indicate preparation and intent: "Men of Israel, listen to me" He had picked his words in advance. This was a different Peter from the one who had himself denied he'd even known Jesus, denied he had been associated with him and had fled from the scene of his arrest and brutal treatment and left him on his own. The Holy Spirit had certainly stiffened his sinews and summoned up his blood.

Certain things come across from the first exchanges Peter had with his fellow Jews, on the day of Pentecost and thereafter. One was the knowledge he and his fellow apostles and disciples had of the Scriptures. It was extensive and detailed. Joel, for example, whom Peter in the account Luke has given us quoted from first, was a minor prophet, and that might well tell us that in preparation for this moment Peter and his colleagues had scoured the whole of the Scriptures for passages that said what they felt had to be said. What it was that they had agreed had to be said would also have been an outcome of the debates, indeed arguments, they had had in the temple and the synagogues in Jerusalem with their fellow Jews over the nine days since the Ascension. The two opposing sides must have argued passage after passage, line after line, over the prophecies, they must have taken the texts apart. The passage from Joel just did not come from nowhere; it had to be known and it had to be relevant. The evidence is all there that in the nine days following the Ascension the whole group, apostles and all the disciples, with women among them (Acts 1:14), made careful preparations, both logistical and scriptural, for the moment when, after the Spirit had descended upon them, they would make their move, go out and engage with the people of Jerusalem, pilgrims as well as residents.

Luke tells us what then actually happened.

> They were all filled with the Holy Spirit and began to talk in
> other tongues as the Spirit gave them power of utterance . . .
> The crowd gathered, all bewildered because each one heard the
> apostles talking in his own language . . . They were all amazed and
> perplexed, saying to one another: What can this mean? Others
> said mockingly: They have been drinking sweet new wine. (Acts
> 2:4–13)

In other words, things did not go to plan, and instead of an eager reception
they were met with mockery. Initially anyway. And before they had
even got into their stride, it knocked them off their stride. The apostles
and colleagues had plunged into the crowd full of enthusiasm, totally
confident. For all we know they might well have stationed themselves in
different parts of the crowd, or they could have gone from one group to
another. Whatever way they went about it, they surely were brimming
full of confidence, preaching and arguing excitedly and noisily; and
to their own amazement as well as that of the crowd, they found that
everyone, no matter where they came from, was able to understand what
they were saying. But decidedly there must have been a strong element
of confusion too in the way they spoke, maybe they were just too eager,
saying too much too fast, because someone in the crowd, looking at them
and listening to them, shouted out that they must have been drinking. The
rumour spread like wildfire as rumours do in a crowd. Mockery deflated
them, it took the wind right out of their sails.

But Peter kept his head, maybe he had stood back and watched as
the rest of the group, or some of them, had streamed out into the crowd.
He might well have felt completely let down at first by enthusiasts who
possibly were spoiling what had been intended. He had to retrieve the
situation. He strode forward, maybe he got the Eleven together in a tight
group around him (Acts 1:14) and at the top of his voice he shouted:
"Fellow Jews. Give me a hearing. Listen to what I have to say." He shouted
for quiet and for order. He must have bellowed it out any amount of
times. Somehow his voice carried. Maybe all twelve of them shouted
for it together. They got some degree of order and attention, enough for
Peter to get a hearing.

He dealt first with the mockery. He knew he had first to scotch the taunt of them being drunk if they were going to be listened to and not laughed at and jeered. "These men are not drunk," he shouted. "It's only the third hour of the day." There is something about the phrase "these men" which could suggest he was pointing to a particular number of his colleagues who weren't going about things the way he wanted, but he did not disassociate himself from them. He defended them. "The third part of the day" was part of how the Jews divided up the day, it approximated to our nine o'clock in the morning. "No!" he shouted at the people who were mocking them. "No! They're not drunk. Nothing of the sort. This is what has been spoken through the prophet Joel." It requires no effort of imagination to visualize the quizzical looks on the faces of the crowd on hearing this—Peter's defence of the over-the-top spirits of some of his colleagues by calling on one of the prophets.

The verb used in the Septuagint translation of the Joel passage, ἐκχεῶ, means "pour out" like one "pours out wine", like from a bottle. Either it was just pure coincidence or he was replying in kind. We just do not know enough about him. "God says," Peter shouted back, "this will happen in the last days. I will pour out upon everyone a portion of my spirit." In other words, Peter could be saying, "Yes, they're drunk all right but not with alcohol. They're drunk with the spirit of God." And possibly, just possibly, there was even something more than that in what Peter was saying. Possibly, just possibly, Peter looked at his colleagues who had been accused of being drunk, and in them he saw something else.

> Your sons and your daughters shall prophesy; your young men
> will see visions and your old men will dream dreams. Yes, I will
> endue my slaves, yes even my slaves, both men and women with
> a portion of my spirit. And they shall prophesy. (Joel 3:1–2)

In choosing this text it is possible—possible, not guaranteed but possible—that among Peter's colleagues mixing in with the crowd there were the women of Acts 1:14 too. And maybe Peter, when he said "And they shall prophecy", turned and with a gesture indicated his colleagues, the women included, meaning, yes, some of them might be disorderly and noisy but that was their enthusiasm, that's the disorder of the spirit of God.

But really, we just do not know the details of what was happening. We do not know if in this speech, the first recorded speech made by the Church to humankind, Joel was in fact the only prophet Peter quoted from. At moments like this, when Luke records what Peter said, both on this occasion and at other events, he had a lot of the apostle's preaching or sermons to choose from, as we know from Acts 2:40. What is in the text before us, Acts 2:14–36, would have taken only a couple of minutes at the most to deliver, yet Peter was there all day in whatever street or streets or squares of Jerusalem he went to. We know he started at 9am if not before, and I doubt he let up before 6pm at the earliest. We can be sure that the argument he used in support of his claim that Jesus of Nazareth was the Messiah was the Resurrection and that the evidence for it was that he and all his fellow believers were "witnesses" to it (Acts 2:32); and, as we know from Paul (1 Corinthians 15:6), there were over 500 such witnesses, many of whom would have been resident in Jerusalem and present in the crowd that day. Peter, his fellow apostles, and many other witnesses to the Resurrection out of the 500 such as the women who had been the very first witnesses and the first to tell of it, must have been powerful and convincing. He, and they, how many of them we do not know, also worked dexterously with the Scripture texts, moving for example between different psalms as well as from Joel to the Psalms.

What we have before us is Luke's redaction of what was said by Peter that day, a summary as short as it can get. Luke wasn't writing for all and sundry, he was writing for a readership of believers; he hadn't anything to prove, he was out to inform his readership of some of the basics of how their faith had developed. So it had to be the case that Peter used many more Old Testament texts than just this one quotation from a minor prophet when he spoke to his listeners that day. Luke would have had both oral and written accounts of the events of that all-important Pentecost Sunday in his possession and from them he made his choice of what to put into his history. We have a perfect example of him doing just that, namely Stephen's speech before the Sanhedrin in Acts 7:2–53. That "speech" was Luke's organization of the records he possessed of what Stephen had been arguing day in and day out before "the people, the elders and the teachers of the Law" (v. 12). "This fellow never stops speaking," Stephen's accusers said to the Sanhedrin, "against this holy place and against the Law" (v. 13). There was no way he would have been allowed by either the Sanhedrin members or his angry accusers to make the long argument which Luke records as his speech at this trial. How angry they were is clear from what happened to him. "They were furious and they gnashed their teeth at him . . . they dragged him out of the city and began to stone him" (vv. 54,58). Nor was there anyone taking down longhand whatever he was able to say at the trial—if a trial it was. The speech was put together by Luke out of the preserved records of the speeches and arguments Stephen had put to the Jews before his arrest and his trial; Luke had collected them in preparation for the history he had in mind to write. The Acts contains a number of such literary devices.

We cannot know why exactly Luke gave pride of place to Peter's use of the Joel prophecy rather than others. However, in his Gospel, just before the moment when Jesus died on the cross, Luke describes the scene this way:

> There came darkness over the whole land, which lasted until three in the afternoon; the sun was in eclipse and the curtain of the temple was torn in two. Then Jesus gave a great cry and said: Father, into thy hands I commit my spirit . . . The crowd who had assembled for the spectacle, when they saw what had happened, went home beating their breasts. (Luke 24:44–8)

The Joel text reads:

> I will show portents in the sky above and signs on the earth below, blood and fire and billows of smoke. The sun shall be turned to darkness and the moon to blood before that great and resplendent day, the day of the Lord, shall come. And then everyone who invokes the name of the Lord shall be saved. (Joel 3:4–5)

It is possible that Luke was drawn to record Peter's use of Joel rather than his use of another prophet, because Joel prophetically corroborated how he had himself described the moment of the death of Jesus; or of

course his description of it had made use of Joel's prophecy. Luke was
concerned to point his readership to the total indescribable significance
and magnitude, even the majesty, of the death of Jesus and he found the
manner in which Joel described "the day of the Lord" too enticing not to.

However, interesting though that might be, it is speculation. What
isn't speculation is how magnificently and soundly Joel's prophecy
corresponded with what Peter, his fellow apostles and all the followers
and believers in Jesus, including "the women and Mary the mother of
Jesus and his brothers" (Acts 1:12), knew the Resurrection to be: "the day
of the Lord, that great and resplendent day" The word here translated as
"resplendent" also carries the meaning of making things known, revealing
things. It was a thunderous endorsement and Peter knew it was; and Luke,
with all the notes and texts in front of him, recognized its worth and
singled it out: "the great, the resplendent day of the Lord", ἡμέραν κυρίου
τὴν μεγάλην καὶ ἐπιφανῆ, *dies Domini magnus et manifestus*. It was what
Peter was arguing, standing there before the crowd of Jewish pilgrims, it
was what Peter was shouting out at the top of his voice: "God has raised
this Jesus to life and we are all witnesses to the fact ... Therefore let all
Israel be assured of this: God has made this Jesus whom you crucified
both Lord and Christ" (2:32–6).

And there was something more to it even than that. This Joel text has
something else besides. It started with the declaration: "In the last days,
God says, I will pour out my Spirit upon all flesh" (v. 17); and it finished
with the declaration: "and everyone who calls upon the Lord's name
shall be saved" (v. 21). Luke immediately recognized the immense value
and significance of that single statement, its role in what he was writing
his history for. What Peter was doing in citing Joel at this moment, at
this stage of his own journey towards full understanding of the nature
of the salvation Jesus was delivering, a full understanding which he
would receive in Joppa and Caesarea, was unknowingly proclaiming its
universality: "All flesh ... Whoever calls upon the name of the Lord
shall be saved." Almost definitely Joel himself as well as Peter at that
moment had his fellow Jews solely in mind; but Luke would not have been
reading it so narrowly. For Luke, composing his history some thirty or
more years after that first Whit Sunday, the Joel prophecy anticipated the
realization Peter would in due course experience of the universal nature

of the salvation wrought by Jesus when Peter witnessed the descent of the Holy Spirit upon the members of the Gentile household of Cornelius the Roman centurion.

That is the significance of the Joel prophecy in the mind of Luke. For us two thousand years later there might be an added significance. It is the faith of the Church that what Joel and Luke wrote is the Word of God; but what that means is difficult to render, and it is fools who would rush in where angels fear to tread, if they think there is a straightforward explanation of it. One reliable thing that might be said of it, however, is that what is in the Bible is not ours, we do not own it. It is God's word, not because God composed it or instructed what was to be written but because it is the word of the people of God. There are depths, it is deeper than what we know of it. The first half of the text reads:

> I will pour out my Spirit upon all flesh, your sons and daughters will prophesy, your young men will see visions, your old men will dream dreams. And yes indeed in those days I will pour out my Spirit on my slaves, both men and women, and they will prophesy. (Acts 2:18, cf. Joel 3:1)

Is there in the text, which is the word of God, a meaning which Peter in reciting it and Luke in narrating it, did not themselves see but which we now, in our modern circumstances, can see? "Upon all flesh, your sons and daughters . . . both men and women." Is it the case that in the first statement which the Christian Church, in the person of Peter, the first of the apostles, makes to the world, it gives to women an equality with men? Is Peter by using this Joel text, without being aware of it, equating women with men as recipients of the Spirit of God with the same prophetic office? It is God's word, not ours. We will see when dealing with Philip's missionary work among the Samaritans that Luke will make an emphatic point of the difference between Christianity and Judaism in that the rite of entry into Christianity is the same for women as for men.

What does "and they will prophesy" mean? Was it a teaching office? In Acts 15:32 Judas Barsabbas and Silas, whom the Council of Jerusalem will choose to take its letter to Antioch, are called "prophets", by which is meant "a person who, being filled with the Spirit, speaks with His authority".[7] In 15:22 the two men are also described as "leading men in the community/brotherhood". Peter was employing a text written by a minor prophet who lived sometime 900 to 500 BC in the southern kingdom of Judah, so we cannot presume continuity of meaning. However, Peter was using the word "prophesy" as it was used by the people of his own time and place, namely first-century Palestine, and not of Joel himself; and that is what matters. And judging by the importance within the Church accorded to Silas and Judas Barsabbas, being able to prophesy signified being ἡγούμενους, a person who leads, a leader.

How far can we, how far should we, take this? We will see in due course that Luke, in setting out the crucial differences between Christianity and Judaism, highlights the significance of baptism in contrast to circumcision in establishing the equality of women with men as baptized Christians. It was also the case that he was aware that already in the Church in his time women could be designated prophets. He tells us (Acts 21:9) that in the church in Caesarea the four unmarried daughters of Philip were prophets. Was it therefore the mind of Luke to assert the equality that should exist within the Church of women with men, a church in which women as well as men are called to "prophecy" which implies a position of teaching and leadership?

Peter and his fellow apostles and disciples were in the midst of pilgrims from all over Palestine and the countries and islands of the Mediterranean when they proclaimed that Jesus was the Messiah. Their evidence was the Resurrection. The Resurrection was an event as dramatic as anything that might possibly happen in the sky above or on the earth below. It was a reversal of everything normal and natural and as spell-binding as anything in the prophecy. What he was saying to them was that in the person of Jesus of Nazareth the world, their world, was being turned upside down. Nature was being defied. Peter knew that the Jewish leaders were emphatically opposed to what he would be preaching. It took guts. He had failed in the courtyard of the high priest. This time he would not. He put forward a concise and straightforward argument to the crowd.

> Men of Israel, listen to me. I speak of Jesus of Nazareth, a man
> singled out by God and made known to you through miracles,
> portents and signs, which God worked among you through him

as you well know. When he had been given up by you, by the deliberate plan and will of God, you with the help of lawless men did crucify and kill him. But God raised him to life again, setting him free from the pangs of death because it could not be that death should keep him in its grip. (Acts 2:22–25)

We mustn't read this passage with the mind of later Christians benefiting from, in our case, 2,000 years of development of doctrine. Nor is there time and space here to think out how Peter could say that it was "the deliberate plan and will of God" that the men of Israel had Jesus crucified and what he meant by it. We have to leave some things alone and just attend to issues which are pertinent to the outcome of the Council of Jerusalem some eighteen or so years later. All we can do here is read the texts with just that in mind and try to work out the mind of Peter and his fellow Jewish apostles and disciples a mere ten days after the Ascension. He spoke about "Jesus of Nazareth . . . a man singled out by God". He described Jesus to his fellow Jews as what he understood Jesus to be: "a man". We just cannot expect that the apostles after the Ascension could possibly have gone each day into the temple to tell their fellow Jews that Jesus was God; likewise we just cannot expect that they would confront a crowd of pilgrims on that first Whit Sunday after the Holy Spirit had descended upon them and tell them that Jesus was God. At that moment they just didn't see him like that. Peter called Jesus a man because that was what he understood him to be. He didn't play down the divinity of Jesus because he was afraid that if he had said any such thing to his fellow Jews they would have lynched him on the spot. He spoke to them of Jesus as "a man singled out by God", because that was what at that time he understood him to be, the Messiah yes, a most exceptional man, but still just a human being.

To appreciate what the apostles and all the other first Christians were up against we have to give free rein to our imagination. In contradiction of their preaching that Jesus was the promised Messiah was what had happened to him—he had been arrested, tried and found guilty by the Council of the Jews, scourged, made to wear a crown of thorns, humiliated by having to carry his cross through the streets up the hill of Calvary, stripped of his clothes and laid out across the cross by Roman soldiers, nailed to it, hoisted up between two common criminals, jeered by spectators, abandoned by his followers, only his mother, her sister his aunt, another woman and just one male follower sticking by him, dying slowly, a lance driven into his side, carried to a tomb belonging to someone else. We have to picture all that in our minds. Could such a wretch possibly be the Messiah? And all that would have been well known to a large number of the people of Jerusalem, and some of them were in the crowds the apostles were preaching to. That was what the apostles were up against. One can see the crowds milling about them, shouting out these things. They had to give them an answer.

The one argument they had that really had weight was the Resurrection. Only God could possibly have brought someone back from the dead, Jesus had claimed to be the Messiah, promised by God to the Jewish people. If he had been raised by God from the dead, he just had to be the Messiah. God hadn't even done it for King David. But Jesus hadn't appeared to everyone, just to those who had believed in him before he was killed. So where was the proof he had been raised from the dead? They, and they only, were the proof. They numbered over five hundred people (1 Corinthians 15:6) as well as the apostles. "And we're here, in front of you, we not only saw him, but we also spoke with him, we ate food with him, we received instructions from him, here we are, and we wouldn't be standing here now if it wasn't true."

That courage and conviction was the gift of the Holy Spirit on that first Whit Sunday, the feast of Pentecost. That was one of the two most important things that happened on that "great and glorious day" (Acts 2:20). The Holy Spirit had come into their hearts, he had given them a share in himself. He had poured himself out upon them (v. 17). He had given them "the power of utterance" (v. 4). They "were all filled" (v. 4) with such burning conviction and courage that "on that day some three thousand souls were added to their number" (v. 41). That was what the descent of the Holy Spirit brought about.

What it also brought about was insight into the meaning of Jesus; it brought about the first promulgation of the gospel of the Lord Jesus by the Christian Church to the world. Now, in that declaration, at this stage, there was no assertion of the divinity of Jesus. There is no such assertion anywhere in the Acts, whether by Peter or by Paul or at the Council of Jerusalem or anywhere in Luke's account of Paul's three missionary journeys or during his final visit to Jerusalem or his journey to and imprisonment in Rome. Peter calls Jesus just "Jesus of Nazareth", "the man Jesus" and "God's servant", "holy and righteous" (Acts 3:13–15), when he cures the man disabled from birth in "the name of Jesus", nothing more. He calls Jesus "the Messiah" (v. 20), "a prophet" (v. 23). In 4:27, the whole believing community in Jerusalem in joint prayer to God the "Sovereign Lord, maker of heaven and earth and sea and everything in them" speak of Jesus like this: "The God of our fathers raised up Jesus whom you have done to death by hanging him on a gibbet. He it is whom God has exalted with his own right hand as leader and saviour to grant Israel repentance and forgiveness of sins. And we are witnesses to this, and so is the Holy Spirit given by God to those who are obedient to him" (Acts 5:31f.).

We mustn't be surprised by this. For one thing the author of the Acts was narrating what the apostles at that moment understood Jesus to be. For another he was writing at least 40 years after these events. There just was no need for him writing so long after the Resurrection to make any such assertion, because by that time belief in the divinity of Jesus was the established faith of the Church. As already said, it had been arrived at much earlier. Paul in fact had asserted it with total clarity possibly a mere six or seven years after the Council in his letter to the Philippians (Philippians 2:5f.), though that letter could have been written by him later. Whenever it was written, there is agreement among the scholars that Luke would have been in Paul's company. Luke is not concerned in his account of the beginnings, development and outreach of the Church with the issue of the divinity of Jesus, because by the time he came to write his Gospel and the Acts it was a given. His concern rather was to give Theophilus (Acts 1:1) an account of how the Church developed and how the gospel was preached after the Ascension of Jesus into heaven. Luke is a historian as much as he is a theologian.

Peter's first declaration was to "his fellow Jews" and "all who live in Jerusalem" (Acts 2:14). "The promise is made to you and to your children and to all who are far away, everyone whom the Lord our God may call" (Acts 2:39). What has to be noted is the description of God as "our God". That wasn't Peter playing to his Jewish audience, it was where he was at at that moment. Just as he did not consider Jesus to be God, at that same time he believed the messiahship of Jesus was for the Jews only, that it was to them and them only that the promise had been made and that they and they only were his people. For that reason it was in the context of the Scriptures and Jewish history that he placed the argument for the significance of the Resurrection. He contrasted what had happened to Jesus with what had happened to King David, second only to Moses in importance in the Jewish religion. He argued from the Resurrection that with Jesus we are dealing with someone who was greater even than King David. "The patriarch David died and was buried," whereas "the Jesus we are speaking of has been raised by God, as we can all bear witness . . . exalted with God's right hand he received the Holy Spirit from the Father . . . and all you now see and hear flows from him" (Acts 2:34).

Peter's contention about Jesus therefore pivots on the Resurrection. The Twelve knew that from the very start. But for them it wasn't just its role as the proof of the messiahship when preaching to their fellow Jews that mattered to them. It was much more than that, and what had happened to them was what they wanted to communicate to everyone. It was what knocked them over, knocked them sideways, what convinced them, it was an overwhelming blinding shattering experience. They found themselves in the presence of a man who definitely had been dead and buried and now was alive and in front of them, eating with them, having a barbecue on the shore of the Sea of Galilee with them, showing them his wounds in his hands, his feet, his side. It was that that drove them forward from that moment onwards. It was that intense conviction that they communicated to their fellow Jews when, full of the Holy Spirit on the first Whit Sunday, they preached the messiahship of Jesus. Their total conviction was what did it, and it produced results, it worked. "Those who accepted his (Peter's) word—(his message, what he said)—were baptized, and some three thousand were added to their number that day" (Acts 2:41).

However, what precisely was the apostles' message to all these people? It is at this point that Luke records the all-significant change that had occurred in what must be the most important element of how the apostles and the rest of the believers now understood what the messiahship of Jesus consisted in, what Jesus had died and had risen from the dead for. The change recorded in their understanding is absolutely fundamental, but in Luke's account in the Acts there is nothing that prepares us for it. He gives no explicit explanation of it. He seems to take it for granted, which is understandable as he was composing the Acts many years later; and, anyway, he probably thought the reason was obvious. He began the Acts describing the apostles as asking Jesus when he will "re-establish the sovereignty of Israel" (Acts 1:6). That was the declaration by the apostles of their belief that Jesus was Israel's Messiah and a political one at that, and their proof was their witness of his resurrection. For that reason Peter, addressing the crowd in Jerusalem on Pentecost Sunday, could conclude the speech he made with a firm appeal: "Let all Israel then accept as certain that God has made this Jesus whom you crucified both Lord and Messiah" (2:36). His listeners are described as "cut to the heart" by the argument Peter has put before them and they ask him and his fellow apostles: "Friends/brothers what are we to do?" But startlingly Peter's reply not only says nothing about any restoration of Israel to independence but takes his listeners somewhere else entirely and presents Jesus to them as a totally different sort of Messiah; and Luke does that without any explanation at all. What that tells us is that Luke is moving fast forward to the understanding about the messiahship of Jesus which Peter and the apostles had actually arrived at in the nine- or ten-day interval between the Ascension and Whit Sunday, which Luke abbreviated into a single sentence, into one single exhortation: "Repent and be baptized, everyone of you, in the name of Jesus the Messiah for the forgiveness of your sins, and you will receive the gift of the Holy Spirit" (2:37f.). That was now their message, their gospel, their transformed understanding. The Christian concept of messiahship has become redemption from sin. There is now no mention by Peter of any political understanding at all, and it never gets a mention again. The messiahship of Jesus has become in the space of a mere ten days a spiritual matter, which of course is what it remains to this day.

For the apostles to preach this new understanding of the Messiah on the day of Pentecost, an understanding for which their listeners could have had little, if any, preparation and one which as a consequence helped make the departure of Christianity from Judaism inevitable, and indeed necessary, must indicate that Luke is not presenting us with detail about how the apostles went about their catechetical endeavours on and around this occasion, but rather with the end result. We can have no reliable idea how the people in that crowd understood what Peter meant by what he said to them, especially the notion of receiving the Holy Spirit. It is all too obviously an example of easy usage by Luke of what soon enough became a basic formula in the Christian message. However, that is not the focus here. The focus here in this script is on the "Repent and be baptized, everyone of you, in the name of Jesus the Messiah for the forgiveness of your sins" (Acts 2:38).

As has been said, there is nothing Luke has told us about which prepares us for this. He had first presented the apostles to his readership as associating the messiahship of Jesus with creation of a sovereign and independent Israeli state, which understanding of it nullifies the Christian understanding of the messiahship of Jesus. But of course Jesus's messiahship is the culmination of salvation history. Salvation history is God's plan as from the fall of Adam and Eve to bring about the reconciliation of humanity to himself made necessary by their sin. Their sin is the sin of the world, which the Christian liturgy speaks of. The sin of the world is rejection by human beings of God. God set that right, human beings did not. "I myself will ask after my sheep and go in search of them," said the Lord (Ezekiel 34:11), which is what he did in his Son and the form God's search for humanity took could not possibly have been foreseen. "The Word became flesh" surpasses all possible human anticipation.

The transformation in the heads of the apostles and their fellow believers from Acts 1:6 to 2:38 is so massive and different as to be almost indefinable and indescribable. We are now talking about something fundamentally different from the political aspirations of an oppressed nation. When, at that moment on the day of Pentecost, Peter tells his listeners "that they should repent and be baptized in the name of Jesus the Messiah" for the forgiveness of their sins he is, undoubtedly without being aware of it, opening up the Church, indeed all humanity, to an initial awareness of the reconciliation of human beings with God through the death of Jesus, and then in due course to the great theological themes of redemption and grace. Peter's exhortation to his listeners is the first step taken by the Church in the direction of understanding the true nature of Jesus, the Incarnation, because as the Pharisees themselves had rightly said to Jesus himself, only God can forgive sin. It will be a long road to travel, from the date of the Ascension to the year when Paul wrote his letter to the Philippians, before the Church will begin to talk about the Messiah as God himself, God becoming a human being, the Creator of all becoming a creature, the Lord God Almighty Jesus Christ, for whom, in the words of Christina Rossetti, "a stable, a breastful of milk and a mangerful of hay sufficed, whom angels fell down before, and the ox, the ass and the camel adored".

Peter's reply to the heartfelt question his listeners put to him represented his and his fellow apostles' new understanding of the messiahship of Jesus. Reading the texts as carefully as is possible it would seem that for Luke the explanation for the enhanced degree of understanding they had arrived at was the descent of the Holy Spirit with "a noise like that of a strong driving wind, tongues like flames of fire, resting on each one, and they were all filled with the Holy Spirit". Of course there would have been more to it. Grace builds on nature, it does not replace it. The apostles had made their own preparations for what was going to happen on Pentecost Sunday. The text makes that abundantly clear. Jesus had vanished from their sight and then "two men in white" appeared to tell them they shouldn't hang about. So "they returned to Jerusalem, entering the city they went to the room upstairs where they were lodging", all eleven of them, where "they were constantly at prayer together and with them a group of women including Mary the mother of Jesus and his brothers. And it was during this time that Peter stood up with the assembled brotherhood all around him" (Acts 1:12–16).

He organized the choice of Judas's successor. As their numbers increased, they had to move into larger premises. They had held meetings and prayed together; and in those meetings Peter held a position that looks at least like that of a chairman. They had debated and agreed what the criterion was for any one of them to succeed Judas, but that was hardly the only thing they'd discussed and prayed about in the ten or so days before the feast of Pentecost. They must have discussed everything, debating the Scriptures page upon page and every word they could remember that Jesus had preached to the public and said to them in private (e.g. Mark 4:34). They would have discussed who Jesus actually was, his ministry, his death and resurrection and what sort of Messiah he was. They must have trawled through everything. We can safely assume that 120 men and women, meeting and praying together over a period of some ten days, didn't discuss and decide just on one issue, namely the successor to Judas, even though that is the only item Luke reports on. That would be nonsense. And what's equally sure is that they didn't just confine themselves to only one premises. They had families, they had homes, they had relations and friends, as Jews there was the temple to go to and pray in, there were synagogues throughout the city, there were shops and bazaars to go to to get food, and there they doubtless spoke with fellow citizens who asked them all sorts of questions about what they were up to and what they stood for. In other words, they themselves had put in an immense amount of thought, discussion and prayer in preparation for the descent that first Whit Sunday of the Holy Spirit. It wasn't empty minds that the Spirit of God engaged with but minds assiduously and eagerly prepared for his coming and infusion.

"The promise is made to you and to your children and to all who are far away, everyone whom the Lord our God may call" (Acts 2:39). As Luke enthusiastically makes clear (Acts 2:37), lots of people began to accept the message Peter and his fellow apostles preached to them that day and in the days, weeks and months that followed. The Church grew rapidly both in size and in structure. It was dealing with Jewish people after all, their own people, people familiar with the notion of the Messiah and the prayer life of the temple. They weren't people of a different religion and culture coming at it cold. Rapidly it took on its own shape and created its own communal life, identity and reputation and worship, as Luke describes it to us in Acts 2:42-7. They continued with the prayer life they were all familiar with, namely the temple worship; and where it came to what was a distinctly Christian liturgy, namely the Eucharist, they did that in their own houses, at home one might say, "breaking bread in private houses" (v. 46), which in itself is a most interesting item of information. The modern Church, which has become building-bound and inordinately, indeed excessively, priest-centred, would do well to take note.

Luke presents these early moments so memorably, so touchingly, it is almost as if he felt it were the Garden of Eden recreated: "They held firmly to the teaching of the apostles, to share a common life, to break bread and the prayers. A sense of awe was everywhere and all the believers were together and held everything in common. Selling their possessions and goods they gave to anyone as he had need. Every day they continued to meet in the temple. They broke bread in their own homes and they ate together joyfully and in simplicity of heart, praising God and enjoying the favour of all the people" (Acts 2:42–6). On reading this passage St John Chrysostom was moved to describe this moment in the life of the Church as "an angelic community". "The breaking of bread" is the earliest title of what we call the Eucharist; and the use of the definite article before "prayers" may well indicate that they already had a fixed liturgy.

The harmony, peacefulness and prayerful tranquillity which Luke describes was profound, but it wasn't to last. It is what might have been. Not immediately, but within a chapter, Luke begins his account of the harsh opposition the believers in Jesus of Nazareth as the Messiah now encounter from the Jewish leadership and in due course his account of internal disagreements within the Church, both of which bring on arguments, division and persecution which in turn become the agents of the change and development which were what he wanted his readership to know about.

# CHAPTER 5

# A Significant Miracle in the Temple Precincts

Luke's account, Chapters 3 and 4, of what happened over two days a little later informs us of how and why the break with Judaism began, and, by reading between the lines, we can dig out quite a lot more. The separation was a most crucial event in Church history. It wasn't what the first Christians either wanted or expected. They wanted all their fellow Jews to accept Jesus as the Messiah and they thought that their witness of his resurrection supplied totally convincing evidence, in much the same way—possibly—as the evidence that we are living in a period of seriously harmful human-induced climate change appears irrefutable. Then as now, however, there are others factors besides evidence which influence how people make their minds up about something; and what is evidence for one person isn't necessarily evidence for another. Luke begins his account of how the break developed with a man crippled from birth begging Peter and John for money from the spot at the entrance to the temple where his family brought him and put him every day. In this story the man represents the Jewish people. The Jewish people, as Luke is representing them, are a disadvantaged people because they have not yet accepted Jesus as the Christ. The story is full of significances.

The man sees Peter and John, still keeping to the observances of their Jewish faith, entering the temple to pray. He puts out his hand. Peter replies "Silver and gold I do not have, but what I do have I will give you. In the name of Jesus Christ of Nazareth, walk!" (3:6). As a profession of faith it was as bold as can be, and making it in the temple precincts itself rendered it bolder still. By calling Jesus of Nazareth "Christ" Peter was asserting that the man from Nazareth was the Messiah. But everyone within earshot knew that this Jesus had been put to death. A dead Messiah was of course no Messiah, so it was an assertion that Jesus Christ of Nazareth was alive, had indeed risen from the dead, and that by the power of God himself, which of course was what Peter and the apostles' colleagues had been saying for days to all and sundry in the temple and the city synagogues. A man who died is now alive.

So far their evidence for the Resurrection was that they had witnessed it; now Peter is offering further proof. He'd told the man who was disabled to get up and walk "in the name of Jesus", that is, by the authority and the power of Jesus who is alive; and the man did. "Now, let Israel do the same," he would have said to himself. On his part it wasn't a gamble, it was an act of faith. He was making a public and outspoken declaration of his faith in Jesus as the Messiah who, despite having been put to death, was alive and able to restore the full use of his limbs to a man disabled from birth, and that right in the temple in full view of everyone. There could hardly have been a more convincing item of proof. Peter was explicit that the miracle was being performed by Jesus as the Messiah, the Christ (Acts 3:6).

He then followed it up, without as much as drawing breath, by saying to the crowds in the temple rushing over to him that this Jesus had received "the highest honour" from their God, "the God of Abraham, Isaac and Jacob, the God of our fathers". Peter is firmly identifying himself with the Jewish people, but in dealing with them he pulls no punches. On the one hand, he says to them, they hadn't only repudiated this man to whom God has given the highest honours, not only had him tried in the court of the Gentile Pilate, but they had "killed the author or prince of life", "the one who has led the way to life" (Acts 3:15). By now the apostles and their fellow Christians had put in an immense amount of thinking, discussion and prayer, bringing them to realize that the fact that Jesus was now alive despite having been killed endowed him with a special relationship to life itself. One can easily detect where the deepening understanding of Jesus by the apostles and first Christians was heading.

Peter tells the crowd that the miracle was not their doing but God's in and through Jesus. In itself there is nothing difficult or unusual about it. The way he tells that to them, however, is in content difficult and is expressed in a complicated way. It is the first mention of faith in Jesus and of the role of faith in Jesus. Pístis as from this first mention will feature greatly in all that follows. The text reads: "And by faith in his name his name has made strong this man whom you see and know; and the faith which is through him has given him this complete healing in the presence of all of you" (Acts 3:16). It is a statement which has to be worked through. Peter attributes the healing of the crippled man to the name of Jesus, "Name" stands for power and authority. With that in mind I will expand the translation of what Peter said as follows:

> Because of his faith in the power of Jesus, the power of Jesus has then made this man strong whom you now see before you and whom you know was disabled; and indeed, it is the man's faith in Jesus, a faith which comes from Jesus, which has made him completely well in front of you, for all of you to see. (Acts 3:16)

Peter was making it absolutely clear to the crowd that it wasn't himself and John who had worked this miracle, but Jesus himself had done it; and since Jesus had done it, he had to be alive, and therefore he had indeed risen from the dead, and that was only possible by the power of God, "the God of Abraham, Isaac and Jacob", the God of their ancestors. On the one hand God had glorified his servant Jesus with this miracle while they, the crowd, "had handed him over, 'the author of life' to be killed". And more than that, it was the power—the hand—of Jesus that had worked this miracle; and since only God could work such miracles, it meant that Jesus was acting with the power of God behind him, and therefore God was with Jesus and that meant that they should have faith in him as the Messiah whom all the prophets had foretold (v. 18).

Peter also says it is by faith in Jesus's name that the cripple at the gate has been healed. His words are: "Faith in him (Jesus) has restored this man to complete health." But he also says: "It is the name of Jesus which has strengthened this man." That has to be read to mean that for Jesus to work this miracle there first has to be belief in him on the part of the disabled man. However, Peter will also say when he meets up with the Judaic faction in Jerusalem on his return from Caesarea that "believing in the Lord Jesus Christ" is the gift of God (Acts 11:17). It is offered to us by God, but we must be open to it. We have the responsibility to say yes or no to it. God did not create robots; we have free will; he wants our response. Faith is not an implant. It would be useless if it were.

Peter at this stage of this understanding of the saving plan of God is addressing his fellow Jews (Acts 3:25). That is the theological position he is at. He says that their salvation from sin and their acceptability to God has been achieved by Jesus. He says to them that that has happened to them because they are the "heirs of the prophets" and "are of the covenant that God made with their fathers". But he goes further. For the first time, quoting Genesis 12:3, he says that "in them all peoples on earth will be blessed". However, at this stage that is not what is in his mind. It is what relates to the Jewish people, the people of the temple in front of him, that he was concerned about. That he is concerned about. We know Genesis 12:3 to be a prediction of universal salvation; that, however, is not what Peter is predicting; he relates the whole verse but he is not reflecting on the universalist message it contains. He is a long way still from his journey's end which is Joppa, Caesarea and Acts 15:11. Yet for all that, where Peter has arrived at by this moment represents immense theological progress on his part and that of his fellow apostles. They had done it by means of their study of the Scriptures as they had been shown by Jesus through their Emmaus colleagues (Luke 24:32), by constant prayer (Acts 1:14) and of course the continuing presence of the Holy Spirit among them.

The theological position they had arrived at differed fundamentally from the Jewish faith which was still in their bloodstream. They were engaged in two battles: one within themselves and the second with what the Council of the Jews represented. What the Council of the Jews represented was the belief or faith about the Jewish people which finds its expression again and again throughout all the Old Testament, that they were the one nation about whom he cared, that they were special in the eyes of God, that they, and they alone, were his chosen people: "They shall know that I, the Lord their God, am with them, and that they are my people Israel, says the Lord God. You are my flock, my people, the flock I feed and I am your God. This is the very word of the Lord" (Ezekiel 34:30f.). Really, to be able to fully appreciate what the apostles and first disciples of Jesus had been brought up to believe, the way they saw themselves and their fellow Jews and the rest of humanity, the religious mentality they had to battle with, we should read and re-read, for example, Ezekiel 34–7, written during the Babylonian exile.

> I am gathering up the Israelites from their places of exile among the nations; I will assemble them from every quarter and restore them to their own soil. Thus they shall become my people and I will become their God. My servant David shall become king over them and they will have one shepherd. They shall conform to my laws, they shall observe and carry out my statutes. They shall live in the land which I gave to my servant Jacob, the land where your fathers lived. They and their descendants shall live there forever . . . I will make a covenant with them to bring them prosperity; . . . I will put my sanctuary forever in their midst. They shall live under the shelter of my dwelling. I will become their God and they shall become my people. The nations shall know that I am keeping Israel sacred to myself, because my sanctuary is in the midst of them forever. (Ezekiel 37:21–8)

This is what the apostles had been brought up on, this was their daily bread. It explains Acts 1:6; it explains what the Judaic faction within the infant Church would soon be struggling to preserve; it explains Peter's initial and instinctive reaction to the vision he was to have in Joppa; and it explains what an incredible achievement Peter's speech to the Council of Jerusalem in Acts 15:6–11 represents.

The apostles had inherited the belief that they, and they alone, were the one and only nation God had chosen as his own and that they should live apart from Gentiles. What they were now beginning to understand was that these things were not what Jesus the Messiah was about. They were in fact undergoing a purge within their very selves of what they had been brought up with. What they were beginning to realize was that what mattered most was the forgiveness by God of sin and reconciliation with him through Jesus and faith in him. Jesus's death and resurrection was the "way to life", it was a new sort of "life", a new "way", "the way of salvation" (Acts 16:17) and "the way of the Lord" (Acts 18:25). What that was they were now beginning to understand. Faith in Jesus is what the apostles from that moment on will teach as what matters, but they didn't address it as theologians. They just weren't theologians. There wasn't one theologian among them, not as we know them anyway. Their utterances, such as Luke records as spoken by Peter, were spontaneous and verbally quite simple. The members of the Council of the Jews recognized this the moment they saw them. They were soon to call them "ἀγράμματοί εἰσιν καὶ ἰδιῶται" (4:13), which is variously translated as common men, unschooled ordinary men, illiterate and untrained men, untrained laymen, unlearned and ignorant men, and in the Vulgate "homines sine litteris et idiotae". It wasn't any structured training in the Jewish religion that the apostles exhibited in the temple that day. What they brought to the temple that day was their experience of Jesus, his ministry and his resurrection, their witness of which was now casting a totally new light on everything about him which they had witnessed and heard from him (cf. Mark 4:34) during his life with them. That is what fired them, that and the descent of the Holy Spirit.

It is necessary to realize that the apostles weren't theologians. They hadn't been subjected to any academic training in their religion that we know of. There is no evidence of anything like that in the time of their association with the Baptist; all we know about it is that it might have included periods of fasting (cf. Mark 2:18). Such sessions might also have been occasions when there was some instruction, sermons, debate and discussion, whatever form that might have taken; but of course we do not know if those apostles who had been with the Baptist had attended any such sessions or exercises anyway. They had other things to do as well, wives and children to support, a living to make. Nor do we know how long a period they had been in the company of the Baptist. We do know, however, that Jesus made a point of distinguishing how he went about giving them instruction from how both the Pharisees and the Baptist went about it. He had no time for fasting while he was with them (Mark 2:19), and that would therefore have included those moments when "privately to his disciples he explained everything" (Mark 4:34). However, squaring that with Acts 1:6 is nigh on impossible since 1:6 exposes ignorance on their part of a most fundamental kind.

The majority of the apostles had been fishermen, and, as we know from John 23:3, they returned to their trade after the death of Jesus. The members of the Council of the Jews, "rulers, elders, scribes and priestly stock, doctors of the law and lawyers" (cf. John 4:5), knew in a flash that the apostles just weren't their sort, not by a long shot; it was a case of class difference amongst other things, and possibly that also really worried them as an elite. The apostles had got together, most of them, before they had even met with Jesus; they were unrefined independent heady seekers after the Messiah but untutored. They were much closer to the people than the Jewish elite who populated the Council of the Jews. They weren't metropolitan, they weren't the elite. They had gathered round the Baptist thinking he might be the Messiah; they come across as rough-cut unpolished Jewish enthusiasts, difficult to deal with, unpredictable, quarrelsome with streaks of envy and ambition (Matthew 20:20) and quite capable of outbursts of rash behaviour (Mark 14:47, John 18:10). Then, when push came to shove and Jesus was arrested, every one of them "deserted him and ran away" (Matthew 26:56), though Peter did find enough courage and loyalty to turn and get inside the courtyard of the High Priest (Mark 14:66), but then when confronted denied he even knew who Jesus was.

The only people who stood by Jesus at the moment of his crucifixion were his mother, her sister who was the wife of Clopas, Mary Magdala and a disciple who wasn't an apostle. It was those four who stayed right with him, even as he was crucified, watched him being nailed to the cross, raised up between two bandits, surrounded by soldiers and a jeering crowd; they watched it all; they stood beneath him as he hung there; they watched him die; they helped take his body down from the cross and get it into a tomb. In full view of everyone. But not the apostles; they weren't even there; they'd done a runner; it wasn't even one of them who had the guts to approach Pontius Pilate about the burial. The whole thing is mind-blowing. It takes some thinking out. What saved them was the fact that they kept together somehow, somewhere, and stayed around. They weren't far away. Something in their heads kept them together and nearby. They stayed within running distance of the tomb (John 20:1f.), the women knew where to find them (ibid. and Luke 24), as did the two disciples who had given up on Jesus and took the road to Emmaus (ibid.). It was the women who prepared the spices to anoint the body who met with and spoke to the Risen Lord before any one of them did (John 20:10ff.). However, once the evangelists had mentioned what the women had done in their accounts of the Resurrection, we find that they, the evangelists, immediately transferred the whole story to what the men then did. Regrettable and typical, but there it is. It was a difficult time for both God and human beings. The gospel needed preaching, the Church needed founding and, given the customs of the time, and most time since, it had to be men who did it. There just was no way women, better and braver though they were, could do what the men did. God had to work with what was there. In comparison with the women, as the two genders appear in the Gospel accounts, the men up to that point were second rate, but that was how it was, that was what God had to work with.

By now the apostles and their fellow believers had popular backing—" the people acclaimed them" (Acts 5:13), so much so that when it came to arresting them the captain of the temple guard hesitated to do it for fear of being stoned by the people (Acts 5:26). Every now and then the ruling elite, be it political or cultural or both, lose control; it may be through a revolution or a referendum; and the people they consider barbarians sometimes get inside the gates. The elite don't like it, the gates after all are theirs, they built them and all the obstructions on them, and as happens when referendums don't go the way the ruling and cultural elite want, they pull every trick in the book to change it. In this instance, however, they weren't in control. The Jesus crowd didn't argue the way the Jewish Council members argued; they argued from the effects of a blinding and shattering experience which, as it was described much later by the author of the John Gospel, brought them down to their knees, crying out: "My Lord and my God" (John 20:28). Little wonder they'd been taken to have been drunk earlier on.

Paul will take the theology of faith in Jesus to profounder depths and greater heights, but what we have here in Peter's statement is its significant beginnings. Peter confronts the crowd of people converging on him from all over the temple when they saw the miracle that had been wrought. "Not us," he cries out. "Me and John didn't do it. It wasn't down to any power and godliness on our part. It is the God of our fathers, of Abraham, Isaac and Jacob, who has done it to glorify his servant Jesus. You disowned him, the Holy and Righteous One, you killed the author of life, but God raised him from the dead. We are witnesses of it. It was this man's faith in the name of Jesus (Acts 3:16) that healed him." Peter had an argument to make. It was in two parts. The miracle had occurred, all the crowd in the temple had seen it. They had heard Peter say that the man would be healed in the name of Jesus of Nazareth. That is what had then happened, and Peter tells them that it proved that Jesus had risen from the dead and was alive, and therefore he was the Christ, the Messiah.

The second part then took the matter of the death of Jesus a crucial step further. Jesus did not die just in order to rise again and provide Peter and the apostles with a good reason for claiming Jesus was the Messiah. His death had another purpose. It was redemptive. Peter said to the crowd that the prophets had said that "his (God's) Christ should suffer" (Acts 3:18). Jesus had of course spoken of it a number of times, most notably after Peter's profession of faith (Matthew 16:16). "From that time on Jesus began to explain to his disciples that he must go to Jerusalem and suffer many things . . . and that he must be killed" (Matthew 16:21). Then Peter had been horrified, now he and his fellow apostles are beginning to understand what Jesus was about. It is the start of redemption theology. It is the death of Jesus that brings about the forgiveness of sin. "Repent and be baptized in the name of Jesus Christ for the forgiveness of your sins" (Acts 2:38). Peter had said on Pentecost Sunday, and again now: "Repent and turn to God so that your sins may be wiped out" (Acts 3:19). What we are witnessing is a slow and hesitant journey on the part of Peter in understanding. It reaches its goal at the Council of Jerusalem with the statement he makes in Acts 15:11: "It is by the grace of the Lord Jesus that we are saved." Paul expands and develops this argument in his letters to the Galatians and to the Romans. Paul had been present at the Council and had heard, and then worked on, what Peter had said to it.

There is something else in Peter's speech which merits consideration. He said: "The God of Abraham, Isaac and Jacob, the God of our fathers, has given the highest honour to his servant Jesus, whom you committed to trial and repudiated in Pilate's court—repudiated the one who was holy and righteous when Pilate had decided to release him" (Acts 3:13–14). Peter spoke in Aramaic when he spoke to the servant girl and others when he was waiting in the courtyard while Jesus was being tried, and here too in the temple to his fellow Jews. In his Gospel account of Jesus's prediction that Peter will deny him (Luke 22:34), the word Luke uses for denial is ἀπαρνήσῃ, a word he repeats in 22:57, when Peter denies he had been in the company of Jesus and even as much as knew him: "Woman, I don't even know him." He says that again in verse 60, then in the following verse when he recalls the prediction and went out of the priest's court and "wept bitterly"—that same word for repudiation is used again. One of Luke's main sources is the Gospel of Mark, as it was for Matthew. When recording the prediction made by Jesus to Peter that he would deny him and describing the moment when Peter did betray him, the three use the same Greek vocabulary, as indeed does John in 13:38 and 18:25–7. Obviously the story was so significant, and dramatic, it was passed down word for word across all Christian communities, no matter how scattered they had become. The point being made here presumes that the Greek text is a reliable translation of the actual Aramaic words used when both Jesus's prediction and Peter's denials were recorded and handed down in Aramaic both orally and in writing. Luke was only too aware, when writing Acts 3:13f., of the significance of what he had written, and of the words he was using when writing Acts 22:34 and 22:62.

When Peter spoke to the Jews in the temple (Acts 3:13f.) about how they had repudiated/disowned/denied Jesus, he could not have been anything but aware that he'd done the same himself before they did. He'd disowned Jesus, he'd denied him. If he didn't pause at that moment and hesitate for a minute or two, questioning his own right to preach to anyone on this matter, one would be surprised. One can see him thinking and saying to himself before he spoke: "Don't look at them. Just keep going. They probably haven't heard what I did. I can only hope so." The thought makes one wonder whether it was for that reason he said to them: "My friends, I know quite well that you acted in ignorance, and so did your rulers" (v. 17). Peter had been there. And Luke, writing out Peter's speech to the Jews in the temple, containing the words it did, must have said to himself: "Yes, I know, Peter, but you repented and you more than made up for it, even in the end laying down your life for the Lord Jesus."

Peter then carried on trying to get through to the Jewish people listening to him by appealing to their scriptures, which was the way of argument his audience was familiar with and would understand. He reminds them that the prophets foretold that God's "Messiah should suffer" (Acts 3:18); and that "all the prophets from Samuel onwards with one voice predicted this present time" (vv. 24–6); and he goes so far as to say, and this surely is one thing that must have made the Jewish leadership angry and hostile, that Moses himself had said that "the Lord God will raise up a prophet for you from among yourselves and you shall listen to everything he says to you and anyone who refuses to listen to that prophet must be extirpated from Israel" (vv. 22–4). If anything was going to make the blood of the Jewish Establishment boil that was it. They were being told in no uncertain terms by total unknowns, amateurs, upstarts, ἰδιῶται (4:13), from the distant province of Galilee, that they would be the object of the severest of punishments set out by Moses himself. It was then made even worse by Peter saying—and this in full view of everyone in the temple itself—that Jesus was God's servant and God had raised him from the dead "so that their sins might be wiped out" (v. 19) and "he might turn everyone of them from their wicked ways" (v. 26). That Peter also said to them: "I know quite well that you acted in ignorance, and so did your rulers", hardly made up for it.

It all seems to indicate that considerable bad blood had been building up between the two sides and it was all rapidly developing into open confrontation, as they met up with each other, disputing and arguing, throughout the city, in the temple and the many other Jerusalem synagogues, in the shops, the streets, the squares. They had reached an impasse. For the Jewish leadership there was the impossibility of them acknowledging Jesus as the Messiah when they had collaborated in putting him to death. And it was not helping them, it was in fact infuriating them, that lots of people in Jerusalem "were accepting his word" (2:41), as well as the fact that Peter was claiming that by raising Jesus from the dead God was wanting "to turn everyone of them from their wicked ways" (3:26). Hardly a turn of phrase to win them over. They could see no other way out of the impasse except to have recourse to whatever force their status and powers made available to them. Undoubtedly the apostles for their part were finding it at the least frustrating, and infuriating, that there was this refusal of the Jewish leadership to accept their "witness" of the Resurrection and its logic, and the significance of the miracle that had taken place before the eyes of everyone present in the Temple. Something had to happen, something had to give.

CHAPTER 6

# The Apostles Confront the
# Council of the Jews

The Jewish leadership didn't delay. They came in force into the temple itself, interrupting Peter and John while they were preaching. Supported by the temple officers, they just closed them down on the spot, even bringing some Sadducees along who were happy to cooperate since they objected strongly to any mention of resurrection and afterlife. It must have been a scene and a half, the apostles protesting before being frogmarched out of the temple precincts and into the streets to the local prison, all sorts of people watching with fascination, no doubt cat-calling both sides, probably Christian converts making any amount of noise and protesting, possibly some of them mixing it with the bouncers to get the apostles released. They couldn't. The apostles were kept in overnight, and the trial was fixed for the following morning.

And what a scene that must have been: "The Jewish rulers, elders and doctors of the Law", together with "Annas the High Priest and Caiaphas", and two men whom we have never met before anywhere and never appear again, a John and an Alexander, as well as "members of the high-priestly families" (Acts 4:5f.). It was the same ruling elite back again who had, in Peter's words, "committed God's servant Jesus for trial and repudiated him in Pilate's court" (3:13). That was the trial that Luke had in mind, and this one in its way was a re-run of it, except that this time Peter's part in it was different. Here Peter came good, arraigned before the same panel of judges, making amends for his failure to have stood by Jesus. For Luke the panel represented establishment Judaism, which was the Judaism, as he wants us to appreciate, that the new Christian Church, by reason of Judaism's rejection of Jesus the true Messiah, was now itself about to repudiate. The Church believed Jesus of Nazareth to be the Messiah for whom the Jewish people had waited for throughout its long existence. The Jewish people as represented by "the Jewish rulers, elders and doctors of the Law", who had collaborated with their Roman rulers in his death, had refused, and were still refusing despite the evidence of the Resurrection which had been bolstered by the healing of the cripple, to accept Jesus as the Messiah. It was the beginning of the parting of the ways.

The break with Judaism was not sought, it wasn't wanted, it wasn't even contemplated; it was forced upon the Church. The rejection of Jesus by the Jewish leadership, even to the extent of condemning him to death, was in the unfathomable design of God what brought salvation to the world: "The Messiah is to suffer death and to rise from the dead on the third day, and in his name repentance bringing the forgiveness of sin is to be proclaimed to all nations" (Luke 24:46f.). The rejection by Judaism of what the apostles preached, be it in the temple itself as in this instance or in a synagogue as in Acts 13:16–41, was what forced the apostles to make the break with Judaism: "It was necessary that the word of God should be declared to you first. But since you reject it and thus condemn yourselves as unworthy of eternal life, we now turn to the Gentiles" (v. 46). Nothing so broke the heart of Paul as he tells us in his letter to the Romans, and it was not the hope and vision that the apostles had had for their own Jewish people ever since they had been born, the vision and the hope expressed long ago by the prophet Micah:

> I will gather all of you, O house of Jacob,
> I will bring together the remnant of Israel.
> I will bring them together like sheep into a pen,
> like a flock into its pasture,
> and the place will throng with people.
> Their king will pass before them,
> with the Lord leading them. (Micah 2:12f.)

For the apostles and their fellow disciples, ardent and hopeful Jews though they were, it was not working out that way. Before their very eyes, as they saw it, the house of Jacob was rejecting the Messiah whom God had sent. The days were now upon them, though they did not yet realize it, when, as the writer of the epistle to the Hebrews (Chapters 8 and 9) will say, "The Lord will conclude a new covenant with the house of Israel and the house of Jacob" (8:8), a new covenant in which he will "set his laws in their understanding and write them on their hearts" (v. 10), laws which will not be "matters of food and drink and various rites of cleansing, all just outward ordinances . . . offerings and sacrifices which cannot give the worshipper inward perfection" (9:10). Of this new covenant Jesus "is the mediator. He offered himself without blemish to God, a spiritual and eternal sacrifice. His blood will cleanse our consciences from the deadness of our former ways and fit us for the service of the living God" (v. 14). And this new house of Israel and Jacob, as the prophet Micah foretold, will now be one where "peoples will come streaming in and many nations shall come and say: 'Let us climb up on to the mountain of the Lord, to the house of the God of Jacob, that he may teach us his ways and will walk in his paths.' For instruction issues from Zion and out of Jerusalem comes the word of the Lord" (Micah 4:2). The Church was treading the path to the Council of Jerusalem from the first moment it presented its message to the world. However, at the time of this first trial of theirs before the representatives of establishment Judaism, when Peter and John were standing before the Jewish leadership, they really had no idea what influence newcomers into the Church such as Diaspora Jews, Samaritans and Gentiles would bring to bear upon their own understanding of what Christianity consisted in.

Peter and John now stood before this panel of judges. Not just before them but "they set the prisoners in the middle and began to interrogate them" (Acts 4:7). One can only guess at what was going through the minds of the two apostles at that moment. Three years or so earlier they had been just another crew of fishermen on a lake some one hundred and fifty miles to the north, yes, with a fervent interest in their religion and avid searchers after the Messiah, but still just full-time fishermen with wives and children to support and care for, harming no one, totally unknown. And now here they were, arraigned before the highest religious court in the land, in Jerusalem itself, before the High Priest himself and all this council. They hadn't committed any crime, they hadn't been involved in any rebellion or disturbance, all they'd done was preach their version of Judaism to their fellow Jews. Yet now they found themselves, as the text tells us (v. 7), right in the middle of the Sanhedrin itself, the highest court in the land, and that in the Beth-din, the Judgement Hall. They must have been asking themselves what had hit them.

The judges didn't beat around the bush. They knew what they had to do. They went straight in. They asked the apostles, "By what power or by what name have such men as you done this?" (Acts 4:7). The NET translates it as "have such men as you done this?" The "such men as you" carries a suggestion of disdain, even contempt, whereas some other translations just render it "have you done this?" The NET finds justification for their reading of it through the addition of the pronoun "you" to the verb, and as we will see shortly, the NET's translation certainly fits with the way the Council members regarded these two apostles and their fellow believers, namely as mere laymen and untrained, indeed as uncouth, Galileans, even "country bumpkins".

Doubtless Luke at this moment, being one of the synoptic authors, had Mark 11:27f on the table in front of him, namely "And as Jesus was walking in the temple court the chief priests, lawyers and elders came to him and said: 'By what authority do you do these things? Who gave you authority to do these things?'" Just possibly the apostles themselves made the connection too, though in the heat of the moment, confronted by the whole Council of the Jews, angry and threatening, maybe not.

Peter gave back as good as he got, both barrels. "Filled with the Holy Spirit he replied: 'It is by the name of Jesus Christ of Nazareth, whom you crucified, whom God raised from the dead, that this man stands here before you fit and well. This Jesus is the stone rejected by the builders—you are the builders—which has become the keystone. There is no salvation in anyone else at all. There is no other name under heaven granted to men by which we may receive salvation'" (4:10–12). Those third and fourth sentences (v. 12) aren't just sheer defiance, they must also intrigue the reader. Their theological content just does not follow from what Peter had said in the first two sentences, it hardly belongs there at all; nor does it follow from anything he had said on Pentecost Sunday or in the temple, when the disabled man was healed. Peter argues that the miracle of the cure of a disabled person by invocation of the name of Jesus proves he is the Messiah. Fair enough. However, it is an unjustified leap to go from that to asserting that Jesus alone provides salvation. Furthermore, what exactly does Peter mean by salvation and is his meaning of it understood, let alone shared, by the members of the Council? Had there been in advance of the arrest of the two apostles or overnight in their cells a discussion or dispute between the two sides as to what was meant by salvation? Had there been agreement, or disagreement, between them on the matter?

One cannot but think that Luke is amalgamating various things said at different times by Peter which made sense to his readers some fifty years later, as they do to us today. However, these would appear to be the product not of reporting but of editing. Peter of course said lots of things, many of which were retained in written form or as oral tradition, and Luke may well be editing what he actually did say during his life, though not necessarily on this specific occasion. Verse 12 appears to be an insertion; theologically it is in advance of the things Peter had said hitherto, while it is reconcilable with his pronouncements as from Chapter 10, which are definitely of a later date. It isn't the only puzzling statement.

There is also his mention only a few verses earlier about "the time of restoration of all things" in Acts 3:21. Now, where did he get that one from? What precisely did he mean by it? How does it fit in with where he was theologically at that moment? Is the precedent in Matthew 17:11 and Mark 9:12? There are difficulties with taking as contemporaneous what Luke records of what Peter said to the Jewish leadership at this early moment in his encounters with them. It could well be that Luke is concerned to edit in order to have Peter presenting a fuller picture of Jesus when in actual fact Peter hadn't yet actually reached that moment himself.

We can move forward a couple of hours or so to when, after being discharged with a warning by the Council of the Jews, Peter and John rejoined "their own people" (Acts 4:23), a telling phrase, to tell them everything that the chief priests and elders had said. What is relevant to this point in the reception they received is that they all break out into a prayer of praise to God in which they describe Jesus as "thy holy servant Jesus" (v. 27). It is a much humbler, simpler, much more contemporaneous phrase by which to describe him. It was where they were at that moment in their progress in their faith.

Luke records the dilemma the members of the Jewish Council found themselves in. A miracle had been worked within the temple itself, there was no denying it (Acts 4:16), and they were keenly aware of the big wave of support and numbers of converts among their own people which the apostles were attracting. They had taken a first step towards establishing control over the activities of what was for them a new Judaic sect; they had told them to end all preaching, specifically not to teach in the name of Jesus. The apostles had flatly refused, saying they would obey God, not human beings (v. 19), and Luke expressly remarks on the boldness of both Peter and John and the frankness with which they spoke. The apostles had now become as bold and forthright as it gets. They were changed men. It is a point of interest that Luke uses that same word παρρησία again a few lines later (v. 31) to describe how "everyone" of the two apostles' own people ... all filled with the Holy Spirit listening to what Peter and John told them had happened, had begun praying and speaking "the word of God". All of them, and not just the leadership, were "filled with the Holy Spirit" (v. 31), whose power, presence and work Luke was very greatly concerned with in both his books.

So what Luke has described to us is the first response of the Jewish religious establishment in Jerusalem to the Jesus-of-Nazareth-as-the-risen-Messiah phenomenon. It consisted in rejection and denial (Acts 3:14 and 4:11) followed by an order to terminate any preaching (4:18). It was a response that in turn was met with defiance by believers who experienced increased faith and fervour (v. 31). What is telling is that the apostles and their fellow Christians, every man and woman of them being Jewish, perceived what had happened to Jesus to be the result of collaboration by Gentiles and their own people "against the Lord and against his Messiah" (v. 26). For them it was the betrayal of their own nation, the betrayal of a calling which had begun in Ur of the Chaldees with Abraham. "They, both Herod and Pontius Pilate with the Gentiles, and the peoples of Israel, did indeed make common cause in this very city against thy holy servant Jesus whom thou didst anoint as Messiah" (v. 27). That phrase "in this very city" (v. 27) gives expression to their feeling that they were being betrayed in another way too. Jerusalem itself, their city, the city of David, the heart of the nation, their nation, was where the collaboration between the Jewish leadership and the Gentile rulers had taken place. One cannot appreciate enough how deeply the first Christians resented and regretted that event in their nation's history and equally the break when it happened; and it will be Paul who will give the most intense expression to their feelings. He will say he was even prepared to be outlawed from Jesus, to be ἀνάθεμα, if he could reverse it and bring his people to Jesus. The first Christians showed no hostility in response, instead they felt intense sorrow and disappointment.

# CHAPTER 7

# And the Council Formally Repudiates Jesus as Messiah

It isn't at all difficult to feel the tension in the text and overhear the arguments that were now taking place between the two sides all over Jerusalem and in the surrounding villages, in the synagogues and on the streets and in whatever was the equivalent of today's coffee shops and pubs. The tension was palpable. "Believers in the Lord, numbers of both men and women were being added" (Acts 5:14). "The sick were being carried out into the streets . . . and the people from the towns around Jerusalem flocked in, bringing those who were ill or harassed by unclean spirits, and all of them were cured" (v. 15). The action the Jewish establishment took was inevitable. They saw all too well that their authority and their standing with the people were on the line. They could see that the Jesus from Nazareth had a powerful following. They acted swiftly. "Then the High Priest and all his associates, who were members of the party of the Sadducees, were goaded into action by jealousy. They proceeded to arrest the apostles and put them into official custody" (5:17f.).

Luke tells us someone inside the prison then let them out during the night. He calls him "an angel of the Lord" because of what he did, which is a literary device he employs at least twice. It must have been someone of importance within the Council of the Jews who could give orders to prison wardens, who could order the prison's cells to be opened and, from what he said to the apostles as he led them outside in the street, he must have been a convert and knew what they represented: "Go. Take your place in the Temple, speak to the people and tell them about the words (message) of this life" (Acts 5:20). We will never know who he was or what happened to him but, as it reads, he was not just enabling the apostles to escape but also encouraging open defiance, and in the temple at that. It is highly unlikely he could have got away with what he did, he would have had to answer for it to someone. His description of what the apostles had to preach as "the words (message) of this life" is a significant one, it is insight into what Jesus and his gospel are. Jesus had described himself to the apostles as "the resurrection and the life" (John 9:25) and, as we have already seen, Peter spoke of him as "the author of life" whom the people of Israel had killed (3:15). It all makes one even more curious to know who this man was.

Of course it didn't take long for the apostles to be found and rounded up again; after all they did exactly what their rescuer had told them to do and went back preaching openly in the temple, and they were taken back to the prison. However, the temple police, knowing what popular support they had, had felt obliged to act discretely. They pleaded with the apostles to come quietly, thinking that the crowd might stone them to death if they used force. The apostles cooperated. The details of what Luke tells us happened next are important in respect of his narration of the break between "the way" and "the life"—the Church—and Judaism. One by one the events that followed made the break an inevitability. The Jewish leadership, which had already repudiated and dealt with Jesus by collaborating with their foreign rulers to have him crucified, now dig their heels in by refusing to accept the evidence both of the Resurrection and the miracle of the healing by Peter in the name of Jesus of the cripple in the temple; and by forbidding the apostles to preach and proclaim that Jesus was the Messiah. They take the issue to the verge of its final moment. They have the apostles brought before the Council, and their treatment of them then made a detente a virtual impossibility. The trial and the stoning of Stephen and the persecution that followed it did not help. Reconciliation between the two religious groups became impossible. The violent hostility Paul met from the Jews in Pisidia Antioch on his first missionary journey (Acts 13) illustrates the same. He was left to face death; and later he was explicitly threatened with it again when he visited Jerusalem after his third journey. He had to be defended by the Roman soldiers in the city.

The apostles are stood now before the Council. Annas the High Priest opens the proceedings by reminding them that they had been expressly forbidden "to preach in this name". Instead, he said to them, "you have filled Jerusalem with your teaching, and you are trying to make out that we are responsible for the shedding of this man's blood" (Acts 13:28). To which Peter and his fellow apostles replied: "We must obey God rather than men" (v. 29). It was defiance pure and simple, it was actually inviting the Council members to do their worst.

We just have to stand back and somehow get to feel the dynamics of this confrontation. It was taking place in Jerusalem itself, the city of David, the capital of the nation. Not just that but in and before the highest court in the land, before "the Sanhedrin itself, the full senate of the Israelite nation" (Acts 13:21), all "summoned" to attend. It was confrontation between the ruling religious, legal and academic elite of the Jewish people on the one hand, intently conscious both of its history and their status within it, and a small group of fellow Jews who were followers of the man their judges had put to death and who were now daring to disobey them. It was eyeball to eyeball stuff. Most of the latter were from the way-out province of Galilee, fishermen and such like, untutored in their eyes, mere plebs (4:13), total nobodies, who themselves a few years earlier would never have dreamt they could possibly be standing before the highest court of their religion and nation and defying it. It is perhaps only when we compare the behaviour of the apostles at this juncture with how it had been during the trial and execution of Jesus that we can begin to get some appreciation of the effect of the descent of the Holy Spirit upon them. It was a collective act of defiance. "We expressly ordered you to desist from teaching in that name," said the High Priest. "We must obey God rather than men," replied Peter. He was saying to every member of the Council, the ruling caste, representatives of all Israel, that he and his fellow apostles, non-entities in the eyes of the Council members though they were, represented God, spoke for God, and they didn't. It was as defiant as it could possibly get; and it was a reply that has reverberated down the centuries, inspiring innumerable acts of defiance of political and religious authorities. It rocked and it infuriated Annas and every member of his Council.

The NET translation is "Peter replied for himself and the apostles", which makes Peter the spokesman for the group, which overall throughout Luke's narration from Chapter 1 to 15 he was. However, literally the text is: "answering, Peter and the apostles said." With Luke here making a distinction between Peter and the rest one can see why the NET read it the way they did, namely that the group was accepting that Peter was their spokesman; and that would have been a more practical and economical procedure for any court. However, that was unlikely to have been the case here. Annas might well have preferred it that way but it is extremely doubtful it would have suited the apostles. They were all personalities, they wouldn't have just stood there and said nothing. Peter says as much. When he said to the High Priest about himself and his fellow apostles "We are witnesses to all this", at the least he would have looked at them all first as a way of showing that every one of them was with him, and each one of them would have shouted their assent with all sorts of additional remarks. The real pity is, no verbatim record of what the other apostles might have said exists. One needs only to look at Peter's reply to what Annas first threw at them to know the rest of them couldn't possibly have kept silent. The issues were monumental, terrifically contentious, dealing with the most significant and important matters of their common religion as fellow Jews and of the individual lives of all of them. They would all have joined in, and probably from both sides. And it might well have happened that Annas had first interrogated each one of the apostles individually to see if they all were prepared to defy the order of the Council to desist from preaching about Jesus, to test out how united the group was—or was not. But the Council members were up against it. They could see that the man who had lived for so long with a disability was standing in front of them healed and vocal and there was nothing they could do about it. "What are we going to do with these men? Everybody living in Jerusalem knows that what they have carried out was an outstanding miracle, and we cannot deny it. (How they could say this defies explanation.) But to stop this thing spreading any further among the people, we must warn these men to speak no longer in his name" (Acts 4:16f.). They knew they could not risk punishing the apostles, "because all the people were praising God for what had happened" (v. 18). So they let them go with a warning. On the part of Annas and co it was a massive climb-down.

Throughout this encounter with the apostles and the one that followed, Annas the High Priest did not mention Jesus by name. He just referred to him as "that name" (Acts 4:28). The omission comes over as if he could not bring himself to do it. One can reach out and touch the bitterness and the hostility he breathed into those two words. But of course from his point of view he had some good reasons to feel that way. Jewish people in large numbers "were being added to their ranks as believers in the Lord" (Acts 5:14), his authority was being openly flaunted and people were saying to him and his colleagues, "Look, the men you put into prison are there in the temple teaching the people", and when he sent the Temple Controller to arrest the apostles, the Controller felt he had to do it "without using force for fear of being stoned by the people" (vv. 23–6). There were two other reasons too. "You have filled Jerusalem with your teaching," the High Priest said to the apostles in the dock before him. His side was losing the argument, and that was much more threatening, much more deadly, than anything else. And "you are trying to make us responsible for that man's death" (v. 28). How he, Annas the High Priest, could say that beggars belief but he did. What he was actually doing was revealing his fear of the population of the city and trying to plant the blame for the execution totally on Pontius Pilate and the Roman soldiers.

The Twelve were re-arrested and in replying to the interrogation that followed "Peter and the apostles" gave it to the Council full on. All twelve voices. "You hanged Jesus on a gibbet," they replied (v. 30). It was pretty direct, no holds barred, and this in an exchange edited by Luke to the bare minimum. "You hanged him on a gibbet whom God had made leader and saviour to grant Israel repentance and forgiveness of sins. And we are witnesses to all of this, and so is the Holy Spirit given by God to those who are obedient to him" (Acts 5:31ff.). To their faces they accused the High Priest and the members of the Council of killing the man whom God had sent to Israel as the Messiah; and they, the apostles, were the witnesses to what they had done, and not just them but so was the Holy Spirit. The Jewish leadership, they said to their faces, had defied God himself, and, as would seem to be the implication of what they are saying, for that reason God is now denying them his spirit, his enlightenment.[8] What's more, what they are ascribing to Jesus as the Messiah is in no way political. His messiahship, and hence the messiahship that God intends for the people of Israel, consists in reconciliation of the nation to their God, not any overthrow of foreign rule and achievement of independence.

Luke tells us that the Council members were rendered absolutely "furious" (Acts 5:33, "touched to the raw" in the NET) by these accusations made against them. The anger and the shouting on both sides must have been intense, probably at certain moments quite uncontrolled. One cannot but be reminded of the way in which the scribes who wrote the books of the Chronicles spoke of the sinfulness and apostasies of many kings and judges who ruled over Israel. That could well have been in the minds of both sides as they went hammer and tongs at each other; and so angry and infuriated did the Council members become that some of them called for the apostles to be put to death (Acts 5:33). That tells us everything about the atmosphere and what went on in that chamber. It was a scary moment. In its way the fate of the Church, and as we now know, of humanity itself, was hanging by a thread.

The situation was saved by the intervention of one Council member, "a Pharisee called Gamaliel, a teacher of the Law held in high regard by all the people" (Acts 5:34). Somehow he quietened the uproar, he brought the courtroom to order and he persuaded the members to have the apostles taken outside while they considered what to do, privately, behind closed doors. At this closed meeting he put a proposition to the members; the advice he gave them is well-known, or at least part of it is: "Keep clear of these men, leave them alone. For if this idea of theirs and how it is carried out is of human origin, it will collapse; but if it is of God, you will not be able to suppress it and you may even be found to be fighting against God" (v. 38f.). The debate between the Council members must have been a heated, contentious and vigorous one and probably lasted some considerable time. At Gamaliel's advice they did withdraw the threat of putting the apostles to death, though it is quite likely that they also acted out of fear for their own safety, given how the temple police behaved when they arrested the apostles and begged them to come quietly. The text then reads as follows: "They took his advice and sending for the apostles they had them flogged" (v. 40). One cannot be sure but it could be construed to mean it was Gamaliel that suggested that instead of killing the apostles they should have them flogged. After that "they then ordered them to give up speaking in the name of Jesus, and discharged them" (v. 40).

There are a couple of other things in this. It might be pointed out that the speech Gamaliel made to the Council members containing his advice on what to do with the apostles was made behind closed doors, after the apostles had been taken out of the chamber. So how did Luke get to know what Gamaliel said to his fellow Council members? Was there a Council member who made a record of it and leaked it to the Christians, which some forty years later Luke had a record of, either oral or written? There is also a strange peculiarity in the response of posterity to Gamaliel's speech as distinct from the response to the flogging inflicted on the apostles. His proposal has been regarded as wise and circumspect, while the flogging is hardly ever commented on, when in reality it was a foul act, and if it was his suggestion, he was a cruel politico indeed. However, we do not know if it was his suggestion. Luke records only that he asked his fellow councillors to let the apostles go; so possibly the flogging was a compromise forced on him by them. Whatever, it was savagery; it constituted a gross humiliation and an immense insult to fellow Jews, which is what the apostles were. It adds to the damage the Council of the Jews did to its reputation with the crucifixion. Its members emerge from this incident a scared and spiritually dishevelled bunch.

There is a further question to consider. Why did Luke give Gamaliel's speech so much space? More space in fact than he will be allotting to Peter's speech at the Council of Jerusalem, which was of immense theological importance with undoubtedly much more in it than Luke retained for us? The answer could be of course that if Gamaliel hadn't persuaded the Council of the Jews not to execute the apostles, Christianity could well have terminated there and then. There is nowadays a fashion for counter-factual histories. Such an intellectual venture, one dealing with the Christian Church which would have had its 12 apostles killed off within months of it being founded, would certainly make for an interesting narrative. However, Luke might well have had another motive as well in including Gamaliel's speech in his history, one that does not cancel out the former. He was writing his history a decade or more after the total destruction of the temple and the widespread dispersal by a conquering Roman army of the Jewish people out of the land of Israel. How they survived as a nation even to this day has been nigh-on miraculous. Possibly, though, just possibly, Luke, looking at what had happened to them as of that moment, was thinking how Gamaliel's words about the Christians had turned out to be more applicable to the Jews. They had been battered and scattered into exiled remnants, while Christianity comparatively was flourishing and spreading.

Flogging people is intensely humiliating as well as cruel, painful and barbaric. The leadership of a religion, in this instance twelve good men and true, sincere in their beliefs and not threatening anyone except in terms of argument—if that indeed is a threat—should not have been stripped to the waist and flogged by the armed guards of another religion just because there are differences in belief. The manner in which the Council members treated the apostles had its consequences in that it contributed seriously to the alienation of Judaism from Christianity. One solid piece of evidence for this assertion is to be found in what Luke tells us after the flogging was over: "The apostles went out from the Council rejoicing that they had been found worthy to suffer dishonour—for the sake of the name" (v. 41). The word ἀτιμία is variously translated into English: dishonour, humiliation, indignity, disgrace, insult, public stigma. That is how Luke some forty years later described the way the apostles had been treated by the Council. They had been publicly disgraced, publicly dishonoured, publicly insulted—ἀτιμασθῆναι. To be stripped and flogged isn't just pain, it is also disgrace. Was it done within the confines of the courthouse, confined just to the gaze of the members of the Council and their heavies? Or was it done more openly, with the public as spectators, in order to teach the apostles, their fellow Christians and would-be converts, what was in store for them if they carried on proclaiming Jesus of Nazareth the Messiah? It was official repudiation and rejection by the highest council of the Jewish people of the new way, the new life, preached by Jesus and his closest disciples, and this time it was not being done through the agency of another authority or power but by Judaism itself, by its highest body.

# CHAPTER 8

# Hellenist Jews Now Enter the Church

The doors of established Judaism had been shut firmly into the face of the new movement. Jesus had been repudiated. Luke, however, working to his agenda, now informs us that among the growing numbers of converts there were "those Jews who spoke Greek", who had a complaint against "the Hebrews" (Acts 6:1), who were Christian Jews who lived in Judea and Galilee and spoke Aramaic, which here the New Testament calls Hebrew. The former were Hellenist Jews who constituted for Luke the first outreach of the new church to people, all Jewish still, most of whom lived outside Judea and Galilee, for whom of course Jerusalem remained the physical centre of their religious belief and to which they made pilgrimage. In Luke's narration conversions in Samaria come next and then the Gentiles. These Greek-speaking communities were of course to be found widely across the Mediterranean and the Middle East, they were the "diaspora"; but there were also such families living in Jerusalem and elsewhere in the Holy Land. One indication of that, which Luke gives us, is his account of the plight of the widows of Hellenist Christians who were living in Jerusalem. It can be assumed that a widow would remain in the home she had shared with her husband, and after his death with their children. Those Hellenist Jews who came from other neighbouring countries would most likely have encountered Christians and learnt about their religion when they came to Jerusalem on pilgrimage or when visiting their relations. Barnabas, who came from Cyprus, was such a person (Acts 4:36); as was Simon from Cyrene in North Africa, and his two sons Alexander and Rufus (Mark 15:21). The man from Ethiopia whom Philip converted and baptized (Acts 8:38) was returning home from his pilgrimage to Jerusalem (v. 28) when he encountered Philip.

Luke tells us that a disagreement arose between the two groups, with the Hellenists complaining that their widows "were being overlooked in the daily (food) distribution" (Acts 6:1). What clearly was happening was what always happens wherever two or three people are gathered together sharing an ideology which they believe really matters to society; they argue over it; and even more so when the group has grown to hundreds, indeed, as in this case, to thousands of members. It happens in politics, in art and in business, in everything, and religion is no exception. Given their different backgrounds something like this was inevitable. It was a clash of cultures, a principal component of which was language, which is what Luke directs our attention to. Interestingly the seven Hellenists he does mention all have Greek names, not Hebrew names. Culturally names can matter a lot. Given the standing within Judaism of the important men and women who forged its existence and its identity, one might wonder why the Jewish parents of the seven Hellenists gave them Greek names. Most likely it can be put down to acculturization; Graeco-Roman culture might well have permeated all aspects of their lives, even their religion. It was a powerful and attractive culture, a successful one, backed up by an all-conquering Roman power.

Luke informs us of this dispute which all too obviously ran contrary to the picture of heart-warming harmony he had given us in Acts 2:42–7. That is to his credit. He doesn't, however, describe it quite as darkly as modern day scholarship has done, though saying that Hellenist widows were being denied a fair share of any food that was being distributed is dark enough. The opinion of scholars today is that there was a much deeper cause of division of which the neglect of the Hellenist widows was a consequence, even possibly a bargaining chip, and not the substance. Quite probably the disagreement had roots elsewhere, in the issue that was dividing the infant Church, namely the different perspective the Judaic Christians of Jerusalem had of the messianic mission of Jesus from that which the Hellenist Christians had. One division that existed within Judaism of that period was between those, the Orthodox, who believed that the only place where sacrifice may be made to God was the temple, and the Samaritan Jews who held that God could be sacrificed to anywhere. Orthodox Jews regarded the Samaritans as heretics. The Hellenic Christians Luke mentions here were not Samaritans, though they were fully aware of this division inside Judaism; and it is reasonable to suppose that, as they lived outside Palestine, they probably felt some affinity with the Samaritan position. The Hebrew/Judaic Christians of this early Church could have had a similar theological disagreement with the Hellenist Christians who had now joined them. Possibly some of the former, maybe the majority, were applying to Christianity the division that existed between the Judaic Jews and the Samaritans, namely the belief that the temple was the only place to offer sacrifice to God; and there is speculation that they "were attempting to force the Hellenists into conformity by shutting off common funds from the Hellenist widows".[9] If indeed that was the case, it was putting a quick end to the harmony, to the "one mind" with which "they were keeping up their daily attendance at the temple" and to the "unaffected joy as they praised God", which Luke had made mention of earlier (Acts 2:42ff.).

At a deeper level, however, the issue concerned the universalism of God's saving plan and as a consequence the universalism of Christianity; it was how to understand Jesus. Everything flowed from that. They were all Jews and as Christians they all believed of course that Jesus was the promised Messiah. His resurrection had proved that to them beyond doubt and to a fast growing number of converts. But gradually, through prayer, through the working of the Holy Spirit and through what had to be the case, ardent debate among themselves, the community had advanced from a political understanding of the messiahship of Jesus (Luke 24:21 and Acts 1:6) to this most significant insight, as proclaimed by Peter to the Jewish Council that "there is no salvation in anyone else at all, for there is no other name under heaven granted to men by which they receive salvation" (Acts 4:12), and "He it is whom God has exalted with his own right hand as leader and saviour, to grant Israel repentance and forgiveness of sins" (5:31). There is a tension between the two statements; the former would appear to state that salvation was on offer to all men, the latter speaks of the salvation brought by Jesus as being for Israel.

It is quite fascinating to observe how Luke sets out the stages of the widening and increasing inclusiveness of the membership of the Church. First its membership consisted of Judaic Jews, and then it widened to take in the diaspora Jews who spoke Greek and inhabited and shared the Graeco-Roman culture of the Empire. The next stage was when it was joined by Samaritans, who were Jews but heretical Jews; and finally we have the non-Jews, the Gentiles, beginning with a Roman soldier in Caesarea. It is equally fascinating to see how Luke plots the stumbling way Peter, whom Luke focuses on as representative of the whole Church, comes to accept them all as genuine Christians, one group after another, shock by shock one might say, until that incredibly important, indeed magical, moment when what Christianity actually is finally hits him, and hits him between the eyes, and he cries out: "I now see how true it is that God has no favourites but that in every nation the man who is godfearing and does what is right is acceptable to him" (10:34). God's covenant is now no longer with just one nation but equally with all humanity. God never cast off the Jewish people and his covenant with them. What he did, however, was reveal in Jesus how his covenant from its very start with Abraham (Genesis 17:4–9), and indeed "from eternity" (Ephesians 1:9f.) was intended by him to embrace every nation on earth with exactly the same love and desire. The choice and the covenant are no longer just with the Jews, they are now with all humankind. Paul in Romans 3 treats of this with detail and with vigour. There is on God's part no rescinding of his covenant with the Jewish people, rather, what he has done in Jesus is extend it to embrace all humanity. A mother does not lessen the love she feels for her first child when she has a second, it doubles, it trebles, it just grows child by child.

Seeing the Holy Spirit at work among diaspora Jews, the apostles and fellow disciples like James, the relation of Jesus who was now a leading light in the Jerusalem Christian community, must now at this point have started debating among themselves, be it "at home/in private houses" as after the Eucharist, or more formally after sessions of prayer "in the Temple" (Acts 5:42), whether or not their belief in the messiahship of Jesus was just something for Jews, and Jews only. They must have started to question whether the concern of God for humanity was limited to just one tiny nation. They must have started asking if the rites and the rituals of their nation were the only ones God worked by. They must have begun reading with fresh eyes and increasing interest all those many Old Testament passages which described their God as promising that his covenant with their nation would also be opened up to all nations, not taken from the Jewish people but extended to everyone else. It is a constant theme of the Old Testament prophets that God would never renege on the promises he had made to his people. However, extending them to all humanity does not diminish in the slightest his love for the people he had chosen. Christ, says Paul in Romans 15:7–13, did indeed "become a servant of the Jewish people" in order to prove God's truthfulness and faithfulness when he made promises to the patriarchs, but that in its turn, indeed "at the same time", was "to give the Gentiles cause to glorify God for his mercy". What Paul wanted from Jew and Gentile was this, that "with one mind and one voice" both "may praise the God and Father of our Lord Jesus Christ" (Romans 15:6). What we are looking at in these first chapters of Luke's account is the early Jerusalem Church struggling to comprehend the gospel, trying to make head and tail of the precious cargo it had been entrusted with and recognize it for the miracle message it was, struggling to decide whom it was to be given to and how.

That was the prospect that faced that small band of Jewish men and women. They were a brave bunch. Theirs has been the situation that Christianity has found itself in ever since, time and time again, century after century, sailing into unknown cultures as it spread throughout the world, encountering different peoples, different ways of life and different ways of thinking, and no more so than now. The Enlightenment, the Industrial Revolution, the vast expanse and achievements of science and technology, their achievements in medicine and healthcare and their subsequent impact upon individual and social morality, the progress of universal education, the women's movement, all these developments have presented, and are presenting, an immense challenge to the status and the teaching of the two-thousand-year-old Christian Church, not least because it has been mainly, indeed almost entirely, within what might be called the territory of Christianity, "the West", that those developments have taken place. The Christian mind has contributed immensely to those developments, indeed not only contributed but also by reason of its foundational philosophy greatly helped make possible.

Luke here in his account sets out how four members of the newly founded Church addressed the issue of incorporation of new people, even by implication of new cultures: Stephen, Philip, Peter and Paul. It was their growing understanding of the person of Jesus and the salvation he wrought that led them to address that issue. What he tells us about each of their responses has to be dealt with separately. The response of each of them is invaluable; they interweave and each assists the other. It was Paul who, when writing to the Galatians and the Romans, provided us with an understanding of Jesus and the salvation he wrought which is the most complete. A great amount, however, of what he taught us is outside the scope of this paper since this paper takes the reader only as far as the Council of Jerusalem and both those two Pauline letters were written after the Council. However, they were written soon after the Council, so undoubtedly it was in the discussions that Paul had with Peter and his fellow apostles both prior to the Council (Acts 15:2,4) and during it, that he had the opportunity to develop his thinking. Peter, as already pointed out, initiated redemption theology, Paul developed it.

It is therefore useful just to point to one of the most essential elements of Paul's theology, which in fact is Petrine in its origins, as will be shown in due course. It is also something which Paul takes up and develops out of what, as Luke presents it to us, Stephen says to the Council of the Jews whose supporters, in this instance violent and out of control, were about to stone him to death. As we will see, though Luke represents Stephen as speaking to his Jewish assailants and opponents, what he has to say is directed by him just as much at certain members of the Jerusalem Church. For Paul, as for Stephen, it is crucial how the salvation wrought by Jesus was to be understood. Paul was to write that being a descendant of Abraham was in no way a physical matter or a matter of race, but instead a matter of faith. Specifically and explicitly faith in Jesus. Paul states this unequivocally, as in Galatians 3:15–18 and Romans 2:25–9. What Paul has to say, expressly in Galatians (e.g. 3:16), renders wrong and mistaken present day declarations by a number of Christian theologians that Islam is an Abrahamic religion. To be "Abrahamic" it is not enough to be monotheistic, which Abraham wasn't anyway. He was a polytheist. Paul in Galatians is explicit that for any religion to be "Abrahamic" it must lead to faith in Jesus, which Mohammad explicitly rejects in the Qur'an.

Paul takes the matter further. He puts forward two different representations of what it is to be a Jew (Acts 2:28f.). There is the Jew who is one "outwardly" and there is "the Jew who is one in secret and is circumcised in the heart, in the spirit rather than in the letter (or as the NET translates it, "directed not by written precepts but by the Spirit"

(v. 29)). Paul is making a point. For him in this passage "Jew" stands for humanity, all of whom God became human to save. It is as noble a presentation of "Jew" as is possible. Little wonder Pope John XXIII (1881–1963) said "We are all Semites". Two things stand out. One is that God's saving plan extends to all humanity, it is not race-based. And a second thing is that, because this understanding of "circumcision" is not "in the flesh" but "in the heart, in the spirit", it is given to women as equally and directly as it is to men. The New Covenant is with women as with men. It is not as things are in the Old Testament, "the sign" of which was circumcision and in which "every male shall be circumcised" (cf. Genesis 17:1–15). Women do not receive the salvation offered by Jesus in virtue of their race as represented by the male. When it comes to the salvation that Christ has brought race and gender are of no account. Christ's salvation therefore is on offer to women in the same way as it is to men, through faith in him and baptism.

Paul presses on: "Do you suppose," he asks, "that God is the God of the Jews only? Is he not the God of the Gentiles also? Of course he is if we believe that God is one. And he will therefore justify both the circumcised in virtue of their faith and the uncircumcised through their faith" (Acts 3:29–30). Yes, Paul drew the conclusions so perceptively; and possibly, considering the huge dispute that was to develop over circumcision, no more bluntly than when in Romans 4:12 he points out that "our father Abraham" had faith "while he was yet uncircumcised". It is a most illuminating statement, and it ties in so well with the point we are at in analysing Luke's narration of the progress of the Church towards understanding how the salvation wrought by Jesus was to be understood.

However, as Luke represents the matter, it is the Hellenist convert Stephen who initiated the discussion of it. The Church was finally moving outwards, away from the narrow religious, linguistic and cultural confines of its Judaic origins. Stephen was foremost among the Greek-speaking converts. He was a theologian and he was outspoken. He and his group challenged the Jews more forcibly than did the apostles and elders. Acts 6:1 is therefore a decisive moment in Luke's narrative. It is where, telling us that "the disciples were growing in number", he introduces converts who, though Jews, were a different sort of Jew, a sort to which he himself belonged, either by birth or by conversion to Judaism, before he became a Christian. His language was theirs, it was Greek and the scholars inform us that it was the Greek Scriptures, namely the Septuagint, which he knew and read, and of course used in prayer, as they did. These facts about Luke are most important in understanding what lies behind what he wrote. The converts he now introduces us to are those who like himself "spoke Greek", in contrast to "those who spoke the language of the Jews" be it Aramaic or Hebrew. Language is culture in spadefuls. The impact of Graeco-Roman culture, not least through its two main languages, on Christian thought, has been inestimable.

That historic impact starts here, in this first verse of Chapter 6. What's more, from this point on in the Acts Luke focuses most on the Graeco-Roman membership of the newly-founded Christian Church, particularly Stephen, Philip and Paul, on their statements, their activities and their achievements. Only Peter gets similar treatment, the same degree of coverage, as had to be the case. He was totally crucial to the theological and demographic development of the Church that Luke was concerned with, because, as Luke makes clear, of the unique leadership position he held within the Church and because of the theology he set forth and defended against strong opposition. Luke gives him and his contribution the fullest recognition. However, once Peter has achieved that, namely at the conclusion of the Jerusalem Council, Luke takes him right out of his narrative. He just drops him. It is editorship at its most brutal. What's more, not one single one of the other apostles, all Judaic Christian, figures at all. Yet, Luke must have known about their activities and where they preached the gospel. Some of them would have been alive when he was writing the Acts. At the least oral, if not written, records of at least some of them were known to him. He just cuts them out. And from the moment the Council of Jerusalem concludes its deliberations and dispatches its letter to the churches in Syria, Antioch and Cilicia, his focus is on the development and spread of the Church in the Graeco-Roman world, which take in both Jews and Gentiles.

Jerusalem plays a big role in the final chapters of the Acts but it is in the end the place that Paul has to reject. His "I appeal to the Emperor" (Acts 25:11) can be given a meaning far beyond what Paul intended. Jerusalem's role in the Early Church was at an end. It terminated with the closure of the Council which it hosted. Paul moved on to Rome, Peter first to

Antioch and then to Rome, where both died and were buried. The centre of Christianity moved to a Gentile city, and that was fitting. Gentiles are the bulk of humanity and God's covenant is with humanity. Sitting in his study, whatever kind of study it was and wherever it was, thirty years later, Luke in his mind's eye surveyed the events of those momentous years and the lands of the Near East and the shores of the Mediterranean where the Church of Christ had put down roots and flourished. They mattered most to him. It was them he therefore wrote about. He had travelled those years and those lands in the company of Paul and the small band around him: Paul's wife (1 Corinthians 9:4), Timothy, Titus, Silas and others. All being Jews they almost definitely had wives and children too. Maybe Luke did also though he wasn't Jewish. If only we knew what part their wives and children played in all these happenings and to what extent they participated and whether they accompanied their husbands and fathers in all the missionary journeys of Paul.

Luke had a fundamental purpose in what he wrote and to it he subordinated everything that had occurred in the life of the Church as up to that moment. He tells us what that purpose was with the very last words that he records for us from the mouth of Paul. It was to explain and describe how the gospel, delivered first to the Jewish people, was then given to all humanity. Paul is speaking to the local Jewish leaders of Rome whom he had invited to the house he was staying in under house-arrest. Paul greets them as "Dear gentlemen, my brothers" (Acts 28:17). He told them that the chains that he had to wear in the house were worn by him "for the sake of the hope of Israel" (v. 20), by which expression, as they understood, he meant the expectation of the Messiah. He "spoke urgently" to them "of the kingdom of God, and he sought to convince them about Jesus by appealing to the Law and the prophets" (v. 23) and his argument with them went on "from dawn to dusk". Some of the Jewish leaders accepted his arguments and professed belief in Jesus. The majority did not. They got up to leave, but before they had reached the door he called them back and said to them: "Be it known by you that this salvation of God has been sent to the Gentiles, and they will listen" (v. 29). It is difficult to read those last short words of Paul, "and they will listen", recorded for us by Luke, his companion, without becoming aware both of the intense optimism Paul was feeling and expressing about the reception which the gospel of the Lord would get from the Gentiles, and at the same time the harrowing disappointment he was also feeling about the response of his own people. There is intense pain in those few words. It is not his own beloved Jewish people who will listen but the Gentiles. Instead, his own people "will hear and hear but will not understand, look and look but never see, a people grown gross at heart, whose ears are dull and whose eyes are closed!" (vv. 26f.). He is speaking the words of the prophet Isaiah (Isaiah 6:9f.) to them, and they knew those words so well and understood his intent; and Luke, who never wasted a single word, would never have written down that Isaiah text unless he had been all too aware how Paul was feeling. How much that must have hurt Paul to say those words out loud to the Jewish leaders of Rome as they got up, went to the door and left his house.

To tell that story of how the salvation of God had come to the Gentiles, how indeed they had listened, was why Luke wrote the Acts. He had a tale to tell. The tale he wanted to focus on with all the intensity of a barnacle's grip on the hulk of a ship was what made up the good news of Jesus and how "those who believed in him with heart and soul" (cf. Acts 4:32) came to understand who Jesus was and what he did for humankind. In Luke's mind, looking back some thirty years later, this was what had enabled the Church, starting off as tiny a movement as could be imagined, a tiny mulberry seed, and in the most hostile of environments, not just to survive but also to grow and spread. This is why Luke gave Stephen such a prominent place in his history, making Stephen's defence before the Council of the Jews the longest speech in the Acts, twice as long for example as Paul's speech before the crowd when standing on the steps of the Roman barracks in Jerusalem in Acts 22. Luke employed Stephen almost as much as he employed Peter to put across the fundamental argument he himself was expounding. Stephen's speech therefore has to be examined in every word.

So, we can safely put to one side Luke's explanation of the disagreement between the Hellenists and the Jerusalem Judaic Christians as just being one about provisions for the widows of the Hellenist group. The fundamental issue was what the messiahship of Jesus was about, and the two sides were looking at that issue from different perspectives. What Luke does is spend all the rest of this chapter and the next setting out the argument the Hellenists were making. It was the argument he himself most emphatically supported. He presents the Council of the Jews to us as the opposition, but at the same time what he also has in mind as the opposition is the leadership of the Judaic faction in the Jerusalem Christian community. There's no lack of subtlety with this writer. Yes, the Council of the Jews was bitterly opposed to Stephen, and they let him be stoned to death, but the much more significant argument in Luke's mind was one internal to the new movement. Stephen is the first martyr of the Church. Luke employs him to expound a theology that profoundly influenced the understanding the first Christians had of salvation history.

Stephen was a theological trail-blazer. He and his fellow Hellenist Christians must have spent hours, with each other, with their Judaic fellow Christians and with the Jews, talking and arguing all the issues involved and about the direction the Church should be taking. Luke provides us with the names of seven of the Christian Hellenes: Stephen himself, Philip, Prochorus, Nicanor, Timon, Parmenas and Nicholas "of Antioch, a former convert to Judaism" (Acts 6:5). All too obviously he held the group in highest regard. He knew the huge value of their contribution both to the understanding of the Christian faith and to the astonishing spread of the Church. He would have known some of them personally. Philip for one, as we know from Acts 21:8f., was still alive and active at least twenty years later and was well known to Paul and, as the verse implies, to Luke too. And Luke's remark about Nicanor that he was from Antioch and was a convert to Judaism might well have been added because Luke, like Nicanor, may himself have first been a convert to Judaism. There is agreement also among the scholars that Luke was not from Palestine; like Nicanor he too could have been from Antioch in Syria. Such details are not superfluous to our story. The Scriptures were not written by God; they were inspired by him, yes, but not written by him. They are all written by human beings, and such details ground them and humanize them.

Luke tells us that Stephen's preaching and "great miracles and signs among the people" (Acts 6:8ff.) attracted the opposition of a particular Jewish synagogue, "the Synagogue of Freedmen, comprising Cyrenians and Alexandrians, and people from Cilicia and Asia". These "freedmen" most likely were the descendants of Jews who had returned as *liberti* to

Jerusalem after enslavement in Rome. Cyrene was a province of Libya with Benghazi as its capital. Alexandria was the second biggest city in the Empire, the principal port and the historic cultural centre of Egypt, and had a large Jewish population. Tarsus, Paul's home town, was in Cilicia. Since Luke makes mention of people from Cilicia being members of that synagogue it is likely that was the synagogue Paul had attended when in Jerusalem before his conversion. In addition Paul famously declared he was a citizen of Rome, another reason why he may have been a member of the Synagogue of Freedmen. The line can also be read to say that the opposition among the Jews to Stephen from each of those groups of the Jews coming from those places was not just from one synagogue, but that each of them had their own synagogue in Jerusalem, so the opposition could have come from several different synagogues in all. There were of course many synagogues in Jerusalem.

What comes across is that among the non-Jerusalem/Palestinian, that is diaspora, Jews in Jerusalem, there was widespread, and as it turned out, strong opposition both to Stephen's representation of the messiahship of Jesus and what it would seem he was saying about the place of Jerusalem in worship. He was definitely arousing strong and vocal hostility among the Jews of Jerusalem, whereas the Judaic Christians, the apostles among them, in Jerusalem were not. With the numbers of Christians increasing rapidly and even making a lot of converts among the Jewish priesthood itself (Acts 6:7), resistance on the part of the various Jewish synagogues quickly began to organize itself. From what Luke tells us, however, Stephen was pulling no punches, and they just couldn't hold their own against him; he argued like a man inspired. The resentment of his opponents was so great they had him arrested and, like both Jesus and the apostles before him and Paul after him, arraigned him before the Council.

# CHAPTER 9

# Stephen's Argument and His Trial

The principal allegation against Stephen at his trial was that he had made "blasphemous statements against Moses and against God" (Acts 6:11). We get a better idea of what that allegation consisted in from the brief record of witness statements that had come down to Luke: "This man is forever saying things against this holy place and against the Law" (v. 13). The change in the wording of the allegations from "Moses" to "the Law" is helpful. It better explains what is meant by "Moses". There was among the Jews of course inestimable esteem for Moses, but in the context of their opposition to the Christians the issue was not the personality of Moses but the Law which he represented, its regulations about with whom they may or may not socialize, circumcision, the temple, the days and the great feasts of their calendar, the food they may or may not eat, what might and might not or must or must not be worn, and more besides. Regrettably religion gets this way time and again, too often it becomes obsessive about rules and regulations, feeds avariciously on them and finds getting institutionalized and having its own recognizable identity comfortable. All too often clerics, of all religions, love it. For some it is a way of life, even at times a teaching position and a source of income.

Being a diaspora Jew, and not just as a Christian, Stephen maintained, like the Samaritans did, that the worship of God could take place with full validity and effectiveness in places other than in the temple, and indeed the Holy Land. This, and of course his belief that Jesus was the Messiah, is what drove the members of the Synagogue of Freedmen in Jerusalem to come forward and argue with him, and when they found "they could not hold their own against the inspired wisdom with which he spoke . . . they stirred up the people and the elders and doctors of the Law, set upon him and seized him and brought him before the Council"

(Acts 7:12). It doesn't take much to picture the moment. The verbs Luke uses say it all. The first one conjures up a vision of a gang crowding round poor Stephen, wrestling him to the ground, maybe even kicking him and almost standing on him; the second one has them hoisting him up, grappling with him and grabbing him by both arms, and the third is sharp, direct and harsh, with them forcibly frogmarching him through the streets to the premises of the Council.

There would have been an extensive oral record of his trial based on the memories of people who witnessed it; and in addition there must have been written records, because there are indications that what Luke presents as the speech Stephen made at his trial is, with the exception of the concluding few lines, a well-organized collection of the arguments he had been making to his Jewish opponents. It is difficult to believe that in the frenzy, ferocity and fireworks of his appearance before the Council, which was more a lynch party than a trial, Stephen had much of an opportunity, if any at all, to make the long and detailed arguments that Luke presents to us, difficult to believe he would have been allowed by the angry and hostile crowd surrounding him to get out anything more than a tiny fraction of what Luke reports him as saying. It seems more sensible to treat the speech as an organization by Luke of the arguments which Stephen had made prior to his arrest and of which records had been kept. Luke fully appreciated his significance not just as the first Christian martyr but as what we would call a theologian.

What Stephen had done was challenge in the most fundamental way possible the understanding the Jews had of themselves and of God's intention for humankind, and of themselves in relation to the rest of humankind. Quite understandably the Jews just couldn't take it; for them what Stephen was preaching, and preaching in Jerusalem itself of all places, was both betrayal of what they believed it was to be a Jew and blasphemy by Christian Jews like Stephen against the God of the Jewish people as they understood God to be. Let there be no doubt about it, what he had to say to them was the most fundamental of challenges; and what Luke made clear was that Stephen did precisely that, in the strongest manner possible, to their faces, and for that he was brought before the highest court in Judaism. What the Jews did to Stephen was totally unacceptable. He was brutally murdered. However, it helps to understand why they were so inflamed and angry, why they stoned him to death.

The strange thing about this speech is that it only comes alive as a real speech in the final three verses of Acts 7:51–53, and those final three verses just do not belong to or follow on from the 50 verses that preceded them. The preceding 50 verses are nothing other than a didactic discourse, an uninterrupted lecture, logically moving from historical event to event, each accompanied by a theological interpretation, the sort of thing that was quite impossible at that moment and in the circumstances Stephen was in. He wasn't in some university lecture hall, he was in a court under threat of immediate execution, the place full of angry people. Those three final verses come right out of the blue and they aroused a furious reaction from the Jews. They were the red rag to the bull, even more so when you think how angry with Stephen the synagogue Jews were to start with. All too obviously those three verses indicate to us that, whatever it was he had said to them in his defence, he had been subjected to fierce heckling, noisy objections, unsettling interruptions and threats throughout and he could take no more; he lost control of himself, he just let fly, he just let rip; and what he packed into them, given the outrage felt by his Jewish listeners, was more than enough to have had him hung, drawn and quartered, let alone stoned to death, which was savage and brutal enough. The first 50 verses represent Stephen's arguments with the Jews prior to his arrest, and doubtless he tried to make the same argument in the trial itself, but he could hardly have done that in the balanced and composed manner in which they are here arranged. The final three verses were evidently his outburst after he had been subjected to the harshest of cross-examinations and ferocious opposition and he could take nothing more.

What he burst out with in those final three verses could hardly do anything else except arouse his interrogators to even greater fury. He called them "stiff-necked" (Acts 7:51). The word had resonance, it stung, it had a history. It was a charge made often in the Old Testament against the Jews, not least by the Lord God himself to Moses when, led by Aaron, the Jews made and worshipped the Golden Calf (Exodus 32:9). That was bad enough. But then Stephen called them "uncircumcised in your heart" (Acts 7:51) and that cut right through to the bone. He just couldn't have insulted them more. Circumcision was the rite by which the male Jew entered into his religion, it signified submission and belonging to the Jewish religion in its fullest requirements, without it the male wasn't Jewish; strange as it now seems it was what it was to be Jewish (cf. Genesis 17). But of course Stephen knew that his interrogators were all circumcised, so he wasn't referring to physical circumcision but to a spiritual circumcision. It is for that reason that the NET translates the phrase to read "heathen still at heart", and that translation might well have it right.

What Stephen was saying was that being circumcised was of no significance unless anyone circumcised genuinely strove to live up to what it stood for, and the Jews who were confronting him just weren't doing it; and because they weren't, Stephen was saying that in the eyes of God they weren't his people but instead, without him being explicit about it, they were non-Jews, they were heathens. It was the ultimate insult. (The reader might cross-reference to Hebrews 8:10–13; and also look at Jeremiah 10:26, where the prophet, with damning frankness, speaks of "the nations and Israel" as "uncircumcised of heart".) He didn't stop there. He went on to identify them with the worst elements in their nation's history, with the worst doings of their people, with the most flagrant acts of sinfulness and betrayal of their God that had occurred. He even associates the whole Jewish nation and not just these particular Jewish leaders with that sinfulness: "You always fight against the Holy Spirit. Like fathers, like sons. Was there ever a prophet whom your fathers did not persecute? (cf. 2 Chronicles 36:16). They killed those who foretold the coming of the Righteous One; and now you have betrayed him and murdered him, you who received the Law as God's angels gave it to you, and yet you have not kept it" (Acts 7:52f.). It speaks for itself. Stephen does not come across as someone on a jihad trip seeking martyrdom out of total self-delusion; but the heckling and the interruptions and doubtless all sorts of insults and threats being flung at him had obviously made him lose control of himself. So had his hecklers, but unfortunately for him they were judge, jury and executioner.

The preceding 50 verses are different. They constitute a rapid survey of the history of the Jews from Abraham to David and Solomon. The historical incidents referred to and the statements of various persons quoted make up the arguments the Hellenists like Stephen put to the Jews, which the Early Church stored in its folk memory or put into writing. Luke takes from that record. There is a simplicity about these verses, they do not constitute a high theology, in parts they come across as colloquial and folksy. It is that simplicity and folksiness that lends them authenticity; the way they describe events is undoctored, it is popular art in the way it is told; and the way the Jewish people are spoken of is familiar and affectionate. Stephen speaks about "our ancestors, our forefathers, our nation and our race". The terminology is not of Luke's creation, it is the words of one group of Jews arguing with another group of Jews but both aware of a common identity even when arguing like cats and dogs about what is best for the people to which they both belong. Luke, in whatever form he had them, was selective with regards to the arguments Stephen and his fellow Hellenists had used with the Jews, he put the speech together carefully. He rightly saw the arguments used for what they were, the fundamental reasons why the gospel of Jesus had to be taken to all the nations, namely it was not to Jews as such and not in the land of Canaan but to Gentiles and in other lands that God, speaking and giving directions to Abraham, had first reached out with his plan and his promise of redemption. In the situation that Stephen was in that was a brave and bold assertion, but he and his fellows knew it was essential in respect of the faith to which they had converted.

Luke begins Stephen's defence with the statement: "My brothers, fathers of this nation, listen to me. The God of glory appeared to Abraham our ancestor while he was in Mesopotamia before he had settled in Harran and said: Leave your country and your kinsfolk and come away to a land I will show you. Thereupon he left the land of the Chaldeans and settled in Harran. From there, after his father's death, God led him to migrate to this land where you now live. He gave him nothing in it to call his own, not one yard of land, but promised to give it in possession to him and his descendants after him" (Acts 7:2f.). This account differs from that of Genesis 11 in respect of some details but those differences do not matter here. What matters is what Stephen is intending to demonstrate to his interrogators, that God, "the God of glory" himself (v. 1), did not restrict his intervention to the land of Canaan and the revelation of his glory just to Jews. What he did was reveal himself first to a man who lived in the land of the Chaldeans and to a non-Jew, a Chaldean; and that even when God had him migrating to the land the Jews, his audience, would be living in, God did not give him even one square yard of land to call his own. What is more, even the covenant of circumcision itself was given to the descendants of Abraham when they were living "as aliens in a foreign land" (NET) or "homeless in a country that belongs to others" (N. King). Luke simply has not given us enough explicit information about the debate and argument that had been going on between Christian converts like Stephen and the Jews; we have to extract them from the implications of what he, Luke, tells us that Stephen said at his trial. What Stephen is reported as saying here only makes sense if he had been saying to the Jews, as indeed he must have, that God in Jesus Christ was extending his intervention of salvation beyond the single nation of the Jews to all humankind just as he, the God of glory, had begun his intervention in the first place with a non-Jew, Abraham, and that outside of Canaan. One might wonder if there has been any discussion of that among the Jewish people through the centuries that have followed, down to the present day.

Stephen then moves the clock forward to Egypt. "The patriarchs (the sons of Isaac) out of jealousy sold Joseph into slavery in Egypt but God was with him and rescued him from all these troubles." Again God, Stephen is asserting, is not restricting his merciful and loving concern to any particular place. Rather, it was "in Egypt that our nation grew and increased in numbers". More than that: it was in Egypt, not Canaan, that Joseph and his father Jacob and all his relatives ended their days and were buried, "as all our forefathers did" (v. 15). So, the land of Egypt itself is thereby made holy and precious.

It was in Egypt where Moses was trained "in all the wisdom of the Egyptians" becoming "a powerful speaker and a man of action". More than that, it was "in the desert near Mount Sinai", not in Canaan, that "an angel appeared to him in the flame of a burning bush" and God spoke to him saying "take off your shoes; the place where you are standing is holy ground" (v. 33). That one statement might well be considered the core of Stephen's argument, and it was the crucial Hellenist argument and claim. It is Genesis 1:21: "God saw all that he had made and it was very good." Mount Sinai and all the desert, both outside of Canaan the Promised Land, are holy. It was on Mount Sinai and not anywhere in the land of Canaan that God appeared to Moses and gave him the Ten Commandments. The whole world belongs to its Maker. All land is holy, not just the Holy Land; and that is what the voice of God will assert in a different way to Peter in the vision he will have at Joppa: "It is not for you to call profane what God counts clean" (Acts 10:15). The revelation of himself which God made to Moses was an instance of divine revelation of immense significance and the giving of the Ten Commandments a most important statement of religion, but neither had taken place in Canaan. They had taken place in Gentile land.

The argument is taken further. Moses was ordered by God to return to Egypt, and "it was Moses who led them out, working miracles and signs in Egypt, at the Red Sea and for forty years in the desert". Again, none of the three locations are in Canaan. And what happened in the desert? "It was Moses who, when they were assembled in the desert, conversed with the angel who spoke with him on Mount Sinai and with our forefathers; (there) he received the living utterances of God, to pass on to us." What is more, and this is directly applicable to the schism that existed between the Judaic Jews and the Samaritan Jews and gives us insight into the argument that the Hellenist Christians were having not just with the Jerusalem Jews but also with the Judaic Christians of Jerusalem, Stephen goes so far as to attribute the banishment of the Jews to Babylon, which occurred centuries later, to the way the Jews in the desert "did not bring me (God) victims and offerings those forty years". What Stephen is asserting is that the desert was indeed a place to sacrifice animal victims to God, and not just Jerusalem. The schism between the Judaic and the Samaritan Jews was that the former insisted that animal sacrifice to God should only take place in Jerusalem; the Samaritans counter-insisted it could take place anywhere. One can see in this how the Hellenist faction has been trying, indeed campaigning, to extract the Church from narrow Judaic boundaries, endeavouring to take it to a much wider public, if only at this stage to a different sort of Jew, namely the Samaritans.

The final verses of what is Luke's presentation of the defence Stephen made before the Council drive home his argument even further. The Tabernacle/the Tent of the Testimonies/the Ark of the Covenant itself, the most sacred object in Judaism, was carried by their forefathers in the desert (v. 44), not in Canaan; and Joshua brought it into the Promised

Land when "the nations were dispossessed", and it remained there until the time of David. David it was who asked God to let him build a dwelling place for the God of Jacob but it was Solomon who actually built it. However, says Stephen, in no way did that restrict the divine presence, there is no limitation on where God abides. "The Most High does not live in houses made by men. As the prophet says: Heaven is my throne and the earth my footstool. What kind of house will you build for me? says the Lord. Where is my resting place? Did not my hand make all these things?"(v. 50). And that says it all, emphatically it says it all. Everything, absolutely everything in heaven and on earth is God's creation, therefore God is present everywhere and not just in any one place; and everything that exists is his. In the words of the writer of the Book of Revelation: "You created all things, by your will they came into being and were created" (Revelation 4:11).

The concern of the Hellenist Christians, inclusive of Stephen, was to persuade their fellow Jews to believe in Jesus as the promised Messiah. That was what had happened to them and it had transformed their lives. Yet in all the 68 verses of Luke's account of what happened to Stephen, his activities, his speech and his death, Jesus is only mentioned once by name and that not by Stephen but by one of his accusers (Acts 6:14). However, we can be absolutely certain that Stephen and his fellow Hellenists argued with their fellow Jews about Jesus being the Messiah down to every single detail both of his life and his resurrection and in the Old Testament prophecies. It was all deliberate editing on Luke's part. He considered this particular aspect of the argument being made by the Hellenists to be of the utmost importance. They were arguing that the universality of God's relationship to the world was the basis for the universality of the messiahship of Jesus. They were providing arguments for the universality of God's love of humankind and by implication for the universality of Christianity as against the Jews' one-nation perspective on God. The Hellenist contention was that God had shown in his dealings with and pronouncements to Abraham, the patriarchs, Joseph, Moses etc. that in every place on earth, big and small, there wasn't one square inch of the earth that wasn't his footstool and not one single human being who wasn't the object of his concern. In their arguments with their fellow Jews the Hellenist Christians propounded not just the universality of God's concern for humankind and the sanctity of every square inch he created but also the universality of Christ's messiahship. That is what mattered most to Luke.

There is so much to think about in this speech of defence. It reveals the sort of argumentation over doctrine, practice and purpose that the Early Church was having within itself, let alone with the Jews. Intellectually it was as alive and stormy as any other period in the Church's history. The evidence in it of development of doctrine is stark and obvious. The Hellenists didn't find opponents to their argument about the universality of God's concern for humankind just among the Jews. As Luke will make clear in the chapters that follow there was a strong belief among some of the first disciples that the messiahship of Jesus was for the Jews only. What we have is a small community which is expanding fast, drawing in not just local Jews but also Jews of different cultures and countries. It is a faith community becoming excitingly aware of itself and what it has to offer. Its faith sources were threefold, the Old Testament Scriptures, the historic Jewish tradition in which they were steeped, and their own recollection of Jesus—what he had said to them, what he had preached, what he had done and what had happened to him, all of which they handed down to their children and converts; and all that has to be blended somehow with the diverse, and non-Jewish, cultures from which converts were now being drawn.

What we have here is a community swapping stories, swapping memories about Jesus, searching their Old Testament Scriptures for everything that could be related to him, jointly working out as best they could who and what Jesus was and what the miracles, the Resurrection and the Ascension told them about him. And those who had been with him then had to tell all the new converts everything they knew, lots of them now knocking on their door; and among them a different sort of Jew, the Hellenist, sharing the same Scriptures but with a different culture. Two groups of Christian believers bouncing ideas off each other, putting their arguments to their Jewish neighbours and meeting day-in day-out, at meals, at prayer sessions, at the celebration of the Eucharist and comparing notes, relating experiences, debating with each other, in short all the things that people in the same organization, sharing the same passions, always do. It is so easy to envisage it; and some of them would definitely have written things down, made out agendas and drawn up rotas for action, with members reporting back and assessing outcomes. That's what people do.

There were debates and arguments between them. Wherever two or three people are gathered together there are always disagreements. In various passages Luke makes explicit mention of debates as in Acts 11:1–4; and 11:18 records the outcome of that debate. It was a debate in which Peter achieved a temporary truce and a reluctant silence. Acts 15:6 also records "a long debate, in which both the apostles and elders participated", a debate that turned out to be the most crucial one of all of them. But these are tiny examples of what is really obvious. These people were Scripture-reading people; the ability to write might not have been universal by a long stretch but they had their Scriptures, they loved the written word, scrolls to be read out in the temple services and carefully listened to. Possibly nowhere in all of the Scriptures is this insisted on as much as in chapter after chapter of Ezekiel: "Go to your fellow countrymen in exile and speak to them. Whether they listen or refuse to listen say: These are the words of the Lord" (Acts 2:11). That statement "These are the words of the Lord" is repeated and repeated time and time again. They had prophets and they had literate men and women among them. The written word was absolutely basic to the very essence of the religion they all came from; and of course the Greek-speakers were thoroughly accustomed to the written word, be it in the form of plays or poetry or history or the works of the philosophers. Paul sent out letters, quite a number more than the few that have survived. They all lived in literate societies, both Judaic and Hellenist, not to mention Roman and Persian and Egyptian and others, all making works of art, science, medicine and literature on which all succeeding Western and Middle East cultures, and indeed here and there other cultures too, stand and depend. This is manifestly the case of course with Christianity; it is also equally true of Islam. Mohammad and whoever else collaborated with him on the text of the Koran had no other sources except their own tribal cultures and their personal experiences, to which they added their acquaintance with Judaism and Christianity and borrowed heavily from both, especially from the former .Nothing comes from nothing, *Ex nihilo nihil fit.*

So what we have in this Stephen defence is an extract. One extract from the wide range of debates and discussions going on in the Church in Jerusalem as it found its feet, came to terms with and recognized its own identity and worked out what it believed, a process that, as we have seen already, started on the Day of the Resurrection itself and continues to this day and will not end till "Christ is all and is in all" (Colossians 3:11). "For in him all the fullness of the Godhead dwells in bodily form" (2:9). We still have a long way to go. As yet we see in a glass darkly, "in a distorting mirror; but then it will be face to face" (1 Corinthians 13:12).

In the case of the Stephen defence we are dealing with an Early Church reflection on its faith. There must have been countless such debates on a multitude of issues like this within the Christian community in Jerusalem in which the life and preaching—the gospel—of Jesus and the Old Testament Scriptures were explored and expounded. That is what members of all organizations do, they meet up to discuss and decide all the issues that happen to them and all the issues about how to organize themselves. In the case of the first Christians such issues were their prayer life and the liturgies that go with it, issues of caring for each other as we have seen in Acts 2:44f. and 6:1–3, issues of evangelization which Luke makes mention of again and again, and of course issues of what constitutes their faith and its practice, which is the substantial matter that Luke set out to write about in Chapters 1—15. There will have been many other such documents similar to the Stephen defence but this one, Acts 7:1–50, a composite though it is, survived for all posterity, whereas others didn't. It has come down to succeeding generations of Christians, something he could never have foreseen, because it forms part of a document which the Church under the guidance of the Holy Spirit chose to declare part of its canon.

How important the speech, or rather the passage, was to Luke can be gauged by the simple fact that he makes it the longest "speech" in the Acts, longer than any speech of Paul or Peter. The basic theological point that Luke, Stephen, Peter and Paul make collectively was that as from the fall of Adam and Eve God's plan, "his hidden purpose" (Ephesians 1:9), was universal redemption, to be achieved in Jesus; that God began to execute his plan through the choice of one single nation which "in the fullness of time" gave birth to the Saviour. Salvation history is the story of the journey from the singular to the universal, from one man Abraham and one nation Israel to embrace every human being, all nations, all of humanity. In the defence speech of Stephen Luke demonstrated the universality of God's saving plan by citing some of the actualities of the history of the Jews beginning with Abraham; and then in the chapters that followed, in the speeches made by Peter and Paul, he laid before his readership how God finally made that plan a reality, namely in Jesus Christ. On the one hand Luke's account tells us what a huge challenge to the Jews' notion of themselves the Christian story was; on the other it illustrates how the Christian Jews were escaping out of a racial and spiritual cul-de-sac in the direction of understanding Jesus to be the universal saviour. It would prove to be a hesitant journey as will be well-illustrated by what happened next.

However, before that is described and discussed, we must recognize where it is that Luke has brought us to. As far as Luke was concerned, the moment had been reached when communication with the Jews no longer had any prospect of progress. The Council of the Jews, consisting of the highest religious, legal and academic structures of the nation, had now on two occasions formally repudiated the claim of the Church that Jesus was the Messiah; in addition it had responded to that claim by twice arresting and imprisoning the apostles, by forbidding them to preach their gospel, by threatening them with death only to commute it to flogging them, which was a huge public humiliation, and stoning Stephen, the leader of the Hellenist Christians, to death, in full view of the Jerusalem population. That was terminal in itself; and it was followed immediately, "that very day", by "a violent persecution against the church in Jerusalem" (8:11), which words certainly suggest rage and rioting by the people and not just by whatever sort of enforcement officers of the Council of the Jews could organize.

Rejection by the Jews, both leadership and people, was now total. Dialogue, all too obviously, was no longer possible. Worse, one side had shown violent hostility to the other. We just do not know how such treatment affected the psyche of the first Christians, how deep it penetrated. Accordingly, Luke now closes down that chapter in the history of the Church which he was narrating; and in saying that, one cannot but think back, with regret and sadness, to the words of Jesus speaking to the Jews who were objecting fiercely to him healing the man on the Sabbath who had been disabled for thirty-eight years and who would lie in a crowd of sick people, the blind, the lame and the paralysed, hoping that someone would lift him into the pool at Bethseda:

> The very work that the Father has given me to finish, and which I am doing here and now, testifies that the Father has sent me. And the Father who sent me has himself testified concerning me, but you have never heard his voice nor seen his form/shape . . . You diligently study the Scriptures because you think that by having them you have eternal life . . . These are the Scriptures that testify about me, yet you refuse to come to me in order that you might have life. (John 5:36f.)

Those four statements merit, and require, a lifetime of meditation. What is heartening is to read them in the light of the infinite generosity of God. We may refuse the many invitations he offers but he persists with them and in the end he always finds ways to win us to himself. "You have made us for yourself, O Lord, and our hearts are restless until they rest in Thee" as St Augustine wrote at the beginning of his *Confessions*; and as Francis Thompson wrote in *The Hound of Heaven*:

> Rise, clasp my hand and come!
> Halts by me that footfall?
> Is my gloom after all
> Shade of his hand, outstretched caressingly?
> Ah, fondest, blindest, weakest,
> I am he whom thou seekest.

It is "with unhurrying chase, and unperturbed pace, deliberate speed, majestic instancy" that he pursues us all, and his voice is round about us like a bursting sea.

There was severe recrimination in what Jesus goes on to say to the Jews who were surrounding him, but recrimination was not his last word to them. Quite the opposite, for as Luke records for us among Jesus's final words there is his prayer: "Father forgive them for they know not what they do" (Luke 23:34). It is significant that in Luke's history there is not one single mention of a member of the Church, despite the persecution it had suffered from the Jews, expressing any desire for revenge, indeed any anger. On the contrary "the apostles went out from the Council (which had arrested and imprisoned them, put them on trial, threatened them with death and then commuted their punishment to flogging them collectively) rejoicing that they had been found worthy to suffer indignity for the sake of the Name" (Acts 5:41). They had the attitude of Jesus who, despite the rejection he received from the Jews, could say: "O Jerusalem, Jerusalem, the city that murders the prophets and stones the messengers sent to her. How often I have longed to gather your children as a hen gathers her brood under her wings. But you would not" (Luke 13:34).

As from the first verse of the next chapter Luke turns from the relationship of Christianity to the Jewish people to dealing with the Judaic perspective on God and religion which the members of the Church, all orthodox Jews, had inherited, indeed imbibed, from birth. Christianity now begins to repudiate the Judaic understanding of what salvation from sin and reconciliation to God consists in and, positively, to establish for itself how salvation from sin and reconciliation with God is achieved. It is a journey, a process, internal to the Church itself. The matter arouses "no little (i.e. fierce) dissension and controversy" (Acts 15:2) inside the Church. In it the role of the Law is placed in contest with the role of Jesus. Any reader who might want to cut to the chase at this point in telling the story might turn now to Acts 10:9–16, to 11:1–3, to 11:19, to 15:1–2, and of course to 15:11, to see how and why.

# CHAPTER 10

# Philip Takes the Gospel to the Samaritans

> This was the beginning of a time of violent persecution for the church in Jerusalem; and all except the apostles were scattered over the country district of Judea and Samaria ... Saul was harrying the church; he entered house after house, seizing men and women, and sending them to prison. As for those who were scattered, they went through the country preaching the Word. Philip came down to a city in Samaria and began proclaiming the Messiah to them. The crowds to a man listened eagerly to what Philip said ... and there was great joy ... When they came to believe Philip with his good news about the kingdom of God and the name of Jesus Christ, they were baptized, men and women alike. (Acts 8:1–12)

This short account, pertinent to Luke's purpose in writing the Acts, moves the story significantly in the direction of the Council of Jerusalem for the reason that the persecution which it describes was the catalyst of a most radical change and development of the Church of the apostles, and indeed of the development of Christian doctrine itself. Luke tells us: "As for those who were scattered, they went through the country preaching the Word" (Acts 8:4). In its way it is a strange thing to say without saying a bit more about it as well. Luke had just told us that the death of Stephen was the start of a "huge persecution" (v. 1) and that Saul was "harrying the church, entering house after house, seizing men and women and sending them to prison" (v. 3). You'd think he'd say a bit more, mention a few names at least of those who, despite the persecution that was taking place, defied it and kept on preaching the Word. But he doesn't. All he tells us is about one man. "Philip went down to a city in Samaria and began preaching the Messiah to them" (v. 4). He doesn't even tell us which city it was, and he gives no details of activities anywhere else. The fact that Luke tells us so little when he could have said so much more makes what he does tell us all the more meaningful, all the more significant. At least, that is one way of finding an excuse for his meanness and the paucity of detail.

In respect of the whole ecclesial and theological development which led up to the convening of the Council of Jerusalem and the decision the Church took at it, which was the most important turning-point in its history, Philip's missionary apostolate was a crucial one. That is how Luke presents it to us. His apostolate among the Samaritans is the one which Luke uses to illustrate the descent of the Holy Spirit upon non-orthodox Jews; and following upon that it is, almost definitely, his apostolate to one specific Roman—non-Jewish—family in Caesarea, which Luke describes, that brings about the descent of the Holy Spirit upon the Gentiles and their inclusion into the membership of the Church, which is the new people of God. By the time of writing his history Luke had come to recognize and appreciate the significant contribution Philip had made to salvation history. All the apostles and doubtless dozens of other Christians in the same period would have been doing the same, but it was Philip and his achievements that Luke has told us about. What that comes down to is the fact that it was in Philip's home town of Caesarea that a particular Gentile came to want to become a Christian, and the decision on that, as Philip realized, could only be made by the church leadership. Peter was called upon to exercise judgement. He did just that. That one single event has had outcomes and repercussions, theological and governmental, throughout all Christendom from that day to this.

What Luke is recording for us is how the command of Jesus to the apostles and disciples to take his gospel to the whole world was now up and running. "Begin at Jerusalem" (Luke 24:47) had been the instruction, and that's what the apostles had done. Then, "all over Judea and Samaria", which was where they were now at, and finally "away to the ends of the earth" (Acts 1:8). Luke does seem to have had a special regard for the Samaritans. It is to Luke that we owe the Parable of the Good Samaritan, which with that of the Prodigal Son must be the most well-known and beloved of all the parables; and in it interestingly the Samaritan is portrayed as kindly, compassionate and generous compared to the priest and the Levite who show no concern for a robbed and injured fellow human being at all. They walked by. In Luke 17, where he narrates the healing by Jesus of the ten lepers when "travelling through the borderlands of Samaria and Galilee" (v. 11), Luke brings one element in the story to the forefront of our attention, namely that only one of the ten, a Samaritan, thought to thank Jesus for what he had done for them and to praise God. Pointedly Luke writes: "and he was a Samaritan" (v. 16).

It seems common sense to assume that it was the apostles who proposed to Philip that he should preach the gospel in Samaria because he lived there, or for the same reason he returned there after clearing it with them. It was a significant event in the life of the Church, the first time it had ventured outside of Jerusalem and Judaea, and they would have thought it out carefully and planned it. Philip, they probably thought, was better suited than they were to take the first steps into Samaria because he was a diaspora Jew with a lot in common with Samaritans. They on the other hand by birth and upbringing were Judaic orthodox Jews. Both of them, orthodox and Samaritan, had big problems in their heads about each other. Then one can easily imagine the situation where Philip agreed to the arrangement but on condition that if he did have any success, one or more of the apostles might follow him, introduce themselves on behalf of the Jerusalem church, tell the Samaritans all about themselves and their own personal experience of Jesus, make them feel wanted and welcome and run their ruler over his activities. Taking the gospel to the Samaritans had been explicitly demanded of them all by the Lord himself but that did not make it an easy step to take. It was frontline stuff, real pioneering activity, which is reason enough to think it would have been exhaustively talked over between them all beforehand. Philip was putting his toes into the water on behalf of all of them. A few verses later we read that the apostles, still in Jerusalem, after receiving the reports of progress they'd been hoping for, dispatched Peter and John to wherever it was in Samaria that Philip was working. We may safely assume that was what had been agreed. It would have been collaboration rather than a supervisory visitation. They were all learning the ropes, it was their first venture, the apostles included, outside of Jerusalem and Judaea.

Luke describes Philip as having had immense success among the Samaritans when he proclaimed the Messiah to them. In a number of ways he speaks glowingly of him, and one wonders if one reason for that, besides Philip's ability as a preacher, is that he knew him well, they could well have been good friends. It was at Philip's house in Caesarea that he and Paul stayed upon returning from the third missionary journey (Acts 21:8). Luke speaks of "crowds eagerly listening to him when they saw him and saw the miracles that he performed" (Acts 8:6f.). The "signs and great miracles" (v. 13) which Philip performs include "driving out unclean spirits and curing people who were paralysed and crippled" (v. 13). In contrast Luke attributes only one miracle to Peter, which has already been described, and he makes no mention of anyone else, be they apostles like John or Paul or elders or any of Philip's fellow deacons, with the exception of Stephen (6:8) performing any miracles at all. In Acts 8:6 and 10 Luke also mentions what a riveting speaker he was. There is one additional thing, however, that Luke mentions in his account of Philip's activity in Samaria which has to be highlighted because of its huge significance and importance.

Luke doesn't just tell us that Philip captivated his Samaritan listeners when he was preaching, he didn't just convince them enough to believe "the gospel of the kingdom of God and the name of Jesus Christ" (Acts 8:12); he says something more. He says: "They were baptized, men and women alike" (ibid.). At first glance that last statement might seem to be saying nothing exceptional or particularly noteworthy. Nothing, however, could be further from the truth. What the statement makes mention of is something that set Christianity radically apart and different from Judaism; and more than that, it was also a statement of something that will in the course of time prove to have had a radically progressive effect upon both civil and secular society ever since, right down to our own times. So radical and different from Judaism is it, the apostles and elders, being Jews, must have been aware of its special feature; and in the long term right down to the present day 2,000 years later, it has been so culturally and socially progressive, and universally wherever Christianity established itself, that it is astonishing its immense importance and significance appears to have been overlooked by the commentators.

CHAPTER 11

# "They Were Baptized, Men
# and Women Alike"

What this statement (Acts 8:12) contains is an additional elucidation both of what is meant by the universality of Jesus's saving mission, which is, as repeatedly stated in this commentary on the Acts, the focus of Luke's narrative, and of how Jesus wishes to impart his salvation to humankind. That tiny two-letter word τε is all-significant. It is emphasis, it is deliberate inclusion. Luke's statement could just as well be translated "They were baptized, men and women too" or "they were baptized, women as well as men". Luke does not waste words, not even a tiny two-letter one. What is meant here is that the universality of Jesus's saving mission is as direct and immediate to women as it is to men; it is not mediated to women through men or through any ritual reserved to men such as circumcision; it reaches women as directly as men through a ritual, that of baptism, which is as fully the female's as it is the male's and is as much intended for women as it is for men.

Why did Luke make this emphasis? We can only fully appreciate what a radical departure from Judaism it represented if we look back to Genesis 17. In that chapter there is the clearest and firmest proclamation by Judaism of how circumcision, a male ritual, from which the female of course is excluded, is crucial and central to how it sees the relationship of the Chosen People to God their creator. Circumcision was in Judaism the instrument, indeed the very condition, of the covenant.

> God said to Abraham: 'For your part you must keep my covenant,
> you and your descendants after you, generation by generation.
> This is how you shall keep my covenant between myself and

you and your descendants after you: circumcise yourselves, every male among you. You shall circumcise the flesh of your foreskin and it will be a sign of the covenant between us. Every male among you in every generation shall be circumcised on the eighth day, both those born in your house and any foreigner not of your blood but bought with your money. Thus shall my covenant be marked in your flesh as an everlasting covenant. Everyone uncircumcised male, everyone who has not had the flesh of his foreskin circumcised shall be cut off from the kin of his father. He has broken my covenant.' (Genesis 17:9–14)

Where the Jewish people got this rite and this attitude towards the penis from, who knows? It could in fact have evolved over centuries, in different Middle East tribes, as a male way of asserting their superiority to women or as an expression of appreciation of the importance of producing children or as a hygienic measure to protect procreation and in due course it was given a religious meaning. Who knows? There can be no denying that reproduction is the most important human activity there is. Without it no economic or cultural future of any kind. No man/womankind without it. All fauna and flora of every kind does it as a driving force of existing.

When, however, to reproduction is added the ritual of circumcision as the condition of religious membership as in Judaism and Islam, the female is of course excluded. Ritually she isn't part of the transaction. Women's membership is through a rite performed not upon or with them but upon the male genital. In contrast Christianity by means of its ritual act of membership, namely baptism, expressly repudiates that whole concept, that whole attitude towards and that whole perspective on women, and by implication on men in relation to women.

This fundamental aspect of Christian belief and practice had already been given the strongest and clearest expression possible by Paul some twenty-five or more years before Luke wrote the Acts. Paul was writing to the Galatians, and Luke was with him to witness it, to demand from them that they resist and refuse the Judaizing preaching of recalcitrant Jerusalem Christians who, defying the instruction of the Council of Jerusalem, had travelled to Galatia to win the converts made by Paul to their Judaic understanding of Christianity which included circumcision

and the observance of Jewish dietary laws regarding so-called clean and
unclean foods and Jewish religious festivals. Paul was as forthright in
opposing such a notion of Christianity as could be. What he was saying
was as radical and mind-blowing for a Jew to say as is conceivable. He
wrote to the Galatians: "Circumcision is nothing; not being circumcised
is nothing; the only thing that counts is new creation" (Galatians 6:15).
That statement by a man who described himself as Jewish as it can get
defies and contradicts what the Jewish scribes wrote in Genesis 17 which
was their definition of what it meant to be a Jew. Some years later he
was to say to the mob in Jerusalem screaming for his blood: "I am a
Jewish man . . . educated at the feet of Gamaliel, instructed according
to the strict manner of the Law of our fathers, as zealous for God as
you are" (Acts 22:2–4). He wrote the epistle to the Galatians with total
spontaneity, one idea, even one word, sparking another into existence.
He thought of the mark circumcision leaves upon the male body and,
repudiating its significance entirely, he contrasted it with those scars
on his body which really mattered to him: "From now on," he says "let
nobody ever bother me again (with arguments why the Church should
continue with circumcision), for I bear the scars of Jesus branded on
my body" (Galatians 6:17). What he was talking about was what on his
first missionary journey he had physically suffered for Jesus and the
scars he had been left with when at Lystra he had been stoned and left
for dead by the angry Jews of Pisidia Antioch and Iconium. For Paul
they were the only bodily scars that mattered, not the scar of a removed
foreskin. He clearly had that covenant passage from Genesis in mind
with that reference to the symbolism of the scar made by circumcision.
His statement was deliberate repudiation; the old covenant had been
replaced with the new, and the most ardent of Jews was saying just that.

Even more profound, however, and more directly pertinent to what
Luke is telling us about women being baptized as well as men is how Paul
understood and visualized the full significance of baptism as the rite by
which union with Christ is achieved. He wrote a line to the Galatians,
which is inspired, and inspiring, beyond words: "For through faith you
are all sons of God in union with Christ Jesus. Baptized into union with
him you have put on Christ as a garment. There is no such thing as Jew
and Greek, slave and freeman, male and female, for you are all one person

in Christ Jesus" (Galatians 3:26–8). Forty-one words in the Greek which in a most significant and socially historic manner set Christianity apart from Judaism, and apart too from most other religions such as Islam and the cultures which those religions have generated; a mere 41 words which confer on male and female an equality never before achievable, but which, it has to be said with unutterable regret, when it comes to the attitude of the Catholic Church towards women since that moment and till today in respect of almost everything else relating to women, is still far from being achieved. Equally regrettable is how Paul himself did not make any logical deduction from what he had written to the Galatians when writing his first letter to the Corinthians. He told them in no uncertain terms that women must not address the congregations during the liturgy but must remain "subordinate as the Law directs", and if they have questions to ask, they should ask them of their husbands when they get back home (1 Corinthians 14:34f.). "It is a disgrace," he wrote, "for a woman to address the congregation." He does not say what law he has in mind. If he meant the Law of Moses as he had lived it with Judaism, it does not fit with what he has to say about the Law in Galatians and Romans. He does seem to be reverting unthinkingly to type, which is in no way unusual and is what most people do time and again, and most institutions. We all do. In this matter Paul just reverted to the norms of male–female relationships and behaviour he had been brought up with. We will see in my final chapter how the glorious way the Church in its most recent Catechism speaks about the fruits and effects of baptism in every baptized person is in practice totally ignored by it when it comes to its treatment of the lay members of the Church despite being baptized. Words are so very very easy. However, I must give praise and recognition where it is due. This discussion must be a fair and balanced one. The fact is, and this should be said out loud, that it is the countries where Christianity has been the main spiritual and social civilizing force that women enjoy the most freedom and a greater measure of equality than anywhere else; and that is down to a culture which is based on and derives inspiration from Christianity's sacramental teaching.

The statement "They were baptized, men and women alike" has to be read along with others which Luke takes from the records he had before him. There are the words Peter took from the prophet Joel on Whit

Sunday and proclaimed to the population of the city of Jerusalem and the pilgrims gathered there: "I will pour out upon everyone (ἐπὶ πᾶσαν σάρκα) a portion of my spirit, and your sons and daughters shall prophesy ... Yes, I will endue even my slaves—both men and women—with a portion of my spirit and they shall prophesy" (Acts 2:17f.). There is so much in this. Undoubtedly in the course of his preaching, on the day of Pentecost itself and in the days that followed, when he was spending every minute available to him addressing people in Jerusalem, arguing with them, preaching Jesus to them, pointing them in every other sentence to the fact and the significance of the Resurrection, Peter makes use of any amount of texts from the Scriptures; and as there was a record preserved, be it orally or even in writing, of what he said, as this record of his use of Joel indicates, Luke would have had a number, maybe plenty, to choose from. Yet the fact is, Luke chose the Joel one. And this text says that the Spirit would be poured out on everyone, sons and daughters, women as well as men, and women as well as men will "prophesy", which means that wherever they are not prevented and suppressed, women will receive the Spirit and respond to it like men will. At the least that means that women will be inspired to preach. That must be the meaning of Acts 21:9. Philip "had four daughters who were virgins/unmarried who prophesied". In other words they were evangelists like himself. It must have been some household! One wonders how his wife dealt with it all. But, needless to say, she doesn't get a single mention. The wife doesn't, the daughters do.

Twice Luke includes women in his account of how Saul persecuted the Christians, and his use of the τε with the καὶ is clear emphasis; "Meanwhile he entered house after house, seizing both men and women, and sending them into prison" (Acts 8:3); and "He went to the High Priest and applied for letters for the synagogues at Damascus authorizing him to arrest anyone he found, both men and women who followed the way and bring them to Jerusalem" (9:2). (The NET almost always translates ἡ ὁδός as "the new way" in the Acts. It seems quite reasonable.) There are ways of reading this emphasis on women as well as men being seized and imprisoned. One might be that Luke wanted to show how fanatical Saul at that moment in his life was being as well as being cruel, arresting women as well as men and taking them as captives all the way, over a hundred miles, on foot, to Jerusalem, not least because there is in addition their children to consider. But another might be that Luke wanted to make the point that women were following the Way just as men were and suffering for it just as men were. Was Luke presenting to us a doctrinal element of what he called "the Way", namely the equality in the mind of God of women with men, an element which was to distinguish it radically from Judaism, and also from other religions and cultures? Not only is the universality of Jesus's saving mission to be as direct and immediate to women as it is to men; not only is it not to be mediated to women through men or through any ritual reserved to men; not only does it reach women as directly as men through a ritual which is as fully women's as it is men's and is as much intended for women as it is for men; but through baptism the female is to be involved as much in the life of the Church in all aspects as the male. "There is no such thing as Jew and Greek, slave and freeman, male and female, for you are all one person in Christ Jesus" (Galatians 3:28), whose body is the Church.

One might go further and suggest that the statement of Luke that "they were baptized, men and women alike" has to be read with the first two chapters of his Gospel in mind. In those chapters Luke has a woman in the forefront of his story: Mary. In his account of Jesus a woman is given a most significant focus through being his mother. She is not accidental to the Jesus story, she is crucial to it. It is to Mary that God first reveals what his saving plan for humanity is and it is through Mary that the angel tells us how it will be achieved. Two whole chapters in which a woman is put before us as crucially instrumental in the salvation of humankind. "This child is destined to be a sign which human beings will reject; and you too shall be pierced to the heart" (Luke 2:34f.). The suffering by which her son wrought the salvation of humanity is one with her own. Mary gave humanity the "light that will be the revelation to the heathen and glory to thy people Israel" (2:29-32). What's more, in Luke's account of the Resurrection (23:49-24:53) women play as major a role as men, indeed more so. It is women who tell the apostles that Jesus has risen and are then met with a refusal to believe by the men; and that failure to believe what the women told them is maintained by the two male disciples on the road to Emmaus (24:13-35). Luke in his account of the Resurrection makes such a contrast between how the women disciples of Jesus readily believed and how reluctant the men were. "Why are you so perturbed?" is the challenge Jesus makes to the men. "Why do questionings arise in your minds? Look at my hands and my feet. It is I myself" (v. 38). This might reasonably suggest to us that from the start, in both Gospel and Acts, Luke had in mind the value of women with men, not just in God's saving plan but also in the life of the Church in which God's plan of salvation is enacted. Why should that attitude stop with the Ascension and the foundation of the Church on the first Whit Sunday? Why should the role of a woman as Mother of God and of women as the first evangelists of the Resurrection stop there? It is reflections like this, based on what God's revelation in the New Testament tells us, that make one shudder at the intransigence, the stupidity, the short-sightedness and, in respect of women's feelings, the meanness of the Church's leadership down to this very day.

"They were baptized, men and women alike." Membership of the Church is the same for both. So why should there be any role, any office within the Church, which cannot be carried out by a woman. It is incredibly puerile to argue that since Jesus chose only males as his apostles that is how it should be now. It is patently a silly argument, it just cannot stand up before that assertion of Paul in Galatians that men and women are "one person in Christ Jesus". It insults women, and increasingly it is being considered an insult by more and more women and girls in our day and age. It is sexist and repulsive, and deeply embarrassing. It offends, it drives women away. It denies to the Christian priesthood the distinct vitality and meaning that women can bring to it. It is incredible that in this day and age the first criterion for selection to the priesthood is what kind of genitalia a person has, male or female. In that way the denial of the priesthood to women and the claim that only men can be ordained to that ministry has to be ranked with the role of circumcision in how Judaism understands God's covenant with the Jewish people. It is not Christian. Men's genitalia are there for procreation, not for ordination. However, one might just find some hope and encouragement in the remark of Hans Urs von Balthasar: "Nothing has ever borne fruit in the Church without emerging from the darkness of a long period of loneliness into the light of the community." That is as apt a description as any of what the Council of Jerusalem represents. Luke didn't write "They were baptized, men and women alike" just to fill a bit more space. It was his thought-out message to us; and it is the Word of God.

# CHAPTER 12

# Samaritans are Received into the Church

> The apostles in Jerusalem now heard that Samaria had accepted
> the word of God. They sent off Peter and John who went down
> there and prayed for them, asking that they might receive the
> Holy Spirit. For until then the Holy Spirit had not come upon
> any of them. They had been baptized into the name of the Lord
> Jesus, that and nothing more. So Peter and John laid their hands
> on them and they received the Holy Spirit. (Acts 8:14–17)

Commentators have dealt to the point of exhaustion with this passage
because of the questions and issues that arise from it. My concern,
however, is a limited one, namely in what way what is related here has
a bearing on the Council of Jerusalem and what the Council achieved.
What is related in that connection, in addition to what has just been dealt
with, is that those Samaritans who had professed belief through accepting
the word of God had been baptized (v. 12) and then through the ritual
of the laying-on of hands had received the Holy Spirit. Very importantly,
verse 18 also informs us that their receiving the Holy Spirit had visible
effects by telling us that "Simon saw that the Spirit was bestowed". We
have seen this already in Luke's account of the descent of the Holy Spirit
on Whit Sunday; and in Acts 10:45f. the effects of the gift of the Holy
Spirit are visible, i.e. "speaking in tongues and praising God".

Peter will say at the meeting of the Council that God had shown his
approval of Gentiles being converted and baptized—a fortiori one might
add of Samaritan converts—by "giving them the Holy Spirit as he did to
us. He made no difference between us and them" (Acts 15:9). By "us"
he meant the Jewish Christians he was speaking to; and by the phrase
"giving them the Holy Spirit as he did to us" he meant precisely what he
will be saying in Jerusalem to the Judaic faction about the converts he

had baptized in Caesarea, that "God gave them no less a gift than he gave us when we put our trust in the Lord Jesus" (Acts 11:17). For Peter the response of the Samaritans to him and John laying their hands on them was proof that the Holy Spirit had come upon them. The Samaritans broke into ecstatic prayer and spoke in tongues in exactly the same way as he and John and the other apostles and fellow Jewish Christians had experienced on the day of Pentecost. That was the assurance he needed. He saw the Spirit in the effect the Spirit had on them before his very eyes.

Appreciating this is indispensable to understanding what the Council of Jerusalem was about. What Peter told his fellow Jews there was that their understanding of themselves as the one and only people who were special in the sight of God had come to an end; and that was because "God gave them—the Samaritan and the Gentile—no less a gift than he gave us" (Acts 15:8). This was the new covenant—ἡ καινὴ διαθήκη. In this instance it was with Samaritans, unorthodox Jews, but Jews nonetheless. The next stage was in Caesarea with Gentiles but that stage was the big one, the real changer; and, as Chapter 10 will show us, for Peter to understand, and accept, what was happening there in Caesarea was, after the acceptance of the fact of the Resurrection, the most significant revolution of mind and heart in Christian history. It was to understand and to accept that the gift of the Holy Spirit was for all humanity equally; it was no longer a matter of race, God's chosen people had become all humanity equally, his covenant was with all humanity, and this will be stated with great emphasis in the letters to the Ephesians and the Colossians.

As Acts 8:12–17 implies, at the time when Philip at the apostles' bidding was preaching and converting in Samaria, their ritual was still in a state of flux. However, what is significant is that at this point in the whole turmoil of doctrinal development and understanding that was taking place, there is no mention, not a word, in what Luke tells us about the conversions taking place in Samaria about issues of the Law and any obligations to abide by Judaic observances. It is faith in Jesus that matters.

No mention either of any such issues when Philip meets the Ethiopian eunuch on the road that led from Jerusalem to Gaza, a high official of the Queen of Ethiopia, in charge of her treasury. Luke says he was an Ethiopian who had travelled to Jerusalem as a pilgrim (Acts 8:28). Almost definitely he was Jewish. He would hardly have travelled that huge journey from Ethiopia to Jerusalem and back just as a "God-fearer" or as a proselyte. It was an immense distance, through different countries with all sorts of possible dangers. The footnote to the passage in the most recent Jerusalem Bible, the Revised New Jerusalem Bible 2018, describes Ethiopia as "the most distant imaginable country".[10] Besides which, the man encounters Philip when he himself is reading the prophet Isaiah. In other words, he knew either Hebrew or the Greek of the Septuagint, or both. He wouldn't have needed either for his job in Ethiopia. So it does look as if he was a Jew fulfilling a lifelong ambition to make the pilgrimage to Jerusalem. Philip baptized him on the spot, which isn't something Philip would have done if he wasn't a Jew, since Philip had felt obliged to get the apostles down from Jerusalem to get their agreement to Samaritan Jews joining the Church. The Ethiopian Jew was reading Isaiah; Philip tells him all about "the good news of Jesus" (v. 35); the eunuch declares his belief and that is followed immediately by baptism. "Look," said the eunuch. "Here is water. What is there to prevent me being baptized? Then they both went down to the water, Philip and the eunuch, and he baptized him . . . When they came out of the water, the Spirit snatched Philip away, and the eunuch saw no more of him and went on his way well content/rejoicing" (Acts 8:34–38). No fuss, no hang-ups either side about observing Jewish practices. They obviously were just taken for granted.

What is an additional item of interest, a curiosity, not quite a theological one, is that the man is said by Luke to be a eunuch. How did Philip find that out unless he had some sort of man-to-man chat with him? It probably came out when Philip asked him, as he must have done, what his job was in Ethiopia, and, being told, most likely he then asked him how he could have got the important position he held inside the household of the Queen. The question would have brought an embarrassed smile to the man's face. "O, it wasn't just because I had a head for figures which I have, but it meant she could rest assured I wouldn't create any problems among any of the many maids she had around her." The two of them must have had a bit of a laugh about it, and Luke had kept it in mind and couldn't resist including it in his narrative.

From the texts it is reasonably sure that the apostles, indeed the whole Judaic church, regarded the reception of the Samaritans into the Church through baptism as presenting no major problem. They were Jewish after all. Their baptism wasn't taking either the Judaic Christians or the Hellenist Christians into a spiritual territory which was non-Jewish territory, their inclusion at that specific moment might still have been reconcilable with the narrow and exclusive Jewish notion of the covenant which was still apostolic thinking. Furthermore, as has also been mentioned, the Gospel of John informs us that on being visited by Jesus himself and conversing with him, many Samaritans had come to believe in him as the Messiah. So possibly Philip might have been directed to a district of Samaria that was already susceptible to his preaching, which would therefore have been a sensibly tactical place to start his work of evangelization. The geographical reference in Acts 8:26 might lend substance to this item of speculation. There is even the possibility that Philip was directed by the apostles to the Samaritan town of Sychar where Jesus had stopped for a drink of water at a well and had held the well-known conversation with the Samaritan woman who, having outlived six husbands, was then living with number seven. She certainly was some woman. And in addition to that feature of her, whatever it might have been down to, she was a compelling character, able to get the people of the town to go out and meet with Jesus. John tells us that "many Samaritans of that town came to believe in him because of the woman's testimony", even to the extent of declaring him "in truth the Saviour of the world" (John 4:29). Whoever she was, she certainly was a missionary for Christ second to none. A pity we've never known her name.

Stephen's speech and Philip's apostolate, two Hellenic converts, constituted a radical departure, they provided a much-needed push towards turning Christianity eventually into a religion open to universal membership. However, that only really came about when the next step was taken, when Gentiles started asking for membership. It could well have been that it was Philip who had first brought the Church into the situation where it had to confront that issue, namely with Cornelius the Roman centurion and his family and some fellow officers.

Verse 40 might well be more informative than previously ever realized. Luke concludes his account of Philip's evangelist activities among the Samaritans and with the keeper of the Ethiopian treasury by telling us: "When he came out of the water, the Spirit snatched Philip away and the eunuch saw no more of him but went on his way a happy man; Philip appeared at Azotus and toured the country, preaching in all the towns till he reached Caesarea" (Acts 8:39–40). Azotus was in central Judea, due east of Jerusalem, well south of Samaria, situated on the main route to Egypt from Sidon in the far north of Palestine. Caesarea was on the coast in Samaria which separates Judea from Phoenicia. As it reads geographically, after being in Samaria preaching to Samaritans Philip went south back into Judea, and then continued his missionary work, well in advance of the missionary work of Paul with which we are all well acquainted. For him to preach in all the towns until he got from Azotus back home to Caesarea would have been a gargantuan achievement; there was any amount of towns between Azotus and Caesarea. Maybe Luke is exaggerating somewhat but that hardly matters. What does matter is to appreciate that in Philip the Church had one almighty missionary worker whose astonishing dedication to proclaiming his faith in Jesus has never received the notice it deserves. And if Philip was doing this, it is certain he did not work alone, he just couldn't have; he'd have back-up from Jerusalem and fellow Christians with him; and it is equally certain that what he was doing was being done across Judea and into Galilee by others, not least the apostles. One thing we can be sure of, that when just a few years later the church in Antioch took the decision to send Barnabas and Saul to Cyprus and on to Asia Minor on what we call Paul's first missionary journey, as a local church it wasn't alone in what it did. Other local churches would have been doing it too in other directions. The Antioch initiative was the only one Luke told us about. The direction of travel from Jew to Gentile had begun.

# CHAPTER 13

# Journeying towards the Gentiles

It is now helpful if we look at certain major trends and areas of debate and discussion in how the Church moved out of its initial, and racially narrow, confines into Gentile territory. We know from Acts 16:10 that Luke was with Paul on his second missionary journey, or at least for part of it, and with him on his third journey, between the years 50 to 58. In that period Paul wrote the First Letter to the Thessalonians, the earliest New Testament writing that there is, followed by Galatians, Philippians, Philemon, 1 and 2 Corinthians and Romans, the seven letters in the Canon which are now agreed to have been written by him. Luke sailed with him from Rhodes via Patera in Asia Minor across the Mediterranean to Tyre in Phoenicia and finally to Caesarea to conclude the third missionary journey. He stayed with Paul when, against all advice from friends, Paul travelled on to Jerusalem where he was arrested by the Roman commander to save him from being killed by a hostile mob. Paul was put into "shackles with two chains" (Acts 21:33), being transferred in due course, again for his safety, back to Caesarea where he remained a prisoner for two years. When he turned up in Caesarea in chains and a prisoner, one might ask if any of the Christians there visited him and reminded him that if he had had the sense to listen to them when they advised him to steer well clear of Jerusalem (v. 12), he wouldn't have got himself into the mess he was now in. Throughout all of this Luke stayed with him, and then sailed with him to Rome only to get shipwrecked off the coast of Malta and then find themselves within an inch of being killed by the ship's sailors. He remained with him in Rome when he was taken into house-arrest to await trial before the Emperor Nero. It is not known if Luke stayed with Paul till he was executed in the year 65. It is strange that he makes no mention of Paul's death which happened in Rome. He knew about it. But that's Luke, some of his editorial decisions defy normal logic. It could be of course that he had intended to write a third book but never managed it, or he did and it got lost.

Luke therefore was able to listen to every word uttered and read every line written when Paul was doing his missionary work and developing his theology, inclusive of his refutation in Galatians of the version of Christianity which was being preached to Paul's own Galatian converts by the Judaic faction, members of which, defying the decision of the Council of Jerusalem, were still determined somehow to restrict Church membership to Jews, either Jews by birth or Gentiles who adopted Jewish religious practices such as circumcision. It could even have been Luke to whom Paul dictated Galatians, at least until that moment when he took the pen off his scribe, whoever it was, and wrote the final verses himself (Acts 6:11–18). The most important comment on and application of the decision of the Council of Jerusalem is Paul's letter to the Galatians.

What Peter and Paul had in common is of immense significance. Both had the closest and most intimate acquaintance with Jesus, though of course in different ways. Both had been traditional, and indeed ardent, Jews. Paul had been what might be called a fanatical Jew as Luke tells us in Acts 9:1–3, and as Paul himself tells us in Acts 26:4f. and Galatians 1:13–15. He'd attended Jewish theological schools, including one in Jerusalem under the direction of Gamaliel, and he never ceased to welcome the company of fellow Jewish scholars and debate the scriptures with them (cf. Acts 28:23–8). Obviously he greatly loved those sessions, it was his upbringing. Peter himself, however, unlike Paul, was no scholar, but the theological insights he had and the theological arguments he made, never abstractly but in response to events and to the argumentation and the pressure forced on to the Church by the Judean faction, proved to be absolutely fundamental to all future Christian theological development and the basis of what we might call Pauline theology. That emerges from what the Acts tell us and what is contained in Galatians and Romans. Peter had been an ardent seeker after the Messiah, had associated himself with John the Baptist in this search for the Messiah, very likely with the Essenes as well, and had formed his own small group of Messiah-seekers, which included his brother Andrew and close friends and fellow fishermen. He did not have the literary schooling or the formal training in Judaism that Paul had, but doubtless he had learned a lot from those associations and from his discussions with the members of his group. When Jesus chose his twelve apostles, he didn't choose without careful consideration of possible candidates. He chose associates of John the Baptist (cf. John 1:35ff.) and others close to, maybe even belonging to, the Essenes.

Both Paul and Peter had had an intimate acquaintance with Jesus. We know of course what Peter's was. It was so intimate, so close, that, as Matthew narrates (Acts 16:22), he could forcibly grab Jesus by the arm and remonstrate with him. Peter lived, spoke, ate, walked, looked on, listened to, argued with Jesus for two to three years, day after day. Jesus crossed the Sea of Galilee a number of times on his boat and slept in it at least once. Peter saw him arrested and from inside the Jewish Council's premises maybe saw him being mocked and scourged, and from a discrete distance might have watched him carry his cross to Calvary. He was not one of the people who accompanied Jesus, watched him being stripped, then nailed to the cross and hung up between two thieves. At best he looked on from a safe distance. He also of course was a witness to the Resurrection and what he witnessed in the forty days between Easter Sunday and Ascension Thursday is all well known.

There were other people there on Good Friday. Some taunted Jesus mercilessly, there were the Roman soldiers who crucified him and the two thieves crucified with him. But besides them there were the people closest and dearest to him, such as his mother and the disciple whom Jesus loved, who stood at the foot of the cross. They heard his last words; they witnessed the death of God. They witnessed the salvation of humankind. Humanity in all its variety was represented there, men and women, saints and sinners. Of the seven who were followers of Jesus, except for Mary the mother of Jesus, we know little, about some of them nothing at all, not even the names of some of them. They would have helped Joseph of Arimathea take the body down from the cross, and together with Nicodemus and Jesus's mother clean it with spices and wrap it in strips of linen cloth and take it to a garden nearby and lay it in a tomb not yet used for a burial.

Paul did not have the sort of acquaintance with Jesus that Peter had. His was different, it came about differently. Paul tells us he "saw" Jesus (1

Corinthians 9:1). "I must make it clear to you, my friends, that the gospel you heard me preach is no human invention. I did not take it over from any man, no man taught it me; I received it through the revelation of Jesus Christ" (Galatians 1:11f.). It was the risen Jesus that appeared to Paul, not just on that one occasion on the road to Damascus but repeatedly over a much longer period (cf. 2 Corinthians 12:2–4). In the same letter (15:8) he tells us Jesus "appeared even to me" just as he had to Cephas, to the Twelve, to over five hundred of the brethren, to James and to all the apostles.

How extensive, how detailed, were these encounters which he had with Jesus? There is that intriguing passage in 1 Corinthians 11:23, where he tells us that it was the Lord himself who instructed him about the Eucharistic rite: "For the tradition which I handed on to you I received from the Lord himself that the Lord Jesus, on the night of his arrest, took bread, and after giving thanks to God, broke it and said: 'This is my body which is for you; do this as a memorial of me'. In the same way he took the cup after supper and said: 'This cup is the new covenant (sealed) in my blood. Whenever you drink it, do this as a memorial of me. For every time you eat this bread and drink this cup you proclaim the death of the Lord until he comes'." This really makes one think about the degree of knowledge of his life on earth that the risen Jesus communicated to Paul. If this detail was told to Paul by Jesus, what else did he tell him about himself? And how important and significant a liturgical action the Eucharist must have been to Jesus given that he revealed it to Paul himself and revealed it in such detail.

There was an interval of some years, maybe as many as ten years, from the moment of Paul's encounter with Jesus on the road to Damascus till he began to engage in his missionary work. Soon after his conversion he escaped from Damascus where the Jews had hatched a plot to kill him. His fellow Christians lowered him down the city wall in a basket. He then went to meet the apostles in Jerusalem but in due course, being the person he was, he got himself embroiled in arguments with Greek-speaking Jews there, doubtless in the way and on the same themes as Stephen before him. Besides, he must have been regarded by them as a traitor to the Jewish religion. His opponents, similar to what happened to Stephen, got a plan together to murder him. Little wonder that "the brethren" in

Jerusalem packed him off to Caesarea and saw to it that he got on a boat to Tarsus (Acts 9:30). Most likely they were afraid to try to get him there overland; it meant going through Judea, probably too risky. It was then some five years before Barnabas, while he was in Antioch at the request of the church in Jerusalem, used the occasion to travel to Tarsus to bring Paul to Antioch. Barnabas himself, being like Mary his sister a convert from Judaism, had judged that the church of Antioch was one which would suit Paul, and together he and Paul "lived in fellowship with the congregation and gave instruction to large numbers" (Acts 11:26).

There can be little doubt that in addition to earning his living probably as a tent-maker which enabled him to support his wife and the children they most likely had, whenever they were with him, he also spent those five years in Tarsus in prayer and in study of what he had learnt about Jesus from the apostles and fellow Christians in Antioch and Jerusalem and from the mystical communion he continued to have with him (2 Corinthians 12:2–4). We might speculate about how Barnabas managed his relationship with him. The two got on together all right but what about the visions Paul was continuing to have? If any one of us were a university lecturer in physics, and a colleague claimed he or she had had, and was still having, sessions with the long-dead Einstein, who was appearing to him and conversing with him about matters scientific, how would one deal with it? Politely excuse oneself, dial 999 and ask for an ambulance? If English medieval historians attending their annual conference at Battle near Hastings found that one of their number was going about saying he was holding regular conversations with the Winchester clerk who edited Great Domesday, how would they deal with him? Would they break into their publicized agenda and invite him to give a lecture? Or would they ring up the psychiatric wing of the nearest hospital? When Paul "gave instruction to large numbers", he must have told them of his experiences since in his letters he refers to them and even used them to justify his claim to be an apostle (1 Corinthians 9:1). How did they deal with it and with him? How did they relate to such a person? And how did Barnabas and the Antioch community?

Before his first missionary journey, which was probably from the year 46/47 to 49, Paul had had many years in which to meditate long and hard on his new faith and communicate with the Risen Jesus. We can be sure that it was for him a time of profound mystical meditation and dialogue with Jesus. "I know a Christian man who fourteen years ago (whether in the body or out of it I do not know—God knows) was caught up as far as the third heaven. And I know that this same man (whether in the body or out of it I do not know—God knows) was caught up into paradise and heard words so secret that human lips cannot repeat them" (2 Corinthians 12:2–4). The levels of mystical encounter with the Risen Lord, of which this would seem to have been the highest, must have been varied; and what Jesus communicated to Paul about himself, his life on earth, his teachings and his mission we can only work out as best we can from what Paul has left for us in his letters. However, if 1 Corinthians 11:23 is anything to go by, Jesus provided Paul not just with a mystical understanding but also with positive details of himself and his life on earth, even with the words he used over the bread and the wine at the Last Supper. There again, however, it is possible that Paul might have confused what Jesus told him about himself and what he did and what he wanted, with what the apostles and others told him about Jesus in the many conversations he had with them. We know from 1 Corinthians 9:1f. that he was under pressure to justify his claim to be an apostle: "Am I not an apostle? Did I not see our Lord?" Anyone can easily picture him shouting this to the person whom he was dictating the letter to. Clearly in anger and frustration. Pressure together with a veritable avalanche of information from lots of different sources might have been too much for him to put everything into the right mental box.

It was at the start of Paul's second missionary journey that Barnabas drops out of Luke's account of the transformation of "the way" from being a narrow Judaic grouping into a trans-national church. The contribution Barnabas made to that achievement was both crucial and immense. There can hardly be any doubt he continued his involvement in it but in what way we do not know. He was no longer relevant to the story Luke was telling, so we learn no more about him. He was a Greek-speaking Jew, of the tribe of Levi, from Cyprus who went to live in Jerusalem, as did Mary his married sister, and it was in Jerusalem that he became a Christian as she, and presumably her husband, did. Acts 4:36f. informs us that he owned a "field/estate", which he sold, giving the money to the community. His sister and her husband owned a house in the city big enough for "a large number" of fellow Christians to hold services in (Acts 12:12), and just possibly it was in her house that the Council was held a few years later. Barnabas achieved considerable status within the Jerusalem Christian community, and his role in the story of the expansion of the Church into pagan territory and non-Jewish cultures was crucial. That he fell out with Paul immediately prior to the second missionary journey has wrongly overshadowed and detracted from the immense contribution he made to the growth of the Church, not just numerically but, more importantly, theologically. For example, it was his intervention into the arguments going on in the Antioch church about admitting Gentiles into membership that paved the way, maybe even initiated, the solution reached at the Council of Jerusalem; and undoubtedly, absolutely undoubtedly, it would have been his innumerable conversations with Paul that, like what Peter preached, decided and spoke with Paul about, helped put what we call Pauline theology into Paul's head. No man is an island, not even Saint Paul.

With Acts 9 Luke moves the mission of the Church from restriction to the Jews in the direction of the Gentiles. He does it with his account of the conversion of Paul on the road to Damascus as Paul himself remembered it and of course told Luke about it, doubtless many times in the innumerable conversations they had in the years they were together. In addition Paul recounts it twice himself, once in Jerusalem when he was under arrest and surrounded by a mob howling for his blood (Acts 22) and again in Caesarea before King Agrippa and Queen Bernice (Acts 25). In his Jerusalem account he has Ananias saying something different from what Luke recounts him saying in Acts 9. Then in his Caesarea account Paul omits to mention Ananias altogether and substitutes Jesus as the person speaking to him. The differences are most intriguing, and their explanation throws considerable light on what understanding we should have of our Christian belief that our Scriptures are the word of God, who never errs. There can be no correct understanding of what is meant by our belief that the Scriptures are the Word of God without understanding the role of the Church, the Body of Christ, which decided which writings composed the canon. That, however, is a matter which requires its own elucidation and is not directly pertinent to the purpose of this paper, which is to describe how the Council of Jerusalem came about, and why, and what its significance was.

There can of course have been no real doubt that in Paul's mind there was a real sense of mission to the Gentiles in addition to his mission to the Jews, even though in actual fact he probably preached more to his fellow Jews than he did to Gentiles. His circumstances made that inevitable. At the same time it has to be said that it was Peter, despite what Paul says in Galatians, who did the spadework and provided the theological leadership in the Church's apostolate to the Gentiles. It was Peter who, assisted by Philip whom Luke calls "the evangelist" (Acts 21:8), brought about the conversion of the first Gentiles, namely the Roman centurion, his family, household and some of his fellow officers; and it was he who then took on the Judaic faction within the Jerusalem/Judean church and formulated and applied the theological justification for what he had done, not just in baptizing Gentiles but also in laying it down that they did not have to adopt Jewish religious practices such as circumcision as a condition of church membership.

Of great significance in respect of this assertion that Peter's theological input was the fundamental one is one line of what Paul said to King Agrippa and Queen Bernice. He is telling them what the Lord said to him on the road to Damascus. As pointed out already, it is not what Luke reported Ananias to have said; this version of the event says a lot more. However, it is just one line that at this juncture merits attention. The Lord says to Paul: "I am sending you to open their eyes (the eyes of the Gentiles) and turn them from darkness to light, from the dominion of Satan to God, so that they may obtain forgiveness of sins and a place/ inheritance with those who are sanctified by faith in me, καὶ κλῆρον ἐν τοῖς ἡγιασμένοις πίστει τῇ εἰς ἐμέ" (26:18). Those last three words in Greek, that final phrase, four words in English, and in the Vulgate "per fidem quae est in me", is precisely the statement of Christian faith which Peter pronounced and declared at the Council of Jerusalem. At the Council Peter stated: "ἀλλὰ διὰ τῆς χάριτος τοῦ κυρίου Ἰησοῦ πιστεύομεν σωθῆναι καθ' ὃν τρόπον κἀκεῖνοι—we believe that it is by the grace of the Lord Jesus that we are saved—sed per gratiam Domini Jesu credimus salvari" (15:11). With that one short statement Peter gave to the Church the required understanding of the who, the what and the why of Jesus

Christ and of its own distinct identity. It is what Paul was to build on and expand magnificently in Galatians and Romans. In developing the theology of the achievement of the Council of Jerusalem in those epistles Paul was permanently and indescribably brilliantly and profoundly dealing with that most basic of all Christian theological beliefs. It is faith in Jesus as saviour from sin and its consequences, which is alienation from himself, that God wants from people, all people, all humanity. The Jewish people belonged securely and forever to God, but they now share that equally with the rest of humanity. For the Church, whose first members, like Jesus himself and his mother and his foster father, were Jews born and bred, to make this decisive break and understand that all peoples were now chosen equally with themselves, was the hardest of hard realizations. For the apostles it was as hard as hard could be, as hard as stone. It went against every grain in their body. But at the Council of Jerusalem they achieved it.

In his letters to the Galatians and the Romans Paul develops and refines the issues, as do the authors of Colossians and Ephesians, as will be shown. Interestingly Luke, though he witnessed Paul writing or dictating his letters, makes no mention of them at all or of this issue in his record of Paul's second and third missionary journeys. That omission, like so many more of Luke's editorial decisions, is really hard to understand. The problems in Galatia, Corinth and Rome which Paul's letters dealt with were so important, indeed most plainly in Galatia so massive, they must have preoccupied him and his companions for months on end, they must have impacted on the missionary journeys so much. It is therefore most difficult to understand why they did not get any mention at all in Luke's record of those journeys. Luke just excluded them. As said, he was, and is, the most ruthless of editors.

# CHAPTER 14

# Visions and a Delegation
# in the Town of Joppa

The Church throughout Judea, Galilee and Samaria was left in
peace to build up its strength. In the fear of the Lord, upheld by
the Holy Spirit, it held to its way and grew in numbers. (Acts 9:31)

There was a cessation of the persecution being inflicted on the Church,
when the Jews turned their attention to stopping the Emperor Caligula
having a statue of himself erected in the temple. One thing we can read
into verse 31 is that, though Luke is confining himself in his narrative
on the whole to describing the evangelical work of Peter, Paul, Barnabas
and Philip, there was a lot going on elsewhere throughout the different
provinces of the Holy Land undertaken by the other apostles and
members, and, as he tells us, successfully. Peter's situation was that he
was leading and living, praying and working with a growing group of men
and women, all Jews, who, himself included, had it as their inherited all-
encompassing cultural and religious perspective that their nation alone
was God's chosen people. He had already welcomed Samaritan Jews into
the Church, as we have seen; and with converts being made among Jews
in great numbers in Judea, Galilee and Samaria (Acts 9:31), he set out on
a tour "to all places" (v. 32)—which took in Lydda, Sharon and Joppa. All
three places were in Judea, with Joppa on the border with Samaria. The
next port north of it was Caesarea at the northern extremity of Samaria.
There is no knowing if Caesarea, immensely important as it turned out
to be in the history of Christianity, was on Peter's intended itinerary. And
as that itinerary took in "all places", and as there would have been many
villages en route, one can surmise that the apostles and other colleagues
in Jerusalem were creating a network, indeed an organization which

sensibly required some degree of government. Luke only tells us that Peter went on this visit to Christian communities in the territory of Judea between Jerusalem and Joppa, a distance of some forty miles. That does not exclude similar journeys with the same intent being taken to other groups of Christian communities by some or all of the other apostles. However, Luke's focus on Peter in this respect as well as in others, which he has given us already and will continue to do so until Acts 15:11, does definitely give the impression that by the time he came to write both his Gospel and the Acts Peter was pre-eminent among the apostles. For the purposes of this script we need do no more than just refer the reader to Acts 9:32–43 for a description of his activities in Lydda; it is Joppa and Caesarea, 10:9–48, that matter.

In Acts 8:40 Luke supplies us with this information that, after his conversion of the Ethiopian eunuch, who "went on his way rejoicing, Philip appeared at Azotus and toured the country, preaching in all the towns till he reached Caesarea". Azotus was some thirty miles due east of Jerusalem, near the coast. It was about another thirty miles south of Caesarea. There were a lot of towns and villages between Azotus and Caesarea, where finally, going by Acts 21:8, Philip had settled and married. His wife, whose name is not given, bore him three daughters "who did prophesy (or possessed the gift of prophecy)", so like their father (21:8) they were evangelists. Luke also tells us that when he and Paul, returning from the third missionary journey, lodged at their house they were "unmarried/virgins". Like with their mother their names are not given, regrettably. There is a fair amount of information here about Philip. As has been said, he was well known as an evangelist; there were a lot of towns and villages between Azotus and Caesarea and he preached in all of them (v. 40), which indicates a huge amount of zeal and dedication. Furthermore, going by the fact that at the date of the conclusion of the third missionary journey, approximately the year 58, Luke would be calling him "the evangelist", we can infer that he had been preaching and converting in and around Caesarea since the conversion of the Ethiopian and was still doing it. That title, "the evangelist", tells us a lot about his reputation within the infant Church.

Luke informs us that "at Caesarea there was a man named Cornelius, a centurion in what was known as the Italian Regiment. He and all his family were devout and God-fearing; he gave generously to those in need and prayed to God regularly" (Acts 10:1f.). God-fearers were people who followed Jewish practice and belief but did not formally convert to Judaism. Cornelius was a Roman name; he was a Roman officer but the office of centurion was not a principal one. He and his troops were stationed in Caesarea, there to maintain and defend the Roman Empire. He was in other words as Gentile as they come. He had his family with him, and servants and a circle of friends (v. 24). He and all his family were known to be "devout" (v. 2), and they attended the Jewish synagogue to join in the prayers. Cornelius gave generously to help poor Jewish people. He was both a "God-fearer" and a giver of alms to the needy. Whether or not he had it in mind to convert to Judaism we do not know. Some scholars read verse 28 to imply he did not.

Luke gives us just an outline of what happened. He tells us that it was while Cornelius was attending a Jewish hour of prayer he had a vision of an angel. "He distinctly saw an angel of God who came to him" (Acts 10:3), telling him to send a messenger to Peter in Joppa to summon him to Caesarea to meet him; and the angel gave Cornelius directions where his messenger would find him in Joppa. Cornelius did as instructed. He called in two of his servants, and one of his officers who was a religious person like himself, told them about the vision he had had and sent the three of them off to Joppa to bring Peter back with them to Caesarea. One is inclined to think Cornelius included one of his officers in the delegation to make it clear to Peter that he had to come. We can put some flesh on these bare bones.

As has been pointed out already, Luke liked angels. The Greek word also means messenger. It is a matter of judgement what it was exactly that he had in mind each time he used the word, either an angel or just a messenger. Textually it would seem to be an angel, since Luke tells us that Cornelius saw the "angel" "distinctly" (NIV) or "clearly" (NET) and that "he stared at him in terror". However, it could well be that Luke, recognizing the importance of the event, knowing it was of the highest significance, that it was a breakthrough moment, decided to describe it in a way that he felt gave it the solemnity it merited. It could be that the "angel of God" was Philip, that he was God's messenger to Cornelius. That is much more likely. Would Almighty God send an angel, something totally alien to the culture and the individual mind of a pagan Roman soldier, to do something someone like Philip could do perfectly well? Hardly. Here the application of Occam's razor makes perfect sense—"entia non multiplicanda sunt sine necessitate". In the Caesarean synagogue Cornelius would have heard the preaching, the arguments, the discussions between the Caesarean Christians and the Jews; and Philip might well have been in the forefront of that encounter. In the synagogue Cornelius could have watched, listened and then conversed with Philip himself. He could have been impressed by what Philip had to say, so impressed and influenced he went to him to talk to him a lot more about it all. Philip would have spoken with him and his family and told them about Jesus so successfully that Cornelius asked to be baptized. Philip, however, was aware that, with Cornelius being a Gentile, any outreach in that direction was another category altogether, a step he himself could not take, one that needed the highest Church authorization. So he told Cornelius he'd have to get in touch with the man at the top, with Peter, who at that moment was in Joppa. He would have told Cornelius about the status Peter held within the Church and how he had got Peter and John to come from Jerusalem to visit the Samaritans whom he was converting to put their stamp of approval upon them becoming full members of the Church.

Philip, being on the church network which was now operating from Jerusalem, across Judea, into Samaria and easily as far as Antioch (cf. Acts 11:22), obviously knew where Peter was, knew that he had come up to Joppa from Jerusalem after visiting any number of other towns and villages, staying here, staying there: "He is staying with Simon the tanner whose house is by the sea" (v. 6). This tells us that there was organization, Peter might have sent out the details of his itinerary in advance, there would have been communication between the churches, even as far apart as Caesarea was from Jerusalem. There could have been information available about who might be staying with whom and where exactly. Philip knew that Peter had got as far as Joppa. Joppa was on the boundary between Judea and Samaria. The fact that Cornelius had to send an officer there to bring him to Caesarea might indicate that Peter hadn't been intending to travel any further north; otherwise Philip might have suggested to Cornelius that they wait till Peter came up to Caesarea or somewhere nearby.

Meanwhile, Peter in Joppa was having a vision as well, but of a different kind. There may well have been, at least in part, a personal origin to it. He could not but see that there was the issue of Church membership being offered to Gentiles, that the messiahship of Jesus might now be offered to non-Jews. It is possible that Peter meeting up with the Christians of Joppa before the delegation from Cornelius arrived on his doorstep could have been influenced by them. The Christians of Joppa, a coastal town, a port open to the comings and goings of Mediterranean shipping, with a constant mix and traffic of people and cultures, and miles from Jerusalem, would not be sharing that city's cultural and religious insularity and narrow conservatism. Objectively the culture and the religion of Israel, despite its immense importance to us, was just one out of many in that great and varied region. Peter had been staying "many days" (Acts 9:43) in the company of Joppa's Christians. There can be little doubt, mixing all the time in a thousand different ways as they would be with Gentiles from all over the Mediterranean basin, from Spain to Palestine, from North Africa to southern Europe, that the Joppa Christians, Jewish though they were, would have been thinking and talking to each other and with Peter about what standing Gentiles might have in the saving plan of God; and he for his part would have the command of Jesus echoing in his head that the gospel had to be taken to the ends of the earth. The vision he was about to have just didn't come from nowhere, the issue must almost definitely have been on his mind. How momentous it would prove to be in its actual outcome and its implications could not be foreseen. It easily ranks with Paul's vision of Jesus on the road to Damascus for the reason that Peter himself gives us in Acts 10:28 and 34. With it "God showed me that I should not call any man impure or unclean". The implications of that Christian proclamation were simply immense, and as significant now as it was then.

Peter, Luke tells us, was hungry, he started making something to eat, but somehow he fell into a trance when doing it; and in it he had a vision of a huge sheet being let down from the heavens full of creatures of every kind, "all kinds of four-footed animals as well as reptiles of the earth and birds of the air" (10:12). He heard a voice from heaven telling him to kill and eat them. Peter, the devout Jew, was appalled. His head was still full, understandably, of the attitudes to things he had been brought up with.

In the case of the Jewish people, then as now, food was an important religious issue. Foods that are taboo serve to give people a powerful sense of difference from other people. It was, and still is, an instrument of self-identification and of differentiation from others. Some religions seem to need this; not all, however. That was how it worked then with Jewish people, and still does.

"Surely not, Lord," exclaimed Peter. "I have never eaten anything that is profane and unclean" (Acts 10:14). The divine rebuke Peter got in reply was: "Do not call anything profane that God has made clean" (v. 15). This encounter happened to Peter three times, which has its own interest, since Peter denied Jesus three times, and after his resurrection Jesus asked him three times if he loved him. The gravity of the message to him can hardly be exaggerated. Nothing God has created is unclean and God has created everything; it is human cultures that create taboos, all sorts of them, generally about clothing and food, even people; and of course the males of some cultures and religions impose them on and around girls and women partly to keep control of them. Religious taboos are of course of interest to sociologists but they also alienate one people from another. Religious leaders sometimes prefer it and maintain it where they can. Taboos can start for such good common sense reasons as hygiene or comfort or business but can then develop into and be kept going as instruments of tribal or religious or national identification and create barriers between peoples. The long loose clothing, for example, Muslim men wear in the warm Middle East makes good sense. However, to wear it in colder climates such as northern Europe to assert a distinct and different religious identity is to be divisive. As is the way Muslim women are often made to dress. It does not serve God in any way at all; God does not need any of it.

Peter as a Jew had taken a direct hit. God had told him in no uncertain terms that within the Church, in "the new way", he was to repudiate the Jewish religious distinction between kosher and non-kosher foods. The theological reason was given in the vision, and it was simple and straightforward: "Do not call anything impure/common/profane that God has made clean" (11:9). The author of the first letter to Timothy set out the Christian perspective on the issue excellently. Speaking harshly of the people who preached "abstinence from certain foods", he said: "God created them to be enjoyed with thanksgiving by believers who have an inward knowledge of the truth. For everything that God created is good. Nothing is to be rejected when it is taken with thanksgiving, since it is hallowed by God's own word and by prayer" (1 Timothy 4:3f.). This is as profound as it gets. The reason God gave to Peter is unanswerable, and one might well think that it is so obvious that the Jews, and indeed other religions, should have seen it for themselves centuries before. They hadn't, however, and anyway, it helped towards preservation of a distinct religious and national identification. Not eating certain foods, wearing distinctive clothing, removing foreskins, wearing skullcaps or beards, having womenfolk cover up their hair or their figure, wearing dog collars or cassocks and much more besides, they can all help to make people feel different, and they do all sorts of things for many religious leaders. God has no need for any of it and with the command to Peter firmly repudiated it.

For Peter, whose cultural and religious mentality harboured many such taboos, what the vision and the voice that accompanied it told him to do was a tremendously difficult directive, and he was still trying to cope with it and its implications when the messengers from Cornelius arrived at his door. It was as if, staggering to get to his feet, he was hit this time with a well-aimed and ferocious punch right between the eyes. There were Gentiles at the door of the Jewish Christians he was staying with; and they were about to order him to accompany them to Caesarea to the home of another Gentile. It could hardly get much worse, since, as Peter will explain to Cornelius, "It is against our Law for a Jew to associate with or visit a person of another race" (Acts 10:28). Luke doesn't describe Peter as metaphorically flat on his back as a result of the first instruction, he kindly describes him as "still wondering about the meaning of the vision" (v. 19), when the Roman centurion's delegation knocked on the door of the house, presenting Peter with an even bigger Jewish religious taboo to wrestle with, a much more serious one in fact, one which today we can acknowledge to be a racist issue, namely mixing with a foreigner. There is nothing in God's creation, indeed nothing in God, which justifies any cult of difference and separation between peoples, indeed the opposite is the case.

The Holy Spirit immediately intervened to help Peter; and what he said to him is significant. He said: "Go with them without any misgivings for I have sent them" (Acts 10:20). There are differences between scholars about elements of Luke's narration of this event, but certainly we can read it as informing us that the Spirit of God (v. 19), in whatever form it took, told Peter he may travel to Caesarea in the company of Gentiles, meet with Cornelius the Roman centurion and be welcomed and taken in by his household (v. 22) despite it being against the Jewish religious law of the time. From verse 23 we can see that Peter responded positively to the arrival of the three men at his door. He "invited the men into his house to be his guests". For him, a devout Jew, inviting them in like that, making them his guests and giving them food and lodging, demonstrates on his part an openness to the issue and an ability to change of mind. Jesus hadn't chosen Peter to be the rock on which he would build his church without insight into his character. On the following day, strengthened by his openness of mind, but doubtlessly apprehensive and worried, he set out for Caesarea with the soldiers, taking a number of Joppa Christians along with him.

The number was six (Acts 11:12). They were all "from the circumcision" (10:45), i.e. "of Jewish birth" (NET). In Acts 10:23 Luke had first described them simply as "some members from (the congregation) at Joppa". It was not, however, without a reason that a mere 22 verses later he specified that they were more than that. The translation this writer prefers is "those of the circumcision party", which is how Luke will henceforth describe them, as indeed he does a few verses later in Acts 11:1–4. It was a group within the Church which emerges as a vigorous opposition faction, wanting all Gentiles upon conversion to Christianity to adopt Jewish religious practices and the Law and who subject Peter to a hostile interrogation (11:1–4) upon his return to Jerusalem from Caesarea. Later they will create havoc among his Galatian community converted by Paul. The description of the six men which Luke uses, if we translate it as "those of the circumcision party", would indicate that the Judaic faction within Christianity was already in existence and its members were recognizable and organized; and Peter was aware of them. It is strikingly similar to what Pope Francis is encountering today within the Curia and elsewhere, a group who are resisting change and fomenting opposition to what he is saying and doing as he takes the Church into our modern age.

Peter was also aware that he had to tread carefully. He knew perfectly well that him just being in the company of Gentiles, let alone considering receiving them into the Church, if that thought had entered his head after speaking with them, would raise the hackles of some members of the Jerusalem community to which he would have to report back. For that reason he might well have felt he needed witnesses for whatever might be about to happen. He chose these six. They would accompany him to Caesarea, and after Caesarea back to Jerusalem. As already said, Luke describes them as "believers (in Jesus as the Messiah) belonging to the circumcision group". Peter must have already have been well aware of the faction in Jerusalem prior to the visitation he was making to the Christian communities in such cities as Lydda and Joppa; and there can be little or no doubt that he chose six such men to accompany him to Caesarea so that they would be witnesses to whatever might happen in Caesarea with the Roman centurion and his family. He figured—rightly (cf. Acts 11:18)—that if the faction proved sceptical about what he might have to tell the Jerusalem community on his return, they would at least believe the witness of their own kind.

The message of the vision was that all nations inclusive of the Jewish nation were in the one same sheet, all sharing existence together, with none of them unclean or profane, all of them made by the same hand, the hand of God, all clean, none of them common, all equally special in the eyes of their Creator. It really is a most powerful image, it is a message, it is a statement of exceptional morality given the age when it was pronounced, indeed even for today. It was the new covenant between God and human beings. With this vision and with the instruction God gave to Peter and the reason he gave for it, God showed us all what sort of world he wants from us. What happened here and what was said was a new covenant, a new heaven, a new earth. Nobody God has made is common and unclean, absolutely nobody. No one is inferior to anyone else. No matter who we are, no matter what wealth or what poverty, what gender, no matter the language, the culture, the intelligence, the colour, whatever it is that differentiates us, we, "creatures of every kind", are all in the same "great sheet of linen cloth". God's revelation is lowered from heaven to earth to reach all its "four corners".

To fully appreciate what a revelation it all was to Peter, and indeed appreciate what it said about him that he could take it on board and act on it, we need to look at the Scripture that till this moment had guided him and his colleagues, the Scripture he had read and absorbed into his mental make-up from childhood. He was not Greek-speaking diaspora Jewish; he was not Samaritan Jewish; his upbringing was strict Judaism; and now he was a Judaic Christian. The temple he had worshipped in other than his synagogue in Galilee was the one built under Ezra and Nehemiah when the exiles returned from captivity. Their scriptures were his scriptures and in them there were the terribly harsh strictures of those two minor prophets against foreigners, especially foreign women. Speaking of the Jewish people Nehemiah boasted: "I purified them from everything foreign" (Nehemiah 12:30), and he said that King Solomon "was led by foreign women into sin" (v. 26), while Ezra even forced the male population who had married foreign women to get rid of them and the children they had had by them. "We have committed an offence against our God in marrying foreign wives, daughters of a foreign population. But in spite of this there is still hope for Israel. Now, therefore, let us pledge ourselves to our God to dismiss these women and their brood . . . and let us act as the Law prescribes" (Ezra 10:2f.). This was racism as bad as it gets, blatant, cruel and ugly.

Nehemiah lived about 500 years BC. What he and Ezra said and did constitutes only two short books of the Bible, but they would have been read and commented on as required in both the temple and in every synagogue. Some elements therefore of its mind and mentality will have carried though to the Jewish people living in the first century AD, and the development of a Judaic faction within the community of the first Christians, demanding of the first convert Gentiles that they live by the Law, is evidence that it did. It was the mentality that Peter now had to deal with. He dealt with it in an exemplary fashion. As we have just seen, the delegation from Caesarea had told Peter what they had come for and who had sent them. His response to his Joppa vision of the sail sheet let down from heaven was to make them welcome, and they stayed overnight. They were allowed to share the same household; and the next day he had set out with them for Caesarea.

But Peter was in territory he had not anticipated. Travelling with a delegation of the Roman military, and that in the sight of anyone and everyone who happened to witness it, must have unsettled him severely. It must have been for him the strangest of company to be in. For the most obvious of reasons both as a Jew and as a Christian he'd be regarding the Romans with immense suspicion. They must have figured in his head as the representatives of foreign rule, often an oppressive foreign rule, made infinitely worse by what Pontius Pilate had done to Jesus and how Caligula had been threatening to desecrate the temple. It was about 40 miles from Joppa to Caesarea, and Luke tells us they did the journey within two days. And that in itself must give rise to intense curiosity in whomever reflects upon it. Two days of travelling for Peter in the company of a small group of Romans, who were not only "devout", but interested in his religion and dispatched for that reason to bring him to Caesarea. We can only imagine the sort of conversations they had. The Joppa experience and the delegation from Caesarea must have got Peter to think on the issues and help put him into the frame of mind, the openness of mind, that the approaching meeting with Cornelius was going to require of him.

He arrived in Caesarea a couple of days later, travelling in the company of the six fellow Christians from Joppa and the Roman soldiers sent by Cornelius to fetch him. By the time he reached Caesarea he would have understood the full significance of the vision he had had. During the journey he would have discussed his vision and its implications with his companions. He had come to understand that the vision he had had concerned much deeper issues than just Jewish dietary regulations and their distinction between kosher and non-kosher food stuffs and that such regulations no longer had any religious significance. There was a much more important matter at stake. "You are well aware," he will say to Cornelius the Gentile Roman soldier and his household, "that it is against our Law for a Jew to associate with a Gentile or visit him" (Acts 10:28). He had been told who Cornelius was, and particularly that Cornelius attended Jewish synagogues and had learnt a lot about Jewish religious and cultural practices. Cornelius would most likely have experienced the discrimination a number of times when doors were shut in his face and his company avoided. But Peter will say to his Gentile listeners: "God has shown me that I should not call anyone impure and unclean" (v. 28) and, understanding the deeper meaning of the Joppa vision, "I now realize that God accepts men from every nation who fear him and do what is right" (v. 35). What happened at Joppa then was a turning point in human history. It was repudiation of racial narrowness; and it enabled Christianity to become a world religion.

# CHAPTER 15

# Peter's Declaration and Gentiles Baptized

Cornelius had organized "a large gathering of his relatives and close friends" (Acts 10:24). It was to be a meeting of historic importance, but it began, as Luke presents it, with an episode simultaneously amusing and significant. To Peter's huge embarrassment, Cornelius in front of everyone strode out and bowed to the ground before him. The Greek word generally means "worshipped". Some scene! A Roman officer bowing to the ground before a Galilean fisherman. Whatever Philip had said to Cornelius about Peter to persuade him to meet with him we can only imagine. Whatever it was, it was enough to persuade the Roman officer to take the step of sending a delegation down to Joppa. That in itself was an indication of the status Peter held within the burgeoning church. But Peter himself was horrified and immediately he went over to Cornelius and raised him to his feet. "Stand up," he said, "I am just a human being like anyone else" (v. 26). When one reflects on how self-important some of Peter's successors have been, how pompous, how full of their own importance, how they both adorned and loved their self-image and revelled in their status, one can only regret that the example and the words of Peter have not always been their guide. Fortunately his present successor, Francis, has repudiated all of that.

What happened then is in effect the core of the message Luke is telling in this his history of the beginnings of the Church. He tells us that, "while talking with Cornelius" (v. 27), Peter was taken from the courtyard to where "a large gathering of people" was waiting for him. Cornelius must have interested a fair number of his fellow Romans, and Jews from the Caesarea synagogues, to come to the meeting, and Philip will have done the same with fellow members of the town's Christian community. Of what Peter had to say to them, of the dialogue that must have ensued, of his answers to the huge number of questions they will have asked him, Luke tells us little. How little becomes even clearer when we glance down the page to Acts 10:48 and we read that at the request of the gathering, "Peter stayed on with them for a few days". A lot must have been said, a lot of questions asked and answers given during those few days about Jesus, his life, his teaching, his death, his resurrection, his family, his mother, who he was, his relationship to God, his significance and about Peter's fellow apostles. Acts 10:34–43, however, is the briefest of outlines. An immense pity. What I for one would give to have been there to make a record of every detail Peter said to his Roman hosts, to hear how he, for example, explained to a Gentile the long and complex history of the relationship of Jesus to the Jewish people and them to him. Yet, certain things do stand out. They are incredibly significant, but they are hard to summarize; and every reader will have his or her own way of dealing with them.

One concerns the way Peter decided to repudiate what was a fundamental dogma of the Judaism of that time and affirm in its place what are fundamental dogmas of Christianity. One such Christian dogma is: "God has no favourites" (Acts 10:34); another is his reason for asserting it (v. 35); and a third is what he calls "the good news of peace through Jesus Christ who is Lord of all" (v. 36). These important matters, however, are preceded by what Peter has to say first to the large gathering of people who had assembled to meet and listen to him. His situation at that moment was delicate and difficult. There were two groups of people in the room he was in, each with their own concerns, and somehow, if he possibly could, he had to reach out to both of them. First and foremost there were the Gentiles in the person of Cornelius and his family and fellow officers, and there were also his fellow Jewish Christians. Jewish Christians at this moment in the history of the Church were made up of two groups. There were those who constituted what might be called the Judaic Christian faction. This faction agreed with Gentiles becoming Christians if they adopted the practices of Jewish religious life, and Luke called them "believers belonging to the circumcision group" (v. 45). Then there were those Jewish Christians like Philip who wanted Gentiles to be admitted into the Church without asking them to adopt the practices of Jewish religious life.

As of that moment in Christian history what the circumcision faction were about to be asked to accept was unthinkable. To appreciate how hard it would be for them, and how much they were being asked to accept, one needs to look at verse 45. That verse relates what happened to them when before their very eyes they saw the Holy Spirit coming down on the Gentiles in the room they were all in. Luke tells us, "they were totally astonished", ἐξέστησαν. The noun generally refers to something being taken from its proper place. In respect of a mental state it means becoming out of one's mind either through sheer astonishment or fear. From it we derive the word "ecstasy". Here it is much more than just being surprised, it is total amazement. The Holy Spirit before their very eyes was breaking with their ingrained concept of themselves, of their nation and of their God. It is difficult not to believe that Luke chose this word deliberately. They were blown away by what they saw; it was mind-boggling for them. They witnessed the effects of the Holy Spirit coming down into the minds and hearts of Gentiles in the same way as they themselves had been experiencing it, and with some of them, as we know from what Peter says in Acts 15:11, as they had experienced it on the first Pentecost.

Peter was all too aware of this. He was also fully aware that the Judaic faction had members present at this meeting who would report back to their leadership in Jerusalem, which, as Acts 11:1 tells us, is exactly what they did. They had their report of Peter's actions in Caesarea back to Jerusalem before he himself got back there. So he begins, one might say, by getting his retaliation in first. "You yourselves are well aware," said Peter to everyone in the room but possibly, just possibly, fixing one eye on the man or the men in the room sent there to do the reporting back, "that it is against our Law for someone who is a Jew to associate with or visit someone of another race" (Acts 10:28). One might call what he was talking about the Nehemiah/Ezra position. With that statement Peter is affirming that he is fully aware of the implications of what he is about to say and do. He is telling them all in no uncertain terms that he is as much a Jew as any of them, that he is someone who knew fully well what the Law was that he as a Jew was supposed to live under. He is also fully aware that as a Jew he is going to defy it and he is going to give the reason why. However, he is also of course speaking to the Gentiles and any fellow

Jewish Christians in the room who did not belong to the circumcision
faction. He wants them to be fully aware in what way, and why, faith in
Jesus as saviour both supersedes and terminates the Mosaic Law.

"I need not tell you that a Jew (such as himself) is forbidden by his
religion to visit or associate with someone of another race. Yet God
has shown me clearly that I must not call anyone profane or unclean"
(Acts 10:28). In a word, Peter bluntly opens up with a statement that
repudiates a fundamental religious belief and practice of his own people.
This is a man speaking who had spent all the years of his life to date
zealously seeking the Messiah of his people, the Jewish people, believing
his people, and only his people, were God's people, and strictly following
the dietary and communal laws of his inherited religion; yet now here
he is repudiating that whole notion, bravely, firmly telling his audience,
some hostile, what he now believes. Cornelius and his group must have
often come up against this mentality among their Jewish acquaintances
and Peter was now acknowledging it in himself. He tells his audience,
his fellow Jews first and foremost, that it is God himself, their God, the
God of their own people, who has shown him this, and shown it to him
clearly, namely in the vision of the sheet containing animals of all kinds,
kosher and non-kosher, let down from on high before his very eyes. He
had read that vision rightly.

The leader of the apostles, the rock on which Jesus said he would
build his Church, had understood that there is nothing kosher and non-
kosher in the eyes of God and that nothing made by God, the maker
of all things, is "unclean and profane", absolutely nothing. No beast
is unclean. That declaration alone, dealing just with the superficiality
of kosher food, constituted one hugely significant departure from the
Mosaic Law. However, the vision was saying something even more radical
to Jewish ears, that there is no unclean human being of any kind. There
are no divisions of humanity in the loving eye of God. That is what Christ
and Christianity stands for, says Peter, to this assembly of people. Till
now Peter and his fellow Christians had accepted the Jewish division of
humanity as Jews and Gentiles. That division had been repudiated and
abolished in Jesus Christ. It will only be a mere three or four years later,
in his letter to the Galatians, that his fellow apostle, Paul, as ardent a Jew
as himself, will say exactly the same thing: "There is no such thing as

Jew and Greek, slave and free, male and female, you are all one person in Christ Jesus" (Galatians 3:28). Paul learnt from Peter.

Throughout all of this Peter must have been experiencing all sorts of emotions. He's in Caesarea, very likely a town he'd never been in before. In the territory of an imperial Roman garrison. Totally new territory for him to put it mildly, a place he would have considered hostile till this moment. In front of him a large gathering, not just fellow Jews but Gentiles, some of them Roman army officers, assembled to meet with him and hear what he had to say, a mere fisherman from one of the smallest provinces of a mighty empire. And till this moment the religion he belonged to was just a tiny Jewish sect; but now Gentiles, including officers and ranks of the Roman military, were asking about it; more than that, they were ready to join it. He must surely have had in mind at that moment those post-resurrection words of Jesus who had brought him to this place and to this moment: "You will receive power when the Holy Spirit comes upon you and you will bear witness to me in Jerusalem and all over Judea and Samaria and away to the ends of the earth" (Acts 1:8).

He asked Cornelius: "What was your reason for sending for me?" With Luke still using the device of saying it was an angel, Cornelius replied "a man in shining robes" (Acts 10:30) had appeared to him who had told him to send for him. Cornelius then asked Peter what he and everyone in the room was bursting to know: "We are all here before God to listen to everything that the Lord had ordered you to tell us" (v. 33). In other words, Cornelius was aware of the issue Philip wanted Peter to settle. Philip had had no difficulty welcoming the Samaritan converts, which he had made, into the Church through baptism because they were Jewish, but this was something again. He had made Cornelius aware that it was something else to offer baptism to Gentiles. It was also a recognition by Philip of Peter's authority within the Church when he told Cornelius that Peter had the authority to pronounce on the matter; and the way Cornelius puts the question to Peter clearly indicates what degree of authority to resolve such a fundamental issue of faith Philip believed Peter to have: "We are all here before God to listen to everything that the Lord had ordered you to tell us" (v. 33). Peter can authoritatively speak on behalf of God. That was the mind of the foundation Church, presented to us by Luke; and what Peter will now say to Cornelius will be what the Lord has ordered him to say. It will be ground-breaking, it will be a revelation in more ways than one. It was a careful and considered reply.

By prefacing it with the phrase "opening his mouth", Luke indicates that what Peter was about to say was significant. He does not use the phrase anywhere else in this way in either of his two books. Peter knew all too well that he had to be as careful as he was authoritative in what he said. He was aware of the likely resistance among some of the Judaic Christians in Jerusalem to it when he returned there. So it was with a deep breath that he began. He replied to the request of Cornelius with the declaration that is 10:34, which ordained the whole route Christianity was to take as of that moment and over all succeeding centuries, influencing the course of human history. He said: "I now see how true it is that God has no favourites, but that in every nation the man who is god-fearing and does what is right is acceptable to him. He sent his word to the children of Israel and gave the good news of peace through Jesus Christ who is Lord of all." A more literal translation might be: "Of a truth I perceive that God is no respecter of persons (or God is not one to show partiality) but in every nation he that fears him and works righteousness (or does justice) is acceptable to him. He sent the word unto the children of Israel, preaching good tidings of peace through (by) Jesus Christ. He is the Lord of all."

Luke crowds so much into this brief statement. What it does is summarize what Peter said to Cornelius over the few days he was with him before he returned to Jerusalem. For example, while Luke does not clarify at all what Peter meant when he spoke to Cornelius about "working righteousness", Peter himself would have done. He would have had in his head the Jewish notion of it which required observance of the Law and Jewish practices, but expressly he was going to make it clear that was not what he was going to demand of the centurion. Neither does he require that anyone asking to be baptized had to be racially Jewish. Peter explicitly states that God "accepts", which must mean "approves of", anyone from any nation. God, says Peter, requires just two things for that acceptance: fear of him, which implies belief in him, and living in a righteous and just way. Peter would have been told in advance that Cornelius was a man of prayer (vv. 1, 30) and a man who helped the poor (19:2). So it seems safe to presume that the righteous and just way of life Peter had in mind was one of normal everyday kindness and the fulfilment of one's family and civil duties according to one's conscience. Of course any such person had to believe in Jesus but that was the sort of person who would be acceptable. What Peter is saying is that anyone like that qualifies for baptism. It simply is difficult to believe Peter himself, in making that statement, had more in mind than that.

He then moved on. We must look at the second and third sentences of what Luke records him to have said. What Luke is telling us is that Peter explained everything about Jesus, such as belief is required in Jesus to be the one who was anointed with the Holy Spirit and with power (Acts 10:38), that he rose from the dead (v. 40), that Jesus is "the one designated by God to be judge of the living and dead" (v. 42), and that it is in and through his name that the forgiveness of sins is given (v. 43). An immense amount of explanation must have been required in all this, and to it there has to be added the unfamiliarity of concepts that a Gentile would experience. However, what doubtless helped was the fact that Cornelius had for some time been attending Jewish services in the local synagogue.

Peter's statement, confirmed by the immediate descent of the Holy Spirit upon "all who were listening to his message" (Acts 10:44), was a declaration by the Church in his person that there was now no one chosen people, rather there was a new covenant in which the whole of humanity is one chosen people. The people of every nation are all equally loved by God. Yes, God spoke his revelation of himself first to the people of Israel. But now through Jesus Christ, who is Lord, not just of the Jewish people but of all peoples, the gospel of peace, which is the reconciliation of man and woman to God, is to be offered to everyone in like and equal measure. In its way it is the first declaration of racial equality. That made it possible, by removing a most significant obstacle, for the Church to become universal. Forty years later, circa the year 95, the author of the Apocalypse, taking a verse of a liturgical hymn, which he calls "a new song", addressing "the Lamb with marks of slaughter upon him", proclaimed: "Thou wast slain and by thy blood didst purchase for God men of every tribe and language, people and nation. Thou hast made of them a royal house, to serve our God as priests and they shall reign upon earth" (Revelation 5:9f.). God's love of humanity has no restriction and the redemption achieved by Jesus is universal. The Church has travelled an almost unbelievable journey from the narrowness and meanness expressed by the apostles in Acts 1:6.

However, there may be more to it; we can take Peter's statement further. As has been shown, he was setting out the requirements for baptism and church membership. His words, however, are not just his. They are in the Canon. He says: "God has no favourites but that in every nation the man who is god-fearing and does what is right is acceptable to him." What does it mean to be "god-fearing/reverencing God"? Likewise what does it mean to "do what is right/work righteousness/do justice"? The requirement "God-fearing" would seem to be straightforward. It requires a belief in the existence of God for starters. But is it so simple? We all know people who are atheists or agnostics, people who do not believe God exists or they cannot be sure. At the same time we know them to be good people, sometimes immensely good and kind. But they are not "god-fearers" as Peter meant it; they simply do not believe in God. The question then arises: what sort of being is it, whom we call God, who would find such people unacceptable just because they do not believe in him? Hardly the Christian God. It is the Christian belief that God is the greatest good, goodness itself. Is to want what is good and to strive for it not the same in the end to want and strive for goodness itself, which is God? People who are good and kind to others and work to achieve it are close to God whether they believe in him or not. God does not need our belief in him but he does want our welfare. All goodness comes from God, so all the goodness of good people are expressions of himself. They are all therefore acceptable to him.

Paul, in his letter to the Romans some eight to ten years later, addresses the issue of how we will be judged by God "on the day of God's wrath, the day when his righteous judgement will be revealed" (Acts 2:5). He says: "God will repay each person in accordance with his deeds" (v. 6). Using the same word that Peter used in Caesarea he writes: "God has no favourites" (v. 11). Paul undoubtedly picked that up from Peter. He puts forward this reason: "When Gentiles who do not possess the Law carry out its precepts by the light of nature, then although they have no law, they are their own law for they display the Law inscribed on their own hearts. Their conscience is called as witness. Their own thoughts argue the case on either side, against them or for them, on the day when God judges the secrets of human hearts through Christ Jesus. So my gospel declares," (v. 15) he says. That gospel is that God will judge everyone with the love and compassion which he has revealed of himself in Christ Jesus. God knows "the secrets of human hearts" (v. 16). Whoever has acted according to the law they feel in their own hearts, they will have acted according to their conscience, they will through the grace revealed in Christ Jesus receive "glory, honour and peace" (v. 10). "The living God" in the words of the author of the first letter to Timothy, is "the Saviour of all people" (4:10), his saving grace exists for every single man and woman. "God," says the author of John's Gospel, "did not send his son into the world in order to judge it, but for the world to be saved through him" (3:17). God is love first and foremost. His is an immense "wealth of generosity, clemency and forbearance" (Romans 2:3). We can all therefore "set our hope on the living God" (1 Timothy 4:10).

What we have here is not just the declaration that baptism is available to all human beings, all tribes, nations, languages and ethnicities, and that this is the new covenant in which the whole of humanity, and not just one nation, is God's chosen people; but we also have the declaration that God in Christ is the saviour of all men and women, both the living and the dead, all who live now and all who have gone before and all who are yet to be born, every single human being, be they believers in God or not, believers in Jesus or not. Jesus is "Lord of all". Therefore all people who live by the light of their conscience can receive forgiveness of their sins.

It is right therefore to apply the statement of Peter: "God has no favourites, but that in every nation the man who is god-fearing and does what is right is acceptable to him" not just to people seeking baptism as he intended it, but to all humanity, even to the tiny child dead from Ebola, unbaptized, shunned and buried hurriedly, untouched in its illness and its death by any human hands, handled with a spade, shovelled into a shallow grave and left without a gravestone or maybe even a single prayer; and to the countless millions upon millions who have never heard of Jesus Christ, or will never hear of him. All humanity is the object of his love, his sacrifice, his suffering, his death and his resurrection. He died for all men and women past, present and future. And we might also extend Peter's statement to our modern concerns, which are good concerns, by saying it is also a declaration of the equality of all humankind and a denunciation of racism, probably the first such declaration ever.

Luke provides us only with an outline of what Peter said to his Gentile audience (Acts 10:36–43) with whom he stayed a few days longer, and what is interesting about it is the difficult questions it raises not just for us, but, one would think, for himself also, and the Gentile converts. He says of Jesus that "God anointed him with the Holy Spirit and with power" (v. 38). One cannot help but wonder what his Gentile listeners made of such a statement. They didn't have the grounding and the upbringing in the vocabulary and the basics of the Old Testament scriptures which converts from Judaism would have had. What, for example, was meant by "anointing", and how is anyone anointed with the Holy Spirit and with power? What power? Was it the power to "heal all who were oppressed by the devil" which Peter said Jesus possessed? Was that what Peter meant when he said that "God was with him (Jesus)"? What did Peter mean when he mentioned the devil? Were there devils in Roman mythology that Cornelius might relate to? What would a soldier in the Roman army make of that? Then there is the Trinitarian element. What did Cornelius make of the statement "God anointed him with the Holy Spirit and with power"? Not with "his spirit" but with "the holy spirit". And with what power? In the time Peter stayed with Cornelius and his family, a few days it seems from the text, he must have been asked any amount of questions such as these. What answers did Peter give? If only a record had been made. When, as Luke tells us, it "astonished the believers, who had come with Peter and were circumcised, that the gift of the holy spirit should have been poured out even on Gentiles" (v. 45), what did they do, what did they say to him? What did Cornelius and all the people in the room where Peter was speaking themselves make of it when the Holy Spirit came down upon them, and they found themselves "speaking in tongues of ecstasy and acclaiming the greatness of God" (Acts 10:44–6)?

Many such questions arise but what are the answers? After 2,000 years we believe we know it all and confidently we just read on. About the mind and understanding of Peter, however, the mind of the Gentile converts, the mind of the circumcised Christians, as at that moment, we can only guess; and there is something else to think about. As has been said, there is no explicit assertion by anyone in the Acts that Jesus was God. By now, however, some statements have been made which would not make sense unless by this point in the life of the infant Church there was at least an initial perception of his divinity, an intimation of something. Jesus is here being spoken of as Lord of all (Acts 10:36) and as designated by God as the judge of the living and the dead (v. 42); and, significantly in the context of the Jewish faith, that belief in him brings about forgiveness of sins "through his name" (v. 43); and, as Luke, narrating all of this, has already informed his readers, Jesus just prior to his Ascension had told his disciples that it is he who will be sending to them the gift his Father has promised (Luke 2:49 and Acts 1:4), which is the Holy Spirit (Acts 1:5, 8). It is difficult to believe that by this time the first believers in Jesus weren't already deep in conversation and discussion about what the implications were of what they were preaching. It is easy for us to say that these concepts were pointing towards something divine about Jesus, but the first Christians were at the start of it all, and it would take the Church another 400 years or so to arrive at a somewhat satisfactory answer, with quarrels, schisms, heresies and divisions occurring every inch of the way.

Luke is concerned to describe what happened as Peter was speaking, because it was to have the most important bearing on the argument Peter will put forward later at the Council in Jerusalem. Luke writes: "The Holy Spirit came upon all who were listening to the message. The believers who belonged to the circumcision party who had come with Peter were astonished—ἐξέστησαν—that the gift of the Holy Spirit had been poured out even on the Gentiles. For they heard them speaking in tongues and praising God" (v. 44f.). We are at a huge disadvantage when we read this because we have rarely if ever experienced this sort of happening, though one might say that when in deep prayer and meditation or in some liturgical moments, some church music and rituals and gospel choirs, we feel ourselves taken in that direction. It is an intriguing passage. In it Luke records that the Jewish Christians who had accompanied Peter from Joppa, six circumcised men, were astonished to witness the effects of the descent of the Holy Spirit on the Gentiles in the room. It might not have been like some form of "fire" over their heads like what had happened to the apostles and others on the feast of Pentecost, but they witnessed the Gentiles in the room speaking "in tongues" and ecstatically praising God. The six Joppa Jewish Christians recognized it as something that had happened either to them, or if not to them, then to fellow Christians, clear evidence that these Gentiles had received the Holy Spirit just as Jewish Christians had already done. The six men were more than just "astonished". They experience "ecstasis". It knocked them sideways. Peter knew all too well what misgivings his Jewish colleagues were still harbouring, and he was able there and then to confront them with the most significant of arguments. They were dumbfounded, they were flabbergasted. Luke did not use that word lightly. He used it to express how till this moment it had been unthinkable for Jewish Christians even to entertain the idea that non-Jews could be the object of the saving power of the Messiah as much as they were, that Jesus was the Messiah for non-Jews as much as for them. For them it certainly was a mind-blowing moment—ἔκστασις—and in its way it dramatically exposed how tight was the hold the inherited Judaic notion of a one-nation Messiah had on the minds of the first Christians. It took the direct intervention of the Holy Spirit to dislodge it. Peter and John had witnessed it when they went into Samaria at the request of Philip. Now it was happening again but this time with Gentiles.

It was also something more. If it may be so expressed, it was synchronized action on the part of Peter and the Holy Spirit. Peter declares that "God has no favourites but accepts men from every nation", and in demonstration of that assertion he proclaims Jesus as "Lord of all . . . God's appointed . . . judge of the living and the dead" and that "everyone who believes in him receives forgiveness of sins through his name". Then, as he says it, the Holy Spirit in what can only be described as approbation of Peter's assertions descends in that very moment upon the Gentiles. Peter, witnessing it, seizes upon it and asks in a ringing voice "Can anyone keep these people from being baptized with water? . . . They have received the Holy Spirit just as we have". There was no more to be said. "Just as we have" is the decisive statement. Gentiles had received the Holy Spirit exactly as they, Jewish men and women, had. The new covenant which embraced all humanity had arrived; the old one which was for Jewish people only had come to an end. That was it. And "so, he ordered that they be baptized in the name of Jesus Christ" (Acts 10:48).

There is significance too in Luke saying "he ordered". Peter was aware of the authority vested in him; and no other apostles were with him. In the face of misgivings on the part of his fellow Christians, some of it outright opposition, he in his own person, individually, took a decision of fundamental importance. That is how Luke relates it to us. And so, the deed was done. All misgivings were to be set aside. The distinction God had once made "between Egypt and Israel" (Exodus 11:7) was no more. "The secret of Christ" was at last revealed, "that through the Gospel the Gentiles are joint heirs with the Jews, part of the same body, sharers together in the promise made in Christ Jesus" (Ephesians 3:5). And that promise? It was that they would be part of "the vast throng which no one can count, from every nation, all tribes, peoples and languages" who "stand in front of the throne and before the Lamb" (Revelation 7:9).

# CHAPTER 16

# Peter Confronts the Circumcision Faction

The deed was done, and Peter had done it on his own authority. He had "ordered them (Gentiles) to be baptized in the name of Jesus Christ" (Acts 10:48). He had been accompanied by six Joppa Jewish Christians. Certainly by the time he reached Jerusalem he knew he was going to face criticism and opposition from members of the Church in Judea and especially in Jerusalem. For that reason he kept the six with him, because they were witnesses of what had happened in Caesarea, useful witnesses, witnesses of that moment when the Holy Spirit came down upon the Gentile party. He knew he would be needing their evidence in support of the decision he had taken (11:12). The reference to the apostles in 11:1 would seem to imply that Peter had not involved them in what he did in Caesarea. However, that was hardly his fault. When he had left Jerusalem to visit the Christian communities in Judea and Samaria, he had had no way of anticipating what would happen to him while in Joppa, no way of knowing there would be three Roman soldiers knocking on his door to tell him to pack his bags and accompany them back to Caesarea, no way of knowing he'd be ordered by yet another voice in his ear to do as they asked. There really had been no way he could delay that summons and make the soldiers wait while he sent messages to Jerusalem to any of the other apostles to join him.

The distance from Caesarea back to Jerusalem was at least fifty miles. Most likely Peter travelled on foot, a three-day journey, right across the Roman province of Judea which took in Samaria, through the plain of Sharon, on to Jerusalem. Acts 11:1 tells us that "the apostles and brethren throughout Judea had heard that the Gentiles had received the word of God", so doubtless he was asked about what he had done in Caesarea by the different Christian communities en route. By the time he reached Jerusalem he would have known that a reception committee was awaiting him in Jerusalem and what he was up against. What he had done amounted to some serious departures from what up to that moment he and all his fellow Jewish Christians believed was obligatory for them as Jews. The Christian community in Jerusalem was waiting for him: "So when Peter came up to Jerusalem, those of the circumcision argued with him and said: You went into the house of men who had foreskins and ate with them." (Acts 11:1–3).

Luke presents us with three parties awaiting Peter in Jerusalem: the apostles, the members of the Jerusalem church and "those of the circumcision". Now, since all the male members of the whole Church as up to the moment when Cornelius and company had been baptized were circumcised, the passage can be read to mean that all the members of the Church in Jerusalem had gathered to meet him, with some ready to argue with him and critically question him. All the members of the Church would of course have been more than eager to know what precisely Peter had done and why, because for all of them what he had done was one huge step for the Church to take. It affected them all. They were all Jews, they were all involved. They would have been familiar with speaking with those Gentiles whom they called "God-fearers" and those they did business with, but they drew a line at sharing meals with them. They were brought up to keep themselves apart. That was, and it still is, a preservation tactic used by some religions and their leaders then and now and all centuries before and in between. The injunction takes all sorts of forms. And being Jews, their heads were also full of notions of kosher food and such like, as we saw when Peter had his visions at Joppa, which can also erect obstacles, even barriers, between people of different cultures. Given all that, it was perfectly normal and understandable that on hearing what Peter had done in Caesarea and how he had mixed with Gentiles, not just going into their houses but even sharing meals with them, they were all wanting him to explain it to them. Undoubtedly, as Acts 11:1 indicates, his fellow apostles too wanted to know the details of what had happened in both Joppa and Caesarea, and one can easily visualize Peter calling them together at the first opportunity after getting back to Jerusalem to tell them. The Caesarea event brought the whole issue of the relationship of Christianity and Judaism to the fore. There were big issues to resolve. It wasn't at all just an issue over rituals, food, and observance of festivals, it was profoundly theological, it was a controversy over the very nature of salvation from sin and reconciliation of women and men to God. Fundamentally, the whole issue was to come down to this: how does God confer the grace of salvation on humanity? Is it through rituals such as the Law or is it through faith in Jesus Christ as saviour? No apostle features as a member of "the circumcision faction". How many of the Christians in Judea and Jerusalem belonged to it we do not know. However, the phrase indicates that it was an identifiable group, a strong and sizable body in fact. It would seem to consist of two groups. From Acts 11:19 we can conclude that one group believed that no Gentile could become a Christian; while another, which appears to have been led by James, a member of the extended family of Jesus, accepted that they could but to do so they had to adopt the religious observances of the Jewish people. Peter is here dealing with the latter.

Interestingly, in order to get a useful insight into what Luke really intends to convey to his readership by means of the one single verse Acts 11:1, it is helpful to look at some of the different ways it has been translated into English. The King James Version reads: "And when Peter was come up to Jerusalem, they that were of the circumcision contended with him, saying 'Thou wentest in to men uncircumcised and didst eat with them'" The Revised International Version reads: "When Peter went up to Jerusalem, the circumcised believers criticized him and said 'You went into the house of uncircumcised men and ate with them.'" The Revised New Jerusalem Bible is the same. However, Luke did not write "uncircumcised men" but "men who had foreskins" (11:3), which is how Nicholas King translates it. Additionally the RIV adds the word "believers", presumably in order to make it clear that the criticism made of Peter came from fellow Christians, not from unconverted Jerusalem Jews. I would think that the RIV wishes it to be clear that the dispute was internal to the Church. However, it misleads. All the male Christians in Judea and in Jerusalem at that moment were circumcised. Consequently the phrase "circumcised believers" tells us nothing extra about them, whereas Luke used the phrase "those of the circumcision" precisely to identify them. The NET reads: "When Peter came up to Jerusalem those who were of Jewish birth raised the question with him: 'You have been visiting men who are uncircumcised' they said, 'and sitting at table with them.'" The phrase "of Jewish birth" is an interpretation, not a translation. It extends the intent of the original phrase "those of the circumcision" to take in all the Jerusalem church members, not just those who belonged to a faction who were insisting on all converts adapting to Jewish religious practices. It is as misleading as the RIV.

The Vulgate is much better; it reads: "cum ascendisset autem Petrus in Hierosolymam disceptabant adversus illum qui erant ex circumcisione, dicentes quare introisti ad viros praeputium habentes et manducasti cum illis." This says plainly what the Greek text itself says bluntly, that the men whom Peter mixed and ate with "had foreskins". The word "circumcision" is not as raw, while "having foreskins" is bluntly visual and all the better for it. It tells it as it is. Nicholas King's recent translation does so as well. The word "circumcision" is the transliteration of the Latin but it does not have the impact on the English ear that the "cutting around" of the Latin word would have on the ear of the Latin speaker. *Beschneidung* in German does the job pretty well. In English "circumcision" is polite, whereas "having a foreskin" is visual. Paul in Galatians 5:12 puts it very bluntly, but in most translations that verse is not translated with the crudeness with which Paul wrote it. To ask a man if he has a foreskin might well be met with a different reaction than if he is asked if he has been circumcised—if, that is, you asked him it in the first place. Besides, there is possibly something more to it again. It could well be that the members of the Jerusalem circumcision faction who described the Gentiles whom Peter ate with as "having foreskins" were not just being blunt but also deliberately offensive. The phrase might read as a sneer. It is better therefore to translate it literally and hide nothing and keep the different possibilities of meaning in play.

What is it that Luke is saying to us in this one single verse? First, he was making it clear that the Jerusalem church members who confronted Peter, arguing with him over his behaviour in Caesarea, were a distinct group, one he called "those of the circumcision" or "the circumcision faction". Referring to them henceforth as the circumcision faction would seem appropriate. They presented Peter with three objections to what he had done in Caesarea: the men he had dealt with there weren't circumcised but had foreskins, he had entered their houses and he had eaten with them. If Gentiles were admitted into the Church, they'd be uncircumcised, which was unacceptable to the faction. The fact was, though, if Peter had abided by the Jewish regulations as the faction's objections would have obliged him to, he would not have been able even to converse with them, let alone convert and baptize them. Religions can be ingenious in creating all sorts of problems for people.

If only we knew how this meeting between Peter and the members of the faction was conducted! Where was it held? In a house or room where other people could attend besides Peter and his six Joppa Christians and his interrogators led by James? Was it open to all the Christian membership in Jerusalem if only to observe and listen to it? Or could they take part in some way or other. We know from Acts 11:1 that at least some of the other apostles were there in Jerusalem, and they would have been more than interested to hear from Peter what he had done. So they most definitely would have attended the meeting. Regrettably their names are not given, but we can be sure that it wasn't just a private meeting between Peter and members of the circumcision faction. One wonders what the initial attitude of the faction was towards him since he was recognized by them, and indeed the whole community, as spokesman for the apostles. Acts 11:2 gives the impression there was some degree of hostility on the part of the interrogators towards Peter; the question they put to him was blunt and critical; and if the phrase they used to describe the Caesarea Gentiles "men who had foreskins" was a sneer and an expression of contempt, how deep did their suspicions of Peter extend? He had a lot to deal with.

His reply was to tell his critics fully what had happened to him to justify what he had done. He told them about the threefold vision he had had of creatures of all kinds and how the voice from heaven had thrice repudiated their Jewish belief that there were some creatures and some foods that were unclean. "Do not call anything impure that God has made" (11:9). He then told them that the Spirit had instructed him to accept the company of three men from Caesarea, whom his interrogators knew to be Gentiles, then go back to Caesarea with them together with his six fellow Christians and to the house of the man who had summoned him at the command of an angel. The way Peter told the panel of interrogators what had happened was such as to make it absolutely clear that God was directing every single aspect of it and that at all times he Peter was acting in obedience to God's wishes. "What I did in Joppa and in Caesarea," Peter says to them, "in no way, not in any single detail, was at my initiative. It was God's from start to finish." "Even to the extent," said Peter, "that as I was speaking to this Cornelius and his household, before my very eyes, and to the utter astonishment of my six Christian companions here with me from Joppa, the Spirit of God came down on these Gentiles, exactly as he came down on us that first day, that feast day of Pentecost, here in Jerusalem. Ask my companions, all six of them, they witnessed it, they will tell you. Yes indeed, God has given these Gentiles the same gift that he gave us, you and me, on that day, because they believed in the Lord Jesus Christ just like we did. The gift of the Holy Spirit was poured out on these Gentiles because of their faith in Jesus just as it was poured out on us. We witnessed them speaking in tongues and praising God just as we spoke in tongues and praised God on that day. And this gift of the Holy Spirit, visible to everyone present, was total proof that I was right to say: 'Is anyone prepared to withhold the water of baptism from these persons who have received the Holy Spirit just as we did ourselves?' (10:47). Their faith in Jesus is our faith in Jesus, yours and mine. Our faith is their faith."

Peter must have looked at his interrogators one by one. He asked them: "Who was I to think that I could oppose God? Who was I to oppose what clearly and definitely was what God wanted?" He could see that they knew they could no longer argue with him. God was with him, they hadn't a leg to stand on. He bent towards them. He was fully aware of the authority Jesus had conferred on him. "So I ordered that they be baptized with water in the name of Jesus Christ." No objection was then raised by his interrogators. Instead they "praised God saying: 'This shows that God has granted life-giving repentance to the Gentiles too.'" We cannot exaggerate the significance of this moment in the history of the Church when the first Gentiles were baptized, not least because the Church in the person of Peter had arrived at the right understanding of the messiahship of Jesus. Peter had pushed open the door to universal evangelization.

There is something more to be said. Regrettably it has long been the custom to ascribe the enunciation of biblical theology mainly to Paul and the author(s) of John's Gospel. Peter has always been put into a much lower theological bracket, indeed if in any bracket at all.[11] However, what emerges from this analysis of these events in Joppa and Caesarea, followed by the confrontation in Jerusalem, is that in the person of Peter we have an understanding as profound as it gets of the essentials of Christian belief and theology, and that occurring when neither Paul nor the John author(s) were yet on the scene. Neither as yet had contributed a single word. This whole event, namely Joppa, Caesarea and the confrontation in Jerusalem, taken with the ground-breaking argumentation of the Hellenists, especially Philip and Stephen, laid the foundations for the Church's understanding of the universality of the redemptive mission of Jesus. The spadework had been done by Peter and Barnabas and the Hellenists; and of the Hellenists, as per what Luke tells us, particularly Philip and Stephen. Peter, Barnabas, Stephen and Philip initiated the charge; and Luke has described to us the hostility and misunderstanding Peter and Stephen were confronted with. They battled through, with one of them getting martyred for taking the argument direct to the Jews, and, as we are seeing here, the other one being met with harsh suspicion and disagreement from within his own Christian community. What Peter told his Judaic Christian audience was that no human being is inferior to another in any way at all, that all are equal in the eyes of God, that God has the same concern and love and regard for all of them, that Jesus was Messiah for all humanity, that the distinction between Egypt and Israel (Exodus 11:7) was no more. That is Christianity, the new covenant, the old one has passed away.

Joppa, Caesarea and Jerusalem were the three places where this all-important development in the life and history of the Church took place, and we can never do sufficient justice to their, and its, importance. Luke was all too aware of it but in his customary way he just relates it and then leaves it to his readership to appreciate it. And, curiously, very curiously, he concludes his narration of it almost tongue in cheek. As we have seen, he narrates how the circumcision faction reacted to Peter's explanation and defence of his actions with: "When they heard this (what Peter had told them), they had no further objections and praised God saying: 'Indeed, God has granted repentance that leads to life even to the Gentiles'" (Acts 11:18). It would appear from that that as from that moment all would be sweetness and light, harmony and unity of purpose on the matter among all the Church members. Nothing of the sort. In the following verse, verse 19, he shows how and why. He moves his narration to Antioch.

# CHAPTER 17

# Antioch Opens the Doors of
# the Church Even Wider

Antioch was then in Syria, it stayed that way until the early twentieth
century. It is now in the extreme south east corner of Turkey. Today its
name is Antakya. Both the political arrangement that placed it in Turkey
and the change of name are a great pity. It is situated on the River Orontes,
and its port was Seleucia. Its position made it attractive to both the later
Hellenistic and the Roman Empire. It was founded towards the end of
the fourth century BC by Seleucus Nicator, one of Alexander's generals,
who named it after his son. It was incorporated into the Roman Empire
in 64 BC; it was declared a "free city"; and it was heavily favoured by the
Romans by reason of its geographical position. Its population grew to
half a million at one stage. It was the centre of Hellenistic Judaism at the
time of the Second Temple Period and had a large Jewish population
at the time of Christ. It is not idle to speculate that, by reason of the
cosmopolitan composition of its population, it was a very different city
from Jerusalem, and for that reason whatever Christian community it
eventually had would be different from that of Jerusalem. No one could
have foreseen how much Christianity would grow and spread, so it is
only with hindsight that we can see how unsuitable Jerusalem was as its
centre. It did not have the intellectual, cultural and religious vivacity and
openness of Antioch and of course of Rome.

Antioch has a most significant place in the history of Christianity, not
least as one of three patriarchates of the Church along with Alexandria
and Rome, in the first four centuries. Its theological contribution to
the development of Christian doctrine was not just immense, it was
fundamental, strategic and permanent. It made a crucial contribution

to deciding what direction Christianity would take in its relationship to the religion which it had come from, namely Judaism, by bringing the Church to the point where it had to define in what ways Christianity was distinctive and different from Judaism. As a consequence it helps us to understand better both the significance of Judaism and what questions should be asked about it, particularly today given the foundation of a Jewish state and the sort of state it is becoming. The Christian community of Antioch, working out of its own experience, together with the experiences of Peter, supplemented by the input of Barnabas, Philip, Stephen and Paul, enabled the Church of the apostles to arrive at an understanding of the relationship Christ had both to Judaism and to the non-Jewish world. The needs, the composition and the attitudes of the early Antiochian Christian community contributed crucially to the process by which the Holy Spirit enabled the Apostolic Church to understand what that relationship was.

Luke, as we have seen, tells us that: "Those who had been scattered by the persecution that had arisen over Stephen travelled as far as Phoenicia, Cyprus and Antioch, telling the word to absolutely no one else but only to the Jews" (Acts 11:19). In other words, this group of Jewish Christians wanted Church membership to be restricted to members of the Jewish race. Today we would unhesitatingly call that racism. But Luke also tells us it wasn't only these highly conservative Jewish Christians who went to Antioch: "But there were some of them, however, men from Cyprus and Cyrene who went to Antioch and began to speak to pagans ("Ελληνας) as well, telling them the good news of the Lord Jesus. The power of the Lord (literally, the hand of the Lord) was with them and a great multitude became believers and turned to the Lord." (v. 20). ""Ελληνας" is to be distinguished from ""Ελληνιστὰι" in the New Testament, the latter is used when referring to Jews born in the diaspora and speaking Greek, the former to pagans who spoke Greek.[12] "Ελληνας gets different translations. In the Jerusalem Bible it is Hellenists, in Nicholas King it is Greek-speakers, in the New International Version it is Greeks, and in the King James it is Grecians, and so on. I prefer "pagans" as in the New English Translation, because that is what this whole issue before the new Church was actually about. Hellenist Jews had had no problem being accepted into the Church as we have seen. The issue was the Gentiles, that is pagans. The way Luke arranged his narrative creates a problem, as the note to this verse in the Revised New Jerusalem Bible points out: "Aggregation of Gentiles at Antioch may well have preceded Peter's action in Acts 10 but the order of narration disguises the fact."

From Luke's narration we know that the gospel had already been preached in the island of Cyprus and in Cyrene, which is a province of Libya (main city Benghazi). The Simon who helped Jesus carry his cross came from Cyrene (Mark 15:21), and the way Mark makes mention of Simon's two sons Alexander and Rufus implies that both of them were members of and known to the Rome Christian community for whom he was writing his gospel towards the end of the 60s after the Nero persecution. The new Jewish converts to Christianity in Cyprus and Cyrene would have lived in a cosmopolitan environment, they would have mixed daily with Gentiles to an extent almost definitely unknown to the members of the Jerusalem church, they would have had friends as well as work colleagues among them just as people of Jewish descent have today throughout the world, with the exception of some of those, some not all, who live in the modern state of Israel. The Jewish communities and synagogues of that time in the Jewish diaspora had close contact and dialogue of a religious nature with some Gentiles whom they called "God-fearers" such as Cornelius and his household. Evidence of this is supplied in Acts 13:16,26,43,50. Verse 43 informs us that the Jews of Pisidia Antioch made converts/proselytes to Judaism of Gentiles. It is therefore quite reasonable to conclude that diaspora Jews who had converted to Christianity would feel no hesitation in taking the gospel to people outside of the Jewish faith. On coming to Antioch they just carried on in the same way, taking the gospel to their non-Jewish neighbours; and, as we see from the text, with great success. Luke in saying that "the power of the Lord was with them" is making it clear where he stood on the matter, but the chronological order of his narrative needs an adjustment.

He continues: "The news reached the ears of the church in Jerusalem; and they sent Barnabas to Antioch" (Acts 11:22). Now, if what was happening in Antioch was what had already happened in Caesarea with Cornelius and his household and which had been approved by the Church in Jerusalem with "everyone giving praise to God" (v. 18), there just wouldn't have been any need to send Barnabas to Antioch to inspect and report back. Obviously something different was happening, something more than just the Caesarea development that a Gentile was able to become a Christian. What was happening was the next, and the final, step in bringing about the breach with Judaism and in terminating the Judaic understanding the Church had of what "laws" governed the behaviour and the religious practices of Christians.

The pagan converts in Antioch just weren't buying into Jewish practices, be they circumcision or food regulations or observation of Jewish festivals or whatever. Why should they? It wasn't their culture. It wasn't their culture of gender, their sort of cooking; it wasn't how they conducted their affairs and how communally they celebrated. Time was being called on the practice of the Law within Christian communities. The Antioch church was in fact proposing a decisively wider interpretation of the salvation wrought by Jesus which Peter had spoken about to the Jewish Council in 4:12, a salvation which extended to all humankind with no dependency whatsoever upon Judaic practices or Jewish identity. When Peter had told the Jewish Council that there was no other name under heaven granted to human beings than that of Jesus by which we may be saved (Acts 4:12), his understanding of his own words was to take on a meaning he had not at that stage dreamt of.

The converts in Antioch forced this rethink. One can easily imagine the situation. Men from Cyprus and Cyrene (interestingly "natives of Cyprus and Cyrene" in the NET), brought up in cosmopolitan cultures, had arrived in this most cosmopolitan of cities and felt very much at home. They've obviously been eating, enjoying life, sharing life and leisure, working and trading with non-Jews as a matter of course and they continued to do so in Antioch. They were converts themselves, like Luke himself, who fully understood them. They unhesitatingly preached the gospel of Jesus to their non-Jewish neighbours; they made converts; and the converts, unfamiliar with Judaism, saw no reason to buy into it. Why should they? They looked at the gospel they had received, it is one of salvation through Jesus, not of salvation through such Judaic practices as circumcision, dietary laws, observing this or that festival, in their eyes strange, foreign, unfamiliar practices. These converts would have been told about such sermons of Jesus as the Sermon on the Mount and heard of a different way of living the religious life in a number of important ways than the Judaic one; and what's more they either would have, or might have, heard about Jesus expressly repudiating major aspects of the Jewish moral creed (Matthew 5). And being non-Jews they doubtless asked themselves the question, as any ordinary normal person would, what reason could there possibly be for a believer in Jesus to adopt the practices of the people who not only had rejected him but had put him to death and had persecuted his followers. That really must have been an ever-recurring issue in all their conversations. When, as Luke tells us, they believed and "turned to the Lord" (Acts 11:21), it was not any narrow Judaic understanding of him they turned to. The new wine of Jesus could no longer be kept in the old wineskins of Judaism.

This "news reached the ears of the church in Jerusalem and they sent Barnabas to Antioch" (Acts 11:22). Barnabas, who had a sister named Mary married to a fellow Cypriot who lived in a large house (12:12) in Jerusalem, was himself from Cyprus. He had therefore the same background as the Jewish Christians who had gone from Cyprus to Antioch. He also had the best of good Jewish credentials, he was a Levite (4:36). He was fluent in both Aramaic and Greek, both languages commonly spoken in Antioch. It was therefore a good choice by the Jerusalem church leaders. Now, though Luke does not actually say that Barnabas was sent to Antioch to resolve the disagreement the two Christian groups had about whom they should preach the gospel to, it is the only reason that makes sense. He went there to arbitrate.

If Barnabas did resolve the disagreement between the two groups, we are not told, at least not explicitly. It comes over as strange that Luke could have told us about the huge disagreement in Antioch within the one congregation (Acts 11:26) over a doctrinal issue of immense importance and that Barnabas was sent there to deal with it, and then not provide us with the details of the outcome. All he reports about the visit of Barnabas is that, "being a good man, full of the Holy Spirit and faith", he "saw the grace of God at work", and he "was glad and encouraged them all to remain true to the Lord with all their hearts", and that "a large number of people were brought to the Lord" (13:22–4). It does read as if he was successful in achieving harmony within the Antioch church; and "he then went off to Tarsus to look for Saul; and when he had found him, he brought him back to Antioch. For a whole year the two of them lived in fellowship with the congregation there and gave instruction to large numbers" (11:25f.). Whether or not Barnabas had slapped down the Jewish Christian faction who only preached to fellow Jews, we do not know. Most probably he didn't, he does not seem to be that sort of person. He comes across as kindly and considerate, a man of empathy. I would think he spoke quietly and sympathetically to the extreme Jewish Christian faction, with understanding of their concerns. I would think he probably brought them round at least to the position being taken by those members of the circumcision faction who were not so extreme. Obviously when he left Antioch for Tarsus, he was in a position to assure Saul that he'd find in Antioch a congregation that was congenial and welcoming and that he could instruct both believers and converts in the understanding of the Christian faith that his mystical communion with Jesus from the moment of his own conversion had taught him.

Luke's Greek vocabulary describing this matter is informative. He employs the word συναχθῆναι to tell us that Barnabas and Paul settled in comfortably in Antioch: "συναχθῆναι ἐν τῇ ἐκκλησίᾳ." The NET translate it as "they lived in fellowship with the congregation". It seems to indicate that Paul found himself spiritually at home in Antioch. It seems reasonable to assume that Barnabas, whatever way he dealt with the relationship of the two groups, was happy enough with the outcome and felt he could leave the city and travel the 50 miles to the town of Tarsus where Paul was, to find him and bring him back to Antioch, to stay there and preach there for the next twelve months. Luke (Acts 11:27–30) informs us that the Antioch community during this period, concerned about predictions of famine, made a collection to help their brethren in Judea and put the money they raised into the charge of Barnabas and Saul to take it there and give it to the elders in Jerusalem. In other words, the two men were highly thought of and trusted by the Antioch Christian community, as was their stance on evangelization.

Luke tells us something else: "For a whole year Barnabas and Saul lived in fellowship with the church and taught great numbers of people; and so it came about that it was first in Antioch that the disciples got the name of Christians" (Acts 11:26). Regrettably various English translations such as the King James version ignore the causal connection which Luke intended his readership to know about. It is an error. They just state: "It was in Antioch that the disciples were first called Christians", when it does seem from the actual text that Luke is making a connection between what and how Barnabas and Saul taught and the name people hearing it gave, perceptively, to the Antiochians who were converted. The Revised New Jerusalem Bible (p. 256) makes this comment: "The Gk word has a slightly contemptuous ring. It was probably a nickname, 'Messianists'." I doubt it. Instead, it could be that the Antiochian Christians were called Christians, because in the preaching of Barnabas and Paul Christ figured predominantly, that what was preached by them was belief in Jesus as the sole Christ/the sole Messiah, that it is he who saves and who forgives sins and not any performance of the Law. A causal connection between the preaching and teaching done by the two men and the attribution of the name "Christian" to the disciples of Jesus might rightly be deduced from how Luke positions the two statements.

The Christians could have been called Jesus followers or Nazareans, but they weren't; they were called, and are called, Christians. The Greek word Χρῑστός means "anointed", it was the Greek word used for Messiah, as in Peter's speech to the crowd on the day of Pentecost (cf. 2:36), and in what he said to Cornelius in 10:38: "God anointed Jesus of Nazareth with the Holy Spirit and with power", and elsewhere. What Peter had said to the membership of the Church in Jerusalem as in 11:5–17, especially vv. 15–17, had been taken up by Barnabas and brought by him to Antioch and to Paul. It became the most significant and conspicuous part of their teaching to the disciples in Antioch. It was what distinguished Christians from Jews. What Barnabas and Paul must have given immense emphasis to in their teaching to all the Antioch church members was precisely that, that each believer was christened, made an anointed one, made messianic. "You are anointed—christened—with the Holy Spirit and with power, you are messianic, you are Christian" is what Paul and Barnabas might well have said to their congregation; and the name might have stuck. The rite of baptism, by which we become members of the Church, is an "anointing"; it is being made to be like Christ and to belong to him by the Holy Spirit and power. This should be said with emphasis to the parents and family of every child brought to the font to be christened; and every youngster going forward to receive the sacrament of confirmation should be re-taught it. A baptized person is an anointed person. The English word "christening" is a truly profound rendering of the meaning and the effect of the sacrament.

Luke makes no mention again of any faction, not even in Jerusalem, that wanted to restrict evangelization to Jews. That it had to be universal was now agreed. However, there was something else, another issue, which still had to be resolved. Though the Judean/Jerusalem circumcision faction had accepted (Acts 11:18) that any and all Gentiles/non-Jews could be baptized and become Christians, its members were adamant still that the Christian way of life had to be Judaic. This would lead to "fierce dissension and controversy" (Acts 15:2) within the Church. Before it would be addressed and resolved, however, two other matters of great importance occurred to dominate the attention of the Church: persecution and mission.

CHAPTER 18

# Persecution by Herod: The Rift with Judaism Widens

Chapter 12 could easily be read quite superficially, as just giving us a filler of a narrative before Luke gets into the more important accounts of Paul's first missionary journey and of the Council itself. Nothing, however, could be further from the truth. Luke is a subtle writer. The subtleties in this chapter are of prime importance, they are theological, and their significance should be understood and digested.

In addition to the threat of hunger facing the Jerusalem church members, Luke now narrates the persecution they then underwent at the hands of Herod Agrippa. We are in the year 41/42; a Jewish kingdom under Herod had replaced direct Roman rule, bringing with it the persecution of the Christians in his kingdom. According to Josephus, Herod was a zealot and hostile to Christians.[13] The Judean Christians suffered harshly for their faith in Jesus. For all the Judaic conservatism of a faction of them and the problems it caused within the Church, they were faithful Christians, prepared to suffer for their belief in Jesus. Many of their fellow Christians, undoubtedly whole families, were being driven from Jerusalem into Samaria, Galilee and Antioch, and now under Herod the apostle James the Greater, brother of John, was beheaded (Acts 12:2), and Peter was arrested and imprisoned.

Herod's intention was to have Peter executed too. All too obviously Herod was going for the top leadership of the Church in Jerusalem and Judea, figuring that the removal of the two apostles would leave the Church leaderless, disorientated and likely to lose membership and fade away. For reasons best known to himself, Herod spared local lesser leaders like James, a relation of Jesus, who will figure in the Council of

Jerusalem. Luke tells us that Peter escaped from prison, while, as Luke describes it, Herod then gets the comeuppance he deserved by dying in a most ignominious manner, namely being eaten up by worms (Acts 12:23). In contrast "the word of God continued to increase and spread" (v. 24). Herod's death occurred five years before the Council, enabling Peter to return to Jerusalem without fear of arrest or indeed harassment from the Jewish leadership.

Where the other apostles were by this time and what exactly they were doing, some ten or so years after the Ascension, we just do not know. One might speculate that they had got well away from Judea before Herod began his persecution, as Herod arrested only Peter and James. Luke provides no details though doubtless he would have known a lot about them, not least because he would certainly have met up with them as he journeyed with Paul between Jerusalem, Antioch, Asia Minor, Greece and Rome; and in addition would have heard plenty of stories about them. He excluded them from the history he was writing because they did not figure in the theological development he wrote his account to describe, and he wanted to restrict himself to the two people who mattered to his narrative and, from what sources we have, contributed most, namely Peter and Paul.

Luke's account of Herod's persecution of the Jerusalem Christian community in Acts 12:1–3 contains some significant features. Herod was proceeding with some care. There was a sizable Christian presence in Judea and Jerusalem, and he had to test the water. He arrested Peter only after he was sure his persecution of the Christians, even the extreme step of beheading James, had the support of the Jewish population. It is likely that he had it in mind to make a more elaborate show of the execution of Peter. He was aware obviously of Peter's leading position within the Christian community. Luke then gives us the details of Peter's escape from prison, describing it as by means of direct divine intervention, with Peter, up to a certain point, thinking it was all a dream until, reaching an iron gate leading into the city, he found himself walking down one particular street where the angel left him. "Then Peter came to himself: 'Now I know it is true,' he said, 'the Lord has sent his angel and rescued me from Herod's clutches and from all that the Jewish people were expecting'" (Acts 12:11). One might just observe in passing that Peter has a real liking for using the phrase "Now I know it is true" when it comes to saying something important. This is at least the third time so far. As usual with Luke, there is more to this episode than meets the eye.

The first thing to observe is how he represents Peter as being treated differently by God—"the Lord"—from how James was treated. James was arrested and beheaded, and that was that. No divine intervention, no angel of the Lord intervening to get him out of prison and save his life. Nothing. But with Peter everything. Despite him being guarded by as many as "four squads of four soldiers each", he is enabled to escape. The guards are put into a deep sleep, his chains and handcuffs just fall off him, and an angel leads him out of the prison, all the doors opening before him, including the outside gate despite its armed guards and heavy padlocks, with nobody in the whole prison noticing a single thing. One might interpret this escape in a different way. Peter's escape must have been an inside job. Someone either in Herod's court or in Jerusalem's police or judiciary department was secretly favourable to Peter and his fellow Christians or possibly, given how securely he had been imprisoned and the numbers of guards he had to get past unseen, he had the help of more than just one insider. Herod fortunately had taken his time over dealing with Peter (Acts 12:4), intending to put him through a public trial, and that gave this insider or insiders time and opportunity to organize. Herod obviously came to suspect as much when the following day, when Peter's escape was discovered, he organized a search and had some of the guards executed. He could easily have had the wrong men killed. Luke has represented Peter's escape as being down to divine intervention because of his position in the Church and the leadership he provided.

There is a second important feature of this Herod–James–Peter story. Luke has informed us that Herod was encouraged to arrest Peter when he saw that his execution of James had the support of the Jewish people (Acts 12:3). Up to this point he had described all hostile response of the Jews to the Christian gospel as coming from the chief priests (4:1), the Jewish rulers, elders and doctors of the Law, which included the High Priest and his family (v. 5) and his colleagues (5:17) and the Council of the Jews (v. 33 and 6:12). He now informs us that with their support for the beheading of James and the arrest of Peter the Jews as a people were endorsing the repudiation of Jesus and the persecution of his believers. The recognition of this by Peter as a final and fateful step in the relationship of Christianity and Judaism is made clear in what he says on his escape: "The Lord has sent his angel and rescued me from Herod's clutches and from all that the people of the Jews were expecting." Peter was a Jew through and through. He had been a Jewish zealot, an ardent seeker after the Messiah, a man who, despite being in the company of Jesus for three years, still at the moment of the Ascension thought Jesus to be the person who would do what all the Jews were expecting the Messiah to do and re-establish independent rule. Now Peter speaks in such a way as to set himself apart from belonging to the people of the Jews. He does not say "the Council of the people of the Jews" or "the Herodian faction within the people of the Jews" or make any such differentiation; he says "the people of the Jews". And what is more, he speaks of them as distinct from himself; and given what he himself is, that is some statement. We are on the verge of what can be described as the most decisive moment in the history of Christianity. The die has now been cast. It is as sorrowful as it is significant, as significant as it is sorrowful. Luke is demonstrating in what he tells us in this chapter how the Jewish people as a nation, by choosing to repudiate this new movement, which had come from within their own ranks, choosing even to persecute its leadership in order to destroy it, made the break a necessity. That fateful choice preoccupied Paul when he wrote his letter to the Romans. In his letter, written as a Jewish person full of love of his people but conscious that God's covenant was now in Christ equally with all humanity, he expresses his overwhelming sorrow about the choice they made (Acts 9:2); and he prays from the bottom of his heart that it will not be forever (10:1,11,28–32). Luke, Paul's companion, was intimately aware of that.

There is logic to the Lucan narrative. The break with Judaism has happened; not wished for, not engineered, it has happened. Now what? What does the Church do now? Where does it go? The universality of the redemption achieved by Jesus is now understood; that gospel had now to go somewhere. Luke concludes this section, this chapter, of his narrative in this way: "And Barnabas and Saul returned from Jerusalem" (Acts 12:25), to Antioch. The decision what the Church would now do next will be taken, not in Jerusalem, but in Antioch by its Christian community.

# CHAPTER 19

# Prophets, Teachers, Liturgy
# and Debate in Antioch

Luke has told us that Barnabas and Saul, once they had handed over the contributions made by the Antioch church members in support of their fellow Christians in Judaea during the famine predicted by Agabus (Acts 11:28), returned to Antioch, taking John Mark, the nephew of Barnabas, with them. It is the church in Antioch that is now our interest, and Luke helpfully gives us some indication of what sort of Christian community it was and what was going on there; we can assume that the Christian communities in other towns were experiencing similar growth and development. He tells us: "There were at Antioch, in the congregation there, certain prophets and teachers, Barnabas, Simon called Niger, Lucius of Cyrene, Manaen, who had been at the court (or was the foster brother, or brought up, depending on the translation) of Prince Herod, and Saul" (Acts 13:1). Whether it is a complete list of prophets and teachers in the church of Antioch at the time, who knows? They could be the only names Luke could remember; they could also have been the names of people familiar to his readership, some of them alive still. They tell us something about what was going on in the Antioch Christian community. There were prophets and teachers, and "they ministered to the Lord and they fasted" (v. 2). As always, there is more to these verses than what first meets the eye, and it helps if first we place both ministries, as best we can, within their community and liturgical context.

From a careful reading of both Acts and Paul's letters we can find that the Christian life of this early Church was different from our own. Its prayer life seems to have had lots of spontaneity and vigour like the Pentecostal Movement today. The description "Pentecostal" denotes liveliness and openness to the spirit either of the congregation or the readings or the sense of occasion as if the Holy Spirit itself was active among them, as it was on Pentecost Sunday. Our Catholic congregations in the Western rite today are often the opposite. They are staid, predictable and controlled, which is as many church leaders want them to be. Young people often find them boring. Mind you, we might well feel uncomfortable, and the clergy unsure and worried, if there was in a parish "a group of prophets". We are far away from what those early communities did and experienced, like when the Holy Spirit came down among them as happened in Jerusalem (Acts 2:1–3), Samaria (8:6f.,16f.) and Caesarea (10:44–8). In this respect, Chapters 12, 13 and 14 of Paul's first letter to the Corinthians are both fascinating and informative. He speaks to "the congregation of God's people at Corinth" and about "the gifts of the Spirit" (1 Corinthians 12:1), and what he says to them gives us an interesting insight into their communal and prayer life.

The list of the gifts of the Spirit that he writes to them about is a list second to none, though being just a list extracted from what he says, it does not do justice to what must have been the congregational reality that Paul describes and writes about with so much detail, enthusiasm, warnings, instruction and theological interpretation. He speaks of "gifts", such as wise speech, the ability to put the deepest knowledge into words, faith, healing, the power to work miracles, prophecy, ability to distinguish true spirits from false, ecstatic utterance and the ability to interpret it, apostles, prophets, teachers, miracle workers, ability to help others, the power to guide them, the gift of ecstatic utterance of various kinds, faith, hope and love, praising God in the language of inspiration, singing hymns as one is inspired to sing (see 1 Corinthians 12—14).

Corinth most certainly was some lively congregation, full of spontaneity, a long way from the congregations I experience. It is the gift of ecstatic utterance that he discusses most, which possibly tells us that it was a major feature in the prayer and liturgical life of the Corinth congregation. His explanation of all the aspects of that life that he writes to them about is not just a plea for unity but also as profound and enduring as it can get: "Now you are Christ's body, and each of you a part of it (in the NET a limb or organ of it)" (1 Corinthians 12:27).

What were these Christians to whom the title "prophet" was given? What did Luke intend by it? Peter on the day of Pentecost, standing up before a great assembly of Jewish pilgrims, had quoted from the prophet Joel, who said that God "will pour out his Spirit, and their sons and daughters will prophesy, that he will endue even slaves, both men and women, with his spirit, and they will prophesy" (Acts 2:17f.). So the notion of prophet was a real part of the thinking within the Christian Church. There is no question that the Infant Church was charismatic in that time and again Luke describes to us how its membership positively thrilled and erupted with the descent of the Holy Spirit upon them, speaking in tongues and praising God with immense vitality, in Jerusalem (Acts 2:1–3), Samaria (8:6f.,16f.), Caesarea (10:44–8) and elsewhere. And, as we have seen, Paul relates (1 Corinthians 12:27f.) that it had its apostles, prophets, teachers, miracle workers, members with powers of healing, members who spoke in different kinds of tongues. Its liturgy and its prayer meetings must have been lively, to say the least. Here, however, Luke just says that there were prophets and teachers in the Antioch church. What did he mean by those two functions?

The designation "prophet" was obviously a recognized status. Luke tells us in Acts 15:33 that two Jerusalem Christian prophets were Silas and Judas called Barsabbas. They "were prophets themselves", and they were going to be appointed by the apostles and elders at the coming council to take its decision contained in a letter to the churches of Antioch, Syria and Cilicia. Luke describes them as "leading men among the brethren" (v. 22). So the designation really meant something. When Paul in Ephesus met with newly baptized Christians and laid his hands on them to bless them, the Holy Spirit came down upon them and "they spoke in tongues of ecstasy and they prophesied" (19:6).What was it that they did? The four unmarried daughters of Philip in Caesarea had the gift of prophecy (21:9). What was it about them to be so called? Then there was Agabus from Judea who had foretold a world-wide famine and turned up a few years later (21:10) to warn Paul about what the Jerusalem Jews would do to him if he went there, a warning that Paul ignored (v. 21). Paul himself makes mention of prophecy as a gift in 1 Corinthians 12:10 and another seven times in the same epistle. The two predictions made by Agabus were what we today would understand by prophesy and he is the only one mentioned like that. The sensible way to read it, it would seem, is that the title prophet was an omnibus term meaning acting in what we would call a charismatic fashion and preaching with eloquence and gusto, predicting divine reward for good behaviour and punishment for bad. That is what the Old Testament books of prophecies were mainly about. The warnings they contain are basically reminders of what will happen to people in general and the Jewish nation in particular as a result of their behaviour. On this basis the prophets mentioned as above in the New Testament were preachers, and their prophecy role, which was recognized within the Early Church, was some form of preaching; and if it followed the OT pattern, it was one of admonition and charismatic. We can only speculate, but that seems reasonable.

Luke also says there were "teachers". He distinguishes the role from that of the prophets in the community, so there was a difference. He knew what it was and so did his first-century church readership, and doubtless we should read it just for what it says, that the church in Antioch held teaching sessions, presumably outside of liturgical services, for the instruction in the Christian faith of its members. This would be in their houses; and as the designation "teachers" as in verse 1 appears to be a formal one, the sessions themselves could have been formal and organized in various ways.

The list of the five preachers and prophets Luke provides us with is enticingly interesting. Barnabas from Cyprus, Saul from Tarsus in Cilicia in Asia Minor, Manean, which is a Jewish name, who had been in the court of King Herod and possibly, depending on how the mention of him is translated, his foster brother, Lucius from Cyrene in North Africa, his name being a Latin one, which could indicate either a Jew with a Latin name, which was not uncommon, or a Gentile, and Simeon, a Jewish name, who was also called Niger, which could well indicate he had a noticeably dark skin. They come across as an interesting mix, men with different cultural backgrounds, one from Asia Minor, one from an island in the Mediterranean, one, maybe two, from Africa, and one from Palestine, with the Greek language in common but some of them able to speak Latin and Aramaic as well, possibly also a language local to their place of birth and upbringing; and some of them Hebrew. Antioch certainly was a cultural and ethnic melting pot within the Empire.

We are not dealing here with the sort of people whom the Council of the Jews dismissively thought they were dealing with when they arrested the apostles, calling them "common, ignorant people" (Acts 4:13), who actually proved to be anything but. We are dealing with men who collectively came with a massive cultural hinterland. In the space of a mere 15 years, Christianity had expanded its membership quite incredibly; it was already of its own volition starting to reach out, as Christ said it must, to "every nation" (Matthew 28:19), and that ultimately was the drive which in the year 49 made the calling of the Council of Jerusalem not just necessary but also a monumental breakthrough. Antioch was becoming its own Christian intellectual centre, separate from Judea and from Jerusalem, which for the time being was to remain the locus of ultimate Church authority.

Preachers and teachers in Antioch. It does not take much to imagine what was going on. Discussion, debate, argumentation, what everyone does, especially in the first years of the life of any new movement, be it political, religious or cultural. There are thousands of instances of this happening in human history. One has only to think—just a few examples—of the Levellers and the Diggers, the huge debates in the American colonies involving men like Tom Paine as they argued about the sort of political society they were creating, the intensity of argument in the French Revolution, the rival theories of the Bolsheviks and the Mensheviks between Lenin, Trotsky, Kerensky and others, the religious debates at the time of the Reformation, 95 theses being nailed to the door of the Castle Church in Wittenberg, definitely a historic door—but no longer there! Taken down and carted away, possibly chopped up and used for firewood! An immense pity. One wonders if the original document which was nailed to the door survived. Doubtful. There is a copy in the church itself. One fascinating feature of it is that it is in Latin, and each thesis is syllogistic, written in the style of argument that prevailed in the medieval schools, be they the Sorbonne, Bologna, Padua, Oxford, Cambridge, Salamanca, right across Europe. Aquinas, Abelard, Ockham, Albert the Great, Bonaventure, Scotus, Grosseteste, Anselm, all the "schoolmen" of hundreds of years of European intellectualism, in which Martin Luther himself was schooled.

When it came to argumentation, early Christianity, as we see in Luke's narrative, addressed it head on; and indeed Christianity has been that way ever since, right to the present day. Don Cupitt described it excellently:

> History shows that a faith like Catholicism is a continuous living stream of community life and devotion, thought and debate, which has been evolving and changing from its very beginning and has always embraced a variety of standpoints.[14]

It is a description worth pondering. Living things which cease to change die. Disagreement and debate was a feature of Christianity from its very start. Luke was aware of it. He informs us that what made the church in Antioch call on the apostles to convene what has turned out to be called the Council of Jerusalem was "sharp dispute and debate" among its members (Acts 15:1f.). That debate was between Paul and Barnabas on one side and "men down from Judea" on the other. In Jerusalem it was between Peter and the Circumcision Faction. The issue was monumental: what is it that achieves reconciliation of humanity with God? And when the apostles and elders met in Jerusalem, it was only after "much debate" (15:7) that the matter was settled.

What were the sources of the teaching, the preaching and the argumentation that was taking place in Antioch, and indeed in every Christian centre now springing up around the Mediterranean? Undoubtedly, the Jewish Scriptures and the records they themselves had, both oral and maybe written, of the life and the words of Jesus, and the endless discussions among themselves on how to interpret what they read and what they had received by way of oral tradition. What form did the teaching sessions take? They would have been held in houses, but how? It all must have been lively and exciting, a prayer life together, an intense intellectual life together, ardent study with men like Barnabas and Saul, who had met, lived and spoken with the apostles and the first disciples in Jerusalem and elsewhere, who would have told all and sundry about their first-hand experience of Jesus. The Christian community of Antioch must have been a veritable cauldron of discussion and debate, of preaching and praying and fasting, with inputs not just of the Judaic Jewish perspective but also from diaspora Jews and from the growing number of Gentile Christians, all of whom had different perspectives.

What Luke tells us in Acts 13:1 is that Antioch was in respect of Christian development intellectually and spiritually a vibrant centre and sufficiently independent of Jerusalem to be able to take important decisions, such as the one we will be dealing with in this account. One can never be sure, but probably by and large Jerusalem was mono-cultural with an homogeneous and uniform population, solidly Jewish and of course Judaic in its religion and culture. It was through the prism of their one nation history as God's chosen people that they looked out onto the world. What else could they do? But not so Antioch. It was a place with immense ethnic and religious variety, a melting pot. For that reason its Christian members thought differently, saw things differently and had different problems to deal with, as Luke himself recorded in Acts 11:19–21. And they made a decision of historic significance. It was the Antioch church, not Jerusalem, that instructed Barnabas and Saul to take the Christian gospel into the Gentile world.

# CHAPTER 20

# To Cyprus: The First Missionary Journey to the Gentiles

Luke tells us that the Antioch Christians held "fasts and offered worship to the Lord" (Acts 13:2). The word used by Luke for "offering worship" is of great interest. It is leitourgéω, a word taken from the Septuagint. From it we derive the word "liturgy". Luke tells us that it was while the five men whose names he gives us, prophets and teachers, and doubtless others, "were keeping a fast and offering worship to the Lord, the Holy Spirit said: 'Set Barnabas and Saul apart for me to do the work for which I have called them'" (v. 2). The Holy Spirit is recorded as himself speaking. As far as I am aware, this is only the second time in the New Testament, where it is the Holy Spirit who speaks; and if it is the case, it just might greatly enhance the significance of this divine command being given to the church in Antioch. "Then after further fasting and prayer, they laid their hands on them and let them go" (v. 3). Luke was fully aware of the great significance of the decision that the Antioch community had arrived at; it was arrived at by prayer and fasting, and of course with no end of discussion between the church membership, with the Holy Spirit working intimately within them all.

The "work" which the Holy Spirit wanted Barnabas and Saul to be set apart for is not actually specified but the Antioch community obviously had no doubt what it was. They were restless. Through prayer and discussion they had come to the realization that it was time to bring an end to the restriction of the gospel to its demographic and geographical heartlands and take it out to all diaspora Jews wherever they might be living, and to the Gentiles. The Antioch Christian community was made up of both Jewish and Gentile people, located just where the Holy Land met up with the Gentile world. As we will see when Paul and Barnabas arrive in Cyprus, and as Paul himself will say in Pisidian Antioch in Asia Minor, the decision was to preach the gospel first and foremost to the Jews; and as we have seen in the case of Caesarea there were Gentiles associating themselves with the Jewish religion and attending their synagogues.

Luke emphasizes that the decision was made with the help of prayer to the Holy Spirit and fasting. He says that twice in two successive verses. He goes further. He says that the decision was made within the performance of their liturgy: "while they were worshipping the Lord" (Acts 13:3). It is by a liturgical action that the two men are so appointed, namely by the laying-on of hands. It is a pity that there is no record of what exactly this liturgy consisted in, with what readings and prayers, what they believed the laying-on of hands meant, who exactly laid their hands on their heads, if it was everyone who wanted to or was it just community leaders, and if so, in what capacity. Most likely the readership Luke was writing for would have been acquainted with it all. Luke says the two men were "sent on their mission by the Holy Spirit" (v. 4). Whatever the details were, it was liturgically carried out, it was seen for what it was, a solemn moment with all in attendance sensing the presence of the Spirit.

They took the road to the port of Seleucia and boarded the boat to Cyprus, doubtless accompanied to the quayside by members of the community. It was an historic moment with what were in due course to be world-wide consequences. The newly founded Christian church in Syria was tiny; and its Antioch branch maybe even smaller, and in terms of comparison to the world around them it was as indistinguishable and obscure and unknown as it could get. Yet, for all that it took it upon itself to behave in an exceptional way. Its members had a belief. It was a belief that a man, unknown to 99.999 per cent of the world's population, who had been crucified as a criminal with the leadership of his own nation against him, in a small province of a huge empire, was that world's saviour. Quite frankly, on the surface it was laughable, it was astonishing that this small, obscure, Antioch community could put two of its men, maybe accompanied by their wives and children, on a boat in the Syrian port of Seleucia to start to take that belief to the rest of the world. It was an incredible venture, one almighty act of faith.

The Antioch church was now in the position, it had arrived at the theological juncture, where it could itself open up a new evangelical front in church expansion. It is worthwhile delaying the story in order to establish who was responsible for this theological breakthrough. It almost always comes across that it was down to Paul first and foremost. After all, it was Paul who was to become known through his missionary journeys as the apostle to the Gentiles, a title we have looked at already, and questioned; and to those journeys and his journey to Rome Luke devotes about half of his Church history. Furthermore, Paul himself tells us in Galatians 2:9 that James, Peter and John had shook hands with him and Barnabas over an agreement that the two of them should "go to the Gentiles", while those three "pillars" of the Church would go to "the circumcision", the people who had been circumcised, to the Jews. It is, however, difficult to make head and tail of this statement of Paul's. It had been Peter, not Paul, who, as we have seen, had established for the Church the universalist understanding of the mission of Jesus; it had been Peter who had brought the first Gentile into the Church, it had been him, again as we have seen, who had confronted "the circumcision faction" in Jerusalem and Judea; and throughout the period of these achievements Paul hadn't been involved, he hadn't been on the scene at all, he had been a long way away in Tarsus in Asia Minor.

The only way to make sense of what Paul asserts in Galatians is that it was in reference to some later meeting between him and Peter, James and John, most likely in Jerusalem, possibly at the Council of Jerusalem itself, which was after Paul's first missionary journey. By then he had a proven track record of going out to the Gentiles, if only because the Jews of Pisidia Antioch had first kicked him and Barnabas out of the city, and his abilities and his total dedication to this apostolate were acknowledged. Yet, whenever this meeting between Paul and the other three took place, the agreement they shook hands on was plainly understood by them to be only a temporary one. Peter for example, Paul tells us in Galatians 2:11, went to Antioch where the Gentile Christians were at least a large minority in the church, if not in fact the majority, and there is the strong oral tradition that he became its bishop. There is the reference in 1 Corinthians 9:5 to Peter (Cephas in the text) which indicates that he was known to the Christians of Corinth as being there or thereabouts accompanied by his Christian wife, and of course he travelled on to Rome, where he became its bishop and died a martyr.

Paul did not originate the apostolate to the Gentiles. It was arrived at before he became a person of influence within the churches; and if there are four people to whom it should be attributed they are Philip and Stephen, Peter and Barnabas. Stephen's contribution has been described. It was Barnabas who went as the representative of the apostles in Jerusalem to Antioch to persuade the community there to preach to the Gentiles, when some Jewish Christians, fleeing persecution in Jerusalem, went there and confined their preaching "only to Jews and no others" (Acts 11:19). It was of course Barnabas who brought Paul back from Tarsus to Antioch; he first involved him in giving Christian instruction to the large numbers of people wishing to join the Church (v. 26); and he accompanied Paul, initially it would seem in a leadership role, on the first missionary journey. He had had therefore plenty of time and opportunity to speak with Paul on the issue of the conversion and baptism of Gentiles by the time they boarded the ship which took them to Cyprus on the first leg of their missionary journey. That was an Antioch decision, not a Jerusalem one, but once Peter had arrived back from Caesarea and made it plain to all that the Gentiles were welcome in the Church, we just do not know if the other apostles and others didn't then take the same action too in all sorts of other places.

Our records are that it was in the synagogue in Pisidia Antioch in Asia Minor that Luke records Paul's first contribution to the matter, namely his forthright and outright statement to his Jewish brothers and sisters. When the two men reached Pisidia Antioch in Asia Minor, they first went to the local synagogue, and there they preached to the Jews. Paul said to them: "You must understand, my brothers, that it is through him (Jesus) that forgiveness of sins is proclaimed to you. It is through him that everyone who has faith is acquitted of everything for which there was no acquittal under the Law" (Acts 13:39). Then, as Luke narrates it, it was only after the Jews rejected their preaching, answering it "with violent abuse" (v. 45), that they turned to the Gentiles: "Paul and Barnabas were outspoken in their reply: 'It was necessary that the word of God should be declared to you first. But since you reject it and thus condemn yourselves as unworthy of eternal life, we now turn to the Gentiles'" (v. 46).

But despite them making that ringing statement, the next thing they actually did on escaping from the violence threatened against them was in fact to go to the synagogue in the nearby town of Iconium (modern-day Konya in Turkey) and preach there to their fellow Jews, and that was the pattern of Paul's missionary strategy from first to last, to preach first in the local synagogue whichever town or country he was in. However, as Luke narrates these events to his readership, there is one thing that Paul said to his listeners that Peter has not been reported as saying. It is his pronouncement, above recorded (Acts 13:39), of the inadequacy of the Law. That will quickly become a significant, and contentious, issue, and coming from Paul, it will make life dangerous for him (cf. Acts 21:21–31). But it is unlikely that it originated with him. It was one inevitable conclusion that all the discussions being held in both Jerusalem and Antioch will have come to before he and Barnabas left for Cyprus. Paul inherited what had been achieved in those discussions, and what he received from Peter as a result of Peter's experiences in Joppa and Caesarea. Paul's contribution, however, which was to prove monumental, was to think it all through and develop it with immense depth and perceptiveness both in his preaching of the gospel in Asia Minor and Greece and in his letters to the Galatians and the Romans.

The Church in the persons of Paul and Barnabas now embarked on its first missionary journey into the Gentile world. They were embarking on a fateful journey, boarding a ship for a voyage they could not know the outcome of. It was the bravest of ventures, in human history one of immense significance.

At the Syrian port of Seleucia the two men had a choice. They could go north to Asia Minor or sail west to Cyprus. They chose to sail to Cyprus. About why they did not choose to go north to Paul's home province of Cilicia and home town of Tarsus, which he himself called "no mean city" (Acts 21:39), we can only speculate. Probably they chose Cyprus because it was the homeland of Barnabas, who was at that moment the senior of the two men. In Luke's text, when the two are mentioned together, Barnabas is mentioned first until they have completed the Cyprus section of their journey and they are in Asia Minor, the change appearing first in Acts 13:13, when they get to Pamphylia, where Mark the nephew of Barnabas leaves them and returns to Jerusalem. Luke says of Paul, and presumably Paul told him so, that he felt that Mark had "deserted him" (Acts 15:38). In 13:13 Luke then uses the phrase "Paul and his company", and the next time he writes "Paul and Barnabas" (v. 42 and again in v. 46). Luke alternates the order of names in Acts 14 and 15, but it is the case that as from the moment they land at the port of Perga in Asia Minor, if indeed not before when in Cyprus, Paul is the principal of the two.

Cyprus was a good place to start. Barnabas had family there, so they knew they would get the welcome and the accommodation, the bread and board they needed for the start of this new venture. There was a diaspora Jewish population with its synagogues, which would be secure bases to launch out from. The Cypriot population itself, however, was of course overwhelmingly Gentile, a population with a long and profound cultural history, but it was not totally virgin missionary territory for Christianity (cf. Acts 11:19f.). It was on one of the most frequented sea lanes of the Mediterranean, totally integrated into the Roman Empire, peaceful, without an occupying army unlike the provinces of Asia Minor.

We might also ask whether Paul and Barnabas were accompanied by anyone else besides John Mark, the son of Mary who was the sister of Barnabas. We know that Peter was married, not least because Jesus healed his mother-in-law (Luke 4:38–40), which makes it all the more ironic that the Church led by the successors of Peter insists on clerical celibacy, which was first introduced as a pragmatic measure to avoid inheritance liability. From 1 Corinthians 9:5 we know that Paul was married. Was his wife with him? We know she was later on in Ephesus when he wrote to the Corinthians. Barnabas would have been married too, that was a taken-for-granted element of Jewish life. 1 Corinthians 9:5 is of immense interest. There Paul tells us that Peter and the rest of the apostles and the brethren of Jesus were married and were accompanied by their wives. What were their names? What contributions did their wives make to their preaching of the gospel and the founding of local churches? How many children did they have? Did they travel together as families? Is that one reason why Paul put such an insistence on himself working for his living no matter where he was? Was it to support his wife and children? Where did the wives live, and die? What happened to their children? It is a crying shame we know nothing about them. Mark 5:21 gives us the names of the two sons of Simon of Cyrene who helped Jesus carry his cross, and that in such a way as to suggest they were both members of the Christian community in Rome for whom he wrote his Gospel and who had survived the persecution inflicted on them by Nero. Simon of Cyrene, however, was not as big a character in the story of the Early Church as Peter, Paul and the other apostles, yet we are told nothing about their children, let alone their wives.

So, from the Syrian port of Seleucia the two men sailed to Cyprus. They spent maybe as much as two years there, from 45 to 47. Yet, despite being there that length of time Luke's account of them in Cyprus is incredibly brief. In fact, though Paul and Luke traversed the whole island, from one end to the other, from Salamis to Paphos, there isn't any account at all of what they actually preached. All Luke tells us is that "they proclaimed the word of God in the synagogues of the Jews" (Acts 13:5), nothing more, and nowhere else but in synagogues. No detail whatsoever. No detail about the sort of arguments they used, the sort of appeal they made. It's not till they are in Pisidian Antioch in Asia Minor after they have left Cyprus that we find out what that appeal was. Doubtless at the start Barnabas would have been besieged by family members wanting to know why he had become a follower of Jesus, who, they would probably have known, had been put to death by the Roman authorities with the full backing of the Council of the Jews, not quite the sort of thing to win adherents easily.

In the synagogues, beyond reasonable doubt, it would have been the resurrection of Jesus, for which Luke tells us that there was "many convincing proofs" (Acts 1:3), that Barnabas would have relied on most in his explanation of his conversion to Jesus. Foremost among those proofs was of course the witness of the apostles among whom the risen Jesus had walked, ate and spoken, and it is likely that Barnabas himself had been one of the "more than five hundred witnesses" mentioned by Paul. There is nothing in the texts which excludes that possibility. In addition, there was Paul's own mystical encounter with the Risen Lord which he would have spoken about and which would have dovetailed with the witness of the apostles with great effect. In Acts 17, Luke records how Paul operated, preached and argued in the course of his second missionary journey, and we can reasonably assume it was a pattern of evangelization that had been started and established in Cyprus. The second journey took Paul and his companion Silas across into Europe. They reached Thessalonica, they went to its Jewish synagogue; and Luke tells us: "Following his usual practice Paul went to their meetings and for the next three Sabbaths he argued with them, quoting texts of Scripture which he expounded and applied to show that the Messiah had to suffer and rise from the dead. 'And this Jesus', he said, 'whom I am proclaiming to you is the Messiah' Some of them were convinced and joined Paul and Silas; so did a great number of God-fearing Greeks and a good many influential women ('of the prominent women not a few')" (Acts 17:2–4). As an aside, one might express a regret that Luke did not tell us more about these women, who they were, what their names were, what it was that made them prominent in Thessalonica and why he included them separately in his short list of converts.

The two men just had to start where as Jews they knew they had an affinity with their audience. They were now on their own, they weren't in the company of fellow Christians like in Antioch, they'd left that comfort zone, they naturally had a lot of learning to do, they had to find their feet in the totally new activity they had taken on. Gentile territory as well as fellow Jews was their goal but, it would seem, they had the sense to know they couldn't just walk into it and hold forth, and probably they didn't know how to anyway. From what information we have from Luke, namely Acts 17:17, it does not look as if Paul addressed Gentiles outside of the protecting arms of a synagogue till he was in Athens, first "in the city square" and then, famously, in the Areopagus, in the course of his second missionary journey. Leaving Antioch to carry out the work of evangelization, he and Barnabas had to start somewhere and the synagogue which was attended by interested Gentiles was the natural springboard.

There are, however, two incidents in the 18 to 24 months the pair were on the island that Luke does tell us about, even if they are all he does tell us about. One was Saul's change of name to the Latin Paul, which could well have been done with the mission to the Gentiles in mind. The second incident was when the two men, on arriving in Paphos, the capital of the island, found themselves opposed by "a sorcerer, a Jew who posed as a prophet, Bar-Jesus/Elymas by name" (13:6) who tries to prevent Paul converting Sergius Paulus the Roman proconsul. Sergius Paulus was, says Luke, "an intelligent man" (v. 7) who most likely got to hear about them and what they were preaching through Jewish contacts in a Paphos synagogue. Like Cornelius in Caesarea who summoned Peter to him, Sergius sent for the two men "because he wanted to hear the word of God". One can easily imagine Paul and Barnabas putting their heads together to decide how to approach him, an audience as different as chalk from cheese from those in Jewish synagogues. Sergius was the first non-Jew, the first Gentile, we know about whom Paul converted.

The sorcerer was in the retinue of the proconsul, and "he tried to turn him from the faith". Paul deals with the sorcerer so harshly, using language so violent, that the poor man had a stroke and went blind and was so paralysed he had to grope around for someone to lead him away by the hand. It was hardly a Christian way for Paul to treat him, even if Luke describes Paul as being "filled with the Holy Ghost" in how he behaved and Paul himself putting the collapse of the poor man down to him "being struck by the hand of the Lord". However, that's what Paul did; and it all so astonished the proconsul that "he became a believer, deeply impressed by what he learned about the Lord". What he saw of the behaviour of Paul in respect of this incident seems rather objectionable. Fortunately, Christian doctrine and the attitudes it demands of Christians preaching to non-Christians have developed since then. God isn't into cruelty, and the sorcerer was entitled to his own personal take on religion. Sergius the Roman proconsul of Cyprus and Cornelius the Roman centurion in Caesarea represent something of immense historic importance. Within three hundred years Christianity was to become the official religion of the Empire; and they were the first Romans, together with the wife and family and household of Cornelius and some of his officers, whose conversion is recorded. The difference between the two of them, the proconsul of a province and a centurion, in respect of class, wealth and power, was of course immense.

Other than those two incidents Luke tells us nothing about what the two men did and what they preached all the time they were in Cyprus, only that "they preached the word of God". There is no reason to think they were on their own. Salamis was within regular sailing distance of Seleucia, and it was a day's journey or so from there back to Antioch. Cyprus was peaceful, no occupying army was required by its

Roman masters. Communication with the church of Antioch by Paul and Barnabas over the eighteen months to two years they were there would undoubtedly have been frequent, both to report back and receive suggestions, possibly even with one or other of the two men themselves making the journey and returning. They may well have left their wives and children in Antioch in the safe keeping of the church community and revisited them on and off. There is no good reason to think that at least during this Cyprus stage of their journey they weren't joined on and off by fellow Christians from their mother church of Antioch or the more senior church in Jerusalem.

# CHAPTER 21

# Confrontation and a Watershed Moment in Pisidia Antioch

Their decision to leave the island and sail to the mainland of Asia Minor would have been made together with the church in Antioch, with Jerusalem possibly involved, and the senior members of the island churches such as at Paphos, where they sailed from. There was a lot of thinking to do, not least what route to take once they landed at Perga. They would have given consideration to the logistics of such a journey, taken advice on whom to contact, given a lot of thought to the abiding issue of how to sustain themselves and not just live off what church members there might be there already, if any. And there would have been concern about language. The organizers of the venture would have talked this over time and again. Cyprus was not Asia Minor; the ruling class in Asia Minor spoke either Greek or Latin or both, but in the towns and villages the ordinary people probably did not, but it was to them as well that the gospel was now being taken. Among the strategies Paul and Barnabas decided on could well have been, after making converts of Jews in these towns and villages, to commission them to reach out to the people of those places in the language they spoke, which doubtless in everyday life the Jews of Asia Minor spoke too. But there again, Paul himself was from Tarsus, a town in the Asia Minor province of Cilicia. Did he know, could he speak, any of the languages of the non-Jewish, non-Greek and non-Latin-speaking population of Asia Minor, present day Turkey? Who knows? But possibly.

But even if he did, how would he approach people who had no connections with the Jewish religion from which Christianity originated, no knowledge of its history and its Scriptures, no notion of a promised

Messiah, who would have had a completely different culture, a completely different perspective on life, a different god or gods. It was this stark situation that made it necessary for him and Barnabas to work out of the synagogues to which some "God-fearing" Gentiles came in search of a more satisfying and fulfilling spirituality than that offered by their own culture. The synagogues were the springboard, there was nothing else. Paul and Barnabas were taking the gospel into unknown and foreign religious cultures, where it could, and at times did, present a threat to a received way of life. For example during the second journey, when he and Silas had barely set foot in Europe and the town of Philippi was the first place they went to, a young female fortune teller spotted them and latched on to them: "The girl's owners seized Paul and Silas and dragged them to the city authorities in the main square and bringing them before the magistrates they said: 'These men are causing a disturbance in our city; they are Jews; they are advocating customs which it is illegal for us Romans to adopt and follow.' The mob joined in the attack" (Acts 16:19–22). The real motive for their arrest was they were seen by the girl's owners as a threat to their income since her fortune-telling brought them an income, but at the same time the incident illustrates how race and culture could be invoked. When one thinks about how foreign, alien and different religiously and culturally Christianity was to the non-Jewish people of Asia Minor, and indeed all the other lands within the Roman Empire, it is a miracle that it was to achieve the mass conversions it was to experience.

It was with all this in their minds, and much more of course, that Paul and Barnabas embarked on a ship in Paphos in Cyprus for the town of Perga in Pamphylia in Asia Minor, and from Perga they made the journey on to Pisidia Antioch, which today is the town of Yaivic in the Turkish lakes region, part of the province of Isparta. Pisidia Antioch was an important military and cultural base of Rome in Asia. It had a long history up to and through the Hellenistic period and to its colonization by the Romans and retired Roman soldiers. Paul, being from the neighbouring province of Cilicia, would have known about it, as he would have known which towns had a Jewish community and a synagogue which was attended by non-Jews/Gentiles who were interested in the Jewish religion—the "God-fearers". Acts 17:2 informs us how the two men went about their work, a strategy established no doubt during their missionary work in Cyprus. They would first pay a visit to the local synagogue, let the people in charge know who they were, then probably depending on the circumstances ask if they could at some point address the congregation, then take their seats, listen to the readings from the Law and the prophets, and wait upon events, wait to see what interest they aroused in the congregation and take it from there.

Pisidia Antioch had a large Jewish community, large enough anyway according to Luke for an event in their synagogue to attract widespread attention across the town. He tells us that on the second Sabbath, only a week later, when Paul and Barnabas had returned to the synagogue to restate the case they were making, "almost the whole city gathered to hear the word of God" (Acts 1:44). This statement makes one wonder if they had attracted such audiences when they were in Cyprus. However, whatever they did in Cyprus, it did not bring about any such drastic event as was about to happen in Pisidia Antioch; an incident which is represented by Luke as changing the basics of their approach to evangelization. It put the two men in a position where they could make a helpful contribution, as we will see in Acts 15:4, to the deliberations of the Council of Jerusalem.

So Paul and Barnabas entered the synagogue in Pisidia Antioch and introduced themselves to its officers. As total strangers they would of course have been noticed. They told the officers who they were and why they'd come to their synagogue, and undoubtedly said they would like to address the congregation. Most likely the synagogue people would have been interested to hear them since no doubt they would have said they wanted to speak about someone they believed to be the Messiah. They then took their seats, listened to the readings and joined in the prayers. They were invited to preach "an exhortation" (Acts 13:15), some words of encouragement, to the assembled Jewish people, and, significantly for Paul and Barnabas, to those Gentiles who were also there.

Paul got up and, looking for the congregation to be quiet, made such a gesture with his hand that whoever witnessed it remembered it and put it in the Church memory bank so that Luke thirty or more years later makes mention of it. What Paul then said to that synagogue audience could hardly have been the "exhortation" its leaders were expecting. It runs from Acts 13:16–41. He stood up, with that gesture he demanded attention, and he began to speak: "Men of Israel and you who fear God, listen to me" (v. 16). We see from this that as well as speaking to his fellow Jews, he was also addressing his Gentile listeners. However, for most of the speech it is to his fellow Jews that he speaks, as when he says that God "chose our fathers", a phrase that would exclude those people in his audience who were Gentiles. They most likely would have been used to it. They were in a Jewish synagogue after all and they would have taken it for granted.

But we now need to pause before we proceed. The scholars are of the opinion that it was Luke, not Paul, who composed this speech. Raymond Brown has no doubt about it;[15] and perhaps that becomes most obvious in verse 23 where, without providing any information at all about who Jesus was, without any prior mention of him, he is suddenly mentioned, and described or offered as "the saviour of Israel". A lot is left out, too much taken for granted. Luke after all was not present when Paul spoke this first time in this synagogue. Whatever Paul said there, Luke himself didn't witness any of it. However, he was with Paul on his second missionary journey which was only a matter of four years later, and that one revisited the towns of Lycaonia, Pisidia and Phrygia such as Pisidia Antioch, and naturally Paul would have described to him what had happened to him there, as would the town's Christians who had witnessed it.

There is more to it than that, however. Even if the speech was composed by Luke, it could still be a reliable account of what Paul actually said, not so much in verbal details but certainly in respect of content. Luke must have heard Paul preach in synagogues on innumerable occasions through the second and the third missionary journeys. Composing a copy must have been an easy thing for him to do. Furthermore, the Christological material in the speech re-occurs in Paul's letters as does, significantly, the vocabulary and ideas about justification in verse 39 which Paul expands on in his letter to the Romans. What is also interesting is that it is uncomplicated in content and Judaic, which would correspond to the degree of development that Paul might have reached at this moment in his life as a Christian. What's more, there are two details mentioned which convey some authenticity. Luke commences with: "Standing up, Paul motioned with his hand" (v. 16) and concludes with: "As Paul and

Barnabas were leaving the synagogue, the people invited them to speak further about these things on the next Sabbath" (v. 42). For these reasons it seems reasonable to take the speech at the least as a fair representation of how Paul would have addressed a Jewish audience with a sprinkling of Gentiles in it in a synagogue at this early stage of his evangelical ministry.

He starts with the exile in Egypt. From Egypt God rescues the Jews and leads them out into the desert and into "the land of Canaan, the land he gave them as their heritage", where first they lived under the Judges and then under King Saul, who was followed by David, and, he says, cutting directly to the chase, it was David "from whose seed God, as he promised, brought to Israel a saviour, who is Jesus". At this point one can easily imagine Paul standing high above his audience, almost opening his arms to take them all in, not just the Jews but the Gentiles there too: "My brothers, you who come from the stock of Abraham and the others among you who revere God, to us has the message of this salvation been sent" (Acts 13:26). As I read him, when he says the words "to us", he is saying: "It is to our generation, to us now, at this time, both Jewish and Gentile, that God's message of salvation has been sent;" and he will express that same message five or so years later, though differently, when in Galatians 4:4 he writes about "the fullness of time".

Paul could see all too well the doubts in the faces of the Jews in his audience, doubts which he had to address, and with some skill he turns their doubts and objections into evidence. Yes, Jesus was indeed rejected by the people of Israel, by both rulers and people, and condemned to death by them. But that was because they did not recognize him and did not understand the predictions of the prophets even though the prophets were being read out to them Sabbath after Sabbath. Therein, says Paul, lies a proof that Jesus is Israel's saviour, because that is precisely what the prophets had said would happen. It was precisely by rejecting him and condemning him to death that Israel, both people and their rulers, made good the words of the prophets. And there was something else. When Jesus had been taken down from the gibbet and laid out dead in a tomb, "God raised him from the dead" (v. 31), and proof of it lay in the fact that "he appeared to those who had come up with him from Galilee to Jerusalem". They, said Paul, are "his witnesses to the people" (v. 31). Furthermore, that had not happened to anyone else in all of the history of the Jewish people, not even to David. The uniqueness of the resurrection of Jesus is proof that he is the Messiah.

And then there is the conclusion. In part it is Petrine, as was in many other ways the body of the speech, namely when he tells his audience: "My brothers, I want you to know that through this man (Jesus) the forgiveness of sins is proclaimed" (v. 38). One might look back to Peter's statement on the feast of Pentecost (Acts 2:38), and again when he stood before the Council of the Jews (5:31). And in part also the conclusion looks forward to Paul's theme in the letter to the Romans, that of justification: "And through him everyone who believes is justified from everything you could not be justified from by the Law" (v. 39). This statement about the inefficacy and inadequacy of the Law in respect of salvation is here made by Paul at the very outset of his missionary career. It is stored up, one might say, and used against him some ten years later, in effect by James speaking for the Judaic faction in Acts 21:21 at the conclusion of his career, when, against the advice of his friends, he arrives in Jerusalem.

One can readily admit to the proposition that verses 38 and 39 were an addition made by Luke to verses 16 to 37 which are pre-Joppa, pre-Caesarea, pre-the Antioch debate in how they present Jesus and his salvific role. That could well be. But the story they tell about Jesus is solidly Judaic. They present Jesus as he could readily be understood by good solid traditional Jews. It could well be the case that what Paul was doing was adapting his preaching to where mentally his Jewish audience in Pisidia Antioch were at. After all, Pisidia Antioch was a long way from everything that had been happening in Palestine and Syria; and what had been happening made up a long and significant list of events which is instructive and illuminating to draw up and look at, not least because what they are leading up to is about to happen.

There had been the persecution of the apostles by the Jewish leadership and the repudiation of the new Christian movement by that leadership; the theological input of the diaspora Jews into the Jerusalem church; the message of the speech made by Stephen before his martyrdom at the hands of the Jews; the apostolate of the deacon Philip among the Samaritans; Peter's visions in Joppa; his attendance upon a Roman centurion in Caesarea; his magisterial pronouncement before Cornelius and the conversion and the baptism of Cornelius and his household; his defence of his decisions before the circumcision faction in Jerusalem; the divisions and the debates in Antioch; their resolution brought about by Barnabas; the beheading of the apostle James by Herod, almost as a gesture of solidarity with the Jewish people, followed by the arrest of Peter; and finally the decision of the Antioch church to take the gospel to the Gentiles. All this, certainly at first glance, was a long way, hundreds of miles away, from the lives of the Jews and people of Pisidia Antioch. Yet it was what had brought these two Jews, Barnabas and Paul, to this synagogue in this city in Asia Minor.

We need to appreciate what was at stake. Christianity wasn't just taking itself out of its place of birth, it was also deciding what its relationship was both to the Jewish faith and to non-Jews. From the Jewish religion Christianity emerged as from a womb; and that is no glib metaphor. Look at the first lines of Matthew's Gospel. It begins with "a table of descent of Jesus Christ, son of David, son of Abraham", and he presents that descent to us in three sets of 14 generations from Abraham up to "the birth of the Messiah". That Jewish religion, however, had formally repudiated Christ and Christianity and had persecuted it, because it sensed that Jesus, as Messiah, stood for something that was essentially inimical to its understanding of itself, namely its belief that God's covenant was solely with the Jewish nation. Yet, the fact was that all the first believers in Jesus were themselves zealot Jews; Peter, for example, had been the leader of a cell of Jewish zealots seeking the Jewish Messiah, and one of the apostles, Simon, was as Matthew tells us "a member of the Zealot party" (Matthew 10:4). This new religion was therefore confronted by two serious conflicts, one with its parent religion which was not hesitating to persecute it, and one posing an equal threat to its existence, namely a membership divided as to whether or not to insist on it retaining the identity of its Jewish origins. Yet, the only people who could resolve this second issue were themselves ardent Jews. Down to their last gene the first disciples were Jewish, that identity which found its total expression in codes and rituals and practices of all kinds. We saw it in Peter's reaction to the visions he had in Joppa.

As for Paul's speech to his synagogue audience in Pisidia Antioch, there were two different reactions to the speech; it attracted support among some of his listeners, it aroused violent opposition among others. The synagogue leaders were impressed, and intrigued and curious; possibly it was the first time they had heard of Jesus, and they asked Paul and Barnabas to come back and speak about the same matters the following Sabbath. Indeed "many Jews and devout proselytes" (v. 43) followed them out into the street, keeping up the dialogue, giving Paul and Barnabas the opportunity to urge them to "hold fast to the grace of God" (v. 43), by which was meant, presumably, that they should keep their minds open to what they had heard or even maybe, if some of them had been converted by what Paul had said, they should hold fast to what they now believed.

However, the following Sabbath, Luke tells us, "almost the whole city gathered to hear the word of God" (v. 44). We can take this estimate as poetic licence on the part of the author; Pisidia Antioch was not a Jewish city; we can assume he meant a great lot of people turned up, the sight of which roused the anger of "the Jews" who "were filled with jealousy and contradicted what Paul said with violent abuse" (v. 45). Luke hasn't mentioned any such reaction before when the two men were in the Cyprus synagogues; it could well be that what triggered it this time was hearing what Paul had said the previous Sabbath about the inadequacy of the Law and, in effect, how Jesus as Messiah hadn't just replaced Moses and his Law but had brought a totally new dimension to "forgiveness of sins" (v. 38), namely the fundamental assertion Paul made, which was destined to have a long and influential journey throughout all Christian history: "You must understand, my brothers, that it is through him that forgiveness of sins is being proclaimed to you; it is through him that everyone who believes is justified from everything you could not be justified from by the Law" (v. 38f.). A wave of outrage greeted this statement.

The conflict of beliefs was so fierce that Paul and Barnabas had to "shake the dust from their feet" (v. 51) and escape to Iconium. However, they left a strong group of converts behind (v. 52); and Paul made that most dramatic and memorable statement right into the faces of his Jewish opponents: "Right," he shouted at them, "it was necessary that the word of God should be proclaimed to you first. But since you reject it . . . behold! We now turn to the Gentiles" (v. 46). But did they? Did they then stop preaching to the Jews and start preaching just to the Gentiles? This is such a well-known statement, one which has ever since been closely associated with Paul. It contrasts his mission with that of the apostles. But is it what he actually did? In the Galatians he will write: "They (Peter, John and James the elder) saw that I had been entrusted with the task of preaching the gospel to those who had foreskins (the Gentiles—that's how he described them, men who had kept their foreskins!) just as Peter had been to the circumcised . . . For God who was at work in the ministry of Peter as an apostle to the circumcised was at work in my ministry to the Gentiles . . . They agreed that we (himself and Barnabas) should go to the Gentiles and they to the circumcised" (Galatians 2:7–9). As it reads it is misleading. It simply was not what happened, it wasn't what Paul then did.

It is not to be understood as if Peter and co were agreeing that as from the time when they had this conversation, probably during the Council of Jerusalem, that they would confine their missionary work to the Jews only. In the light of the Joppa and the Caesarea events and bearing in mind what Peter had argued and asserted before his Judaic interrogators in Jerusalem on his return from Caesarea, and what he had to say at the Council of Jerusalem, and knowing a little of his activities in Antioch and Rome later on if only by way of oral tradition, it makes no sense to read this assertion of Paul in his epistle to mean as from the moment of the Council Peter preached the gospel only to Jews. No sense whatsoever. If read in that way it would both misrepresent and denigrate Peter and the apostles. What the assertion can only mean is that Peter and co acknowledged that Paul's mission was decidedly more Gentile-orientated than theirs was. Nothing more than that. One crucial difference between Paul and Barnabas on the one hand and Peter, John and James the Elder on the other was that they were diaspora Jews, not Palestinian, be it Judea or Galilee. Greek was the language of Paul and Barnabas; and the Empire with all its bustling languages and peoples was their milieu. It wasn't a division of labour that was agreed, it was an acknowledgment of some degree of a different emphasis.

And that becomes clear from everything Luke has to tell us about Paul during the rest of the Acts. No sooner had Paul told the Jews of Pisidia Antioch that he and Barnabas were turning to the Gentiles (Acts 13:46) and no sooner had they shaken the dust of the place from their feet, than they went to Iconium, where: "they went into the Jewish synagogue" (14:1). So much for turning away from the Jews! On the second missionary journey Luke tells us that on crossing into Europe and getting to Thessalonica Paul "as his custom was went into the synagogue and on three Sabbath days reasoned with the Jews from the Scriptures" (17:1). Then going on to Berea he and Silas his companion "went to the synagogue of the Jews" (v. 10). Furthermore, "every Sabbath" in Corinth "he held discussions in the synagogue" (18:4); and "when Silas and Timothy came from Macedonia, Paul devoted himself entirely to testifying to the Jews that Jesus was the Messiah" (v. 5). In Ephesus "he argued with the Jews" (v. 19). Again in Ephesus during the third journey he stayed three months arguing "boldly" (19:8) in the synagogue. In other words Paul never deviated from the missionary strategy he had started out with in Cyprus with Barnabas of using the synagogue as a base and a launching pad. It was still the only sensible and workable missionary strategy. Furthermore, straight after the third missionary journey he went to Jerusalem, taking part in a ritual of cleansing, after which he was arrested and kept in detention for two years. Finally, on arriving in Rome under guard and in chains, within a mere three days he had organized a meeting with "the leaders of the Jews" (28:17); and Luke tells how that initial meeting expanded into even bigger meetings with "large numbers at the place where he was staying" (v. 23) and at these meetings "he spoke urgently of the kingdom of God and sought to convince them about Jesus by appealing to the Law and the prophets" (ibid.). He did all this for two years "with a welcome for all who came to him, proclaiming the kingdom of God and teaching the facts about the Lord Jesus Christ" (v. 31). So we can conclude that in no way did Paul stop preaching the gospel to the Jews and devote himself solely to the Gentiles. From everything that Luke relates about him it is crystal clear that he was, right to the moment of his death, as much an apostle to the Jews as he was to the Gentiles.

However, there was one real difference in respect of this matter between him and Peter. Paul was a man of the Empire, he famously declared himself a citizen of Rome, and that "by birth" (Acts 22:28). He had a real feeling for the Gentiles. Throughout the chapters just quoted Luke also tells us that he preached to them, indeed to large numbers of them and to their womenfolk. For example there was Lydia from Thyatira (16:14), who dealt in purple fabric, whom he converted and baptized;

she was a Gentile. He mixed with Gentiles, spoke with them and got into trouble with them, like he did over the slave girl in Philippi who was a fortune teller, making a tidy profit for her owners; and in the shrine of Diana in Macedonia. It is surely correct to say that Peter could hardly have done what Paul did before the Court of Areopagus, "in the city square before casual passers-by and Epicurean and Stoic philosophers" (17:17) and deliver the sort of argument Paul made on seeing "an altar bearing the inscription 'To the Unknown God'" (v. 18). Paul was at home with Gentiles. He had been brought up with them. He was indeed an apostle to the Gentiles. However, he began, continued with and ended his days with an apostolate to the Jews as well.

The harsh rejection by the Pisidia Antioch Jews that Paul and Barnabas experienced was indeed a crucial moment. One feels, re-reading the text of the event, that it was a wake-up call. Their eighteen months or more in Cyprus, moving from synagogue to synagogue, do seem to have gone smoothly, and possibly some complacency had settled in. Then, unexpectedly, they had been repulsed in no uncertain terms in Pisidia Antioch and that pulled them up short and reminded them of what their "instructions from the Lord" were: "I have appointed you to be a light for the Gentiles and a means of salvation to earth's furthest bounds" (Acts 13:47). What they did and what they achieved in the three or four towns in Asia Minor which they visited was to be the basis of their input into the Council of Jerusalem, when they were called upon to tell the apostles, elders and others attending it about "all the signs and miracles that God had worked among the Gentiles through them" (15:12).

What is also interesting in what happened to them in Pisidia Antioch is what it revealed about the Jewish population in that city, something that emerges about it elsewhere too. Luke informs us that "the Jews stirred up feeling among the women of standing who were worshippers and among the leading men of the city. A persecution was started against Paul and Barnabas and they were expelled from the district" (Acts 13:50). In the next city, Iconium, "a move was made by Gentiles and Jews together with the connivance of the City authorities, to maltreat them and stone them. They got wind of it and made their escape to the Lycaonian cities of Lystra and Derbe and the surrounding country, where they continued to spread the good news" (14:5-7). However, "then Jews from (Pisidia)

Antioch and Iconium came on the scene and won over the crowds. They stoned Paul and dragged him out of the city, thinking he was dead. The disciples formed a ring around him and he got to his feet and went back into the city" (14:19).

These details inform us that the Jews of these cities were well-settled, integrated and accepted and that they were on good terms with the town authorities. Possibly they also held local authority offices. There was no reason why they shouldn't have been part of the local Establishment—unless like the Judaic Jerusalem Christians, who made up the circumcision faction, they held to the Mosaic ruling that they should not socialize with Gentiles, which they most definitely were doing. It does appear that these Asia Minor/diaspora Jews had none of the scruples the Jerusalem Jews had about mixing with Gentiles. They were able to represent Paul and Barnabas as incomers disturbing the religious status-quo and with it the civil status-quo, both their own and that of the local Gentiles. One doubts they would really have had any truck with pagan religions, but it was probably convenient to them at least to appear sympathetic if only to get the local non-Jews onside in dealing with these two men. Something much the same had happened to Jesus in Jerusalem. The High Priest and his Council had used the Romans to try to terminate Jesus and his message altogether.

What also comes across from these incidents is the power of Paul and Barnabas as speakers. In three places Luke makes mention of the crowds within the towns who came to listen to them and reacted to them, which was all the more reason why they aroused opposition from the local religious and civil establishments, pagan and Jewish. In addition, both men were as tough as nails. They had been driven out of Pisidia Antioch (Acts 13:50); they had fled from Iconium, when "a move was made by Gentiles and Jews together with the connivance of the city authorities to maltreat them and stone them" (14:5); and Paul had nearly been killed and certainly been left for dead in Lystra (v. 22); but nothing daunted them. They went on to the town of Derbe and they then, amazingly, just turned round and went back to Lystra, Iconium and Pisidia Antioch "heartening the converts and encouraging them to be true to their religion" and warning them that "to enter the kingdom we must pass through many hardships" (v. 22f.).

The first missionary journey was now at an end. They returned to Perga and went on to the port of Attalia to take a boat back to Antioch, "where they had been originally commended to the grace of God for the task which they had now completed" (v. 26). How different they were from us today, what different circumstances they were in! We live in a world where the faith they preached is well known around the world and powerful. We can go out confident that we have a huge international back-up behind us. They preached it when it was totally unknown, the faith of a tiny few. No internet, no telephone, no emails, no television, no newsreels, no supporting governments, no supporting structure, nothing, reaching nobody except the people they met face to face in this village and that city. Their faith was simply incredible, they preached it as salvation for the entire world when 99.999 per cent of the world had never heard of the man they believed to be their saviour nor cared to. And as for the notion of "salvation"—well, how many people in the world they had preached it to cared about it for a start? The salvation most people cared about was protection from illness, accidents, robbery, droughts and floods, the health and welfare of their children, and from the wars the powerful waged all round them.

For all that, "when they arrived back, they called the congregation (of the church in Antioch) together and they reported all that God had helped them to do, and how they had thrown open the gates of faith to the Gentiles" (14:27). "To the Gentiles" who made up most of humanity! These two men in the eyes of the vast majority of the people living in and around Antioch were totally insignificant, yet they were saying they had gone out and presented all of humanity with a completely alternative sort of existence, not just here and now but for eternity. And a tiny group of men and women living in Antioch believed them. What arrogance or what faith, what a perspective or what utter self-delusion, depending on how one sees it.

C H A P T E R  2 2

# Antioch Appeals to the Apostles
# Against the Circumcision Faction

Now, one might have thought that, given Peter's authority, the declaration he had made, the explanation he had given upon returning to Jerusalem from Caesarea and the fact that the Judaic faction had expressed their satisfaction with it (Acts 11:18), the problem some Jewish Christians had with Gentile converts receiving baptism was settled. But nothing could be further from the truth. The faction hadn't given up, they reneged on what they appeared to have said after their discussion with Peter, even to the extent of travelling outside of their own community into Syria: "Now certain persons came from Judea and taught the brethren: 'Unless you are circumcised according to the custom of Moses, you cannot be saved'" (15:1).

That was as fundamental as it could get, in effect substituting the observance of the Law, above all circumcision, for belief in Jesus as saviour. Yet, the members of the faction did believe that Jesus was the Messiah. Luke in the very sentence in which he condemns them by calling them Pharisees says they were believers (Acts 15:5). There is, however, no record of what for them exactly Jesus's messiahship consisted in, what it was for. Neither is there anything in the speech to be made by James the Elder at the Council meeting, their leader, that helps to elucidate this matter. It is noticeable that in that speech, as we have it, he does not mention Jesus at all while he does mention Moses. It all makes one supportive of the critical opinion Luke definitely had of the members of the faction. As just mentioned, he called them Pharisees. In his Gospel he tells us that Jesus explicitly called the Pharisees hypocrites (Luke 12:1), and in Luke 11:37–52 Jesus spares no detail describing what many forms the hypocrisy of the Pharisees took. Luke also recorded that at the meeting in Jerusalem, which the faction had had with Peter on his return from Caesarea, they had given him their full support and made the declaration that what he had said and done there meant "that God has granted life-giving repentance to the Gentiles also" (Acts 11:18). Possibly Luke recorded that statement of theirs in order to enable his readership to compare it with what in fact they were doing and saying in Antioch and what they said to the Antioch delegation when it arrived in Jerusalem for the Council meeting (15:5). They said one thing to Peter when he returned from Caesarea, and now said and did the exact opposite in Antioch.

We are not talking about anything shallow and superficial here, we are addressing the most important article of Christian belief, namely faith in Jesus as sole saviour. It wasn't a difference over marginal matters but theological difference at its most fundamental. What the faction wanted was for the Church to be Jewish both in faith and in observance. They had compromised in that they were now prepared to admit Gentiles into church membership, but they wanted them to adopt Judaic religious practices, to be circumcised and told to keep the Law, otherwise they couldn't be saved (Acts 15:1, 5). In effect, the faction wanted Christianity to be no more than a sect within Judaism.

Peter knew what was at stake. He will make that clear in his speech to the Council. It was a choice between Jesus and the Mosaic Law. The decision of the Council, given in the letter they were to send to Antioch, describes what the members of the faction were doing in frank and devastating language, as will be shown. Paul in his letter to the Galatians is both incisive and blunt. He exposes the faction comprehensively. He says that what they were preaching to the Galatians amounted to "a different gospel" (Galatians 1:6), and he states: "If anyone, even if we ourselves or an angel from heaven, should preach to you a gospel at variance with the gospel we preached to you, let him be anathema . . . I repeat, let him be anathema" (v. 8), which can be translated as "an outcast from Christ". It is in Galatians 5 that he is clearest. He follows what Peter had said at the Council and damns the Faction's attempt to impose the Law on Christians as "burdening them with the yoke of slavery" (v. 1); he warns his Galatian converts that "if you let yourselves be circumcised, Christ will be of no value to you at all . . . you will be alienated from Christ, fallen away from grace. For to us, our hope of attaining that righteousness which we eagerly await is the work of the Spirit through faith" (v. 5). Could anything be clearer than this? Paul is telling the Galatians that to accept circumcision in order to be saved is to reject Jesus as saviour, making Jesus "of no use" to them: "Christ will profit you nothing" (v. 2). He is so taken by the seriousness of the issue that at the end of the letter (6:11–16) he reaches out to his scribe, possibly it was Luke himself, snatches the pen and in his own hand writes: "Circumcision is nothing, not to be circumcised is nothing. The only thing that matters is new creation" (6:15).

And there is then that so subtle a statement of his, so full of meaning. He wishes peace and mercy on everyone in Galatia who takes what he has written as their guide, and adds that he wishes peace and mercy too "to the Israel of God" (v. 16). In using that expression he is totally radical in every original meaning of the word. He transforms the concept utterly. Paul, a Jew, a man who was to describe himself as "belonging to the strictest group in the Jewish religion, a Pharisee" (Acts 26:5), is here saying that in God's new creation, in the new Israel of God, the Israel God wants and has been his plan from eternity, the Law and all the observances that go with it, even including circumcision, count as nothing, and the only thing that does count is Christ and belief in him. He is saying something that would have been totally impossible for him even to imagine before meeting Jesus on the road to Damascus. He a Jew of Jews is saying that God's Israel is now not just the Jewish people but those who believe in Jesus no matter what tribe, what people, what language. It is a new Israel, a new creation, open to all humanity, of which the people of the Jews are a part, beloved of God indeed but no more and no less than the rest of mankind. In Galatians 2:21 he cries out: "If righteousness can be gained through the Law, Christ died for nothing!"; and his fundamental point, the belief he hangs everything on, is "God justifies the Gentiles (his own beloved Galatian converts) by faith" (3:8). "Those who have faith are blessed" (v. 9). "By faith we receive the promise of the Spirit" (v. 14).

There is another significant angle to what the members of the faction were asserting which needs to be highlighted if only in order to be repudiated. Luke 8:12 states that when the Samaritans whom Philip had been preaching to had come to believe "his good news about the kingdom of God and the name of Jesus Christ, they were baptized, men and women alike". What Luke was intending to convey when he wrote that statement has already been discussed, namely that Christian baptism is for both men and women. Women are given salvation as human beings as men are, and by means of the same rite and sacrament as men are given it. That is the Christian faith, our Christian faith. With baptism women enter precisely the same way as men do into the death and resurrection of Jesus; unlike the role circumcision has within Judaism, women do not become members of the body of Christ, which is the Church, through any instrumentality or agency of the male.

The Judaic faction in Jerusalem and Judea therefore was fundamentally undermining the significance of Christian baptism, in Christ, as Paul will say, and will say it explicitly against the members of this faction in the letter to the Galatians: "in Christ there is no male and female" (Galatians 3:28). The members of the Circumcision Faction, Christian though they were in believing Jesus to be the Messiah, but shallow in their understanding of what Christianity stood for, were transferring to women, indeed to the Church, the sexism of the Jewish religion. Not that the Jewish religion is alone in being sexist. In no way. Sexism was in all cultures of that time and is alive today in most religions. Just to take Christianity as an example: in the largest Christian churches half of their membership is denied access to the priesthood on grounds of gender. It is a fundamental misconception. Male genitals are for procreation, not for ordination. However, there is an important difference on this matter between Christianity on the one hand and Islam and Judaism on the other. With Christianity it is not a matter of dogma despite all or any papal statements; it is only a matter of time till women in the Catholic Church can be ordained to the priesthood and that will bring the sexism we Catholics have to live with at present in that respect to an end. But can modern Judaism, will modern Judaism, ever terminate the sexism that is entailed in their belief about circumcisions? And can, or will, Islam ever repudiate those verses of the Qur'an (4:34) which say that women are inferior to men while still maintaining that God wrote the Qur'an?

What the Circumcision Faction was doing was offensive and insensitive. Its membership must have known how unacceptable to the

Antioch Christians their assertions were. There was no way they wouldn't have known about what Barnabas had achieved in Antioch some four years earlier, and that since then both him and Paul, who had been preaching among the Gentiles in Asia Minor, had been happily settled in Antioch with fellow disciples a fair amount of time already (Acts 14:28). We shouldn't beat about the bush on this one. The faction was behaving outrageously. They were as insensitive as it can get. So it is little wonder they were met with "sharp dispute and debate", with Luke expressly saying that it was Paul and Barnabas who confronted them (15:2). The pair of them must have been tearing their hair out. It is not difficult to picture the scene; they were almost back to square one, the argument must have overflowed into prayer meetings, household meetings and whatever was the Antioch AD 49 equivalent of a coffee house or a pub frequented by the Christians of the city. In the end there was only one thing to do; the Antioch Christian community decided to send a delegation of its members, led by Paul and Barnabas, to go to Jerusalem "to see the apostles and elders about this question" (ibid.).

Luke does not tell us how agreement was obtained by the Antioch community from the apostles that such a meeting of apostles and elders should be convened. The apostles would have already been aware of the trouble and dissension in Antioch and likely also the church community would have asked them before it elected its delegation for the meeting if and how they would deal with it. The apostles after all were entering new and unfamiliar territory with this proposal that they possessed the authority to rule definitively on the matter, not least for the reason that, from what we know from what Luke relates to us, they had never done such a thing before. Doubtless they first convened separately and asked this question about themselves. That would seem to be implicit in the formula they put into the letter they sent to Antioch at the conclusion of the Council, namely: "It is the decision of the Holy Spirit and ourselves" (15:28). Both their employment of the word "ἔδοξεν" and their assertion of the participation of the Holy Spirit in and endorsement of their decision-making tell us that they gave the whole matter a lot of thought.

What the Council of Jerusalem did wasn't just to send a decision back to Antioch. Of equal importance was the decision of the apostles about themselves that they could rightly and legitimately, with full authority, do just that. Therewith they made a statement about the Church for all successive generations. It gave direction to the Church in its decision-making; it affirmed that there is authoritative leadership in the Church which is at one with the Holy Spirit; it locates that leadership within the Church; and it affirms that the Holy Spirit is present in the Church, inspiring and guiding. Christians believe that the Acts of the Apostles are part of the Word of God. Luke who wrote the Acts decided to leave out an immense amount of the Council's deliberations, but under the guidance of the Holy Spirit, he left in enough guidance for all future generations of Christians.

And so the apostles and elders in Jerusalem decided to hold a meeting "to look into the matter" (15:6). No agreement had been reached between the two sides in Antioch, so it was referred to Jerusalem for a final, a definitive, resolution. This would have suited both parties. For the Judaic faction Jerusalem was their heartland, where they had a lot of support, they might have felt they'd be playing at home. For the Gentile or non-Judaic faction members in Antioch there was Peter in Jerusalem, who, they would have known, would be supportive. He had already made it perfectly clear to the Circumcision Party (11:5–17) precisely where he stood on the matter and why, and of course that would have been made known to the Antioch church. The status of Peter was accepted by all. However, in the weeks and days leading up to the moment when "the apostles and elders would decide this matter" there was a lot of "fierce dissension and controversy" (15:2); and indeed up to the very day, indeed the hour, it was held, there would have been any amount of lobbying of him by one side and arguing with him by the other; and that could account for the suggestion of impatience, even annoyance, that would appear to be present in what Peter had to say to the Judaic faction when he made his speech at the Council.

What in reality it came down to was this: the newly founded Christian Church had now to decide definitively and authoritatively between two opposing propositions. One was to declare that salvation from sin (and sinfulness) was a gift of God through faith in Jesus Christ achieved by his death and resurrection, available to all humanity; it was to declare that Jesus Christ was "the lamb of God who takes away the sin of the world" (John 1:29). The other proposition was to say that salvation was achievable through the carrying out of the Law, above all through males, whatever their racial background, accepting circumcision and conforming to the religious culture and practices of the Jewish people. What the first Christians were confronted with was a profound alternative, one which for them was contrary to all their mental upbringing, that God himself was meeting them in Jesus, that it was his doing, not theirs, and that that meeting was not brought about by a long trek through religious rituals. For the first Christians it amounted to the mind-blowing realization that the old Covenant was at an end, to be replaced with the new Covenant, given by God in Jesus to all mankind, one that was irrespective of any nationality, race and culture. Peter in his speech at the Council would address that question, and address it definitively.

The Antioch delegation consisted of Paul and Barnabas, whom the community appointed, along with others whose names are not given. "They were sent on their way by the church and they travelled through Phoenicia and Samaria, telling the full story of the conversion of the Gentiles. The news caused great rejoicing among all the brethren there" (Acts 15:3). Now, there may well be more to this seemingly straightforward statement than meets the eye. The delegation of course would have been given a big send-off with all sorts of instructions about what to say and what to argue at the meeting with the apostles. And so they set out, and Luke specifies the route they took. It was the coastal route through Phoenicia, which was Gentile territory, and through Samaria, which was a province of heresy in the eyes of the orthodox Jews. As Luke makes clear, in both Phoenicia and Samaria provinces they found they were among friends. They would have had total sympathy and support from the Christians there who were delighted to hear about conversions of non-Jews made in Asia Minor. And it was likely that they weren't at all surprised to hear the account Paul and Barnabas gave of how the Jews in Pisidia Antioch, Lystra and Iconium had treated them. One might imagine them saying to the two men: "Well, what did you expect? Did you really think you could say the things you were saying in their synagogues and expect to get away with it. Wise up, brothers!" But they would then have been wined and dined and positively lionized. It is so easy to picture the reception the delegation would have been given, applauding them as they arrived and clapping them on their backs as they departed, with cries of: "Give it to 'em, brothers. When you get to Jerusalem, give it 'em straight; don't let them old stick-in-the-muds hold you back, tell them they've got to move on. Heavens above, they don't think, do they, that us so-called Gentiles should go in for circumcision and live like Jews? No way! When you get there, just make it perfectly clear to them that we're as much Christian as they are and we've no need to be Jewish." The situation makes one think about what Paul was to write to the Corinthians: "Christ is indeed a single body but has many members, and all the members are one body, for in one Spirit we were all baptized into one body, whether Jews or Greeks, when slave or free, with all drinking of the one Spirit, but the body is not made up of one organ but of many, the foot is not the hand, it is not the ear ... You are all the one body of Christ but each a limb or organ of it" (1 Corinthians 12:12–27).

With all these shouts of encouragement echoing in their ears, knowing how much the newly converted were placing their trust and their hopes in them, the Antioch delegation strode on and reached Jerusalem. It was a turning-point moment, one which was going to happen again and again in the history of the Christian Church. Christianity for the first time, but by no means its last time, though this time being the first time was the decisive one, had to decide where it stood in relation to the cultures of its fellow human beings. It had emerged within one culture and was now taking members in great numbers from other cultures. The culture it had emerged into the world from was that of Judaism; and Judaism identified its culture with its religion. It identified the constituents of its culture with the divine when in reality in whole or in part they were man-made: circumcision, kosher food, this festival and that festival, based on the changes in the agricultural year, attitudes towards women based on superior male physical power and/or the role of women in procreation, attitudes towards other nations and so on. The Judaic element in the Jerusalem church, as Luke records and as we have described, had confronted Peter when he returned from Caesarea after baptizing Cornelius and his household. God himself, as Luke described it to us twice and as Peter described it to the Judaic party, had admonished Peter with the vision of the sheet let down from on high containing everything that moved and wriggled and squawked and burrowed and flew. Nothing God has created is unclean, and that applies not just to birds and fishes and insects and bugs and the beasts of the woods and the fields but to all fellow human beings as well. That was some statement. That was some rebuke. The newly converted Christians of Syria, Phoenicia, Samaria, Cyprus and Asia Minor had their own cultures, and they could see no earthly reason why they should give them up and take on that of the Jews.

Little wonder that, as Luke tells us in Acts 15:3, the Antioch delegation passing through Phoenicia and Samaria "caused great rejoicing among all the brethren there". The advice of Pope Gregory the Great to Augustine of Canterbury as recorded by Bede in Chapter 30 of his *History of the English Church and People* is pertinent. "They—the English—are no longer to sacrifice beasts to the devil but they may kill them for food to the praise of God and give thanks to the Giver of all gifts for his bounty." In other words, wherever possible, the way of life of a people on becoming Christian should be retained. It is also interesting that Luke does not mention Judea when he listed Phoenicia and Samaria as two provinces where the Antioch delegation got a resounding reception, even though to get to Jerusalem it had to travel through it. Was the reception in some villages in Judea or from individuals here and there unwelcoming? Maybe here and there it was even hostile. The Circumcision Faction would definitely have had members in Judea.

# CHAPTER 23

# The Antioch Delegation
# Arrives in Jerusalem

As it turned out, the delegation reached Jerusalem, to be met with a warm welcome from one group and hostility from another. "They were welcomed by the church, the apostles and the elders" (Acts 15:4). It sounds like they had the support of the bulk of the membership of the Church in Jerusalem, the apostles included. Their support mattered. However, "Some of the Pharisaic party who had become believers came forward and said: 'They must be circumcised and instructed to keep the Law'" (v. 5). This was the Judaic faction and Luke was really expressing what he thought of them when he called them Pharisees. It was deliberate. After all, it was Luke who had recorded for us in his Gospel what Jesus had himself said about the Pharisees: "Beware of the leaven of the Pharisees; I mean their hypocrisy" (12:1). Luke is here invoking the Lord himself against them; and their hypocrisy in his eyes would consist in them presenting themselves as Christian when in fact in this most vital matter they were not. They were Christian in that they believed Jesus to be the Messiah. That, however, was not enough. To be Christian fully was to believe in Jesus as saviour without any requirement to observe the Law. The perspective the faction members had on justification and salvation, which they were preaching in Jerusalem and Judea and trying to impose on Antioch, was a harmful leaven. Luke had been with Paul three or more years after the Council at the moment when Paul had exploded in anger and wrote his fiercest epistle on hearing that members of the faction had gone into Galatia in defiance of the decision taken on the issue at the Council to try to persuade Paul's converts to adopt the Law if they wished to be saved. Luke was there when Paul dictated that epistle, and may even have been the one taking dictation from the apostle.

It was, then, both support and opposition that met the Antioch delegation on its arrival in Jerusalem. Before the Council meeting was formally started, there must have been any amount of discussion and argument, talk and disputation in every Christian household in the city, every church gathering, everywhere, entered into by every teacher, apostle, elder, married couples and families over dinner tables. That is how human beings behave; it was both natural and inevitable. The Antioch delegation must have roamed the meetings; Paul and Barnabas must have been in demand, with the members of the Judaic faction doing the same thing. It is not wild to believe that both sides met in debate here, there and everywhere, and the debates must have been intensely contested.

If beforehand in Antioch, as Luke reports in Acts 15:1, there had been "fierce dissension and controversy" between Paul and Barnabas on the one side and on the other the advocates from Judea of "circumcision in accordance with Mosaic practice"; and if the Christian communities in the provinces of Phoenicia and Samaria had welcomed and greeted the Antioch delegation on their way to Jerusalem with "great rejoicing" (v. 3), then how intense and widespread must the argumentation in Jerusalem itself have been, as the apostles made preparations for the meeting which would decide the issue. Luke, with his customary terseness and reserve, simply said: "The apostles and elders assembled to look into this matter" (v. 6). The atmosphere within the Jerusalem church must have been electric. The meeting naturally had its own dynamic, there was a lot at stake; and as best we can we have to work out what those present at it understood its status to be.

First of all the meeting was called and convened by the apostles and elders (Acts 15:6). They had done so because the issue had been referred to them for resolution by the brotherhood who made up the Antioch church (v. 2). That says three things: that the members of the local Antioch church accepted that they themselves were not empowered to resolve the matter, that they believed that the apostles and elders located in Jerusalem were so empowered and that the apostles and elders themselves believed they were so empowered. That is endorsed by verse

23. That verse restricts this empowerment to the apostles and elders. There is a fourth consideration. Having been asked by the church in Antioch to decide the issue as in verse 1, the apostles and elders did not go about it in any private manner. They held a "long debate", and verse 22 indicates that the apostles and elders were not the only people present at it. Luke tells us that "the whole church" (v. 22) agreed at the conclusion of the Council to choose representatives to send to Antioch together with Paul and Barnabas to convey to it the decision they had made. That might indicate that attendance was open to everyone. But did it include the women members of the Jerusalem church? We just do not know. Paul and Barnabas followed Peter's speech by describing "what signs and miracles God had wrought among the Gentiles through them" (v. 12), and to listen to them "the whole assembly became silent". The word assembly or crowd indicates a lot of people. How open to the Church membership we do not know, but it was certainly open to some extent and not just confined to the leadership. There is a reliable clue in the apostles' letter to the churches with which they concluded the meeting. It makes an interesting distinction between the two decisions the Council took. The second decision, as will be shown, was a doctrinal one and it was taken by the "apostles and elders" (v. 28). The first one was administrative, namely who would take the letter to Antioch, and that decision is described as having been taken by "the apostles and elders with the whole church" (v. 22). That definitely implies a much wider attendance than just the apostles and elders.

Luke tells us that once the Council was convened, there was "a long debate" (Acts 15:6). How long we just do not know. One day? Two days? Three? We do not know. It could well be that it was held in the house of Mary, the sister of Barnabas, which was big enough to hold a "large company" (12:12). Which apostles were there? Which elders? Of the Twelve we know that one was dead, James the elder brother of John who had been beheaded under King Herod (12:2). Which of the remaining eleven were at the meeting? While the only one mentioned is Peter, it is possible that Galatians 2:9 informs us that John was present. The only elder mentioned is James, the head of the church in Jerusalem, leader of the circumcision faction and a relation of Jesus, probably on his mother's side. All Luke gives us is two contributions, one from Peter and the other from James, together with the mention that Paul and Barnabas were called upon to describe their experiences in Cyprus and Asia Minor, though he does not give any actual details of what they said. But he hardly needed to. He had after all described their experiences and their missionary efforts in those two countries already. Luke also provides us with the text of the letter they agreed to send to Antioch. As a record that is all we have. We do not know how many drafts it went through. There is nothing casual about it, and its vocabulary is precise and carefully chosen. Despite what James and some Jerusalem church members did later (cf. Galatians 2:12), the letter makes the point that in the Council itself the decision the apostles and elders came to was "a unanimous one" (v. 25).

Though the letter states that "the whole church" was in support of the decision it conveyed to the churches of Antioch, Syria and Cilicia, Luke restricts mention of the names of participants just to Peter, James, Paul, Barnabas, Silas and Judas Barsabbas, but of course he had a good knowledge of who was there even though he most likely hadn't been there himself. He'd been in the company of Paul during his second and third missionary journeys and on Paul's visits to Antioch after both journeys; he was with Paul when Paul took the decision to take the gospel into Europe (Acts 16:11); he stayed with him after the third journey and accompanied him on his disastrous visit to Jerusalem; he remained with him during the two years he was under arrest there, and he was with him on the sea voyage to Malta and Rome and during at least the start of Paul's captivity in Rome. In all that time and in all those different places and circumstances he must have met with at least some of the apostles and the elders, and indeed others, who had been at the Council. What's more, Silas who attended the Council (15:22–32) was also with Paul on his second journey, and hence with Luke and there can be no doubt that the two of them, and Paul, and others too, talked about the proceedings and the significance of the Council time and again, place after place, the way people in such circumstances always do. The Second Vatican Council took place from 1962–65, over fifty years ago, and some of the people at it, either members of it or their theology assistants, known as *periti*, which is Latin for experts, can doubtless still be found talking about it to all and sundry as if it were yesterday. There can be little doubt whatsoever either that in the fifteen to twenty years between the death of Paul and his writing his Gospel and the Acts, Luke would have lived in or at least met with a number of church communities. He would have had every opportunity to hear detail upon detail about the Council, not least from the apostles themselves whom he must have met time and time again. The four-verse introduction to his Gospel, where he makes it plain he had done detailed research in order to write "a connected narrative" (v. 4), and where he informs us that he had also researched "the traditions handed down to us by the original eyewitnesses and servants of the Gospel" (v. 2), might well be considered testimony that he also would have made sure he possessed a wide, detailed and reliable knowledge of this important meeting before he wrote about it.

# CHAPTER 24

# The Council of Jerusalem is Convened

We can imagine the degree of ferment that the first Christians felt as the day of the Council approached. It wasn't just belief that was the issue, though as we will see that is what Peter addressed; it was also about the practicalities of a religious life, some of them everyday practicalities. A group of Judaic Christians, clinging to their Jewish way of life, wanted to impose on all Christians such things as circumcision, rules about what can and cannot be eaten, about whom one can meet and associate with, about the days and the ways of observing religious festivals and much more. Undoubtedly, by the year 49 the Jews themselves, for sheer common-sense reasons, had grown out of observation of the myriad of minutiae that any ruling priesthood can inflict on people, such as we get the flavour of in the books of Leviticus, Numbers, even Deuteronomy, and Nehemiah, but many of them were still being practised and simply were foreign and unacceptable to Christians of other cultures. They were, in Paul's words, "the yoke of bondage" (Galatians 5); they were fetters, purely man-made and serving no purpose in the matter of the relationship of God and man. Peter had already said so, as in Acts 11:5, and will be saying it again to the faction members in the course of the Council itself: "Why do you now provoke God by laying on the necks of these disciples a yoke which neither we nor our fathers were able to bear?" (15:10). What is also of interest is how both Peter and then Paul use the same words such as "yoke" when addressing this issue. A commonality of vocabulary had been established when it came to discussion of the issue. Words matter. An agreed vocabulary makes debate possible, it indicates a shared understanding.

In all of this monumentally important matter the basic issue is faith in what has been achieved by the Lord Jesus. That is what Peter will set before the Council: "We believe we are saved through the grace of the Lord Jesus" (Acts 15:11). Somewhere between fifteen and thirty years later the writer of the letter to the Hebrews will say: "Jesus Christ is the same yesterday and today and yes indeed, forever. So do not be swept off your course by all sorts of outlandish teachings. It is good that our souls should gain their strength from the grace of God and not from scruples about what we eat, which have never done any good to those who are governed by them" (Hebrews 13:8f.). Advice many a religion would do well to consider. And on that same basic theme Paul teaches: "In Christ Jesus neither circumcision nor un-circumcision has any value. The only thing that counts is faith expressing itself through love" (Galatians 5:6). Paul enlarges on this in Galatians 5:22f., when he writes about the "fruits of the Spirit". And on that same basic theme Paul teaches: "In Christ Jesus neither circumcision nor un-circumcision has any value. The only thing that counts is faith expressing itself through love ἐν γὰρ Χριστῷ Ἰησοῦ οὔτε περιτομή τι ἰσχύει οὔτε ἀκροβυστία ἀλλὰ πίστις δι' ἀγάπης ἐνεργουμένη" (Galatians 5:6). It is that "δι' ἀγάπης ἐνεργουμένη" which Paul enlarges on in 5:22f. that Luther and Calvin did not adequately take into account when formulating their doctrine of justification. It was a most regrettable, and fundamental, oversight on their part. The preaching of the Judaic faction on this issue amounted to nothing less than the total undermining of the significance of the death and resurrection of Jesus. Luther went to the other extreme. How the whole issue would impact on the religious life of each individual was also dealt with by Peter (Acts 15:10), and, following him closely, by Paul in Galatians 4:8–10 and 5:1. What was becoming more and more evident to Peter and his fellow apostles with every passing day was that the Judaism of their upbringing was incompatible with their following of Jesus.

What was happening was that the differing cultural perspectives of the Antioch Christians and the Jerusalem/Judea Christians were having their effect upon the new Christian religion. Antioch was the Empire's third largest city, a huge melting pot of different peoples, languages and cultures, a city vital in matters of trade within the Mediterranean basin. Jerusalem was nothing like that, it was so different, narrow and limited in comparison. The latter would confine Christianity to the Jews and those Gentiles who took on the Jewish way of life, the former would offer the Church to the world and every nation, embracing all cultures. Yet each in its own way came together in this matter. It was Antioch that requested the Council; it was at Jerusalem it was held; it was in Jerusalem the apostles wrote down the decision of "the Holy Spirit and ourselves"; it was to the melting pot that Antioch was that they sent it by letter. The divine journey of salvation was from the singular to the universal, God chose one nation as the vehicle of salvation to all nations.

"After a long debate Peter stood up" (15:6). Wherever it was held, whoever was present, whatever way it was organized, the first thing the Council did was hold that long debate. The word ζητήσεως is also translated as discussion and questioning, both of which can suggest a different sort of dialogue between the groups. Luke doesn't tell us one single thing about it other than that it happened, let alone who the speakers were and what they said. He restricts himself to relating just the concluding speeches of the representatives of the two sides. However, he had already spent 14 chapters of the history he was writing taking us through what had led up to the debate, what the issues were and who the participants were, so he undoubtedly felt his readership had been sufficiently informed, and besides some of them would have been present at it and many others would have heard lots about it by word of mouth anyway. For all that, it would have been more satisfying if he had brought in other personalities, with their names, and given us a broader description of the dynamics and the flavour of the event.

I believe that given the seriousness of the issues and who were present the debate must have been as fiery as it gets; and deeply emotional. They were Jews from head to toe, all of them, and always had been, and, indeed, never ceased to be. They all knew what was being asked of them, and one cannot but feel immense sympathy. The covenant between God and Israel, their nation, which made them special, made them the Chosen People, was being given to all nations; and circumcision, which for them symbolized that election, and their days of celebration and their rules and ritual of eating, and much more, all part and parcel of their very being, what they had learnt at their mother's breast and lived every day for all their lives, all that was now being declared unnecessary in how they related to their God. No one should have any doubt whatsoever that they were all being called on to make a break within themselves mentally, spiritually and physically which was as gut-wrenching as could be. It was no easy break they were being asked to make. Their Judaism had the most tenacious of holds on them.

We must make no mistake about it, what was achieved by these first Christians in the Council of Jerusalem and what Peter stood up before them to ask of them (Acts 15:7–11) was nothing short of heroic. We are all in their debt; and when it comes, as it now has done again in the history of the Church, to a similar situation we should learn from them. They are the foundation Church. They and its membership came from as conservative and as inbred a position as any in today's Church. For that reason they have set us an example. They put the Church and people first before their own instincts, they responded to the promptings of the Holy Spirit. This will be attended to later, but it does no harm to say here and now that all those people within the Roman Curia, not all of them of course but enough, those conservative forces within the Church who are digging in now in order to frustrate Pope Francis, the successor of Peter, a pope who is aware of the plight and the anguish of men and women caught up in the entanglements of our modern secular culture, can learn from the example set by the apostles and first Christians at the Council of Jerusalem. What does not change is doomed to lifelessness. As John Henry Newman wrote, "to live is to change, and to be perfect is to have changed often". Today's church leadership is being called to renounce some of their most ingrained ways of thinking and doing, ways inherited over centuries and taught them, accepted by them and practised by them as unchangeable, which, however, are not all unchangeable but in many cases are products of their times and not of the essence of the faith. Indeed they are proving to be irreconcilable with what our faith in our time is required to be. New times create new perspectives, different understandings. The apostles did it, today's church leadership now has to do it. There is nothing more being asked of the present church leadership in this matter than what was asked at Joppa and at Caesarea of Peter and of all the apostles at the Council of Jerusalem. At the Council they were faced with people who were resisting changes in the laws that gave expression to the only way of life they had known, a way of life which had been the lifeblood not just of themselves but of the apostles as well. Like the apostles today's leadership must "be led by the Spirit"; they must not just be "under the Law" (Galatians 5:18). "As we live by the Spirit, let us also walk with the Spirit" (v. 25).

The assertion made by members of the faction to the church members in Antioch that "unless you are circumcised in accordance with the Law you cannot be saved" was what was debated. It was about what salvation was. It was therefore as fundamental a disagreement over what Christianity was as one can possibly get. Luke had used two words to describe what happened in Antioch, namely dissension or argument and searching, inquiry, investigation. Luke describes them as "in no way small", but in different versions this is also translated as sharp and fierce. In verse 7, however, he uses only the one word "investigation", and not "argument", for the session that took place at the Council itself before Peter rose to speak. Luke describes that investigation as "big", which again gets various translations such as "much questioning" and "a long debate". Something might be read into this. It could mean that in addition to the very sharp debate that took place in Antioch between the Judaic faction, which wasn't just Judean in its membership but also had support in Antioch itself (cf. Acts 11:19), and those represented by Paul and Barnabas (15:2), there was also an investigation, namely each side had recourse to the Scriptures for the proof it wanted of the stand it was taking. Maybe Luke wanted to make the point that the dispute in Antioch was not just bitter argument but also, given the seriousness of what was in dispute, a very serious consideration of the Scriptures, particularly what kind of Messiah was to be expected, his relationship both to the people of Israel and the rest of humanity, the nature and the future of the covenant and the status of the Law. It was Christianity that was at stake in this Council.

# CHAPTER 25

# Peter's Speech

Luke completely leaves out any mention of whatever anyone else had to say except Peter and James; and even then, if there is one speech in all 28 chapters of the Acts which he summarizes ruthlessly, it is Peter's at the Council. Peter stood up to address the most fundamental issue of the Christian faith. He was repudiating what constituted the faction's whole idea about Jesus and what salvation consisted in and how it was achievable, and for all of that Luke allots him a mere five verses. Peter didn't get to his feet after the "long debate" (Acts 15:6), which must have been as stormy and passionate as it can get, just to utter five short sentences, but Luke focuses, ruthlessly, on what mattered most in what Peter had to say. It is an abridgement second to none, it is a masterpiece in distillation. What Peter had to say at the Council of Jerusalem was a statement of Christian belief of inestimable importance against the arguments of the Judaic faction which not only would have reduced Jesus to a figure of very secondary importance in God's plan for the salvation of mankind but would also have bound Christianity to Judaism as a mere sect.

In the Greek text, Peter's final words, as terse as it gets: "No, we believe that it is by the grace of the Lord Jesus that we are saved, and so are they" (Acts 15:11) are the summation of the Christian belief about salvation. The salvation of men and women, be they Jews or Gentiles, both from sin and the consequences of sin, has been wrought by Jesus, by nothing and nobody else; that is the Christian belief. On that briefest but solidly and absolutely rock-like statement of faith Christ founded his Church, and in it one of the people at the Council, Paul, listening to Peter, heard what was to be the foundation and framework of his own teaching. Paul built on Peter. His letters to the Galatians and the Romans are expositions of Peter's final 13 words, the last words of Peter which we have a record of.

The brevity, bluntness and baldness of the way Luke records Peter's speech lend it authority. Peter got to his feet; he stood up before the whole gathering; "he addressed them". "Addressed" as in the NET, the Revised New Jerusalem Bible and the NIV is far preferable to the "said" of the KJV and the "told" of the recent N. King translation. "Addressed" does justice both to the content of what Peter said to the Council members and to how he said it. He had risen to his feet, he looks at them all, and his tone of voice, which is eminently decipherable from the text, is authoritative and solemn. It is the defining moment of the Council. He faced the members of the Judaic faction seated before him, he told them in no uncertain terms that the version of Christianity they were trying to force on the Gentile converts was wrong. This is so important that what Luke has preserved for his readership from the original text has to be put in front of the reader with a literal word-by-word translation.

The statement is the first time in the life of the Church that the Church addresses its own membership in the person of the apostle, whom Luke, event by event, speech after speech, has presented as its leader, who authoritatively declares what its faith is on this specific but fundamental point. It is a declaration of the Church to the Church, nothing less. From the moment of the first Whit Sunday, the Pentecostal moment, the Church has been expanding its membership. First, its membership was orthodox Jews; it was then extended to Samaritan Jews, which caused some initial theological concern but they were reasonably smoothly accepted. Their males were already circumcised; and for the faction, as long as that was the situation, there basically was no problem. There were other important and defining elements such as dietary laws, observation of certain festivals, not mixing with non-Jews and suchlike to be dealt with, but circumcision was the most decisive defining feature and requirement as set out in Genesis 17:1–14. It was "the sign of the covenant" (v. 11) between God and Israel. And if we turn to Isaiah 52:1, we can get a further insight into the isolationist and divisive force that circumcision was to the mind of the Jewish people: "Awake, awake, O Zion, clothe yourself with strength. Put on your garments of splendour,

O Jerusalem, the holy city. The uncircumcised and defiled will not enter you again." Possibly that final sentence says it all.

As a consequence, what happened in Joppa, Caesarea, Antioch and Asia Minor, where Church membership had been extended to uncircumcised non-Jewish Gentiles, presented the most fundamental challenge possible to the understanding these Jews had of what the Messiah and God's people meant. The debate, disagreement and division within this Infant Church was a most natural and inevitable outcome. The Christian Church is an assembly of human beings, not of robots. Peter had thought, or at least had hoped, he had settled it when he returned from Caesarea to face the faction in Jerusalem. He had won their agreement to admitting Gentiles into Church membership only to be confronted by a twist in the tail. They were now coming up with what he rightly perceived to be a fundamental misrepresentation of the meaning of salvation. They wanted Gentiles to adopt Jewish religious practices as the condition of salvation; those practices, not Jesus, were the requirement for the forgiveness of sin and salvation. Just possibly the news the members of the faction had received when Paul and Barnabas returned from Asia Minor to Antioch that the two men had thrown "open the gates of faith to every Gentile" (Acts 14:27) had proved to be one bridge too far for the Judaic faction. After all, Cornelius, though not it seems a proselyte, was a "God-fearer", attended synagogues, presumably took part in the prayers and attended to the welfare of poor Jews in Caesarea. But throwing open the doors of faith to all and sundry among the Gentiles, "the uncircumcised and defiled", was going too far. Whatever the reason was, there was now recognition by the Church membership that this basic issue of faith had to be decided by its leadership.

It provides an important pointer for all succeeding generations: that in the life of this new Church there were leaders, whatever word might be used, that they have the authority to make decisions, and such matters cannot be left to drift, that there has to be unity of belief and practice on a major issue of belief. There simply was no acceptance here in this founding body when it was confronted, not with something minor or just arguable or somewhat different, but with a fundamental and decisive issue, that the Church could allow itself to live with conflicting views and practices. The founding body of Christianity, when it came to a fundamental issue of faith, was not "a broad church" if by that is understood toleration of differing beliefs which concern the fundamentals of the Christian religion. This is never a simple matter. Our faith develops and deepens in understanding and has to respond to changing times and cultures. Some wrong departures from the established norm are easy to spot, other departures are not and often have to prove themselves and sometimes they do. In the end, however, it is the successors of the apostles who in due course decide. The request made by the Antioch community, a local church as per Acts 15:2, was not fortuitous, it was incredibly instructive for all future generations of Christians as to how in such serious circumstances matters should be conducted; as was the response of the apostles to it. The authority of the apostles to decide was acknowledged and appealed to, and the formula used by them: "it appeared good to the Holy Spirit and to us" (v. 28) defined it. And it is inconceivable, it just would not be common sense, that the authority they exercised at Jerusalem died with them and was not transmitted.

Peter's four statements have to be carefully examined.

*1. "Men, brothers, you know that in the early days God made his choice among you that from my mouth the Gentiles should hear the word of the gospel and believe."*

What does this mean? In its way it can be taken as simple and straightforward. Or is there more to it than what meets the eye, as very often is the case in Luke's narrative? Is Peter saying no more than that, when he was in Joppa, God told him that he was to preach the gospel to the Gentiles despite all the reservations he had as a Jew, so that they might come to believe; and that is what he then did in Caesarea. We can be sure everyone attending the meeting would have had the benefit of hearing about all the details of what happened to him in Joppa and Caesarea, precisely what God had said to him in Joppa, and what had happened in Caesarea, what he had preached and done there, and that the outcome was that for the first time Gentiles had been preached to, had believed and had been baptized. Is the statement just that or is there more to it? How do we read Peter's opening statement made to his fellow

Jewish Christians that it was from him, out of all of them, that by God's choice the Gentiles should first hear the gospel?

The answer given to that question by Lumby in his detailed commentary on the Acts (cf. bibliography) is that God's choice of Peter shows Peter "to be putting himself and his fellow apostles on the same level with the whole Christian body which he is addressing. God might have chosen whom he would to receive the instruction of the sheet let down from heaven . . . and with the phrase 'by my mouth' he may not seem to be claiming a distinction for himself as the one chosen of God for this work. Peter is careful to call himself no more than a mouthpiece of God".[16] Dr Lumby, whose theological position is Anglican and Protestant, is as well aware of the theological implications of different ways of interpreting this statement by Peter as anyone can be, and, as will be evident from his comment on it, comes down firmly on the side of the interpretation that what Peter says about himself should not be read to suggest he has any special leadership status among the apostles or the Christian body generally.

Such an interpretation is very hard, however, to justify. The evidence does not support it. We must first look at the way Luke introduces what Peter has to say. "The apostles and elders met to consider the question. After much debate Peter stood up and addressed them" (Acts 15:6f.). Luke clearly intends to present Peter's judgement of the issue at the very least as an important statement; in fact, as the Council's letter to the churches will inform us, the decisive one since it is the one it sends to Antioch. Emphatically Peter reminds his hearers of the position he holds in the Church. In this matter, he says, God, who indeed could have chosen any one of them, particularly any one of the Twelve, to make the Joppa revelation to and then to carry out in Caesarea what it stood for, actually chose him specifically because of the position he held by God's decision within the Church. I would suggest, for the reasons that follow, that Peter knew why, they all knew why. He knew, they all knew, what his position and status was among them; he knew, they all knew, how in different ways Jesus had singled him out during his ministry, as in due course was to be recorded in the gospels, specifically in Matthew 16:18 and John 21:15.

The evidence is as follows. As we have seen, Luke presents Peter time and again as leader and spokesman for the apostles and the Church, firstly in the meetings they held immediately after the Ascension, at one of which under his chairmanship and direction they elected Matthias to succeed Judas Iscariot, then when addressing the Jewish pilgrims on the feast day of Pentecost, then in the temple, in performing a miracle, then on both occasions before the Council of the Jews when they were twice arrested and imprisoned, in Samaria when Philip made converts, and most significantly in Joppa which was followed by speeches and events in Caesarea. Luke goes on to describe Peter's decision-making role in Jerusalem when confronted by the Judaic faction after Caesarea. It is because of all of this that it is not reasonable to read Peter's statement to the Council merely as one anyone else could have made. It is correct, of course it is, that God could have chosen another apostle for all these things but God didn't; and it was in the presence of the other apostles that Jesus said to Peter that he was the rock on which he would build his church and that to him he would give the key to the kingdom of heaven. It all amounts to an immense donation of authority and status. All the above items which I am putting forward as evidence have to be considered together. It was God's doing, not Peter's. God's choice of him, not just on this occasion but over a long period and in many critical moments and events, as Luke narrates, endowed him with an authority no one else had. He was himself fully aware of it. That is the very point of his statement in Acts 15:7. With hindsight we can say that that verse is one of the most important verses in all the Bible. My reading of it seems quite reasonable. Peter's opening words to the meeting are an assertion of his possession of the authority to rule on the issue before it. As we will see, his statement in verse 11, the words he uses, show precisely that. It is a separate matter, however, one which does not concern us here, whether or not his authority was handed on at his death to anyone else, and if it was, how and to whom.

In the circumstances that the Church was in as originating in Judaism the decision to open the membership of the Church to Gentiles required authorization. That was given by God through Peter, and everything followed from it. Joppa and Caesarea were where it happened, Joppa because of what was said by God to Peter, and Caesarea because of what Peter did in response, which was endorsed by the Holy Spirit (Acts 10:44–48); and that was what enabled Barnabas and Paul to go out and "open the door of faith to the Gentiles" (14:27) in Cyprus and then in Pisidia Antioch, Iconium, Lystra and Derbe in Asia Minor.

2. *"And God, who knows the heart, bore witness to them by giving the Holy Spirit to them just as he did to us. And indeed he made no distinction between us and them, cleansing their hearts by faith."*

But Peter hadn't gone through long hard debates with the faction before the Council was convened not to know that there was something more to what it was arguing for than whether or not Gentiles could be admitted through baptism into the Church. Be it reluctantly or not, the faction, certainly not the majority of its members, were no longer opposing that anyway, and, given how the Church had already developed, they could do nothing about it. But Peter knew, and this had been argued with them hour after hour before the meeting started, that they had something else in mind, and he was now going to settle that with them as well. What they wanted was a different sort of church from what he had brought the Gentiles of Caesarea into, and he wasn't having any of it; and he had his reasons and he had his proof.

There has to be some clarity, as best as we can get it, about what the Judaic faction stood for, at least to the extent that we can ascertain it from what Luke in the Acts and Paul in Galatians and Romans tell us. What the faction wanted was a church which believed that God's way to mankind and mankind's way to God was the practice of the Law. We have to re-read the texts given to us: "Some men came down from Judea to Antioch and were teaching the brothers: 'The Gentiles must be circumcised and required to obey the Law'" (Acts 15:5), "Unless you are circumcised according to the custom of Moses, you cannot be saved" (v. 1). James the leader of the faction was later to describe its adherents as "zealous for the Law" (21:20). They held that a man is justified in the eyes of God and reconciled to him, not by faith in Christ Jesus but by observing the Law (Galatians 2:16), and in particular through the rite of circumcision (Acts 15:5) as set out in Genesis 17, with other rituals and prescriptions as already listed and described; that a man receives the Spirit not by believing in the gospel preached to him (Galatians 3:2–5) but by observing the Law; and he is saved not through the grace of the

Lord Jesus (Acts 15:11) but by observing the Law (v. 1). In contrast the Church in the person of its apostles preached that it is by faith in Christ Jesus that we have received the Spirit (Galatians 3:14) and have become sons of God (v. 26), that it is through the grace of the Lord Jesus that we are saved (Acts 15:11), and that we are reconciled to God by the grace of the Lord Jesus, namely his death and resurrection. The letter (vv. 22–9), which, as we will see, the Council sent to their fellow Christians, their "Gentile brothers", in Antioch, Syria and Cilicia, described in no uncertain terms the irreparable damage to their faith that the faction would have brought about if it had got its way. All that was what Peter had to deal with, which he was now doing in what he was saying to the Council, a speech drastically reduced by Luke, regrettably. However, Luke has left us enough to be able to appreciate the seriousness of the issue.

We really have no definite idea what form the argument between the two sides took as the Council proceeded, whether it was noisy and intemperate or polite and restrained despite the gulf of difference between them. One would certainly hope it wasn't language-wise as unfettered as chapter one of Paul's letter to the Galatians, but in fairness to Paul he had every reason to lash out in that letter. Members of the faction, despite what had been agreed at the Council, had journeyed all the way to Galatia to press their beliefs on his converts. They were replacing Jesus with the Law. If at the Council he had spoken to the members of the faction in the same way, the argument between the two sides must have been a very angry and bitter one. However, Barnabas was there to restrain him and Peter, going by Acts 15:12, would have assured Paul he'd have every opportunity to have his say. It is interesting, however, that Luke with that verse tells us that "the whole assembly fell silent as they listened to Barnabas and Paul". Possibly that implies that the meeting had till then in fact been noisy and tense, with all sorts of interruptions when someone was speaking. What was at stake was the very nature of the Church and the role of Jesus in God's plan of salvation. The dispute was serious, very serious, it was precisely what Peter addressed himself to. For him salvation was in and through Jesus, nowhere else. Jesus saves humanity, nothing else does. Jesus reconciles man to God, nothing else does. As we can say it now, though I doubt Peter saw it this way at the time, God reconciles men and women to God. The argument he put to the meeting has to be understood.

"God, who knows the heart," Peter said to the meeting, "shows that he accepted them (the Gentiles) by giving the Holy Spirit to them just as he did to us (Jews)." There are two things to note here. One is, Peter and his circumcised fellow Christians, who accompanied him first from Joppa to Caesarea and then to Jerusalem, had witnessed the descent of the Holy Spirit upon Cornelius and his family and fellow officers. "While Peter was still speaking these words, the Holy Spirit came on all who heard the message. The circumcised believers who had come with Peter were astonished (taken out of themselves) that the gift of the Holy Spirit had been poured out even on the Gentiles, for they heard them speaking in tongues and praising God" (Acts 10:44–6).

What Peter wants his audience to realize, especially the members of the faction, is that the Holy Spirit had descended on people who had not been circumcised, who had never observed the Law, some of them might possibly have never even heard of it. In other words, in view of what they all saw happening, God's gift of the Spirit was in no way dependent on being Jewish and observing the Law. And in that argument there was on Peter's part, on the part of a Jew faithful to his upbringing and faith, the hard, difficult, almost unacceptable implication, that that applied to his listeners too, the great majority of whom, if not all of them, were Jews. That is the really big thing Peter and co had to consider and accept. For all their upbringing, for all their years of faithful observance of the Law, they too hadn't received the Holy Spirit on that fateful day, that glorious day, on Pentecost Sunday, because they were Jews and because of their religious behaviour to date, but purely by the grace of God through belief in Jesus. Peter's words were: "God showed his approval of them (the Gentiles) by giving the Holy Spirit to them as he did to us." Think about it. Over a thousand years of circumcisions, of all sorts of other rituals, of temple worship and prayers, of hanging on to belief in him throughout all kinds of trials and disasters, had most certainly prepared Jews for the form reconciliation with God took, but none of it, either individually or collectively, had brought that reconciliation about. God himself had, through the death and resurrection of Christ. This statement of Peter made an immense impression on Paul, and his reflections on it are to be found in his letter to the Romans, especially Chapters 4 to 7. They have to be read and re-read, and read out loud. The Gentiles in Caesarea had received the Holy Spirit just as they had done. If God "made no distinction between us and them because he purified their hearts by faith", it meant that it wasn't their observance of the Law, no matter how long his fellow Jewish Christians had observed it, but it was by the pure gift of God of faith. It doesn't take much for us to imagine what the members of the faction felt when Peter said that to them, and said it bluntly to them.

Significantly, this phrase "God who knows the heart" occurs only twice in the Acts, the first time in Acts 1:24 when the eleven apostles are praying for guidance when making their choice of Matthias as the replacement for Judas Iscariot. Peter is stating that God, who knows the mind and intentions of everyone, is affirming that in their hearts and minds the Gentiles who have professed faith in Jesus are as genuine and sincere as they themselves are. They too have received the gift of the Holy Spirit from God and the proof of that is what he Peter and others witnessed in Caesarea, how they responded to that gift, how they behaved in their response, just as he and his fellow Jewish Christians did on Pentecost Sunday and the Samaritan Jews did before Peter's and John's very eyes (Acts 8:14–17). The presence of the Holy Spirit within them was revealed and proved by how they behaved. In truth, Peter is saying to his Jewish audience, God is treating these Gentiles as he has treated himself and his fellow Jewish Christians, in exactly the same way, producing exactly the same responses which prove that God was working in them in exactly the same way as he had worked in their hearts and minds. Whatever gifts God has given to his Jewish people he has given to Gentiles, even the gift of his Holy Spirit itself. The Holy Spirit had descended on Whitsunday upon them all "in tongues of fire, resting on each one of them and they were all filled with the Holy Spirit and they began to talk in other tongues as the Spirit gave them power of utterance" (2:1–4). That was a defining moment, a moment of immense and indescribable significance. But, says Peter, it was not the only one. The same happened again with the Gentiles. The gift of the Spirit, the descent of the Holy Spirit upon them, was the same for them as the descent of the Spirit was for the apostles and for the very first Christians on the day of Pentecost; "The Holy Spirit was given to them as He was given to us."

What Peter is saying has the widest possible implications. He is saying that our salvation and the descent of the Spirit upon us and into us is not in any way our achievement. It is purely God's gift, on offer to everyone, even the little child who knows nothing about it, dying from Ebola, totally unknown and abandoned in West Africa, with its parents and family members dying all around it, a child of no significance, naked and suffering, unaware of itself even—about that desolate child he is saying to us that its baptized state is the descent of God the Holy Spirit upon it, as full and replete with grace as everything that happened to the apostles on that first Whitsunday. It is one almighty statement. It is both the most resounding assertion of spiritual democracy ever, and the most uplifting. A great crowd of pilgrims, Luke has told us, from Parthia, Mesopotamia, Judea, Cappadocia, Pontus and Asia, Phrygia and Pamphylia, Egypt, and Libya, from Rome and Crete and all across Arabia, "peoples drawn from every nation under heaven" were there in the temple square in Jerusalem to meet them when the apostles emerged and proclaimed the gospel to them, while only gloved and fumigated hands wielding a spade, faces hidden behind masks, shovelled the little dead body into a broken box or onto discarded pieces of contaminated clothing and hurried it away and buried it in a shallow grave, forever unknown. But, says Peter, speaking to us across the ages, that child is known to God, God knows the child by name, the child is with God, and the Holy Spirit of God dwells in it as much and as lovingly and as intensely and as intimately as in the highest and the mightiest as we rank them; and now dwells with God and sees him as he is, and forever.

God knows us all by name, we are all, no matter who we are, dearer to him than any sparrow, his spirit embraces us with his love as dearly and eternally, as passionately, as ever this child's grief-stricken mother and father and brothers and sisters did. God, Peter is saying to us, does not ask what nation we come from or what land or country we live in. "God has no favourites" (Acts 10:34). Paul repeated that very statement, as we have seen, in Romans, and before that there is his proclamation in Galatians: "there is no such thing as Jew or Greek, slave or freeman, male and female, you are all one in Christ Jesus." Luke is always so concise, so curt, so compressed in his style it can positively hurt. He leaves it to his reader to jump the gaps and connect up the themes. He now follows up with Peter's words: "And indeed God made no distinction between us and them, cleansing their hearts by faith." Peter is now addressing the issue the Council was convened to deal with, namely to choose between the Judaic understanding on the one hand and his understanding on the other, of what it is that brings about reconciliation of humanity to God.

Peter asks his audience to recall what he had told them about the vision he had had at Joppa. The hunger he had felt at that moment stood for the hunger of mankind for salvation; and on offer at that moment was a choice between the kosher food being prepared in that Joppa household and the food lying and wriggling in the sheet let down from heaven. The kosher food represented the Jewish people, the creatures in the sailcloth represented all of humanity in all its variety, Jew and non-Jew, male and female, slave and freeman.

As up to that Joppa moment it could have been that Peter himself had believed that what was on offer from God through Jesus was salvation to Jews and anyone else who conformed to the Jewish way of life and to no one else. There is nothing in what he had preached up to the Joppa moment that ruled that out. But in Caesarea Cornelius had fallen on his knees before him and Peter made him stand up. "I am a man like anyone else," he said to him. Then, "Still talking to him Peter went in and found a large gathering. He said to them: 'I need not tell you that a Jew is forbidden by his religion to visit or associate with a man of another race; yet God has shown me clearly that I must not call any man profane or unclean'" (Acts 10:28). He had pondered on the Joppa vision and the words he had heard as the sheet descended and hovered before him. Journeying between Joppa and Caesarea he had come to understand that the salvation brought by Jesus was not dependent at all on observance of the Jewish way of life or any physical or cultural or religious association with Jews or Judaism, that the contents of the sheet stood for all humanity which included the Jewish people, but included them just as it included any other, no more, no less.

The Christian Church in the person of Peter was making its choice. Peter was all too aware of this. He is forthright in both understanding and obedience. "God made no difference between them and us," said Peter to his fellow Jews. It is most emphatic. "What we are," Peter says, "they are, and what they are, we are," and that coming from a zealous Jew is one great statement. "It was faith and not observing the Law that purified our hearts," he says. "And in the same way it is faith and not observance of the Law that purifies and will purify the hearts of Gentile Christians." Only a couple of years later Paul will say the same thing to his Galatian converts who were under immense pressure from recalcitrant Judaic elements from Jerusalem, men he calls "outcasts" (Acts 1:8). He says it with a most incisive addition of phrase: "If we are in union with Christ Jesus circumcision makes no difference at all, nor does the absence of it. The only thing that matters is faith, achieving its effects through love" (Galatians 5:6). And that is the New Testament statement that could have reconciled both sides in the Western Church in the early sixteenth century, that Galatian statement, and would have if there had been eyes to see and ears to hear.

3. *"Now, therefore, why are you tempting God by putting a yoke upon the neck of the disciples which neither our fathers nor ourselves were able to bear?"*

Peter would surely have been taking his time, what he had been saying had to sink in, the Judaic faction needed time and for that reason he will shortly call on Paul and Barnabas to describe exactly what they experienced on their first missionary journey in Cyprus and Asia Minor and how the Gentiles there converted to faith in Jesus. We can easily visualize him at this point in his speech, pausing to look at all his fellow Christians assembled before him, wordlessly saying to them: "Now, there you have it. That, brothers, is it. I can allow no deviation on this matter. What I have said to you, God said to me. Yes, we are Jews but that is not what matters any longer. We have seen that in the way the Spirit of God showed itself to be in Gentiles despite them not adopting anything prescribed by the Law. What matters is faith in Jesus, he has removed all differences between us and everyone else, the Gentiles are us and we are them, their faith is as good as ours and they are the objects of the concern of God and the salvation achieved by Jesus as much as we are."

We have to see that assembly of people for what it was. Really, a tiny gathering, minuscule, a few dozen, maybe a few more, as tiny a number of people out of the millions inhabiting the planet as one can get, who believed that a man who died a few years earlier in a most dreadful manner died for every single soul who had lived and was living and will live, anywhere and everywhere, believing that their faith in him was the one faith that mattered for the whole world. Not one single person in that gathering was of any importance as far as the rest of the world was concerned, not one was known outside of his and her family and friends and the tiny religious group that they now belonged to. Anyone looking in out of curiosity from outside the room and listening a little while would have thought they were weird, and their faith one monumental piece of arrogance; and as for the god they were talking about, well there was neither sight nor sound of it, him or her, nothing other than a figure of their own creation.

It is with the words "Now why do you persist in tempting God" (Acts 15:10) with which he then continues that Peter makes it absolutely clear whom specifically he is addressing. He was choosing his words carefully. He could see that the faction, or at least some of them, were still resisting, and to them he addressed one of the harshest criticisms possible within the Jewish religious culture and history. He accuses them of "tempting God" (KJV) or "challenging God" (NET) or "testing God" (NIV and King), "putting God to the test" (Revised Jerusalem). The people he was addressing his words to in the room knew exactly what he was getting at, and he knew they did. The faction knew exactly what the implication of his words was. He was accusing them, before the whole assembly, who were now listening with bated breath, of distrusting the guidance of God and consequently of disobeying God's revealed will. There wasn't a soul in the room that missed his intent or failed to identify whom he was addressing. They were all Jews who knew their scriptures and their nation's history.

Peter was invoking Psalm 95 (Hebrew numbering, Greek numbering 94). It consists of eleven verses. Luke gives us only a little of it, no more than the one verse and the bit that is given above. We cannot be certain of course how much of the psalm Peter himself actually quoted to them, we will never know. One thing, however, is certain, there wasn't a soul in the room who wouldn't have recognized the relevance the psalm had for what they were concerned with; and Peter had already made it clear that he was speaking with the authority of God himself, that his voice on this matter was God's voice. It is helpful therefore if verses 6 to 11 of the psalm are quoted.

> Come, let us bow down in worship, let us kneel before the Lord our maker; for he is our God and we are the people of his pasture, the flock under his care. Today, if you hear his voice, do not harden your hearts as you did at Meribah, as you did at Massah in the desert, where your fathers tested and tried me, though they had seen what I did. For forty years I was angry with the generation. I said "They are a people whose hearts go astray, and they have not known my ways". I declared an oath in my anger: "They shall never enter my rest".

Peter was pulling no punches, his message to the meeting was crystal-clear: anyone persisting in challenging the declared will of God to open up membership of his people to Gentiles, without imposing conditions that are impossible to meet, was committing the sin of the Israelites at Meribah and Massah in the wilderness, the sin of sheer obstinacy to God's declared will. Meribah and Massah—two places, two events, that resonated in Israel's story. The hearts of the people thinking of doing this have gone astray, they themselves will no longer belong to God's people, it will be they who will cease to live in the peace and the restfulness of God's household. If, says Peter, if we Jewish people are to remain within the people of God, we must leave the desert of our inherited understanding of what God's people now is and enter a new Promised Land in which the Gentiles now live as full of the Holy Spirit as we are. Gentiles, says Peter, are now God's people and God's flock equally with all and any Christian of Jewish origin. There is now in God's eyes neither Jew nor Gentile but only one person in Christ Jesus the Lord. Let no one underestimate what it took for Peter to say this. Hundreds of years of the Jewish faith flowed through his veins. Yet, his words were as blunt as they could get. It was God, not they, who decides who are his people and if despite the evidence they hardened their hearts and persisted in challenging and testing him (NET), God would cast them into the wilderness.

One is inclined to think that at this moment Peter recalls to himself how, despite the agreement the faction had given to what he had done in

Caesarea, they had then gone back on it and sent their people to Antioch to stir things up against it. They were not to be trusted. That could be the reason why the phrase he begun this third sentence with, "now therefore", is so important. He had presented the evidence, namely the vision he had had at Joppa, the action of the Holy Spirit upon and within Cornelius and his household members and its effects upon them which he and others had witnessed, the same with Gentile converts in Antioch, Syria and Cilicia who had asked the apostles to resolve the matter, and of course the argument of his own authority with which he had opened his statement to the Council. The evidence was there for them all to see, it was incontrovertible. So: now therefore, he beseeched his fellow Jews within the faction, for your own sakes, for the sake of the Church, for the sake of the Gentiles, accept the evidence and stay with us.

But Peter saw that there was more to it even than just that. For him the issue also revealed the Judaic faction to be guilty of a cruel hypocrisy. Beyond doubt what he had in mind was Jesus's very forthright denunciation, later to be recorded in Luke 11:39–46, of the Pharisees for the cruel hypocritical way they treated the poor, for their neglect of justice, their pride, and above all in respect of Peter's condemnation of them, for "loading people down with burdens they can hardly carry and not lifting a finger to help them" (Luke 11:46). We must also keep in mind that Luke had himself already described members of the Judaic faction as belonging to "the Pharisaic party" (15:5). Peter's strong criticism of them here was that they wanted to impose a version of Christianity upon non-Jewish Christians that was more than what they themselves were prepared to practice, and they were doing it in order to preserve as much Jewishness in Christianity as possible; and that, said Peter, constituted a challenge to God's direction and purpose. It was defiance of God, it could not and would not be tolerated. It wasn't just that any performance of Judaic rituals was not compatible with Christianity if, and this is an important "if", as we shall soon see, if faction members continued to believe them to contribute towards reconciliation with God and justification—"the gift of righteousness" (Romans 5:17). Romans 5 and 10 are required study in respect of this matter. The Council, as we will soon see, will not rule that the rituals cannot be performed any longer, its concern is how they were to be understood. They are not salvific, only

Jesus is. They were to be understood as part of the spiritual tutelage, even bondage, of humanity until "God sent us his own son, born of a woman, born under the Law, to purchase freedom for the subjects of the law, in order that we might attain the status of sons" (Galatians 4:4), by which he meant spiritual maturity and freedom. As Peter said, the requirements involved in the ritual were "a yoke that neither we nor our fathers have been able to bear" (15:10). They were not what Christianity was about. The new wine of Christianity could not be put into old wineskins. God's new revelation has changed everything.

4. "No, we believe that it is by the grace of the Lord Jesus that we are saved, and in the same way so are they."

This is Peter's final statement, the very last words recorded of him in Christian history. With just the one word "no" or "but" he decisively, cleanly and comprehensively rejects the understanding of the Judaic faction of salvation, which had indeed been the one he himself and all his fellow apostles and elders had been born into and had believed. With the few words that follow, as succinct a statement of Christian belief as can possibly be imagined, he sets down what is the true nature of divine salvation. Salvation from sin and reconciliation with God is the work of Jesus Christ alone, and it is there for both Jews and Gentiles in the same way. It is what Paul will develop, expound and preach as from that moment and which the Church has expounded and preached ever since. Therewith Peter is silent. The sentence is his final "credo", it is succinct, it is authoritative; and in its way a very simple declaration. The matter was now closed.

What is important to note, however, is that Peter does not say "But I believe". Instead he says "But we believe". He is speaking for the Church of Jesus Christ, for every generation of Christians who are to follow, which is what his Christ-given status authorized him to do. He is saying what our creed is. With his final words he sends out to the Christians of Antioch, Syria and Cilicia, who represent all humanity, the assurance that they had asked for, that salvation from sin and reconciliation with God was wrought by Jesus on behalf of all men and women, whatever their race or their culture, faith in Jesus, trust in Jesus as Saviour brought with it the grace of the Lord Jesus, the saving favour of the Lord, the divine gifts which Peter had set before the pilgrims on the feast of Pentecost years before in his first public speech: "the forgiveness of sins and the gift of the Holy Spirit" (Acts 2:38). Upholding that, he underwent martyrdom. These words of his, and what he had already done in guiding the Church in its first years of existence as Luke has described them for us, is his gift to us. We are in his debt, all of Christianity ever since and everywhere is in his debt.

## CHAPTER 26

# The Contribution of Paul and Barnabas

It is as if, in the way Luke arranges his account of what happened next at the Council, he was marking the end of one significant stage in the life of the Church and ushering in the next. Peter has now done his job and Luke directs his spotlight elsewhere. Paul and Barnabas now take his place. Peter has laid down, as in indestructible concrete, the singular most important foundation stone on which the Church was built. That done, Luke turns to Paul and Barnabas. Though Barnabas will drop out as soon as Luke's account of the Council's proceedings is complete, as of that moment he and Paul represented the growth and expansion of the Church and the future of Christianity which by implication was what the Council was all about and will now make possible. The two of them had already taken the gospel to the Gentiles. They were of course in no way the only missionaries, then or after the Council had ended and its attendees had departed and dispersed. We know that from many references both in Luke's narration and Paul's epistles. But as of that moment, in that Council meeting, because they had just come back from Asia Minor, they stood out. Peter turned to them; he invited them to tell the meeting what they had done, what they had experienced, and what they had achieved; and "at that the whole assembly fell silent and listened to Barnabas and Paul as they told of all the signs and miracles that God had worked among the Gentiles through them" (Acts 15:12).

Because of the narrative he had already written, namely Acts 13 and 14, Luke obviously felt he had no need to tell us anything at all about what Paul and Barnabas had to say to the meeting. There is something more to it, however. We must keep in mind that the Council of Jerusalem was no spontaneous event, just as, for example, the annual Glastonbury Festival isn't. For Glastonbury and its huge TV audience it looks spontaneous, even at times anarchic. But it is nothing of the sort. An immense amount of planning and preparation go into it. Peter and co had obviously given a lot of thought to how to get a coordinated agenda together. They were taking no chances. They had to see to it that the correct theology of redemption was endorsed and that what the Judaic faction was arguing for was repudiated. Such an outcome, however, could not be taken for granted, and it was for that reason Paul and Barnabas were called upon to follow Peter. The gospel the two men had preached and what they had experienced in Cyprus and Asia Minor, particularly in Pisidia Antioch, lent support to what Peter had already said to the assembly; it was a very powerful supplement to what he had experienced in Joppa and Caesarea, so that by the time the senior Jerusalem presbyter James had the floor the outcome was decided.

However, the members of the faction were members of the Church, and Peter and his fellow apostles wanted them to remain in it. For that reason they wanted them to hear what Paul and Barnabas had to tell them, which till now they, or at least some of them, might not have had the opportunity of doing, at least not in any orderly way. Very likely quite a number of them had heard only snatches as their supporters and their opponents had exchanged opinions in the build-up to the meeting, either quietly or ferociously, in all sorts of places across the city. Not just them of course; everyone in the Jerusalem church and from elsewhere needed to hear it too. Since arriving back from Asia Minor Paul and Barnabas had gone to Antioch and stayed there; and though they had now been in Jerusalem for a few days at least, meeting with members and talking to them, this was the first formal opportunity for members of other churches like Jerusalem to see them and hear them themselves, and possibly especially the members of the faction. Peter and his fellow apostles wanted to keep the faction on board. For that reason it would seem, though this is guess work, what the two men were probably asked to concentrate on was "the signs and wonders that God had brought about among the Gentiles through them" (Acts 15:12). The agenda was not just to give the reasons why the demands of the Judaic faction were a serious misrepresentation of the role of Jesus for humanity, but also to demonstrate that without any performance of the demands of the Law the Gentiles were already benefiting from conversion, were already the object of God's largesse and miracles, that the Spirit was already openly at work among them, that they were finding joy, salvation and meaning in their lives from their belief in Jesus. God was already "working signs and wonders among the Gentiles". The evidence was there for all to see that neither God nor the Gentiles needed the Law for the latter to be full active members of the Church and be imbued with the Holy Spirit.

What definitely comes across from Luke's account of the Council, from the letter that was sent to the Syrian and Cilician churches, is that Peter and co weren't into point-scoring. As we will see shortly, James and his party had to make a massive climb-down on their version of the nature of the messiahship of Jesus. They didn't only get next to nothing out of the Council but they also had to face up to a very positive rejection of their position and their demands, but they didn't have their noses rubbed in it. Peter wanted them on board, the Church wanted cohesion and unanimity, and for that reason the letter was couched in such a way that, though it expressly described how harmful the demands of the faction were, it could not be described as showing the slightest desire to antagonize or alienate or humiliate the members of the faction. Indeed, quite the opposite. They were fellow Christians; they too had taken the brunt of the antagonism of their fellow Jews by openly professing faith in Jesus as the Messiah, and at least one of them, James their leader, maybe even more than just him, belonged to the family of Jesus. In the letter to Antioch there is in fact a degree of compromise, which in Jerusalem later on, as recorded in Acts 21:25, James was to make nimble use of.

Barnabas and Paul must have held the floor for a couple of hours, there must have been all sorts of questions to them from the floor, it was "a large assembly", so any amount of swapping experiences would have happened and any amount of extra argument. The account they gave must have been a really rousing one, instilling immense pride in the assembly, inspiring them and thrilling them at the picture Paul and Barnabas would have painted of them going out beyond Palestine and Syria into other provinces of the Empire, how converts were being made among other peoples, how the gospel of Jesus was already finding acceptance among people who weren't Jewish but belonged to different cultures from theirs. Of course while in Antioch, while en route to Jerusalem, while in endless conversations and discussion in Jerusalem itself, Paul and Barnabas would have given graphic accounts of the violent opposition they met in Asia Minor. But Luke does not say they did that in their Council contribution. He tells us that when called to speak they made mention of the positive, no mention of stuff which could well have been hard for the members of the Judaic faction to hear, could have alienated them and humiliated them and made them resentful. We will never know for sure how exactly Peter and his fellow organizers planned it all. But what we do know is that what they did at the Council achieved unanimity; the text twice makes mention of it and no discordant voice is recorded. And when James follows on Paul and Barnabas, there is no indication in what he says of resentment.

# CHAPTER 27

# The Response of James on behalf of the Judaic Faction

This James was not the apostle James the Greater, who was the brother of the apostle John and who had been beheaded by Herod in the same persecution in which Peter was arrested; nor was he the apostle James, son of Alphaeus. He was, however, a relation of Jesus and an elder of the church in Jerusalem and in due course, as far as one can tell from the texts, he became its leader. Almost definitely he's the person who's described by Paul as a "brother of the Lord" (Galatians 1:19); and belonging to the group of "brothers" of Jesus mentioned by Mark 6:3 and repeated in Matthew 13:55.

A most interesting digression arises out of those two references. If by "brother" in these texts Mark and Matthew meant that Mary was James's mother as she was of Jesus, she would, as in the list given, have had five sons, namely a James, a Joseph, a Judas and a Simon as well as Jesus, and in addition "sisters" (Matthew 13:56). The names of the girls, unlike those of the boys, and the number, are not given, just the plural. It would have been a lot of children for Mary to have had, not least because it would appear from the Gospel texts that she was also a widow. Joseph does not seem to have been with her at the marriage feast at Cana, and, much more significantly, when she stood beneath the cross. If for whatever reason he was still alive at that moment, Jesus would hardly have handed the care of his mother to someone else. All this in mind, Mary would have had very little time to have so many pregnancies given that there is again the belief that Jesus was only in his thirties when he died. They all, at least up to eight or nine of them, not to mention the possible additional very common occurrence of infant deaths and possibly a miscarriage too, would have had to happen in the limited amount of time between her marriage to Joseph and Joseph's death, which does seem from the texts to have occurred before the public ministry of Jesus. To have had all those children in that amount of time would have meant she was very fertile indeed, which of course is very possible, and almost permanently pregnant. What's more, if Mary had provided Jesus with brothers and sisters in such numbers, it is not likely he would have asked someone else at the moment of his death to take care of her. Little wonder the tradition therefore has been to read "brothers" and "sisters" in these texts as "relations", such as cousins. It certainly makes more sense.

Being a family member it could well have taken James some time to recognize and acknowledge the exceptional nature of the personality of one of his relations, some considerable time to accept a cousin as the Messiah, whichever way he and others understood it, and then become his disciple. It can be difficult for anyone to see that sort of thing in someone whom as a cousin you may well have been playing with throughout childhood and boyhood. However, in due course he definitely did recognize it, and he did become a disciple. Not just another one but a very ardent one, and there is more than a glimpse of that in one thing Paul tells us about him. In 1 Corinthians 15:7 Paul lists the people to whom Jesus appeared after his resurrection, first Cephas, then the Twelve, then 500 of the brethren, and then "he appeared to James and afterwards to all the apostles". Now, there are some peculiarities in that list but ignoring that, what is evident is that Paul, who already had reason enough to find James a very difficult character to deal with, made a point of singling out him along with Peter as a named witness of the Resurrected Lord. Of course there are others also so singled out by the writers of the gospels such as Mary Magdalene and Thomas but that makes it no less of a distinction. And we might well bring to mind how significant and special the experience of actually having seen the Risen Lord was to the Early Church. It was the Resurrection, as Peter had argued from the day of Pentecost to the Jews (e.g. Acts 2:31f.) and throughout all his preaching, that provided evidence of the unique significance of Jesus. "The patriarch David died and was buried and his tomb is here to this day . . . The Jesus we speak of has been raised by God, as we can all witness . . . Let all Israel therefore accept as certain that God has made this Jesus, whom you crucified, both Lord and Messiah" (vv. 29–36). The Resurrection was the argument, witness to it was what mattered; and James was as valiant a witness to it as it gets. He underwent martyrdom for it, being killed by stoning by decree of the Sanhedrin, and very significantly, as Josephus reports, was described by his executioners as "the brother of Jesus who was called the Messiah".

At some juncture James became the leader of the Jerusalem church. There is what might well be a clear acknowledgement of it by Peter himself in Acts 12:13–17 when Peter escapes from Herod's prison in Jerusalem. On escaping to the house of Mary the sister of Barnabas and mother of John Mark, who in due course will be accompanying Paul and Barnabas on the first of Paul's missionary journeys, Peter tells her to report his escape "to James and the members of the church". He was still head of the Jerusalem church when Paul some nine years later, just after his third missionary journey (21:18), stubbornly ignored all advice and went to the city and paid him a visit. Paul was persuaded by him to go through a ritual of purification in the temple after James boasted to him—that is how it comes across—about how many "thousands of converts we have among the Jews, all of them staunch upholders of the Law" (v. 20).

In Galatians Paul states that it was this James that sent Jerusalem church members to Antioch when after the Council of Jerusalem Peter was there. Peter, says Paul, challenged by James's people, wavered on the Council's decisions "out of fear of the advocates of circumcision" and stopped eating meals with Gentile Christians and "separated himself from them" (Acts 2:12f.). Paul says it was not just Peter who did this but Barnabas as well and "other Jewish Christians" who behaved with the same "hypocrisy (or) lack of principle". It's as well to keep in mind that Paul was in a very angry mood when he wrote Galatians. That mood might well have been why he used such forceful and colourful language in it and as in Acts 5:12 pulled no punches. In Acts 21 where Luke describes Paul's visit to Jerusalem, Paul's behaviour there does appear to make him unqualified to have criticized Peter and Barnabas the way he had done in his letter to the Galatians for what he says they did when confronted by the Judaic faction in Antioch. Paul certainly seems to have been overawed by James on the occasion described in Acts 21. One observation might be made about it all, that here we are dealing with very normal human beings and the usual human relationships. From start to finish the apostles, as from their selection by Jesus, and Paul and Barnabas and everyone else who played a part in the founding moments of the Church, were all just plain human beings doing their best, slipping and sliding as everyone does, dealing with something infinitely greater than what they could possibly comprehend.

It's only when these elements in the story that Luke is narrating are put together or we extract impressions from between the lines that we can get some appreciation of a wider picture, namely that of the extended family to which James belonged and its internal relationships. For one thing, it was definitely a very religious family. It produced John the Baptist and Jesus, both of them itinerant preachers, both willing to be put to death for their beliefs, one taking on Herod the king and the other defying the Council of the Jews and the Roman governor. It produced James himself. Another member of it was Zechariah, who belonged to the division of the priesthood called after Abijah (Luke 1:5), with Elizabeth his wife, who "was of priestly descent", and "both of them were upright and devout, blamelessly observing all the commandments and ordinances of the Lord" (v. 6). And then of course there was Joseph the foster father of Jesus and his mother Mary. There is enough in just that to give us a good idea how solidly religious and Judaic the whole extended family group was, and to make us wonder how the cousins of the Baptist and Jesus regarded both of them, and how they had got on with them as kids, playing and arguing and fighting and squabbling and all the rest, those four for example whose names Mark and Matthew have given us, the James and the Joseph and the Judas and the Simon, and their sisters, whose names significantly enough are not given. There must have been plenty more.

If one thinks about it, it is not difficult to understand how the members of the extended family would have hesitated, to say the least, to regard Jesus with the same respect and belief as the apostles had who came to know him only after he had become an adult. Little wonder the people of the village of Nazareth, who had known him as infant, child and boy, couldn't get their heads round it all (Matthew 13:54f.), little wonder they held back. Indeed, when one again reflects on it all, it really was a huge intellectual and psychological achievement on the part of a man like

James to come round, as he did, to recognizing and acknowledging that this cousin of his, this former playmate of his, was the Messiah himself, not just the Messiah for the Jews only but, as he says in his speech at the Council, for the Gentiles too (Acts 15:17), or at least for some of them, depending on how one reads that speech. The mention of him that Paul makes in his first letter to the Corinthians, that Jesus appeared to James after his resurrection, might be telling us something more, that there was a close family bond and a special friendship between the two of them, Jesus and James.

And one can well understand too how difficult it must have been for James when asked to agree to the abandonment of the Law and to the significance of circumcision and to the rituals he had been brought up with and had practiced. They had been his way of living his religious beliefs since the dawn of his spiritual consciousness. They were his lodestone, his north star; and there was Peter saying to him, in his face, at the Council, that "It is by the grace of the Lord Jesus that we are saved" (Acts 15:11); and that meant saved by the grace of Jesus, by belief in the man he had as a cousin, whom he had known, a member of the family, whom he had played around with as all kids do at family get-togethers; and not saved by any of the religious practices that had been his way of life and belief, and his cousin's, since their childhood. None of it might excuse him—but probably it does—but he can well be understood, and forgiven, for clinging on to it all like a limpet even after the concessions he had made and the form his climb-down and acquiescence took. What's more, he proved himself to be true to the faith in Jesus that he had embraced, valiantly true. He underwent martyrdom just over a decade later, in the very city whose Christian bishop he had become. Greater love no man has. They are now eternally together.

We can take it for granted that what we have of James's speech is just those parts of it Luke rated as having a direct bearing on the decision the Council had come to and which it would send by way of a letter to the Christians of Syria, Antioch and Cilicia. One might ask why Luke recorded anything from James at all, considering that apostles other than Peter were present and that they undoubtedly made speeches of some kind or other, yet Luke doesn't give us one single word from any of them. We can never be completely sure why but most likely it was because what they had to say was in agreement with Peter, and Luke wasn't into repetition. James, however, was spokesman for the dissenting faction and Luke considered it very necessary to show that he and his group had come on board and that the decision the Council took had unanimous backing.

James's response was a total climb-down. It had to be. It was clear by the time he came to speak that there was no way the Council was going to try to impose Jewish practices on peoples of other cultures wanting to become Christians. Nothing would more defeat the instruction of Jesus to preach the gospel to all nations than that. Not only didn't James get what he and his faction had been demanding but when it came down to it, in his speech he didn't even ask for any of it. They had been demanding, even up to the moment the doors of the Council opened (Acts 15:5), that male Gentile converts were circumcised. Some of them had even refused to preach the gospel to Gentiles (11:19), and, as we saw when Peter returned to Jerusalem from baptizing Cornelius and his household, they had questioned him about keeping company with Gentiles and sharing meals with them (v. 3). None of this appears in what James had to say to the Council, he had dropped it all. Instead he substituted concerns which neither he nor his fellow faction members are recorded as having spoken about before, namely that Gentiles should avoid doing anything which touched on idolatry and they should not commit fornication, both of which matters hadn't been contested by anyone on either side anyway. James's response to the declaration of Peter and to the input of Paul and Barnabas was a face-saver; but at the same time it had its subtleties. It, and he, held his faction together and what he had to say offered them some encouragement.

Unanimity mattered. Luke makes mention of unanimity in Acts 15:22 and it is in the letter itself in verse 25. For that reason, when James says "My judgement therefore is" (v. 19), it almost definitely is him turning to look at his faction and saying to them: "Brothers, this is the conclusion I have come to, this is my advice to you. We just have to go along with what Peter has said to us." James was speaking to the members of his faction. They like himself had to climb on board; they couldn't sail on their own. As leader of the faction he was making a public declaration of submission.

The faction could well have met privately beforehand, as factions do, and decided, most likely under huge pressure from Peter and his fellow apostles, to toe the line. We know from other references to them such as Galatians 3:12, Philippians 3:2, Acts 21:18–29, severally in Romans (e.g. 2:25–29), and elsewhere, that their support for the decision of the Council was neither unqualified nor wholehearted, and indeed that might be read in what James has to say. Furthermore, at the time when Luke was writing, some thirty or more years later, elements of what the faction stood for were re-emerging. That was possibly one reason why Luke wrote the Acts in the first place. Despite, however, whatever reluctance and foot-dragging there may have been on the part of the faction, the pressure in the Council was for a unanimous decision, and James could hardly defy it. Instead he lent it his support, verbally anyway, and though, as I have said, there were apostles and other elders who definitely made speeches of support, for Luke James's speech was important as he represented the faction, the theology and the activities of which had forced the Church to convene the Council in the first place. There are some pro-faction subtleties in it, but essentially it was the climb-down and the statement of acquiescence that the Council wanted and the concession that the Antioch delegation needed to take back with them.

One thing is noticeably absent in what James had to say to the Council. He makes no mention of Jesus, which by any standards is very strange. However, that could just be because what we have is as Luke edited it. Luke is, however, generous in how much he reports of what James had to say. Again, that could be for the very good reason that what James did say amounted to an admission of defeat, even if James himself did not represent it quite that way. That could have been important to Luke if the Judaic faction was to some extent making a re-appearance at the time he was writing his history and he felt that what they had conceded and agreed to at the Council needed to be made known.

It is difficult, if not impossible, not to read what James says here at the meeting of the Council without recalling what he says and does later. Under his leadership of the church in Jerusalem there is a continuation of practices prescribed in the Law within its Christian community, so much in fact that he can boast, and boast very smugly at that, to Paul when Paul visits him in Jerusalem after his third missionary journey some nine years later: "You see, brother, how many thousands of converts we have among the Jews, all of them staunch upholders of the Law" (21:20).

And it wasn't as if James confined the activities of his Judaic faction to Jerusalem. Members of it infuriated Paul when they went uninvited into the community of his converts in Galatia trying to persuade them to adopt the Law; and later they followed Peter and Barnabas to Antioch similarly trying to stop them as Jews from mixing with Gentile Christians.

That, however, all happened after the Council. James knew the score, he knew that he and his faction had to settle with what they could get. He needed a face-saver. There is however no retraction on the part of the faction that is recorded, maybe that was just left unsaid; and it is preceded in verse 14 by James giving his agreement to the judgement Peter had already made and by implication expressing acceptance of Peter's authoritative role in the matter. Nicholas King SJ in his recent translation of the Bible says that "James' speech is not all that coherent".[17] That is putting it mildly. James does use his speech to express support for what Peter had done in Caesarea but he says nothing whatsoever that lends support to the theological explanation Peter had placed before the Council. The reason might well have been that he—James—was under immense pressure somehow to accommodate what he had to say to both sides of the dispute.

He began very positively: "Simon has told us how it first happened that God took notice of the Gentiles to choose from among them a people to bear his name" (Acts 15:14). However, even in that one simple sentence there was a subtlety. He refers to Peter by his Jewish name "Simeon" He might have meant it as a reminder to his audience of the origins of their new faith, a hint maybe that though he and his faction were on the losing side, what they represented was something that should never be lost nor forgotten; and, interestingly, he reminds them all of just that in the final sentence of his speech. He quotes the minor prophet Amos in support of the decision the Council is about to take: "After these things I will return, and I will build again the tent/tabernacle of David, which is fallen. And I will build again the ruins thereof, and I will set it up, that the rest of men may seek after the Lord, and all the Gentiles upon whom my name is called, says the Lord who does these things that have been known for ages" (Acts 9:11f.).

One thinks he might have been more considerate and sensitive if he had chosen a prophecy from someone else. The anger Amos felt against

Israel's neighbouring tribes knew no bounds and he has God declaring: "O people of Israel . . . you only have I chosen of all the families of the earth" (Amos 3:2), which of course was true but was now superseded. There were any amount of other statements in the psalms and the prophets he might have used. He could have shown himself willing to embrace change, "to enlarge his tent, stretch its curtains wide, not hold back but lengthen its cords and strengthen its stakes" (Isaiah 54:2). But he did not. He could, for example, have spoken to his audience these other words of Isaiah: "The Lord has comforted his people, he has redeemed Jerusalem. The Lord will lay bare his holy arm in the sight of all the nations and all the ends of the earth will see the salvation of our God" (52:9f.). He did not.

James's next statement: "My judgement therefore is" (v. 19) has had a reading which all too widely and all too often has been incorrect and misleading. It has been represented as the statement of the person who was in charge at the Council, as its chairman delivering the final verdict. It was nothing of the sort.[18] He was speaking to his faction, he was telling them that, like it or lump it, their notion of what the Christian Church should be had been repudiated by its leadership; he was telling them that they just had to submit, that it was time to throw in the towel—if only for the time being. And from what Luke has given us of what he said, it amounted to a wholesale concession. In what James offered the Council there was no mention of one single item of the demands he and his group had been trying to impose upon the Church; and by saying "We should impose no irksome restrictions on those of the Gentiles who are turning to God" he was conceding to what Peter had bluntly pointed out in verse 10. It was acceptance that the religious culture and practices of the Jewish religion were not to be imposed upon Gentile converts, that in the judgement of the Church, circumcision and the observation of the Law were not necessary for salvation.

What James then went on to propose in his speech was as minimalist as it could get. His proposals amounted to nothing more than what was obvious, to requirements which had to have been already in place. In its letter at the conclusion of the Council, the Council was to call those proposals "these essentials/these necessary things" (v. 28). If essential or necessary items of behaviour, which they were, otherwise the Council wouldn't have so described them, they would already have been demanded of Gentile converts in preparation for baptism; there was nothing new about them at all. They were: "to abstain from things polluted by contact with idols, from fornication, and from anything that had been strangled and from blood" (v. 20). What James proposed was about the avoidance of idolatry and fornication, about both of which there was no disagreement on either side. James was saving face, nothing less, he was showing willing after having had to abandon all the demands on the Gentiles he and his faction had been making. In his speech he makes no mention of those demands at all.

Interestingly, the manuscripts differ as to what was actually proposed. For example, some do not include "from fornication", probably because it was a given anyway, it does not fit alongside concerns about idols, it just was something else. In comparison with the really important theological differences between the faction and the apostles these things were secondary. However, in 1 Corinthians 8:1–10 and 10:19 Paul does show an immense degree of sensitivity for Jewish Christian feelings on this matter; he makes clear how he would have Gentile converts deal tenderly with the scruples of their fellow Jewish Christians. Dietary attitudes were a very sensitive issue, and still are in different degrees and ways with Jews, Hindus and Moslems. Every culture, be it secular or religious, has its habits, customs and addictions about this and that, food usually being one. For the Christian there shouldn't be any such issues: "Allow no one to take you to task about what you eat or drink or over the observance of festivals, new moon or Sabbath. These are no more than a shadow of what is to come. The reality is that of Christ. Why let people dictate to you: 'Do not handle this, do not taste that, do not touch the other?' All of them perish on being used as they are the injunctions and teachings of human beings" (Colossians 2:16–22).

This phrase: "the injunctions and teachings of human beings" is an observation that is pertinent beyond estimation. Religion all too often is a heaving mass, a swelling reservoir, of rules made by human beings and regulations which all too many of its devotees revel in; in food, dress and appearance particularly, they can give them power and control, and clever things to do, they give power to men over women, they make people feel special and different and are often used by the people in charge of a religion to emphasize differences and keep their adherents separate from neighbours and fellow citizens.

The very last thing James had to say also deserves a comment. It reads as a late addition made by Luke but it is of great interest: "For Moses, from generations of old, has had people preaching him in every city and is read in the synagogues on every Sabbath" (Acts 15:21). Plainly it is James's way of acknowledging defeat but he's seen a consolation prize he can put before his followers to give them cause to be a bit cheerful. "Yes, we've lost the argument, brothers, but we haven't lost everything. What's been decided here hasn't got rid of Moses. It doesn't intend that at all. In no way. He and his Law have been preached from time immemorial in all our synagogues here and wherever our people have settled, Sabbath after Sabbath, festive day after festive day, and it will always be that way." James did not know, and of course could not have known, what the future held for the sacred scriptures of the Jewish people. The Church from its very beginning without any hesitation regarded them and kept them for what they were, the word of the people of God, and they did not cease to be so when all humanity were declared by God in Christ to be what they had always been, his people. The scriptures are the Old Testament, they belong to all the world, they are part of the Christian canon, they are read out at almost every single Christian liturgical gathering. The events and characters of the history of the Jewish people have been celebrated in the liturgy, the literature and the songs and music of Christian cultures everywhere ever since. Through their adoption by the Church they have been made known progressively to nearly all the peoples of the world for the last two thousand years, and all the profound religious thoughts of the Jewish people, all their exploits, all the prophets major and minor, have been explored for meaning, and their psalms have become the very prayer of the Church. The fact is, Christianity has given certain main components of Judaism an international use, fame, love and attachment such as no one could possibly have imagined in Jerusalem in the year 49, two thousand years of praise of God and of prayer and ritual across all the world.

However, like Jesus in the Sermon on the Mount, the Church sifts the text of the Old Testament with care, rejecting what is unacceptable to the Christian faith, whatever in it misrepresents God; and that does occur in the Old Testament, for example those texts which instruct the Jewish people to kill and slaughter the peoples occupying the Holy Land. Those texts are put into the mouth of God by the scribes of the people of God in order to justify the dreadful massacres which they themselves relate they committed. They are nothing less than gross misrepresentation of God. God, however, did not write the Bible. The Old Testament texts were written by the scribes of the Jewish people. God allowed what they wrote. Not to allow would have been to represent that people in a way which it was not. In its way their representation of him is an incarnation of God in the words and ideas they had about him as over time their understanding of him progressed to his revelation in Christ. He did not impose, he left it to his people to put it right.

To achieve this in its fullness in the fullness of time the Spirit of Truth inhabited and guided the Church, which, as the writer of 1 Timothy said of it, is: "God's household . . . the pillar and bulwark of the truth" (1 Timothy 3:15). All statements in the Old Testament are revered because they are the words of the people of God as they went through life and history, sometimes fumbling and stumbling in what they did and what they wrote, on their way to the coming of Jesus, the Messiah. The prayers and the psalms, the prophecies and the histories, the songs and the epic achievements, and the disasters, of the Jewish people have permeated Christianity through and through, they flow through us like blood through a living body, they have formed our minds and our cultures. They are us in a million ways.

Peter and his fellow apostles dealt very sensitively with their fellow-believers in the Judaic faction. They were given a genuine hearing. Their arguments were listened to and when they had put forward a compromise, even though it was nothing more than a face-saver, it wasn't cast to one side, but it was incorporated into the letter which was about to be sent to the Gentile converts from Antioch, Syria and south east Asia Minor. There was no way cultural things like circumcision and kosher food, which mattered so much to the Judaizers, would ever find acceptance by Gentile nations who had their own cultures. Besides, many religious practices are just human creations, some can be helpful, others seriously divisive and socially very harmful. Religion today is still full of both of course. The fundamental issue the Council of Jerusalem dealt with was that in the eyes of God no one nation was more loved by him and no one nation was to be treated differently than any other, that salvation from the consequences of sin was wrought by the Lord Jesus Christ on behalf of all men and women, and that it was faith in him that God wants of us.

There is a very short psalm, Psalm 87 (Hebrew numbering), which the Council might well have addressed. Because it is emphatically relevant to the issues before the Council, it might have been read out loud to the whole assembly and discussed. However, what we have of it, the English translations are so different from each other in some of its lines that at first one might wonder if the translators are looking at the same text. The editors of the NET say that "it is disordered" and re-arrange its verses. That is putting it mildly, but I will follow the order it sets out. What matters is the very significant kernel that it contains. I would suggest that nowhere else is the religious relationship of Judaism to the peoples of the world expressed more deeply, lovingly and, theologically, more perceptively and prophetically. The psalm reads: "The Lord loves the gates of Zion, her foundations are laid upon holy hills and he has made her his home. Glorious things are said of you, O City of God. I will count Egypt and Babylon among my friends; Philistine, Tyrian and Nubian shall be there, and Zion shall be called a mother in whom all men of every race are born. The Lord shall write against each nation in his roll of nations: 'This one was born in her.'"

The psalmist is saying that Zion, which is Jerusalem, is especially beloved by God and it is in her that he dwells. She is the City of God.[19] She carries in her, as in a womb, unaware of what is stored in her and what it will lead to, the revelation God intends in the fullness of time to give to the whole of humanity. That revelation is Christ. God's revelation to all nations and races comes to them through her. All nations are considered friends by God, even Egypt where once the people of Israel were enslaved and Babylon to which they were exiled, Zion/Jerusalem is mother of every nation, because in her the rebirth of mankind was begun. We are all born in Zion. That is the prophecy the authors of the epistles to the Ephesians and the Colossians will describe as the mystery and secret of God's eternal purpose which was revealed in Jesus in the fullness of time. This role in the salvation story was offered by God to Zion, to Jerusalem, to the people of Israel, God offered to Israel the role of giving to the world its Messiah, its Saviour. He was born in Israel, in Israel he preached God's gospel to Israel, so that Israel in turn might give it to every race and nation. But Israel would not. It refused the role, it rejected him. Hence Christ's lament: "O Jerusalem, Jerusalem, the city that murders the prophets and stones the messengers sent to her. How often have I longed to gather your children, as a hen gathers her brood under her wings. But you would not. Look! There is your temple forsaken by God" (Luke 14:34). But, Paul asks, "Has God rejected his people? No! God has not rejected the people which he acknowledged of old as his own . . . God's choice stands . . . They are his friends for the sake of the patriarchs . . . For the gracious gifts of God and his calling are irrevocable" (Romans 11:1–36).

CHAPTER 28

# The Conclusion of the Council:
# Letter to the Churches

The arguments had now come to an end, the speeches had been made, and two decisions were made. The first one was to choose two prominent members of the Jerusalem church to be sent to Antioch; the second was a letter to the "brothers" in Antioch, Syria and Cilicia, containing the decisions taken by the Council on the issues it had been convened to consider. A comment first on one aspect of that word. Today we would write "brothers and sisters" or "sisters and brothers", depending. It indicates that we have made some progress in the matter of gender equality, if only a little. If we had been members of the Church then and present at the Council, we wouldn't have found anything amiss at all with saying just "brothers". It was the mentality of that time and place; it was the mind of the Judaism they had been born into and brought up in. However, when some thirty years later Luke wrote his history, it is clear from Acts 8:12 that by then at least the equality of the female with the male in becoming a member had been understood by the Church, and that represented immense progress.

Obviously, at some point, either before the Antioch church had contacted the apostles in Jerusalem to settle the issue that was creating very considerable dissension or after receiving notice that the Council would be held, the churches in the rest of Syria and in Cilicia, the home province of Paul, had joined in in support of what their Antioch colleagues were doing. That the Council members addressed the churches in the rest of Syria and Cilicia as well as Antioch might well indicate that the Judaic faction had been actively promoting itself and its understanding of what the Christian gospel consisted in more widely than just in Antioch. It had to be dealt with before it got out of hand and, in effect, had reduced Christianity to just a sect within Judaism.

The first decision, Luke informs us, the one about which people were to take the letter to Antioch, was taken by "the apostles and elders, with the whole church" (Acts 15:22); the letter on the other hand was written by "the apostles and elders" (v. 23). Is there anything to read into this difference between them? There is. The first decision was an administrative matter involving tactics with no issue of belief in it. The consideration of which men were the most suitable to send to Antioch was a tactical one. The Council members were alive to its sensitivity. Whoever were chosen to take the Council's decision to Antioch had to be seen to be genuinely representative of the authority vested in the Council, to be totally non-partisan and not open to any suspicion of bias. For that reason the Council decided it would not just leave it to members of the Antioch delegation such as Paul and Barnabas to take the letter back with them. Instead the Council chose two "men from among themselves" (v. 22). The description almost reads like the two men, Silas and Judas, were members of a kind of inner committee of the Council responsible for its conduct. The letter also described them as being prominent or having a leadership position "among the brothers", which probably meant the Jerusalem community. Paul and Barnabas would naturally accompany them back to Antioch but it would be Silas and Judas who would formally present the letter to the Antioch community as Jerusalem-based representatives of the apostles and elders in Jerusalem, open it and read it out; and they would explain its contents "by word of mouth", face to face, encourage discussion and answer questions. Silas was to be with Paul and Luke on the coming missionary journeys in Asia Minor and Greece (v. 39), and he is mentioned by Paul in 2 Corinthians 1:19 and 1 Thessalonians 1:1. Acts 15:30 tells us that on reaching Antioch they were met by a big crowd who were delighted with what they heard. The apostles knew how to go about it; it was the right way of doing such things; and it was the news the churches had been waiting for, a decision of immense significance, then and now.

The second decision, however, was different. It wasn't administration, it was doctrine. Its opening words don't only express warmth and oneness with the "brethren who are Gentiles in Antioch, Syria and Cilicia"; they don't only send greetings to them as "brothers to brothers", but they also make it clear in what capacity they are writing to them. Namely as "the apostles and elders". This time there is no such addition as "with the whole church" though that would not have detracted anything from the affirmation of authority that they were about to make. But one senses that the absence of having any such addition in the letter is a silent affirmation of their awareness that vested in them as apostles and elders was authority to pronounce on doctrine, an authority which the membership of the Church accepted. That is explicit in Acts 15:2 which relates the decision of the Antioch membership to appeal to the apostles and elders; and it is formulated by the apostles and elders in the letter itself: "It is the decision of the Holy Spirit and our decision." It is a formula which places this decision in a very different category from the decision whom to send to Antioch with the letter. This was a statement on the Christian faith of a very definitive sort. To make such a statement required status. The apostles and elders themselves wrote it "with their own hands" (v. 23). The phrase possibly means "with great deliberation, after giving the matter a lot of thought". Its importance as a statement of the faith of the Church cannot be exaggerated. It was to be the passport of Christianity into the world.

It begins: "The apostles and elders, brothers, to the brothers who are of the Gentiles in Antioch, Syria and Cilicia, Greetings" (v. 23). First of all, the apostles and elders make it clear they are writing to the Gentile members, not to the Jewish members, of the three churches. Then in the same breath they employ the word "brother" twice in that one sentence to emphasize that the distinction between Jew and Gentile no longer has any basis or relevance, indeed any meaning, in the oneness that baptism gives in Christ, which is precisely how we see it today. Racial or national origins have no relevance at all in Christ. All are brothers and sisters, one father in God, one brother in Christ. If there was one statement in the letter that more than any other must have warmed the very cockles of the hearts of the letter's recipients, that was surely it. From the Church leadership this was an undiluted full-blooded assertion of oneness, brotherhood, unity and identity in Christ Jesus. It was Christian brother and sister speaking to each other, total brotherhood and sisterhood in Christ, total oneness and community in Christ.

This was no quick or easy piece of writing on the part of the apostles and company; it was very carefully thought-out, it had been discussed, every word, as will become clear, thoughtfully chosen. It set out what the character and the essence of Church membership on this vital point should be for good and all. This is where Paul in writing Galatians got it all from, this was Galatians 3:28 half a dozen years before Paul put pen to paper and wrote: "You are all one in Christ Jesus." It took final shape and ultimate expression in Ephesians 2:11–22 and Colossians 1–3, which will be looked at below and which give unsurpassable expression to Christian theology and mysticism, and extend and deepen the content of the greeting which the apostles and elders who made up the Council of Jerusalem sent to their fellow Christians in Antioch. Ephesians 2 and Colossians 1—3 are the Council's short statement developed and enlarged. In the simplest way possible the greeting sent by the Council anticipates the sublimity of the theology of Ephesians and Colossians which then open up an ocean of meaning, unfathomable and immeasurable, out of one fundamental concept, namely: "For he is our peace who made both peoples one" (Ephesians 2:14). And what is more, both letters in this passage reveal how profoundly, indeed incredibly, the theological and mystical thinking and the liturgical language of the Church had developed in the few years between the event of the Council and when, round about thirty or so years later, the epistles were written.

The letter then addresses the issue that the Council was convened to consider. It reads: "Ἐπειδὴ ἠκούσαμεν ὅτι τινὲς ἐξ ἡμῶν [ἐξελθόντες] ἐτάραξαν ὑμᾶς λόγοις ἀνασκευάζοντες τὰς ψυχὰς ὑμῶν οἷς οὐ διεστειλάμεθα", a very literal translation of which is: "Forasmuch as we have heard that certain men who went out from us, have troubled you with words, subverting your souls, to whom we gave no commandment" (Westcott-Hort 1881. American Standard Version 1901). There are two verbs in this statement, which require very careful examination, for which we are dependent on the scholars. The two verbs are: ἀνασκευάζοντες and διεστειλάμεθα.

First the verb διαστέλλω, which in this context means to command, give orders (It is the tertiary meaning in Liddle & Scott, which cites both the NT and the LXX as sources). In the subordinate clause "to whom we gave no commandment" it can admit of two interpretations. It could mean that the apostles are saying that with regard to what the faction members did in Antioch they themselves were in no way involved, it was not their fault, they had neither so instructed them nor sent them there, and that was that. That is not, however, how a number of versions read it. The NET and the NIV for example both translate the phrase as "without any authorization/instructions from us", which does seem more likely. The statement can then be read as a rebuke to the faction members, implying that they knowingly defied the agreement reached when Peter had returned to Jerusalem. There must have been a lot of arguments both before the Council started and during the long debate, which Luke has made mention of, where Peter and his colleagues expressed their anger and disappointment at the way faction members had gone up to Antioch without a word to anyone, with Peter squaring up to James and telling him that the very least he could have done is to have let him know what his colleagues were up to, and where they'd gone with their preaching, and reminding him of the decision they all had reached together when he got back to Jerusalem from Caesarea. There must have been outbursts of real anger in those moments. It does seem inevitable that Peter at some point would have said to James and his supporters: "The very least you could have done was ask our opinion first before your people went up there to Antioch. But you didn't, did you? You acted completely on your own, without any authorization from us. After all, we are the apostles, we're entitled to be informed and to be asked." When "in their own hand" the apostles wrote the letter, it positively demands to be taken as much more than them just saying they weren't responsible. It rings out as a rebuke, and a very stern and conspicuous rebuke at that, and a declaration to the Gentile converts in Antioch, Syria and Cilicia that the people who had given them so much trouble did not represent the Church, had no authorization at all for what they had done and definitely weren't preaching the gospel Jesus had commissioned his followers to preach.

To appreciate the concern felt by the apostles we then have to look at the verb ἀνασκευάζω which they used to describe what it actually was that the faction had been causing in Antioch. It is very important to get its translation right, because one way or the other, be the translation "unsettling/troubling" or "subverting/plundering", it indicates the degree of gravity with which the apostles regarded what had happened in Antioch, and describes what effect on the Christians there they believe it all could have. By means of it the Council expresses the conclusion it has come to about the activities of the circumcision faction, it is its verdict on them. In his commentary J. R. Lumby makes this comment:

> The verb ἀvaskeuάzeiv is found in the N.T only here, and not at all in the LXX. In classical Greek it is applied mostly to an entire removal of goods and chattels either by its owners or by a plundering enemy. The devastation wrought in the minds of the Gentile Christians through the new teaching is compared to an utter overthrow. In L&S it is given as "dismantle, waste, ravage".[20]

For those reasons there can be little doubt that the translations "unsettling", "disturbing" and "troubling" are weak and very inadequate. They mislead by not doing justice to what the judgement of the Council amounts to. Any one alternative such as "subverting your souls" or "hollowing out your souls" or "ravaging your souls" is better as they are correct translations. The decision arrived at by the Council was that what the faction was preaching amounted to a hollowing-out of the minds of the Gentile Christians of Antioch, Cilicia and Syria, a dismantling of what Paul and Barnabas had taught them, of making a wasteland of their souls and their Christian beliefs, of which the most important one in this context is in Christ as the sole source of our salvation.[21]

This has consequences for a reading of the Council of Jerusalem in which for far too long a notion has persisted and should be disposed of once and for all. It is that somehow or other the use by James of the word "κρίνω" (Acts 15:19) halfway through his speech indicates that he was chairman of the proceedings of the Council. The evidence makes short shrift of that opinion, long lived and widespread though it has been. The decision of "the apostles and elders unanimously" (15:23–5) to use the word ἀναοκευάζω to describe how and to what gross extent the preaching of the faction, of which James was the leader, damages and deforms the Christian faith indicates, as I have said above, that James was addressing his following within the Council and advising them to accept its ruling. That some of them didn't, as Galatians informs us, should not surprise anyone. It has happened subsequent council after subsequent council.

The verb ἀνασκευάζω tells us that James as leader of the faction was not at all in the chair but in the dock, and his faction's version of the gospel had been on trial and found, not just wanting, but harmfully misleading; and that he emerged well and truly admonished and reprimanded. The apostles' description of their decision as ὁμοθυμαδὸν might well indicate that in the interests of unity James as an elder, and a very prominent one, put his signature to the letter to the three northern churches. It is anybody's guess whether or not what he had to say to Paul a few years later when Paul arrived unannounced on his doorstep in Jerusalem (Acts 21) shows him to have reverted to the position he had held when leading the faction.

This word ἀνασκευάζοντες addresses one of the three principal theological issues before the Council of Jerusalem. The other two are, first, the mention of "essential matters" (v. 28) and, second, the well-known and highly significant statement: "It is the decision of the Holy Spirit and our decision" (v. 28). Discussion of both will follow. Together all three best convey the meaning behind the decision it had come to. The use of ἀνασκευάζοντες tells us how seriously the apostles were taking the challenge which the faction was making to the very essence and substance of what Christianity was. By describing what the faction was doing as subverting and plundering souls the Council was rejecting their preaching emphatically and dogmatically. In the words of Paul writing to the Galatians, what the faction was preaching was: "another gospel which is really no gospel at all" (Galatians 1:6).

Paul was present when the apostles and elders composed their letter, present to witness the care they took, quite possibly along with others who were fluent in Greek contributing to the choice of words to be used in it. Presumably it was written in Greek, since it was sent to Gentile converts. He accompanied it back to Antioch; he was with Silas and Judas Barsabbas when the two men read it out loud to the Antioch Gentile Christians who had assembled to hear it and he witnessed their exclamations of joy when they heard what it had to tell them (Acts 15:31). The letter didn't just represent total rejection by the Council of everything that the faction had been preaching in the three northern communities, it was much more specific and condemnatory. It damned what they had preached as a "subversion" of faith and doctrine. One needs only read the first chapter of Paul's letter to his Galatian converts to perceive how that notion stayed with him and guided, inspired and drove what he had to say to them. He uses different words but the same ideas with identical bluntness. Members of the faction had infiltrated the churches of Galatia behind his back; they were preaching a gospel totally different from what he had taught them; they were "hollowing out" the minds of the community; they were "distorting the gospel of Christ"; they were "accursed/outcasts/condemned" (Galatians 1:9), depending on the translation one is using.

Peter's declaration that we are justified by the grace of Christ through faith in him (Acts 15:11) was the source and inspiration of Paul's theology of justification, which he set out in his letter to the Romans. Too many commentators, and for far too long, have represented Paul as an independent thinker, have spoken and written much too easily about what they call "Pauline theology", when the source and inspiration of the gospel which he preached and which he wrote about in Romans and Galatians was Peter both before and inside the Council, and the Council's letter to the Gentile Christians of Antioch, Syria and Cilicia. The evidence for that assertion has been produced. What has become known as "Pauline theology" was already in its essential elements mainstream Church teaching by the time Paul wrote Galatians and Romans, in which, however, he took it to new heights and greater depths.

There was however another constituency of Christians the Council had to attend to, whom it could not ignore, namely the Jewish Christians in Syria and Cilicia, who were not just neighbours of the Gentile Christians but fellow believers in Jesus as saviour, sharing the same liturgies of baptism and Eucharist, sharing the same duties and prayer life, particularly the psalms. The letter wasn't addressed to them; they weren't mentioned in it; they weren't within the stated object of its "Greetings" (Acts 15:23). Yet, beyond any shadow of doubt they would have addressed as many questions to Silas and Judas as their Gentile brothers and sisters did, the main ones of course being: "What about us? Where do we fit in? Do we abandon our Jewish customs? Do we continue to circumcise? Are we now expected to eat non-kosher foods? What happens now to the feast-days which we have always celebrated such as Purim, Sukkot, Rosh Hashanah, Passover and Chanukah, all of which you apostles and elders and Silas and Judas Barsabbas and Paul and Barnabas and virtually everyone else attending the Council had themselves celebrated since infancy?"

For that very reason it is unthinkable that the members of the Council did not have their fellow Jews in mind in all the proceedings. They would never have just taken them for granted. There just was no way they'd have done that. Just to take one example: circumcision. Jewish Christians at that moment in time would never have stopped circumcising their new-born sons, no way at all, not even the apostles themselves. After centuries of carrying out that custom it was total instinct, unsuppressible instinct. It still is with Jewish people. It just was their way of life, it still is. And it wasn't just religious, for them it was also party time, it was celebration, and still is, it is their way of welcoming another child into the ranks of the Chosen People; and that nothing like it, no initiation ceremony, happened to new-born girls didn't cause any problem whatsoever, it would never as much as enter their heads. That's how their life was, and by and large still is, and on occasion, as with a mixed marriage, can still lead to bitter argument, even fisticuffs. Who knows where circumcision has all come from originally, and exactly why. That Judaism adopted it as a ritual of massive proportions, such as Genesis 17 describes, tells us nothing about its origins. Just possibly, given the hot climate of the region, it was a hygienic practice across the Middle East and was then elevated at some point in its history by one tribe or other to become a very representative ritual. When one thinks about it, it is astonishing how much being born with a penis can figure in religion, and not just by way of circumcision as in Judaism and Islam but, as has already been pointed out, as a *conditio sine qua non* to becoming a priest or a bishop in some 75 per cent of Christianity.

Luke relates that when the letter was read to the "assembly" of the Antioch church, its recipients "rejoiced because of the consolation/ encouragement/exhortation it brought them (Acts 15:31). One cannot help but wonder how the non-Gentiles, the Jewish Christians, in that very same audience felt. Lumby, adopting "consolation", makes an observation which is pertinent to the problem in hand: "The consolation would be felt both by Jews and Gentiles, by the former because they now knew how much was to be asked of their Gentile fellow worshippers, and by the latter because they were declared free from the yoke of Jewish observances."[22] That is acceptable to a point, but it does not address what must have been of equal concern to the Jewish Christians, namely where did the Council's decision put them. The Gentile Christians now had every reason to rejoice, they had received the instruction they had been hoping for, but, at first glance, the Jewish Christians hadn't got anything out of it at all.

At first glance. The more one reflects upon it all, however, the more one is inclined to conclude that the fact that the Council sent no instruction whatsoever, no clarification at all, to the Jewish Christians indicates that there was none to be sent. They no less than their Gentile fellow Christians had their own culture. From the fact that the Council did not give them any instructions it would seem to be a fair inference to draw that they need not discard it, but that they could retain it just as the Gentiles had no need to discard theirs except those elements, such as the idolatrous practices mentioned in the letter, which were in no way acceptable within Christianity. However, there can be no doubt that what Peter would have told his fellow Jews about his visions at Joppa must have given them a lot of food for thought. It amounted to one enormous challenge to their way of life.

But sometimes things are best left alone. Within reason, and subject to the impact of such teaching as the message of the Joppa vision, Jewish customs could be retained by the Jewish Christians. However, it had to be understood and in no way disputed that, as Peter stated: "Our faith is that we are saved by the grace of the Lord Jesus" and not by any cultural customs, Jewish or Gentile. Cultural customs can be, and indeed over time in many countries did become, ways of giving public expression to their Christian faith, sometimes glorious and imaginative public expressions of the Christian faith as, for example, the way the day of the birth of Jesus, which is Christmas, is celebrated in England with nativity plays, meals, street bunting, carol services etc., or his passion and death is celebrated in the wonderful spell-binding processions in Spain during Holy Week. Those celebrations are not sacraments but they certainly are great sacramentals, they are both immensely enjoyable and very instructive, they are what religion should be. Religion should be alive, and enjoyable.

We know from the Acts itself that the Jewish Christians, or at least some of them, indeed in one church—Jerusalem—a very large number of them (Acts 21:20), did in fact continue with their traditional practices. Within a few verses of describing the response of the Antioch Christians to the Council's letter Luke tells us that on arriving in Lystra and Derbe in Asia Minor during his second missionary journey Paul had Timothy, who had a Jewish mother, circumcised in order to avoid alienating the Jews to whom he was preaching. We can take it that Paul saw no inconsistency between the Council decision he had backed with enthusiasm and how he dealt with Timothy. For him the circumcision of Timothy, we presume, was tactical, but who can be sure? That Paul saw it that way is very obvious from what Luke then tells us in the very next verse, that as Paul and Timothy travelled from town to town in Asia Minor, "they handed on the decisions reached by the apostles and elders in Jerusalem and enjoined their observance" (Acts 16:4). This sentence comes across as one in which Luke chose every word with care, one he thought through.

What Paul did with Timothy was, however, just a single isolated action on his part; Acts 21 describes a situation that was on another scale altogether. It has James boasting to Paul. Speaking of his own church membership in Jerusalem he said to him: "You see, brother, how many thousands there are among the Jews who are believers and who are all staunch upholders of the Law" (v. 20). How James phrases this is quite fascinating; he is telling Paul that the faith in Jesus that was a necessity to be a true Christian was there all right but it need not stop a Jew from "walking in the way of our customs" (v. 21), which was in fact correct, and he warns Paul to expect trouble: "They have been informed that you teach all the Jews who live among the Gentiles not to circumcise their children or live according to their customs" (ibid.). He then seems to have scared Paul enough to get him to take part in a Nazarite purification ceremony.

Or there again he might not have scared Paul at all. Just possibly Paul had gone back to Jerusalem, defying advice (Acts 21:11–14), out of sheer nostalgia. He was getting a lot older. He had totally immersed himself in preaching right across the eastern Mediterranean, just possibly he was feeling his past plucking hard at his heart strings, just possibly he wanted to be back home, spiritually, one more time, relive some of it one more time. Who knows? From this whole episode we can safely conclude that there was any number of converted Jews, not just in Jerusalem and throughout Judea but throughout the diaspora, who kept vigorously to the Mosaic way of life; and it is likely that that practice continued for quite some time and no attempt was made, thankfully, to stop it. Over time, as the non-Jewish population of the Church became by far the major one, Jewish cultural practices such as circumcision and dietary regulations just died away, which cannot be said of the massive liturgical and theological donation made by Judaism to Christianity, which of course is permanent. If no Judaism, then no Christianity. A Jewish girl had to give birth to Christ if there was to be Christianity.

There was, however, something the Council addressed which reveals how thoughtful and reflective it had been. It had said to the members of the faction that they had acted without authorization. That criticism of them was possibly what gave the Council in the person of the apostles and the elders cause to look at themselves and consider and spell out what was the authority they themselves believed they had. In the "long debate" that had gone on between the two sides prior to the Council being formally convened and also during it, the faction members would definitely have contested the right of the apostles and elders to decide against them and would definitely have asked them for evidence or proof why their judgement was to be accepted rather than theirs; and the apostles could not have pointed them to any scripture in their support. There wasn't any. All they had was the mind of the Church, nothing else. All they had was their memory, nothing else, of what the Lord had said to them, their recollection that he had said to them at the moment of his Ascension: "You will be baptized with the Holy Spirit . . . You shall receive power when the Holy Spirit has come upon you" (Acts 1:8), to which of course must be added the very well-known promises of Jesus about the sending and the working within them of the Spirit of Truth and the guidance he will give them, contained in John's Gospel. The assertion they made was "It is the decision of the Holy Spirit and our decision" (v. 28). It is positively startling in its boldness and astonishing in its brevity and theological depth. It is just stated as a fact with no justification or explanation being given, which would imply that it was already the common belief of the Church leadership and its members; and that was authority enough. It was the mind of the Church and that constituted authorization enough.

The verb δοκέω is used by Luke in this way three times within six verses and the translations vary as follows: "It seemed good to", "resolved", "it is the decision of", "it pleased", "was decided", "was agreed". The three instances are: Acts 15:22 "then it seemed good to/then the apostles and elders decided"; verse 25 "it seemed good to us all/we have resolved unanimously"; and verse 28 "it is the decision of the Holy Spirit and our decision". Lumby notes that it is an expression often used in official announcements or with decrees made by an authority.[23] That the apostles and elders were consciously exercising authority is indisputable, that after all was the stated purpose of the letter. That they could claim that their decision was also that of God the Holy Spirit came out of their realization that the promises made to them by Jesus applied to them collectively: "When he comes who is the Spirit of truth, he will guide you into all the truth" (John 16:13), and to Peter individually: "You are Peter the Rock, and on this rock I will build my church and the forces of death will never overpower it, I will give you the keys of the kingdom of heaven; what you forbid on earth shall be forbidden in heaven and what you allow on earth shall be allowed in heaven" (Matthew 16:18f.); and to the instruction Peter received three times from the Risen Lord: "Feed my sheep" (John 21:17).

The apostles were not interpreting a scripture when they made this assertion, the principle *sola scriptura* just does not apply. There was no New Testament scripture to interpret. This assertion of the apostles and elders predates Scripture. By that year, AD 49, not a single New Testament text had been written. The apostles were relying on their memory of what Jesus had said to them and their growing understanding of it, accompanied and assisted by prayer and mutual discussion. There was no other way available to them. Furthermore the singular fact that the Christians of Antioch had sought their decision on what was a profoundly important theological matter, one that went to the core of what Christianity was, and that two other churches, Cilicia and Syria, were as ready as Antioch to accept what the apostles decided and the instruction they gave, indicates that they took their understanding of the Christian faith, not from any scriptures, which did not exist anyway, but from the collective mind of the Church, which was the teaching of the apostles. There just is no other source of justification for the assertion that they made.

The statement of faith made by Peter to the Council "We believe it is through the grace of our Lord Jesus that we are saved" is another prime example. As of that moment there was no scriptural or written evidence for that declaration of faith which he might have had recourse to. He relied on what Jesus had said to him and his fellow apostles and on the understanding of Jesus which he came to in various ways, not least through prayer and the inspiration of the Holy Spirit and through discussion with his fellow apostles and elders. The word of God was working in him and his fellow apostles. "The word working within the Christian soul" is a most mystical concept, it is how the Spirit received in baptism can work in us. Paul says to his converts in Thessalonia a mere year or two later: "The word of God is working in you who believe" (1 Thessalonians 2:13). With his statement in Acts 15:11 Peter could, and did, authoritatively set out what the Christian faith about salvation was; and it was on that teaching, on that assertion made to the Council, that the Council's final decision relied.

The word ἔδοξεν is this time describing the action not just of the Council members but of both the Holy Spirit and the Council members together. No word was used lightly, all were knowingly chosen. What the Council members are saying is this: "The Holy Spirit and ourselves are of one mind on this; what we are saying in this letter God is saying, our mind on this is God's mind; and we know this to be the case. We have the authority to make this decision; and it is the right one." In what must rank as a masterpiece of understatement the Anglican scholar J. R. Lumby, writing in 1904, gave it as his opinion that "the coordination of the Divine Spirit and the human instruments in the preamble of the decree is not a little remarkable" (p. 283). The Council was affirming that its decision on the issue before them was not just theirs but the Holy Spirit's as well. How did they know, how could they make such a claim? It is a startling claim. In the following two millennia that has been the mind of the Church as displayed in the statements of faith made by its councils.

One can immediately see what the resonance of the statement is, can see how it is relevant to controversies in the centuries that follow. We might just consider such councils as Nicaea, Chalcedon and Ephesus. The patriarchs and bishops who attended took it as a given, as what gave them reason for convening in the first place, that the decisions they will arrive at are the Holy Spirit's. They just took it as read that the authority the apostles and elders claimed at the Council of Jerusalem, as related in the New Testament text, had been passed on to them. Its grounds are the words of Jesus: "I will ask the Father and he will give you another to be your Advocate who will be with you forever, the Spirit of truth . . . You will know him because he dwells with you and is in you . . . Your Advocate, the Holy Spirit, whom the Father will send in my name, will teach you everything and will call to mind all that I have told you . . . When your Advocate has come, whom I will send you from the Father, the Spirit of Truth that issues from the Father, he will bear witness to me; and you also are my witnesses . . . When he comes who is the Spirit of truth, he will guide you into all the truth" (John 14:15f.,17,26; 15:26 and 16:13).

That phrase "forever" has immense significance. The Holy Spirit did not cease to dwell in its Church upon the death of the last apostle but remains with it and is at work within it (1 Thessalonians 2:13) until the end of time. The Church in the words of Holy Scripture is "The household of God . . . the church of the living God, the pillar and foundation of the truth" (1 Timothy 3:15)—an understanding of the Church which is not derived from Scripture but anticipates the Scripture that records it. The Scriptures are the documents of the mind of the Church, of the *sensus fidelium*.

The issue before the Council was how the Church was to be understood, whether it was to be universalist or Jewish, and how it was to be presented to non-Jewish nations, as Jewish in its practices or as open to embracing other cultural ways of life. The Council consisted almost totally of Jewish Christians. What it decided, and stated in its letter, was a thoroughgoing rejection of the position taken by the Judaic faction and a firm endorsement of an understanding of the Church and its religious practices as universalist, as open to the cultures in all their forms of all the nations of the world. The apostles and elders made their attitude to the Gentiles and their cultures very clear from the first line of the letter. In it the first thing they did was to send greetings to them as from brothers to brothers, in that way to make an explicit affirmation of the oneness of all Christians, be they Jew or Gentile. They then set out a very strong and explicit condemnation of what some of their own members had done in Antioch. They expressly stated that what these men had preached was a veritable subversion, a plundering and hollowing-out, of Christian belief. The apostles and elders also made it clear that though these people were part of their own membership, they had had no authorization at all from them to do what they did and to preach what they preached.

In order to ensure that the Gentile Christians fully grasped the importance with which the Council regarded the issue and the decision they were taking, they informed them that they had chosen two men eminent within their own ranks, Silas and Judas Barsabbas, to go to Antioch and deliver the letter in person, in order to confirm its contents face to face and by word of mouth. The apostles and elders made a point of saying that Silas and Judas would be accompanied back to Antioch by Paul and Barnabas; and the Council expressed its full support for Paul and Barnabas, describing them both as dear friends and as men who had risked their lives for the name of the Lord Jesus Christ. In speaking so highly of Paul and Barnabas the Council was endorsing what they had preached in Antioch, Syria, Cyprus and Asia Minor and their decision to preach it to Gentiles as well as to Jews and invite them into the Church. What Paul and Barnabas had preached and what by stating their support for them the Council was fully endorsing, was that all people, both Jew and Gentile, were saved by believing in Jesus and not by carrying out the demands of the Law or adopting the Jewish way of religious practice. Salvation was through Jesus only; there was, there is, no other way.

The Council's letter was a very well balanced letter. On the one hand it told the Gentile Christians that they would not be burdened with any of the requirements of the Law which the men who had come up from Jerusalem had said they must also practice. On the other hand they were told there were certain practices, common in their Gentile cultures, such as eating the flesh of animals that had been sacrificed to idols and drinking the blood of animals killed in honour of idols, were idolatrous and therefore incompatible with the faith of the Church they now belonged to.

It is in saying this to their Gentile brethren that the Council introduced a concept which is as pertinent and significant now, two thousand years later, as it was then. The crucial theological issue each time Christianity engages with a culture is to decide what constitutes the "compulsory/essentials/necessary things" (Acts 15:28, different words used in different translations) that God wants of us; and in this instance the Church in the person of the Council of Jerusalem ruled that the Law was not necessary, even though it was their total upbringing, their dearest attachment, they had known little else. It was the most incisive of insights, on their part the bravest of decisions. It is what the Church needs today, immediately, urgently as I will outline in the concluding chapter of this book.

Finally, in what is the first official written document of the Christian Church, Jesus is called Lord and Christ (Acts 15:26). The title Christ affirms that Jesus is the Messiah, and as the letter is being addressed to Gentiles the affirmation is that he is Messiah for all humanity. The title Lord as at this moment in the development of the Church's understanding of Jesus at the very least means that it is Jesus and his gospel that should be ruling minds and hearts and is the source of the grace of salvation. Soon, very soon, however, within a mere two or three years, there is development. Paul declares that Jesus is divine (Philippians 2:5–11) and to him is given the title "Lord" in all its traditional fullness, "the name that is above every name, and every knee should bow, in heaven, on earth and under the earth, and every tongue confess 'Jesus Christ is Lord' to the glory of God the Father".

It is, however, in John's Gospel that the Church proclaims the understanding of Jesus that it finally reached. The gospel was written somewhere between the year 80, which was possibly about the time Luke wrote the Acts, and the year 110. It begins with its Prologue which declares that in the beginning there was the Word, that the Word was with God—that the Word was God—, and the Word became flesh. In their account of the Resurrection and of what the Risen Jesus did and said before he was taken into heaven the Gospel writer(s) describe how and why the apostle Thomas falls on his knees and, in the presence and hearing of his fellow apostles, cries out: "My Lord and my God" (John 20:28). Thomas could not have said this at that moment, none of the apostles would have arrived at that insight so early, but of course he could well have said it later, and, when he did, it could have been recorded. It might also indicate that he was a member of the Johannine school—if, that is, he hadn't already gone by ship to Kerala in the south of India. His exclamation is a most fitting conclusion to an account of the person and life of Jesus which begins: "In the beginning was the word, and the word was made flesh."

When in their letter the apostles and elders said to the Gentile Christians that they were not to be burdened with the requirements of the Law, they were saying to them that the world of Jewish religious practice was not their world, that they rightly had their own cultures, that they could continue to live in them and that the salvation wrought by Jesus was available to all mankind in every culture. "God has no favourites," as Peter had said. For that reason and with that attitude of mind they were able to conclude their letter to their Gentile brothers in Antioch, Syria and Cilicia with a most encouraging and fortifying final word: "If you keep yourselves from these things—any involvement in idolatrous practice and sexual immorality—you will be doing all right. Farewell!" It really was a marvellous way to end their deliberations; and their letter, containing the very simplest of instructions, with no more than a couple of words, with no pious waffle and no long catechism of dos and don'ts, tells the new converts that they should just get on with their lives in the circumstances they find themselves in, in their own cultural environments, believing in the Lord Jesus as sole saviour. Salvation is reconciliation with God; and reconciliation with God is carried out by God.

Christianity is really a very simple religion—as well as the wildest ever conceived. God loves mankind and became one with it, even dying for it. All he asks is kindness to our fellow men and women in return. This has no truck with the mass of regulations we create in order to control behaviour. There has to be regulations but they should be as few as possible; they should be as limited as common sense can make them. God's instruction to us is simplicity itself: "Love God and your neighbour as yourself"; and Paul, confronting the faction that had descended on Galatia to hollow out the minds of his converts and subvert the teaching he had given to their community, described the sort of vibrant form that Christianity should take: "The harvest of the Spirit is love, joy, peace, patience, kindness, goodness, fidelity, gentleness and self-control. There is no law dealing with such things as these . . . If the Spirit is the source of our life, let the Spirit also direct how we live it" (Galatians 5:22–5). To be Christian is those two things: to believe that Jesus is our saviour; and to live the life of his Spirit. Faith without life in the Spirit is dead. Faith and to live by the Spirit in the way Paul describes are God's two requirements.

The valediction to the three churches merits repetition: "If you keep yourselves from these things—any involvement in idolatrous practice and sexual immorality—you will be doing all right. Farewell!" One need only compare it with the closing lines of St Paul's first letter to the Thessalonians written a mere twelve to eighteen months later: "May God himself, the God of peace, make you holy in every part and keep you sound in spirit, soul and body and without fault when our Lord Jesus Christ comes. He who calls you is to be trusted; he will do it. Brothers, pray for us also. Greet all our brothers with the kiss of peace. I adjure you by the Lord to have this letter read to all the brotherhood. The grace of our Lord Jesus Christ be with you." There was nothing like that in the Council's concluding words, no doxology, no mention of God the Father and of the Lord Jesus or the Spirit, no blessings, no gracious and heartfelt prayer for the spiritual welfare of the recipients. Not even Paul's short and simple wish to the Philippians "The grace of our Lord Jesus Christ be with your spirit, my brothers. Amen". Yet in its own way the ending of the Council's letter is a breath of fresh air, very human, no airs and graces, very ordinary, very matter-of-fact, just a cheery farewell. It was business done, and now let's move on; and in that spirit the Council of Jerusalem ended.

There would have been final prayers; they would have carried out the express wish of Jesus to "do this in memory of me" and held the service of the Eucharist, though precisely in what form and with what accompanying prayers we know not, other than the recitation of the words of the Last Supper as Paul informs us in 1 Corinthians 11. And then they departed, to take the Lord's gospel to every nation, even to the ends of the earth. We know the names of only a few of the people who were there; where they all went to we do not know, who went with whom and how they departed from each other we do not know. They themselves left but one record of their meeting, which was to become the most important in the history of Christianity. That record was a letter, a mere 149 words, no more than seven verses, which fortunately was kept safe and was made known to Luke.

The message issued by the Council was that declared by Peter, that what matters is faith in Jesus as saviour. The observance of the Law and of the rituals and prescriptions of the culture of the Jewish people did not convey salvation, they were only preparatory instruments for the moment when "faith in Jesus Christ may be the ground on which the promised blessing is given, and given to those who have such faith. Before this faith came, we were close prisoners in the custody of the Law, pending the revelation of faith. Thus the Law was a kind of tutor in charge of us until Christ should come, when we should be justified through faith. And now that faith has come, the tutor's charge is at an end" (Galatians 3:22). Jesus had come; it was "the fullness of time" (4:4).

The Law of Moses had been replaced by the Law of Christ. But what is the Law of Christ? The Council members had made a monumental choice, a towering decision, between past and future, their own past and the way forward for the Church they were establishing. They had repudiated in themselves, as well as for others, the "Mosaic" mentality of narrow Judaism. Yet they remained Jews, they stayed firmly Jewish. They had no need to change any of that. What had changed in them was not their origins, what had changed in them was an understanding of what was meant by "the people of God". "In truth," as Peter said, "I see now that God has no favourites." All peoples were the Chosen People; and what Stephen had argued, detail by detail, even at the cost of his life, was that the Promised Land was no longer any one country, it was all the earth, God was everywhere in equal fashion, all peoples were the chosen people wherever they were, whatever parcel of land they were standing on, wherever it was. Given what these first Christians were, all this was an incredible change in their minds and hearts; and God's grace alone enabled it. It is something which today's Christians, Jews and Moslems need to reflect on. Jerusalem, Palestine, Mecca, Medina, Rome, Constantinople, Moscow, wherever, have no more worth—but no less—than the humblest village in Outer Mongolia or the poorest most miserable favela in South America or the most deprived and abandoned shambles of a failed inner-city district in Europe or the USA.

That, just that, in its way should be enough to enable us to appreciate the greatness of the Council of Jerusalem, to make us appreciate what a monumental revolution the first Christians had achieved. "Common people/country bumpkins" the Council of the Jews had called the apostles. Nothing could be further from the truth. Through the workings of the Spirit of God within them individually and collectively they had seen through the limitations of the religion they had been born into. They had come to understand "the mystery, the secret, hidden from all ages till now". They had proclaimed the universality of the salvation wrought by Jesus of Nazareth, son of Mary, Son of God. But at the same time they had held on to all the sublime things within the religion of their inheritance which God had inspired for the benefit of all mankind and which the Church has made known, and daily makes known, through its liturgy.

They had been led by the Spirit of God to change the way humanity was to understand its relationship with him. "God is love" (1 John 4:8). He did not create humanity for the purpose of being worshipped, to be declared he is great. He doesn't need any of that. Rather, as God is, God does. Loving explains creation. God created in order to share. And God then went much further: "For God loved the world so much that he gave his only Son, so that everyone who has faith in him may not die but have eternal life" (John 3:16). What God in Christ asks of us in return for the love he has shown to humankind is that "You love one another as I have loved you", which finds such simple expression in what Paul wrote as set out above to the Christians of Galatia in Galatians 5:22–5.

This small group of people, assembled in a house in Jerusalem, almost two thousand years ago, had cast off from their moorings and sailed free, free and equipped to "make disciples of all nations" (Matthew 28:19b), free to preach the gospel "throughout all the world and to all creation" (Mark 16:15), and "to the ends of the earth" (Acts 1:8). That was the achievement of the Council of Jerusalem.

# CHAPTER 29

# The Epistles to the Colossians and the Ephesians

To appreciate better what that achievement of the Council was we need to turn to the epistles to the Colossians and the Ephesians. Who their authors were we cannot be sure, there is discussion and disagreement amongst the scholars. A majority of the scholars consider both epistles to be pseudonymous, the former written some fifteen to twenty years after the death of Paul, about in fact the same time as Luke's Gospel and the Acts, and the latter a little later. There is a case, as will be evident, for thinking that the author of Ephesians, either an individual or a school, might well have drawn on Colossians. Those details about them, however, are secondary. Both letters are in the Canon, they are statements of the Christian faith, that is what matters. What stands out most in both of them is their presentation of what Jesus means for mankind and what baptism and belief in him give to each individual person. What is particularly significant in respect of the story told in the Acts is that their description of belief in Jesus and baptism directly and expressly builds on what had been first said by Peter at the Council and on what the Council repudiated in respect of the role of the Law and Judaic religious practices in God's plan of salvation for humanity. Both letters instruct us in the profundities of that plan for each believing person, but what is required for an adequate understanding and appreciation of it is knowledge of the issues settled at the Council of Jerusalem.

That divine plan Paul called "the mystery/secret" (Romans 16:25). What Paul meant by calling it "mystery" was that, until in the fullness of time when Jesus Christ came, the belief of God's chosen people was that God's saving plan was for the Jews only and was to be achieved through the observation of the Law. However, the truth, "the mystery", after it had been "kept hidden from times eternal", was something startlingly different and, says Paul, it was now "revealed—by the commandment of the eternal God to all the nations to bring them to faith and obedience" (vv. 25–7). The author of the first letter of the two attributed to Peter speaks to us in the same vein: "Remember, you were not redeemed by anything corruptible, neither in silver or gold, but in the precious blood of a lamb without spot or stain, namely Christ; who, though known since before the world was made, has been revealed only in our time, the end of the ages" (Ephesians 1:18–20).

What the two authors of Ephesians and Colossians say about what Christ did for us and what it means to be a Christian, and what is bestowed upon us by reason of our faith in him and our baptism, goes far beyond Luke's record of what Peter said at the Council. They describe the incredible riches conferred by the gift and grace of Christ, and that in a way and to an extent that very likely at the time of the Council Peter and his fellow apostles had not themselves grasped. However, what is also a matter of real fascination and is particularly relevant to this paper is that, even though they are writing up to thirty years later, the two authors do it with explicit reference to the very core of the difference between Peter and his fellow apostles on the one side and the Judaic faction on the other. They give us an even deeper insight into the immense significance of the argument that had raged between Peter and the Judaic faction in the fifteen or more years that followed on the Ascension by telling us more about what had been bestowed on us through Christ and through him alone. They and their communities and schools had clearly devoted much prayer and discussion to it in the years that followed the Council; and the presentation of Christ that they describe is one that should be made known to all Christian believers and to those to whom he is preached.

# Colossians from Chapters 1 to 3

He is the image of the invisible God, the first born of all creation. All things in heaven and earth were created in him and for him. He is the head of the body, the church. God was pleased to have all his fullness dwell in him and through him to reconcile all things to himself, making peace through the shedding of his blood upon the cross, all things, whether on earth or in heaven. He has reconciled you by Christ's physical body in order to present you holy in his sight, without blemish, as long as you continue in the faith, grounded and steadfast. Continue to live in him, Christ Jesus the Lord, rooted and built up in him. In him all the fullness of the Godhead dwells in bodily form. You have been given fullness in Christ who is the head of all power and authority. In him you were circumcised in the putting off of the sinful nature, not with a circumcision done by the hands of men but with the circumcision done by Christ, buried with him in baptism and raised with him through your faith in the power of God who raised him from the dead. God made you alive with Christ. He forgave us all our sins, having cancelled the written code with its regulations. He took it away, nailing it to the cross. Therefore, do not let anyone judge you by what you eat or drink or with regard to a religious festival, a new moon celebration or a Sabbath day. These are a shadow of the things that were to come, the solid reality is found in Christ. If then you were raised with Christ, set your minds on things above where Christ is seated at the right hand of God. For you died and your life is now hidden in Christ. When Christ, who is your life, appears, you will then also appear with him in glory. Put to death whatever belongs to your earthly nature: sexual immorality, uncleanness, lust, evil desires and greed which is idolatry, anger, rage, malice, slander and filthy language. Put on your new self which is being renewed in knowledge in the image of its Creator. Here there is no Greek or Jew, circumcised or uncircumcised, barbarian, Scythian, slave or freeman, but Christ is all and is in all. As God's chosen people, holy and beloved, clothe yourselves with compassion, kindness,

> humility, gentleness and patience. Forgive as the Lord forgave
> you. And above all put on love to bind all together in perfect
> unity. Let the peace of Christ rule in your hearts since as members
> of one body you were called to peace. And let the word of Christ
> dwell in you. (New English Bible)

What an incredible description of Jesus is this statement, what an incredible account it is of what God has bestowed on each individual man and woman in Christ, in whom all the fullness of the Godhead dwells in bodily form (Colossians 2:9). Through baptism we share in that fullness. That is what conversion to Jesus Christ, belief in him, is; it is what should be preached from every altar, from every pulpit, in every church, to every individual Christian. Yet it can only be fully understood and appreciated if there is understanding and appreciation of the Council of Jerusalem. It does not mention the Council but explicitly it deals with the issues the Council addressed and it built its whole message upon the resolution of them that the Council achieved.

## From Ephesians 1—2

In the same way the author of the letter to the Ephesians around the year 90 could not have made the following statement without what had been achieved in their understanding of Jesus by the people who attended the Council, and it is a text which should be put before every Christian time and again and before whomever the gospel is preached to.

> In Christ we have redemption through his blood, the forgiveness
> of sins, in accordance with the riches of God's grace which he
> lavished upon us with all wisdom and understanding. I keep
> asking that the God of our Lord Jesus Christ, the glorious father,
> may give you the Spirit of wisdom and revelation, so that you
> may know him better and the hope to which he has called you,
> the riches of his glorious inheritance in the saints. God placed
> all things under Christ's feet and appointed him to be head over

THE EPISTLES TO THE COLOSSIANS AND THE EPHESIANS 307

all the church which is his body. God raised us up with Christ and seated us with him in the heavenly realms, in order that in the coming ages he might show the incomparable riches of his grace expressed in his kindness to us in Christ Jesus. For it is by grace that you have been saved, through faith. And this is not your doing, it is the gift of God and not by works done. So that no one can boast. For we are God's handicraft, created in Christ Jesus to do good works, which God prepared in advance that we might walk in them. Remember that formerly you who are Gentiles in the flesh and called "uncircumcised" by those who call themselves "the circumcised" in the flesh which is done by hand. Remember that you were separate from Christ, excluded from the citizenship of Israel, foreigners from the covenants of the promise, without hope and without God in the world. But now you are in Christ Jesus. You who were once so far away, have been brought near through the blood of Christ. For he is our peace who has made the two peoples one and he has destroyed the barrier, the dividing wall of hostility by abolishing in his flesh the Law with its commandments and regulations. His purpose was to create in himself one new man out of two, thus making peace. Consequently you are no longer foreigners and aliens but fellow citizens with God's people and members of God's household.

There is something profoundly mystical here. This isn't just theology at its profoundest; it is sheer mysticism, and one can only wonder how the Church in the person of its members, by the time both those passages were written, achieved such an understanding. What a body of people thinking and at prayer the early Church must have been. It is mysticism unsurpassed, it is theology unsurpassed; and both these statements are ours, to read, reflect on, savour and absorb. They should be made part of the baptismal liturgy and one of them with a small adaptation read out loud over the head of every Christian child. It should be read out loud every year at assemblies and meetings and masses in all Christian secondary schools, colleges, universities and chaplaincies in order to make everyone, every single Christian boy and girl hearing them, aware of their incredible dignity and worth, aware of the baptism that constitutes their identity. To do that is to go forward.

It is the vision of the human being that the Church should proclaim, this is what the Church through its parents in the home and what its pope, curia, cardinals, bishops and archbishops, priests and members of its religious orders should be proclaiming from their pulpits and in all written statements. There has to be a worldwide promulgation of this vision, this inspiration, this statement of the incredible dignity of the human being. Visions inspire. What these passages tell us just cannot be celebrated enough, they are what Christ died for, it is the Christian message. It is peace and unity for the whole world.

It is not a notion of religion in which there is force and submission, nor one that is considered to belong just to one people. It preaches none of any of that. It was that understanding that persuaded the Jewish founding members of the Christian Church to break with their Judaic beliefs as to what and who constituted salvation and enabled them to take that gospel to the non-Jews who make up over 99 per cent of humanity. Today Jews are 0.2 per cent of the world's population. There is no reason to think that proportion was different in the year 49. It is a most interesting and helpful statistic. It makes one even more aware of the total inadequacy of the faction's understanding of salvation, of God's concern for humanity. The faction would have taken the Church, in the very years of its infancy, into immeasurable error. The gospel is about universal love and friendship and community. Salvation is God's gift; and it is on offer to all humanity, "It is not strain'd; it droppeth as the gentle rain from heaven upon the place beneath. It is twice bless'd; it blesseth him that gives and him that takes". That is the Christian religion. In Christ God has revealed himself to be loving all mankind, our Creator loving us all, not looking for glory and obeisance from us, not asking us to shout about his greatness, but, incredibly, becoming one of us and dying for us. These declarations, these statements of the epistles to the Colossians and the Ephesians, are the expansion and explanation of what the Council of Jerusalem achieved. They are what the Church of the twenty-first century should now place before all its members and the world today. Each baptized person must have this awareness of himself and herself, of what God in Jesus Christ has changed in them, if the Church is to be reborn and expand further and deeper into the rest of the world, in the many centuries ahead. The Church collectively must make this awareness its life, every Christian must be told about it and it must be preached to the whole world.

# CHAPTER 30

# The Necessity of Change: Christianity in Today's World and Culture

> I lifted up my eyes and there I saw a man carrying a measuring line. I asked him, "Where are you going?" and he answered me: "To measure Jerusalem and find out how wide and how long it is". Then, as the angel who spoke with me was going away, another angel came out to meet him and said to him: "Run to the young man there and tell him that Jerusalem shall be a city without walls, so numerous shall be the men and cattle within it." I will be a wall of fire around her, says the Lord, and her glory within her. (Zechariah 2:1–5)

That is what the first Christians at the Council of Jerusalem achieved. They took away the walls built round and into their minds and with that the walls around their church. They opened up their minds to change and with it they opened up the Church to the world. They were magnificent people. They were open to the Spirit, they lived with the Spirit, they walked with the Spirit; and my interest here is how they showed themselves open to the Spirit. It is hoped that in these pages what they changed from and what they changed to, and what it all represented, and the immense difficulties they had in doing it, have been adequately described. The Church could have been enclosed and narrow, just another Judaic sect; instead they made it a city without walls, open to the whole of mankind, at its heart the fire of the Holy Spirit. That has to happen again. Now.

Trusting in the wall of fire, which is the Spirit that is within her, the Church has to change, it has to open itself up, it has to throw open doors to fresh winds if it is to hold on to its membership, give them solid reason to feel that their Christianity and their baptism are an essential, vibrant part of their identity and equip them to take it into their modern world. That is what matters above all else, that Church members see and feel that their Christianity and their baptism in all aspects are an essential and vibrant part of their own culture and identity, which they just cannot do as long as the Church holds on to certain major components of a culture which are now not just outdated but are also to be repudiated as, in some cases, discriminatory, or they are as Peter described them to the Council "a yoke" which has become impossible to bear, or they are as the Council's letter itself describes them: no longer "essential". The Church has to change, and change seriously, if it is to renew and grow the ministry of its membership; it has to change, and change seriously, if it is to present Christ and his gospel successfully in the cultures of today's world. Church members should not feel ashamed and defensive about what the Church is, but proud and content. To bring about that change is required in today's Church, in today's very different world, because people have changed as a result of the achievements of Western humanity and the direction the West has taken in the last three hundred years and the immense cultural changes it has brought about.

But with the phrase "today's Church" I am confronted by a problem. Which Church? Which Church am I to deal with? There is the Catholic Church, there are the Orthodox Churches, and there are the Protestant Churches inclusive of the Pentecostal Churches. Together they make up 32 per cent of the world's population of 7 billion. Of that 32 per cent the Catholic Church comprises just over 50 per cent and the Orthodox Churches 12 per cent. I am a Catholic. I am very reluctant to suggest changes to the Protestant Churches. One reason is it would be downright impolite to do so, especially for a Catholic when there's enough, more than enough, reason for him or her to try to put their own house in order first. I can speak bluntly to the leadership of my own church. Another reason is that two major changes I will be proposing, which are about how Catholic women and married men are treated, have already happened in the Protestant churches. Nonconformist churches for sound theological reasons have long had women ministers, it is something they simply take for granted. The Anglican Church has now opened up the priesthood to women, and I feel nothing but great admiration for it and immense gratitude for being able on and off to experience how good it has proved. There is then a third reason. Between them the Catholic and Orthodox churches, which hold the same sacramental beliefs, constitute 63 per cent of Christianity, and the Catholic Church, which comprises just over half of all Christianity, finds itself more than the rest in the headlights of modern media in the West. This might be a controversial assertion to make, but it does seem to me that because of its size and universality, and because in the West it has become the main representative media-wise of Christianity as a whole, it is very much in the interests of Christianity generally that the changes that are needed are adopted by the Catholic Church. The Catholic Church is massive both intellectually and in its social, educational, medical and charitable endeavours. Being one of its members I can legitimately address some of its shortcomings and the changes it needs to make in a forthright manner.

The foremost achievement of the Apostolic Church in the year 49 at the Council of Jerusalem, a mere fifteen years or so after the Ascension of the Lord and its foundation on the Jewish feast day of Pentecost, our Whit Sunday, was in their understanding of Jesus and his mission. That is the crux of everything. As an understanding of him it wasn't as theologically capacious and refined as that achieved by later councils, but it was the foundation of all later Christological and Trinitarian achievements. As a result of the understanding of Jesus that they had arrived at the apostles realized that certain dominant features of the religious beliefs, mind-set and practices they had inherited from their Judaic origins and lived by from birth and had presumed would continue, had in fact to be thoroughly re-thought, some even abandoned, even though those practices were what they had thought, and had been taught, were their way to God and God's way to them. They came to realize that Jesus of Nazareth, son of God and son of Mary, was God's way to them and their way to him and nothing else was. Without that achievement they and their fellow Christians could not have gone out and preached a Jesus Christ who could possibly be acceptable to the Gentiles and their different cultures. It took a monumental rethink on their part, a radical transformation of understanding by them of what God's plan for humanity was. That plan Paul was to call "the divine secret, kept in silence for long ages but now revealed and through prophetic scriptures by the eternal God's command made known to all nations to bring them faith and obedience" (Romans 16:25). "All nations", as far as we ourselves are concerned, means the peoples who exist here and now in today's world. It is the only world we live in.

But of course there are many "worlds" out there. There is that of Hinduism, and there is that of the people of China. Together they contain probably a third of the total world population and each of them has its own distinct and cherished culture. There is the world of Islam, another billion people. There are one hundred million Shintoists in Japan; there are many more millions of people who are Buddhist across Asia; and there is the Western world where Christianity is the principal religion but where atheism, agnosticism and indifference to the very notion of religion itself are firmly established and on the increase. However, that is where Christianity is at its strongest intellectually, not least by reason of its long penetration, and indeed development, of Western cultures; and it is Western culture in general and its achievements that do seem, at least in respect of certain major aspects of it, to be influencing, even permeating, all the others, and will continue to do so. How do we present Jesus the Son of Mary, a man from Nazareth, who died almost two thousand years ago, to the peoples who inhabit and live by Western culture?

My main concern here is with his presentation and that of his gospel to this Western population, because it really is the only culture I have lived in and know anything about, though it might well be argued that the issues that exist between it and Christianity will in due course, at least in part, be the future for other populations and cultures too. What can the Church learn from what the members of the Council of Jerusalem did? The Church in the West, inclusive of Australia and New Zealand, is facing severe decline. What should it do? Speaking at this point only very generally I would suggest two things. One is that the Church leadership should perceptively and bravely discard certain attitudes and ways of behaviour and decisions which have accumulated over its centuries of existence and are proving themselves to be a barrier between it and our present-day world; and that will include some which it holds to be of abiding importance, though in fact upon closer examination they will be seen to be products of past cultures and no longer applicable, exactly as the apostles found that the Law was not applicable in the world in which Christ had instructed them to preach his gospel. The second thing is that then in that reassessment and reorganization of itself it takes on those principles and practices of social relationships which its own lay membership shows their approval of by the way they live out their own secular existence.

But where do we start? The canvas is so vast. Faced with the modern humanistic, technological and scientific culture of the Western world, a world populated by highly educated free-thinking, independent-minded people, half of which is female, women who are now standing up and demanding equality with seriously unstoppable determination, the Church has to make some brave and profound changes of mind, attitude and practice. If ever the Church needed vision, needed enlightenment, it is now. The Apostolic Church got it. In Joppa a lamp was lit in Peter's mind. He suddenly saw something and understood something differently and on returning to Jerusalem and being confronted by very hostile "men of the circumcision" his words to them were: "While in a trance I had a vision" (Acts 11:5). If the Church is to be able to take Christ and his gospel to today's world, it needs vision. The vision Peter had came from God. God must now be asked in earnest prayer to supply it again. Reformation is necessary. "*Ecclesia semper reformanda est*—the Church must always be undergoing reform" is an ancient and ever necessary maxim. Every individual Christian who applies his or her mind to the situation Christianity is in in the Western world today, and every individual Christian should, will accept that serious reform is urgently needed. Each of us will have our own individual suggestions about what should be done. All I myself can do is put forward what I myself think must be changed if Christianity is both to hold on to the membership it has at present and preach Christ with success to the rest of humanity. However, to change is very often to discard. What the Church changes into requires as much consideration as what it must discard. I would hope that that clearly emerges from the reasons I will give for the changes I wish to suggest.

I wish to set out first, however, the basic principles I believe must operate if successful and effective changes are to be. There are two fundamental doctrines underlying Christianity. They can of course be put into words in different ways and how I set them out is no more than just how I see them. They are first that Jesus Christ, by reason of his divinity and humanity and his death, resurrection and founding of the Church, which is his mystical body, is the saviour of all humankind, by which is meant that he reconciled humanity to God. Humanity had alienated itself from God, its creator, through sin. Jesus Christ took upon himself the guilt of that sin and by his death and resurrection paid its penalty and reunited man with God. God the Son as a human being did that on behalf of all humankind because he is goodness itself. The second doctrine is that, in the words of Jesus himself, what is required of mankind is to love God and to love our neighbour as ourselves. Love of God and of our neighbour as ourselves is what God wants. As God has stated time and again, he wants "mercy not sacrifice". By "sacrifice" was meant initially the slaughter of animals and birds in the temple in the belief that somehow it constituted worship, and in time a proliferation developed of set rules and regulations of behaviour by which God was to be obeyed. God's interest in us is not in either, that is a trap humanity always falls into. He just does not need adoration and worship, as will be obvious to anyone who gives it serious thought. That is not his nature. God is goodness and giving, and living that is what he wants of us.[24] His interest, if that word may be used, is as expressed by Paul in this letter to the Galatians, in which he is begging them not to fall into the trap of "sacrifice" as I have described its meaning, but to be something else. He writes: "The harvest of the Spirit is love, joy, peace, patience, kindness, goodness, fidelity, gentleness and self-control. There is no law dealing with such things as these ... If the Spirit is the source of our life, let the Spirit also direct how we live" (Galatians 5:22–5). That most crucial insight of Paul into what Christ wants of us in response to the gift of himself which he has made to humankind demands repetition: "There is no law dealing with such things as these." One thing Paul intends by that statement is to say that Christianity is not a religion of regulations but of the Spirit. The reader will make of it what he or she will.

What we have to acknowledge is that over the past three hundred years Christianity has lost an immense amount of its intellectual standing in the West. It has lost out badly to a philosophy of science and of social and personal morality which in the case of some, certainly many, possibly most, of its representatives is atheistic and/or agnostic. An illuminating, if localized, example of this decline in intellectual standing and influence was Christianity's lack of any adequate response to the book *The God Delusion* by Richard Dawkins. *The God Delusion* is a shallow book, in places embarrassingly so, but it gave expression to a prevailing social intellectual perspective, and to the best of my knowledge no one in the English-speaking world put forward any effective refutation. Likewise, I know of no one, except myself,[25] who challenged and exposed Philip Pullman's trilogy despite it being a bestseller among both young and old. Pullman is a good story-teller, brilliant in fact, but his trilogy is viciously anti-religious and explicitly anti-Christian, particularly anti-Catholic, through and through. It was written in part to denigrate and disparage Christianity as much as *The God Delusion*. Both books in their way signalled recognition that Christianity still exercised influence, which might provide a sliver of comfort but shouldn't because both books were written to eradicate it. Both authors want religion to be considered unworthy of serious intellectual consideration and in addition Pullman wants Christianity in particular, especially Catholic Christianity, to be looked on as seriously harmful. Regrettably both ride on a very strong tide.

Times have changed. The times the Church now lives in are radically different not just from those of its foundation 2,000 years ago but also, and possibly especially, from 300 years ago. In the last 300 years, following hard upon the heels of the Enlightenment, which was radical enough, we have had the Industrial Revolution, and now we have a revolution in communication and how it is done which is simply mind-bending. There has been at least two and a half centuries of penetrating industrial, scientific, technological, social and cultural changes, profoundly affecting almost every aspect of intellectual, political, cultural and social life, health, nutrition, entertainment, employment, travel, war, and human relationships, and not least gender and sexual relationships. The last one in that list is massively prominent today. The culture that has developed as a result is the one the Christian population of the West now live in, a culture in fact which Christians themselves have contributed to and have helped create. It is a big part of their culture, they have endorsed a great part of it, and rightly so.

It has been said by historians that human society changed more in the first three or four decades of the Industrial Revolution located in Britain than it had ever done before in all its previous two million years or more of existence. Nineteenth-century German commentators and thinkers called a major aspect of it *Manchestertum*—an ideological commercial and industrial tidal wave—*eine Strömung*—of free trade and political and social liberalism. Friedrich Engels famously described it and its consequences in his book *The Condition of the Working Class in England*, his family made themselves rich out of it. It enabled him to both go out riding with the hounds in the county of Cheshire and keep Karl Marx and his family solvent and out of the workhouse in London. Marx would travel to Manchester on and off to meet with Engels in the—still very visitable—library of Chetham's College in the centre of the city. Bismarck found time and opportunity to pay the city a visit to experience it for himself. It was in all too many respects ugly and brutal, but it was as intellectually driven as it was by commercial motivation. One has only to stand and look a little while at the engineering masterpieces of that period on exhibition in Manchester's Science and Industry Museum to appreciate what was achieved. It was a movement that has gone deep into the modern psyche; it has developed exponentially across the rest of the Western world; it is invading every other national culture; it has brought about deep and immense changes. In the light of that there is something very appropriate in the fact that Manchester and its university have contributed very substantially to computer science and technology which are proving radically transformative in virtually all aspects of our modern world and the lives of every individual.

People are the world which we are discussing; and they have changed. Some of the changes made are good and irreversible. Where across the world people as yet have not changed, whether held back by poverty or politics or the repressive hand of a religion or a dictatorship, they will in due course.[26] Our twenty-first century is in many major respects, not in all of course but in many, the product of those past 300 years. Already in its first two decades there have been radical changes in how people communicate with each other which in turn are having an immense effect on behaviour, morals and politics. These changes demand an adequate response from the Catholic Church. As yet there hasn't been a response that in any way measures up to the changes that have occurred or even shows an adequate awareness of their nature. Instead, in certain most important areas of life it exhibits an excessive attachment to its past, believing in an unrealistic, even at times an arrogant, manner that somehow it is above change, that the moral teaching and the style of government of "the barque of Peter", as admirers of its past call it, can sail majestic and untouchable through all vicissitudes. It just cannot. And it shouldn't. There is a silly boast at times that the Church measures the changes it makes within itself in terms of centuries as if somehow that rightly justifies it to think that it can be slow about change and that it stands loftily aloof and above the rest of mere humanity. It is more than a silly boast, it is both religious snobbery and false pride of a most harmful kind. The reality is that the revolution in how humanity now lives, how it thinks, how it works and in how people relate to each other that has taken place over the last two to three hundred years will grow and develop further while the Church stands in danger of being left centuries behind.

The fact is that the Catholic Church just cannot carry on as it is any longer. As a body, as an institution, in the person of its top representatives, especially the Pope and cardinals, it just cannot continue to impose all the components of the social understanding and the morality which it established to its satisfaction in the centuries before the Enlightenment, the Industrial Revolution and the science and digital technology of the present day. What the Church preaches must be clearly relevant to modern needs. It has to prove its relevance to today's mankind. It is a fifth of the whole human race, it is spread throughout all humanity. Furthermore, "with more than a billion followers the Catholic church is the largest global organization the world has ever seen".[27] Its position is unique. It stands at the beginning of its second two thousand years of existence. It could do an immense amount of good if, in defiance of the opposing forces within it, it could settle on a very serious re-think of itself to contribute to the new ways in which the world it inhabits now behaves.

A lot of the version of science in the Western world, which worldwide is the dominating version, has turned out to be aggressively anti-religious, and its influence on the Catholic membership, indeed on all Western Christianity, has been widespread. Evidence of that is a very drastic, and continuing, drop in attendance at church services and, in the Catholic

Church, in applications to the priesthood, which is bringing about widespread closure of churches and amalgamations of parishes. The fewer the preachers and the smaller the congregations that listen to them, the smaller is the influence that the Church will exercise and the greater is the impoverishment of the education in the faith among the baptized. Undoubtedly the prevailing version of science and of anti-religious humanism influences young and old. Western youth live in that culture. It is their culture in that it surrounds them, they breathe it in. It is a culture which in innumerable ways despises religious belief as outdated, unscientific, unprovable, reactionary and hostile to the enjoyment of living. It contains eminent members who sneer at religion. It is in part a culture, by which is meant a mentality or perspective on life, which sees no reason for belief in God and, accordingly, for an afterlife. It is in part a culture that considers religious practice meaningless and openly represents it as hostile to progress and as mental servitude. Every Western country is experiencing this. In the USA 55 per cent of Catholics went to Mass regularly in 1965; by 2000 only 22 per cent did. In 1965 1.3 million Catholic babies there were baptized; in 2016 only 670,000.[28]

Ireland, for centuries a strongly Catholic country, is an example. A very recent census there revealed that people who say they have no religion are the fastest growing part of the Irish population, with a 74-per-cent increase to 481,388 in 2016. The group makes up 10 per cent of the population and has an average age of 34.[29] The two recent referenda, the one on gay marriage, the second on abortion, have shown beyond any doubt that the hold of Catholic moral authority on the Irish population has departed. Possibly Ireland can no longer be described as a Catholic country but instead as a country with very many Catholics in it. It most certainly has liberated itself from clericalism, which is a very good thing even though it has achieved that step forward over the issue of abortion, which is acutely morally delicate and which the referendum most certainly did not deal with the moral and intellectual refinement that was needed. However, in the mix of arguments, feelings and passion that characterized debate in both referenda, a very strong, but very understandable anti-clericalism played its part, as did utter disgust at the sexual abuse of youth by a significant number of the clergy. One cannot help but think sometimes that if the Irish clergy had put out statements supporting both gay marriage and abortion, the outcomes in each of the two referenda would have been the reverse of what they actually were, or at least near enough.

As far as the Western world is concerned, which has developed a deep and pervasive support for democracy, the Church is out of step. Democracy has not been internalized in the Catholic Church itself even though the Church's theology and its biblical sources are prominent components of its foundation and origin. The equality of women with men is fundamental to it. It is in no way an historical accident that democracy has rooted and developed in countries which have a Christian heritage. Yet, despite that, Catholicism, and with it the rest of Christianity, in the West is losing its intellectual standing. Our technological and scientific culture treats faith as myth and as hostile to reason. In the UK, in the case of the Church of England that has happened already. The British Social Attitudes survey 2018, for example, has found that only two 2 per cent of British young adults identify with the Church of England. It would appear true to say that very many people see no use in religion; they do not attend services, because services no longer mean anything to them. There is both indifference and rejection. What is of equal concern is that, in contrast, in many important respects it is the Western world, where this is happening, that is looked upon by much of the rest of the world as contributing greatly to intellectual, cultural and scientific leadership.

There therefore has to be a resurrection of intellect within the Church if in respect of attitudes to Christianity it is to defeat the anti-religion form of scientism and humanism which, as does appear to be the case, at present dominates Western culture, and infiltrates almost every young mind. All this is known of course to the leadership of the Catholic Church, it is visible and widespread, it stares the local parish clergy in the face at every Sunday Mass when they look at who is there. Those who are there are predominantly the elderly. Young people, though baptized and attending Catholic schools, are absent. Just a few attend but at the very most no more than 5 per cent of the Catholic school population. It isn't defiance on their part, it isn't some sinful or anti-religious mentality, it is because they do not see any need to be there. The Catholic Christian education they are receiving in their schools is failing if success in this matter is to be calculated by church attendance; and church attendance most definitely is one correct way to calculate it. Church attendance offers biblical and eucharistic sustenance without which the Christian spirit will not be sustained. The prayers of the eucharistic rite, its reading of the Scriptures and the sermons delivered, remind, maintain and extend the Christian education received in childhood and as youths. But the youth population of the Church is now not in attendance, and most Catholic school pupils do not appear to consider their baptism as part of their identity. Unless and until they do, whatever Christian education they might be receiving at Catholic schools is failing. The Church presents itself as an institution which defies some of the important basics of the culture they belong to and believe in.

Decline in the Church in many places is now feeding on itself. Interestingly, and tragically, the places where that is happening are the parts of the world where the Church was strongest, where through its immense intellectual input and the humanitarian and civic philosophy which it has imparted to humankind over centuries, it has created the very conditions which now threaten it. Atheism and anti-religious humanism are commonest and are most "missionary" and strident in the countries where Christianity has been the very foundation stone of the culture and civilization which free-thinking needs in order to exist. The Christian belief is that God the Creator endowed human beings with free will and that free will is the sine qua non of morality. Belief in free thinking as a human right and the right way to conduct one's life is a direct consequence of that belief. That is Catholic teaching. It is no accident, no mere coincidence, but a direct consequence of that teaching, that free-thinking is a feature of both modern Christian and post-Christian societies. Free-thinking is what people in today's Western cultures want. They want reasons for doing things, rightly they want to know why, they don't want to do them just because some authority or other, some religious or political system or dictator says so. They want to judge for themselves. People want freedom; and so they should. In sharp contrast there is Islam. For the Islam that we are presented with today, in contrast to Christianity, free-thinking is held to be inimical to its understanding of the nature of religion. Wherever modern Islam has political control there is restriction of freedom of expression and religious choice. The worst example of that is its opposition to the right of a person to convert to another religion. That, among other things, arises from a wrong, and a harmful, understanding of God.

I went to Mass on the second Sunday of Advent 2016 in the church of the parish I happened to be in that weekend, the 10-o-clock Mass, the usual time or thereabouts for Sunday Mass for families. The church had pews enough for at least 300 people. Thirty or forty years ago the church would have been packed for this Sunday Mass. This time no more than forty people turned up, most of them taking the pews in the back half of the church. Barely a soul in the front rows. Eighty per cent of those present were elderly like myself. Just one single mum and her little boy. Other than that not one single family to be seen. Yet the Catholic primary school is located right next door. Such a poor attendance is now commonplace. The church was cold, everyone wore overcoats. The sermon was virtually inaudible because the mike made it a blur. There was no atmosphere, no life, the priest was in his 60s or 70s, he looked tired and dispirited, there was no music.

I also attended Mass on the Feast of All Saints, 1 November 2017, at our local Catholic primary school. The contrast was total. The children came in to the hall, all 200 or so of them, class by class, most of them with their hands clasped as if in prayer, which I very much doubt they were doing. It was communal, heart-warming, happy, with the pupils doing the readings and every one of them singing the hymns by heart at the top of their voices, with every one of them except the youngest classes taking Holy Communion. Behaviour was happy and perfect. Yet in that same parish I attend the family Mass at 10:30am the following Sunday. If there's 10 per cent of those children ever there, it would be a great surprise to me. At least 90 per cent of them don't attend, neither do their families. There is a glaring discordance between church and school which threatens the continued existence of the former.

The evidence of a severe decline in the Western Church in two crucial criteria, namely understanding of and identification with one's baptism, is indisputable. If approaching wholesale absence from the liturgical life of the Church tells us anything it is that Catholic schools in the UK are failing to achieve a conscious belief in and identification with one's baptism in the minds and hearts of Catholic school children who attend them. All I can do here is put forward a few of the things I believe should be done. Whatever is the right path forward, the Holy Spirit will not do it all for us. For God human freedom is his most precious gift. The Holy Spirit collaborates, and he will do it with gusto, but the Church has itself got to think out the path to renewal and resolutely set out upon it. It's got to be that partnership of "the Holy Spirit and us" (Acts 15:28), as the apostles said in their letter to the churches in Antioch, Syria and Cilicia.

Just to give one example. The bishops in the Western world from the Pope downwards are confronted with a massive reduction in the number of priests. It has forced them to close down churches, reduce the number of services on Sundays and Holy Days and redraw parish boundaries. But what are they doing to get more men to apply for the priesthood? They just "pray for vocations", while they persist defiantly in the restriction of the priesthood to celibate males who get fewer by the day. It has to be said, and said bluntly, their prayers are a total waste of time. The Holy Spirit does not answer prayers which defy evidence and common sense, and support a status quo which has no support from either biblical or dogmatic theology whatsoever and are really only intended to give some sort of pious justification to the status they find themselves in, no matter how great a disaster the status quo is proving to be. The Holy Spirit is speaking to us loud and clear in what is staring the Western Church in the face. The day of a priesthood restricted to the celibate, an enforced unmarried priesthood, and a male only priesthood, is over, it's dead; and the Holy Spirit is telling us just that by confronting us with the reality that is the Church today. It is a Church that is emptying itself by its stubbornness, it is itself stripping itself of its priesthood. If the Catholic Church leadership, from the Vatican right down to the local bishop, were a business, they would have been sacked by shareholders and shown the door ages ago. And they know it all right. What is increasingly happening is that once bishops retire, aged seventy five or older, and become what they now are calling themselves "bishop emeritus", which looks grand, some of them write letters to Catholic newspapers and periodicals to let us know how much they really supported the proposal of a married clergy, even female clergy, but felt bound to keep quiet about it when in office. I just wonder how they now have the nerve to do it. Just one of them while in office making a stand and stepping down if need be would have achieved far more. As for their colleagues from the Pope downwards they will all have to answer before the throne of God for their obstinacy, and indeed for their timidity.

The Catholic Church, in this first quarter of the twenty-first century, has to do a Council of Jerusalem. It must separate the "essentials/necessary things" from what is not, and jettison what is outdated or irrelevant or whatever is, as Peter described it, "a burden too heavy to bear" (Acts 15:10). The "barque of Peter", as I have heard Catholic romantics call it, must now like a ship in peril from the sea lighten itself by throwing the dead weight of useless cargo overboard, such as refusal of the priesthood to married men and to women. Bravely the Church has got to apply itself to ridding its membership of the burden of moral demands which it once thought were necessary and are not, and it must, in a positive manner, ask its membership to direct their Christianity to issues which in today's world are crying to God to be dealt with. The Church of the twenty-first century has to sail free; it has to streamline itself, it has to travel light. It has to do a Council of Jerusalem.

We must look at where we are at. The fact is, both in its leadership and right down to parish level, the Church is institutionally sexist. It discriminates against women, and it does it shamelessly, openly and seriously. It is institutionally undemocratic because it is excessively centralized in respect of its government and restricts power and authority to the narrowest number of its membership. It is ruled by a tiny clique of male celibates, most of whom are old, who select each other and exclude all married men and all women from its government even though women and married men make up over 99.99 per cent of its membership. This situation is an absurdity, lacking any rational and theological justification. It is a dire insult to women. The Church is clericalist, it excludes the laity from participation in Church government and in the formulation of its faith and liturgy. Its liturgy is excessively centred on priests, it carries out its liturgy almost entirely around them, it dresses them and parades them in the antiquated vestments of ancient Rome which have no Christian origin and significance whatsoever. The liturgy needs to have life, vivacity, and variety with modern features as much as its ancient features. All that is just some of the modern reality that the Church must face up to if it is to follow the example of the Council of Jerusalem and become relevant and acceptable in today's Western world.

There is widespread alienation of girls and women, because they are excluded from its management and its priesthood. If this mentality towards women, which is flagrantly sexist, were given voice and its measures enacted anywhere else in modern progressive society, the perpetrators would rightly be outed as bigots, brought before the courts and prosecuted on grounds of blatant sex discrimination. The leadership of the Church justifies it artificially and wrongly on so-called religious grounds when all that is nothing more than ingrained sexism, a sexism which permeates through all the life of the Church as in fact it does virtually all human institutions, derived from too many previous centuries. Its leadership is out of touch with modern life, with the cultural, social, educational and employment aspirations and achievements of today's women, with the changes brought about in gender and sexual relationships by the last 200 years of cultural, scientific, technological, political and educational innovation and progress. The Church badly needs the insights and experience of women as well as men, and of both married men and women if it wants to achieve a balanced, genuinely respected, knowledgeable, compassionate, perceptive ability, and indeed a reliable instinct, to teach and advise on such matters as the morality of sexual and medical behaviour and social legislation. If there is one massive wall the Church has erected around itself it is professional celibacy; and that wall wrapped right around it shuts in and shuts out. It confines initiative and imagination about what the Church should be and do to one very little group of males, pathetic in number, incredibly limited intellectually and emotionally because they are so few, and all single-sex at that. All this nonsense must stop.

There has to be on the part of the Church acceptance of modern attitudes towards women, sexual relationships and birth control. The pill is safe, reliable and effective birth control and its availability and usage has changed the Catholic laity's moral understanding of sexual relationships and activity in certain significant ways and in serious measure. On this issue the laity is ignoring, indeed defying, its hierarchical leadership. They see no good reason why sexual intercourse between wife and husband cannot, when they want it to be, just for pleasure and enjoyment. After all, it isn't much to ask in return for the heavy responsibilities of being parents. Only people who by the decisions they have made about their own lives have cut themselves off from that experience, and the pleasures and the responsibilities that it brings, can possibly think otherwise. They, the Pope included, when they outlawed artificial contraception, as they called it, were not fully qualified to deal with the matter. The papacy made a mistake, as popes do on and off, in what it taught in this matter, a mistake that undermined confidence in the Church's teaching authority. It was a monumental blunder. At the very least that mistake and the response of the laity to it should tell the Church leadership that when it comes to judgement on matters of sexual behaviour and marriage, reliance on the opinions of celibate clergy alone is not wise. The involvement of women in the Church's decisions about sexual morality would at the least add a nuance which for centuries has been missing. There is no substitute for experience of the reality of sexual and gender relationships.

We are in today's world; and if the Church is to have a role in it and retain its existing membership and deepen and expand their understanding of their faith and reinvigorate their commitment to it, it simply has to involve them; it has to democratize itself. Its membership are convinced members of today's culture and very many matters of social, moral and political significance, such as gender equality and democratic rule, are their culture. It is what they live with and what they live by. The Church has got to repudiate some major aspects of the past cultures it has lived in and adopt what is good in the cultures its membership believes in and practises.

The main thing the Church has got to get into its head is the basic realization that it is allowing itself to suffer badly not just by being ancient but also by persisting in it. It has spent most of its existence within political cultures that have been, and in many places still are, autocratic in government, such as the political culture of the imperium of Rome, and are sexist in their attitude towards women. Not just the Church, however. Sexism has pretty well been the whole world's, not just the Church's, attitude towards women since whenever, from which it did not, and still has not, escaped. Sexism has penetrated deep into its structures even though, in contrast to other religions, there are in its scriptures, statements which explicitly assert male and female equality. In sharp contrast, over the last century and a half anti-sexism has fortunately found its way into Western thought. However, it is only being fair to Christianity to point out that it has been in countries that have a Christian history that steps have been taken, both real and effective, towards achieving equality of women with men. We can compare the political and social cultures of the West in this matter with countries where Islam is dominant. Islam's attitude towards women, its treatment of women, is repressive. It is founded on the Qur'an which incorporates the sixth- and seventh-century Arabic tribal culture of Mohammad's own experience and way of life. Muslims believe, as the most basic and important item of their faith, that the Qur'an is not the product of any human culture or human being in any way but was composed by God himself, using the Arabic language it is expressed in, and is intended for all mankind everywhere and at all times; and that being composed by God, as they believe, it was not subjected to any cultural influence of time and place. That is the Islamic notion of revelation. It is ideologically opposed to Western culture and civilization. As the direct consequence of that religious ideology the Muslim attitude towards and its treatment of women are that of Mohammad's time and place, that of his seventh-century Arabic tribal culture, and we witness it being enforced to this day, some 1,300 years later, in countries which are controlled by Islam as a religious obligation both upon its adherents and upon non-Muslims.

The Church just cannot carry on living an existence not just distant from but even hostile to what its membership themselves respect and practise in their daily lives. It is a dichotomy that is disabling, destructive and alienating. It is little wonder that attendance at church services is in serious decline when there is sexism in its liturgy, and autocracy and centralism in its government. The Church should have the openness of mind, the courage, indeed the humility, to adopt changes which incorporate what is good in modern culture. Nothing now stops that happening except the obstinacy, narrowness and blindness of some of its aged leadership. Our modern world is inestimably different not just from the century when the Church was founded but from that of a mere two to three hundred years ago. The Church is as much on a journey now as the apostles and fellow Christians were in the year 49; and for that journey our minds must be open minds, no walls around them, despite the opposition of those many members of the Church, some in very high places, who inhabit a theological culture which believes it has already arrived at the finishing line. It most definitely hasn't; and it will never be reached. In the twenty-first century to restrict participation in decision-taking just to members who are male and celibate and usually old, who make up less than 1 per cent of the Church membership, is virtually incomprehensible; it staggers belief; it is nothing less than absurd; it offends; it makes the Church look archaic, out of touch, which in certain very important matters it definitely is. The nonsense must be stopped forthwith. What the Church has got to accept, among many other things, is that to restrict the priesthood and everything that goes with it just to members who have a penis and a scrotum, neither to be used sexually, makes no sense at all. Male testicles are for urination, copulation and procreation, not for ordination.

The Industrial Revolution and scientific progress have had a huge impact on how people live and how they interact with each other, on family life, on male–female and employer–employee relationships. Life has been transfigured. Pope Leo's encyclical *Rerum novarum* (1891) did show that the leadership of the Church was becoming aware of what people were going through, and it was a very welcome and a much needed intervention, even though very late in the day. By 1891, as far as the working classes were concerned, the worst was over. Pretty well on their own throughout the Industrial Revolution they had fought against immense forces of injustice and extortion from employers and their upper and middle class Conservative and Liberal party representatives in governments. Their trade unions, the only organizations that stood up for them, were well established by 1891, and the political parties such as the Labour Party, that would over the next seventy years legislate on their behalf, were already being formed and founded. The contribution the Catholic Church leadership made to that long struggle was minimal, and it should hang its head in shame. I know no evidence that the leadership of the Orthodox and Protestant churches at the time were any better, with the exception of Methodism. "It must be the poore, the simple and meane things of this earth that must confound the mighty and strong" wrote Richard Overton, Leveller, in 1647.

A Church which does not engage with and respond to, and as much as possible in an open and welcoming manner embrace in its own life, all the progress that has been brought into people's lives over the last two and a half centuries, is doomed to exist as nothing more than a powerless sect on the sidelines of global movements in the same way the Church in the year 49 would have stayed if it had remained just Judaic. If it does not incorporate what is good in those enormous changes, it will not be what Christ said it should be, "the salt of the earth, the light of the world". And what a challenge that is to live up to; and what an incredible thing for an itinerant preacher two thousand years ago to say, a person with no power and no cash behind him, someone who ended up nailed to a cross, stripped, laughed at and jeered, a wild and incredibly presumptive thing for anyone to say. Living as he did in as undistinguished a province of the Roman Empire as one can get, totally unknown except to a tiny parcel of followers, speaking a language only a minuscule fraction of the world's population knew about, let alone could speak, him telling his followers that he wants them to be the salt of the earth, the light of the world, well, it's the sort of stuff you'd might just hear one weekend at Hyde Park Corner, where it would be greeted with guffaws and all sorts of barracking and dismissed as silly fantasizing. Yet, for all its seemingly hopeless origins, it's had a marvellous innings and Christ's followers are still at the crease, batting away across almost all the world.

The human being of modern industrial, financial, scientific, electronic, technological and medical changes is not altogether the same moral person as existed before because he/she is now subject to circumstances and pressures never known before, as is the Church itself. One thinks of the much expanded life-span of the people of this twenty-first century, which must become a factor in any reflection on marriage and sexual morality; of the advances made in healthcare and its technology, of robotics and automation, of the internet and its totally astonishing technology, of informational technology and the social internet. The individual human subject is now a dartboard for the arrows of bewildering changes and experimentation and is open to both opportunities and difficulties never before experienced. The preservation of life, now possible where once it simply was not, in old age or indeed at any age, at the point when the prospect is only suffering, or freedom from suffering is only by being fed with morphine by a tube or artificially in some other way even where it defies the natural process, is one such very problematic moral issue. It might not be enough any longer to maintain that God who gave life alone has the right to take it away. That moral dictum is not applied in war. Time and again throughout the Scriptures God pleads with us to exercise mercy as well as sacrifice. Modern medical progress is confronting the moral theologian, be he/she a medic or a theologian, with many very difficult decisions. Looking at the situation positively, it is the case that today's world has been blessed with a great swathe of medical progress, and it is something that the Church must embrace. The Church must not hold back, arrogantly thinking it is the sole arbiter of what constitutes moral progress. It most definitely is not. It must have both the humility and the common sense to recognize that there is very great goodness, intelligence and progress everywhere. It must be open to change. It must be prepared to learn from sources other than its own tradition. The apostles did, they heeded the voice of the Gentile Christians of Antioch, the Church today must.

And now, in my assessment of the matter, another time has arrived in the long life of the Church when it can no longer just coast along reliant on its past. Massive waves are breaking onto its shore, some of which I have attempted to describe, which it can no longer ignore. It has to face modern reality which in the West, and probably throughout its world-wide membership, is making a direct challenge to a number of its structures and some of the components of its religious culture. And it cannot afford to delay either. I am unqualified to pronounce with any great confidence on the measures taken, for example, by the Council of Trent, in response to the demands of the Reformers, but for the Church to take over four hundred years to adopt the vernacular as the language of its liturgy indicates a boneheaded stubbornness, and indeed a theological ignorance, which frankly defy explanation. And it is still opposed to the ordination of married men and women even when its leadership in the person of the Vatican has privately, but not publicly, acknowledged there is no biblical objection to either. Of course there isn't.

The Council of the Jews commanded the apostles "not to speak or teach at all in the name of Jesus" (Acts 4:18). The reply of Peter and John, however, was forthright: "Judge for yourselves whether it is right in God's sight to obey you rather than God. For we cannot help speaking about what we have seen and heard" (v. 20). What we now have in our world is women voting where once they could not, and they changed that by challenging it actively and bravely. In this regard the similarity of resistance between the apostles and the early twentieth century suffragettes is inspirational. It was as believing Jews that the apostles defied the Council which was their own Jewish leadership. As a consequence "the full assembly of the nation of Israel" had them arrested and imprisoned; they escaped but they were soon re-arrested and brought back before the Sanhedrin. "We gave you strict orders not to teach in this name," said Annas the High Priest; to which Peter and the other apostles replied: "We must obey God rather than people." (5:29). They persisted even when threatened with death, which was commuted to a flogging. We all regard their defiance as bold and enlightened action, which is how Luke portrayed it. They emerged from the flogging, "rejoicing they had been counted worthy of suffering disgrace for the Name . . . and they never stopped teaching and proclaiming the good news that Jesus is the Messiah" (v. 41). Their defiance paid off. Without it no Christianity. We are all in their debt just as society today is in debt to suffragette struggles across the world, of which that in the UK was only one. The women of the Catholic Church must now challenge the male hierarchy in just the same way.

They must obey God rather than people. The equality of women with men is what the New Testament expressly teaches; and it is what the membership of the Church has embraced already in their secular lives. The Church must now obey what God has taught us in the New Testament Scriptures. On this matter its leadership has to be challenged as bravely as Peter and the apostles challenged the Council of the Jews, and indeed as bravely as women challenged men for the right to vote. Pope John Paul II forbade even a mention of women priests, let alone any open discussion of the subject. Theologically, denial of the priesthood to women doesn't have a leg to stand on. That possibly was in the subconscious of the papacy when it issued that dictate. Discussion is the last thing dictatorial minds want, so they invoke their authority. The Church desperately needs priests; and as women like any other Christian are entitled to aspire to the spiritual life they feel God has called them to, it can be said that the time has come for effective protest action, for demonstrative action, of the sort the suffragettes carried out. Just arguing about it and petitioning and writing about it are not enough any longer, it is too serious for that. Worse still is when one hears someone saying "We must have a conversation about it". The time for conversations is long past. The ordination of women will put right a serious wrong and terminate the insult and the injustice with which the Church leadership has long treated women. The ban is doing harm within the Church and to its reputation in our modern world. It is time for everyone, lay and cleric, to challenge the intransigence of the Church leadership on this matter.

And intransigent and stubborn it still is. On 30 May 2018, at the time this script was being written in its final form, a Cardinal designate, Archbishop Luis Ladaria, Prefect of the Congregation for the Doctrine of the Faith, issued a declaration that women can never, yes never, be ordained priests on the grounds that that was the teaching of "the ordinary, universal magisterium". Ladaria made reference to an "apostolic letter" of Pope John Paul II in 1994, which, he said, had a "definite character of the doctrine of *Ordinatio sacerdotalis*" and ruled out the priestly ordination of women. One might say to him in reply "So what if it did?" The first Vatican Council neatly established what papal declarations are and what are not infallible and this statement most definitely was not. Generally, when people like this cardinal-designate archbishop, who holds one of the most senior positions in the whole Church, find themselves running out of arguments, they invoke authority as a substitute.

The opposition within the Church to women priests is beginning to feel the pressure and they are arguing back. The struggle is now on, and it is on in real earnest, and the time has come for those bishops, theologians and clergy who support the ordination of women to publicly say so in the long term interests of the Church, whatever it might cost them. The laity should protest too, vociferously, and take to demonstrating their opposition. The apostles made a stand, they set an example which endures. Nothing will do as much for the reputation of the Church in today's world, nothing will make women, young and old, and mainly the young who are the future, re-appreciate and feel identification with the Church they were baptized in, and nothing will do more to shoot the arrow of renewed vigour and enthusiasm into its body and soul as opening the priesthood to women. It will invigorate, enthuse, enlighten and transfigure like nothing else can in matters moral, liturgical, spiritual and mystical. It is the future, no matter how Church forces of reaction oppose it, and if grasped now and implemented, it will transform.

There is, however, a caveat. The priesthood has been exclusively male for 2,000 years. It has very much become in how it visibly manifests itself a male product. Women priests must give thought to what the present priesthood has become and not just assume the same mantle. Collectively, as they find their feet within it as an institution, they should discuss and consider what developments and change and tone they might bring to it. Such collective action by women will bring about many other much needed changes. The diaspora Christians who came into the Church, represented by those seven Greek-speakers of Acts 6, created shock waves, produced argument and brought about change. Women activists, whatever roles and offices they take on, will, I hope, do the same today, as will a married clergy. But of course I know only too well that in all such matters we have to proceed with great care and prudence. No institution survives where its members pick and choose. There has to be leadership; and in the case of the Church there isn't just leadership but there is also the power to bind and to loose "as it is in heaven" (Matthew 16:19). It makes for a very complex matter, knotty and delicate. But that is how life is. It's never straightforward. The laity know that the bishops and the pope are the successors of Peter and the apostles, that is our faith; and they know that there has to be government and leadership and decisions taken about issues of doctrine and morality. We all have to move forward very carefully, but move forward we must. It must always be kept in mind that the Vatican I definition of papal infallibility is also a formal and public acknowledgement of papal fallibility. Nothing less. The limits it placed on any papal pronouncement being infallible are such that logically they imply that all other such pronouncements are fallible and as such are open to amendment in the light of developments. While there has been very many papal statements since Vatican I, there have only been two declared infallible.

Our present world is gripped by dramatic and irresistible forces of global change in electronic technology, medicine, science, ethics, finance, climate, politics and commerce. There are huge ethical issues rising up before our very eyes in such matters as the environment, migration, modern weaponry, employment rights, the fate of animal species, food, the world supply of water, climate change, the poisoning of the oceans with plastics, the distribution of wealth, the health of the poorer classes, the crass difference between the wealthy nations and the poor, the obscene accumulation of incredible wealth in the hands of a small number of individuals, to name just a few. These aren't just emerging massive on our horizons, they are already here. Life on this planet is facing widespread destruction because of the treatment of it by humanity, by us. The Catholic Church "with more than a billion followers, the largest global organization the world has ever seen"[30] has therefore an overpowering moral duty to endeavour to do something about it such as never before. And not just something, but everything it possibly can to involve its total worldwide membership in reversing what is happening, in establishing justice, in eliminating poverty, in saving the environment, in turning world powers from war to peace and disarmament and terminating the threat of hunger, even in places starvation, to the poor and the powerless. The position of the Catholic Church is unique. It is the biggest voluntary international organization in the world. It therefore has one almighty duty, which is to put its vast resource of people into action. Peter invoked the power of God to heal a disabled man begging at the gate to the temple in Jerusalem. For the Catholic Church, inspired by the Pope's recent encyclical on the environment, to motivate its massive membership to tackle climate change because of all the immense harm it will do to people, especially the poor, would be as divine an action, as beneficial, as what Peter did. For example, a call by the Church to all its membership to stop using plastic as we use it now because of the dreadful harm it is doing to the creatures God has made and to our own health, will reverberate across all industry and throughout society. Doing good is what Christianity is about as much as it is about traditional religious activities. "Going about doing good" is how Peter described Jesus to Cornelius. The Gospels actually give much more space to describing the miraculous healing ministry of Jesus than they give to him either in acts of temple worship or in prayer, which is an intriguing consideration.

The ethics of the issues I have listed can no longer just be decided by clerics. The Church desperately needs the input of the laity, women as much as men, married as well as single, and even that of its youth into such matters. They live totally within the communications culture of today in all its diversity as well as in traditional occupations. The knowledge the laity have of right and wrong in today's world is immense. They depend on it; they work in it; they draw their income from it; they bring their families up in it. There has to be not just consultation with the laity, but also their appointment to the bodies which govern the Church, even both to Vatican and hierarchical dicasteries, congregations and tribunals. Nothing less. We must have a modern Church, not the archaic antique which in some ways it has become. If the Church's clerical leadership, numerically so few, not even 1 per cent of the total membership, all male, all elderly, some very elderly, all celibate, think for one moment that they can deal adequately with it in our modern world all on their own, they are living in cloud cuckoo land. Their minds and their experience are just not up to it.

And if any proof of that is needed one need only recall the disastrous error of moral judgement made by Pope Paul VI and his close clerical advisors in *Humanae vitae* in 1967, even compounding the error by declaring the sort of birth control, which it was considering, a mortal sin; and what a dreadful abuse of office that particular aspect of that papal judgement was; and what severe problems of conscience it created for the laity. However, unexpectedly, certain very good things did come out because of that error. It exposed how inadequate the judgement of celibate clerics on sexual matters can be; it roused the laity to resistance, which is of enduring value and must be maintained and extended; and it is testimony to the fallibility of papal judgements. The laity needs to be involved in discussion and decision about all major issues. When we come to look at what the Catechism of the Church has to say about the enlightenment baptism has infused into the laity, it will become clear that the Church must call upon it to contribute to the moral, sacramental and governmental life of the Church. There is a driving urgency about all this, it must be *potius hodie quam cras*, to employ the aspiration written by St Ralph Sherwin in the log book of the Venerable English College in Rome—"today rather than tomorrow".

The sacrament of ordination is additional to that of baptism and bestows an extra grace and standing, in particular to pronounce with efficacy the words whereby bread and wine are changed into the Body and Blood of Jesus. It cannot be disassociated either from the power bestowed on Peter to bind and to loose. However, the first and most fundamental reception of the Holy Spirit is in baptism, and it merits acknowledgement, respect, consultation and involvement. "The baptized are 'a chosen race, a royal priesthood, a holy nation, God's own people, so that they might declare the wonderful deeds of him who called them out of darkness into his marvellous light . . . Baptism gives a share in the common priesthood of all believers."[31] There is more, and it should be made known: "Baptism is God's most beautiful and magnificent gift . . . grace, anointing, enlightenment, garment of immortality, bath of rebirth . . . We call it enlightenment because it radiates light."[32] Contrast that statement with that of Pope Pius X in the first decade of the last century: "The Church is by its very nature an unequal society," he said, "It comprises two categories of people, the pastors and the flock. The hierarchy alone moves and controls . . . The duty of the multitude is to suffer itself to be governed and to carry out in a submissive spirit the orders of those in control."[33] It is a dreadful statement, and reading it one can only wonder what sort of theological education that pope ever had, probably just the dry biscuits of textbook dogma without the life and leaven of the flesh and blood of Scripture.

Contrary to this sad and wrong assertion the massive membership of the Christian churches is, if only it could be involved, a vast ocean of enlightenment, over a billion people enlightened by the Holy Spirit and getting bigger by the hour. What a resource, what an immense reservoir of spiritual knowledge for the Church's leadership to tap into! Church members in almost every country today are now as educated, trained, skilled, knowledgeable as its clergy, they are independent-minded people, great numbers of them with degrees and doctorates, managers of people, managers of business, men and women with all sorts of experience and responsibility in life, in work, in politics, in science, even in war.

That is the modern world; that is the culture that the Church must now embrace, the culture which the Church of the twenty-first century must now accept as existing in all their parishes, dioceses and countries. The Church institutionally has got to know it, understand it, develop and grow within it. It is a culture in which education, both academic and occupational and both combined, is greatly prized, for both men and women. The Church has an educated membership which thinks for itself in any amounts of ways. Its members in their secular lives vote who will be their government; they take part in referenda; they respond to political electioneering; they choose their careers and their jobs; they decide for themselves how many children they will have; they bring them up; they listen to party broadcasts. Their choices are needed, so they are bombarded with adverts which they assess. In none of this, of course, are they able to act with total independence; they are plagued with lies and falsehoods all the time. But they are able to think their own thoughts and make up their own minds. This state of affairs has a direct consequence for their Church membership. They are absolutely not what Pius X considered them to be. They will no longer be obedient to Church demands just because the Church commands this or that. They will assess matters for themselves. That is what they are educated to do; and doing that in their secular existence they will also exercise it in spiritual matters. As Antonio Gramsci wrote in his *Prison Notebooks*, all men and women are philosophers, all of them intellectuals. That is what the membership of today's Church is. Education is universal, and education even up to its tertiary level is commonplace; and that is something the Church's leadership should now respect and build on. If clerics had children, that is what they would want them to be: educated, independent-minded, knowledgeable adults. And that being the case, they should not expect members of today's Church to be anything different. The Church has got to move into our modern age. It just will not hold on to its membership, much less increase it, if it does not. Today's membership will not respond to moral dictates just with meekness; it will not just be submissive. Take for example two moral matters which are now to the fore: cohabitation and divorce. Today's Church membership will hold views on both.

And today there is a massive reason why many, very many, of them might feel they have no good reason to listen submissively to the Church as used to be the norm. Many priests and members of teaching orders have deeply shamed it, and with it the Catholic laity, by widespread sexual and physical abuse of children, which has been accompanied by the efforts of a number of bishops and local heads of religious orders and abbots of individual monasteries to hide the guilty, even to let the abuse continue rather than bring the Church into disrepute. The damage done to the Church has been immense. We also have to ask ourselves what reason does the laity have to take the word of the papacy as gospel when one pope, namely Paul VI, was able to make a declaration on birth control which they themselves, and indeed many priests, consider mistaken. The Catholic Church now has a membership which thinks for itself. That is the outcome of their education. That is what the Church has to deal with. It should welcome and encourage it. It should work to make itself a church of the willing, a church of thoughtful members. That is one most important thing the Church has got to do to itself in our time. That awful understanding of Church, as we have seen Pope Pius X describe it, an understanding of it that runs deep in the clerical psyche and still actually governs Church government and how doctrine is taught, has to be totally repudiated.

And there is another consideration. For centuries the Church has been ruled in all matters by men. Balance must be restored. Women have a different perspective on many matters which, of course, is as valid and perspicacious as that of men. The male is not the female; the female is not the male. The female mind is not the male mind. Women see things differently; they feel things differently; their outlook on life is different; their perspective on things is different. They see and feel things men do not see or feel. Their insight into things is different. Not necessarily better but different. The Church is a very lopsided being. It acts on what its male membership sees and thinks and feels; that is how it directs itself in almost all its doings and responsibilities. To include the female mind and feeling in its understanding of what is morally right and wrong will change and improve theology, improve and change moral theology, change Church government, improve church government, change its liturgy, improve its liturgy. The Church should be both engine and inspirer of this democracy and equality; and if that happens, a change and a transformation of mind and the apparatus of its government would have been achieved, rivalling the achievement of the Council of Jerusalem itself.

The Church's clerical leadership should bear in mind what the New Testament teaches us about what a believer in Jesus Christ is, be he/she lay or cleric. I have drawn the reader's attention already to what the two epistles to the Colossians and the Ephesians tell us about what belief in Christ and baptism bestows. There is also that most significant statement in 2 Peter 1:4, which is just one out of many statements of like content in the New Testament. Its author speaks of "the great and precious promises" freely made to us by God and Jesus our Lord "so that through them you (the recipients of the letter) may share in the divine". It is an incredible vision of what the baptized person has become, it is awesome beyond measure; and if well told and explained to a congregation often enough, it will bring about in the minds of its listeners and readers a transforming identification with Church and sacrament. What's more, nothing more exposes the emptiness and barrenness of the disdain that Pope Pius X showed of people who through the same baptism and the same faith in Jesus share in God's own nature. I hope my purpose in all of this is clear. What was achieved at the Council of Jerusalem, what happened there that made it possible for the Church to take its belief in Jesus and his gospel to the whole world. The transformation of mind they underwent must happen again; and it can.

I will now go into one issue in some detail as, in my judgement, it is directly pertinent to the argument I am making and is an example of an established Church belief that needs to be reconsidered in the light of human development and difficulties in today's world. I do not know how many Christians are involved in it, but it is an issue that is being much discussed. It affects millions of people. One could hardly hope for a better example of what is here being argued for. It concerns the Church's long-established understanding of marriage as "until death do us part". The Church is deeply admired for its firm defence of marriage. However, it is appropriate to ask if it is being excessively rigid in today's world and creating unnecessary alienation and unhappiness. The issue is about rigidity and absolutism in respect of an inherited theological position and a moral code. It takes in a number of situations. Three may be too many to provide, but I will chance it.

A young Catholic woman has got married, in a Catholic church, observing the rites of the Church. The marriage did not work out; it simply failed; they found they were just incompatible. Their breach was so serious that they separated. She was in her mid-twenties, and had forty, possibly fifty or so years of life ahead of her, in which time she could enjoy companionship and re-marry and have the fulfilment and enjoyment of her God-given sexuality and have children. But her local clergy informed her that her marriage remained indissoluble, and if she were to re-marry or enter into a partnership, she would be committing a grave sin. I do not know what she did after that. But I do recall this very well. Another Catholic woman I knew at the same time got married outside of the Church, in a registry office, a marriage not recognized by the Church, which meant she was, in the language of those years, living in sin. That marriage also failed, and she obtained a divorce. But in the eyes of the Church she was not married in the first place; she had not received the sacrament of marriage. So she was then able to marry in a Catholic church with all its rites and celebrations to a fellow Catholic, and she went on to have life with him and children by him. I submit that this difference of treatment by the Church has to be reconsidered.

And as regards the first case, we might recall that God isn't into making lives miserable. Christ never intended any such person as the first one to spend most of her life in such a dismal way because she made a mistake as a young woman. If in her circumstances she merited a separation, and if the period of separation did not work out, then she also merited a declaration that her marriage was dissolved; and she should be told to be wiser next time and get on with life and live it to the full. That surely is Christianity. Peter was given the power to loose as well as to bind, and basic humanity and common sense should be a guide. That, I would propose, is what the laity today would say if they were asked about it, and they, says the Catechism of the Catholic Church, are the recipients of baptism which is "God's most beautiful and magnificent gift . . . grace, anointing, enlightenment, garment of immortality, bath of rebirth . . . We call it enlightenment because it radiates light".[34] The Word did not become flesh and live and die among us to bind us in chains. That is excessive religious legalism. Christian people deeply respect marriage and they want fidelity. But they want it both protected and treated with common sense and fairness. Everyone knows that a mistake in choice of spouse can be made, it is human to make mistakes. Where the mistake turns out to be a serious one, so serious that a period of separation cannot restore it, it is cruel to allow it to shackle a life until death do them part. Very cruel. That just is not the morality Jesus taught. If because of any brutality this young woman had murdered her husband, she could have done time and then walked free, free and able in the eyes of the Church to marry again. And the court, acting with compassion and common sense, would have reduced the sentence because of the abuse suffered. A great pity that the Church does not show the same consideration, the same understanding. My more general point, in line with what I am arguing in this book, is that the rigidity of Church teaching and regulation by an unmarried clergy is alienating its own membership. The Church must consult with the laity and take their advice, which will be based on familiarity with the tensions, stress and development of modern life and, more deeply, based on an understanding of the fragility of human nature.

I move to another person's situation, a Catholic woman who falls in love with a man who has been divorced, not a Catholic, goes to live with him, marries him in the town hall registry office and bears him three children. He was divorced before she met him; she had no involvement with the divorce at all. She has the children attending the local Catholic school; she is utterly devoted to their welfare and to his; she holds down a full-time job, as he does, to enable their children to have a roof over their heads and be well fed and clothed and educated. In other words, she is a very good parent and spouse. But at Mass, though the three children go to Holy Communion, she feels she cannot and she does not, because sharing a bed every night with their father is called a mortal sin by the Church. Can it reasonably be expected of her that to reconcile herself with God and the Church she would have to stop sleeping with her husband? It simply cannot be. Her sleeping with him is part of the life of her children; it is their parents' way of showing love for each other; and that love flows out of the bed into the hearts and formation of their children. It is Trinitarian. Abstention from sexual intercourse is humanly impossible for her; and it should not even be contemplated, let alone actually required of her. She is where she is. Her love for the children and for her husband is where she is. Nothing else can or should be expected of her. There just cannot now be another way of life for her as long as her circumstances remain as they are. And as the author of 1 Timothy tells us: "the woman will be saved through childbearing" (1 Timothy 2:15). If anything merits salvation, child-bearing and good parenthood does. This woman's faith is the Catholic faith; it is the faith she is bringing up her children in; her faith and her love of her husband and her three children count for more in the eyes of God than any subjection to harsh moral teaching. She should be made welcome to Holy Communion; for what she is doing for her children the Church should consider itself honoured to have her. For what she is doing for her children and her husband she is as Christian as it can get.

On 11 November 2016 an organization called Change OK based in San Francisco put out a press release describing the plight of a woman who had been married for 18 years. In that time her husband had turned "violently abusive". She found the strength to leave him and took out a restraining order against him. She thought that the nightmare she was experiencing was at an end. "But two weeks later he turned up at my place of work and shot at me with intent to kill." She had not entered the relationship of marriage for it to turn into a nightmare; the man's cruelty had breached the basic contractual agreements of that relationship; the marriage was at an end. No moral sophistry can possibly justify refusing to acknowledge that this marriage had been terminated and that the woman in question had every moral, as well as the common-sense, right to consider it terminated and, if she wished to, marry someone else. Common sense and basic humanity require that the Catholic Church declare the marriage terminated. The Church should not enslave the individual to a life of misery. The Church has got to do a re-think.

Jesus did not say "What God has yoked together, let no man separate" (Mark 10:9) as a legalism. There can be no doubt that Jesus wanted lifelong unions, absolutely no doubt. That is why he had first invoked the Old Testament in saying "In the beginning, at the creation, God made them male and female. For this reason a man shall leave his father and mother and be made one with his wife, and the two become one flesh. It follows that they are no longer two individuals, they are one flesh" (Mark 10:7–9). But that is aspirational, and mystical. That is not an instruction, that is God's aspiration. It is how God wanted it, and what God wants we must aspire to achieve, because God is not just good, he is goodness itself. Goodness craves goodness. His whole being craves what is good for us. Those words of the Bible about man and woman and their union in marriage must rank among the most aspirational ever uttered. They are about the very wonderful emotional and physical reality of the human being; they are about children. Children are as much the "one flesh" as the act of union itself. It is an image of the Triune God, it is Trinitarian. It is an ideal. That beautiful ideal is the context in which Jesus said: "What

God has joined together, let no man put asunder." Ideals are what we strive for; but they are not what are always achieved.

It really is nonsense to say that a married couple, where one of them seriously abuses the other, are one flesh. That patently is not the case. The contract of marriage has been broken because its principal terms have been seriously broken. Jesus told Peter: "Whatever you bind on earth will be bound in heaven; and whatever you loose on earth will be loosed in heaven" (Matthew 16:19). The Church, going by that statement of Jesus, has the power to declare a marriage is finished. This is plain common sense. Basic human kindness cries out for such decisions. Where the Church does not show it, people are rightly shocked and turn elsewhere, either to another church or from religion altogether. They are left feeling abandoned by the cruelty of cold unfeeling legalism. Legalism has triumphed over humanism. That is not Christian. The Church's teaching on sexuality and marriage has got to be balanced, sensible, liveable and, to use the word Pope Francis wishes us to give consideration to, merciful.

I would propose that the Church's teaching on sexuality and marriage will not be like that until it submits the issue to the judgement of the vast reservoir of the enlightenment bestowed upon the total membership by the sacrament of baptism. To do that in the world as it is today is possible. It is the world of the internet, of global interaction and the dissemination of knowledge, of instant mass communication of information and news, of emails, of skype, of referenda, of mass education, even of university education; and it is an issue the laity do give thought to and discuss. Those celibate Church leaders, cardinals included, who openly oppose Francis, can discuss among themselves as much as they like about what they call "a ratified and consummated marriage between two baptized persons" and rule that "it can be dissolved only by death" and that "if Christians in a valid marriage join with someone else while their spouse is alive, they commit the grave sin of adultery". They can pronounce that there are "absolute moral commandments" which are to be obeyed "without exception" and no "subjective judgement of conscience" can make "an intrinsically evil act good and lawful". Such concepts and such conclusions are to be treated cautiously. When it comes to relationships between human beings, and especially between a man and a woman, the whole idea of acts which are intrinsically good or intrinsically bad should be treated with extreme care. Sex is a minefield. Blame God, if you wish; he created it. To apply the notion of "absolute moral commandments" to the relationship of a man and a woman is hazardous to say the least and it is not a matter which can be decided solely by celibates. The reality of it requires experience of it. These issues aren't easy, not at all, but, faced by harsh realities, the Church has to show mercy and understanding, and when it comes to teaching should bring in those of its membership who know from living in a marriage what the reality is. That is the very least it should do. The Church in its Catechism cannot, or shouldn't, describe the effect of baptism as enlightenment and then ignore it when it comes to the laity. If its leadership doesn't really believe what it writes, and it doesn't in this instance, it shouldn't have written it.

I have gone into detail on this issue of marriage because I consider it provides one clear example of how and where not just Church teaching, but also its attitudes, must be seriously reconsidered if the Church is to speak to the modern world with confidence and success and offer who and what Jesus Christ is and what his gospel is. The Church is now in a world of educated, independent-minded people. I believe it cannot be said often enough and loud enough to the leadership of the Church that the world has changed and that the Catholic population within it too has changed. The Catholic population of the Western world, which, with Christians everywhere, baptism has endowed with enlightenment as the Catechism states and as 2 Peter 1:4 describes, lives in its culture approvingly. We live in gravely changed conditions and circumstances from when the Church's teaching was formulated, and indeed formulated by fellow Church members, and in matters of male–female relationships and sexuality by Church members who are celibate and whose lives were not, at least not directly, affected by many of the formulations that they have made. Every thinking Catholic will have his or her own list of changes they believe should be made, but 99.99 per cent of Catholics are excluded from having any say in anything. That simply is no exaggeration. Furthermore, government in the Church is excessively centralized in the Vatican. Bishops worldwide are chosen by the Vatican according to its own criteria. Women, who make up slightly over 50 per cent of the Catholic membership, are totally excluded from its priesthood, which situation excludes them from local diocese and parish government. No undemocratic, non-egalitarian and sexist organization will thrive in our modern world, and must instead expect to decline when its members approve and practise the democratic, anti-sexist and egalitarian culture of the secular societies they live in. That applies to many other basic ways in which the Church conducts itself. The laity will not put up with the past being imposed on their lives as Christians just because their leadership says it must, they want what they know to be better.

"Jesus," Peter said to Cornelius, "went about doing good" (Acts 10:38). It was by doing good that Jesus attracted people to him. "He went around the whole of Galilee teaching in their synagogues, proclaiming the good news of the kingdom and curing all kinds of diseases and illness among the people. His fame spread throughout Syria, and they brought to him all those who were suffering from diseases and painful complaints of one kind and another, the possessed, epileptics, the paralysed, and he cured them. Large crowds followed him, coming from Galilee, the Decapolis, Jerusalem, Judea and beyond the Jordan" (Matthew 4:18–22). The Church from its very beginnings has followed him in that way ardently, serving the sick and the poor, building schools, clinics, universities, hospitals and refuges of every kind. There is no one organization anywhere and throughout history, even to today, which has done more for the sick, the poor and for education than the Catholic Church; and it is the example of Jesus that inspired what must be one of the greatest Christian cum secular achievements ever, the British National Health Service and the Welfare State. That was the product and outcome of the belief that health, wealth and work should be shared by all for the common good, a belief held by the British Labour and Trade Union Movement and implemented by the Labour Party government in the years 1945–51.

But "going about doing good" should no longer be restricted to health care and education, Christianity's traditional areas of good works. By reason of its worldwide moral power and huge membership Christianity is now positioned to be, and should become, a voice and a campaigner for justice and against wickedness worldwide in all its forms, not just what directly harms our fellow men and women, like poor wages and bad employment conditions, but what also harms them indirectly, like the destruction of the environment. Climate change is already doing great harm, especially to the poor and to people living in countries where there is drought and where crops and food are then made hard or even impossible to grow. Contrived low wages, dangerous working conditions, unjust employment regulations, serious air pollution, racial discrimination, paying women lower wages than men when doing the same work, destruction of rainforests for gain, the over-fishing of the world's seas, discrimination against women, making weapons of mass destruction, exporting weaponry to governments engaged in wrongful wars, the list is a very long one. They are doing as much harm to people as ill-health, poverty and denial of education. They are what the whole of Christianity—Catholic, Orthodox, Protestant and Pentecostal—must denounce together, from every cathedral and church and chapel across the world, from every possible pulpit. Christianity must unite to put things right wherever it can and, with this drastic change of attitude towards such matters, no longer just leave them to secular governments.

When it comes to environmental matters, which are immense in today's world, a papal encyclical like the *Laudato si* of Francis I, superb though it was, is not enough. From every pulpit in every diocese and parish there is a voice that must be heard. The Catholic Church, first and foremost because of its size and universality, must be in the forefront of the defence of the environment; and it must openly and institutionally work for peace, campaign against war, modern slavery and women and child trafficking, racism and sexism and for gender equality, and demand fair wage structures, good working conditions and fair employment legislation. All this it can speak out for from its pulpits and altars and call the total church membership to action. That is what all Christian youth would strongly welcome and identify with. The Christian religion should loudly and openly be as much about getting a roof over the head of every family, the education of every child, girls as much as boys, equality for women, defence of the environment which God created and of all creatures in it, the availability of decent health practice paid for by everyone for everyone, as it is about its religious services. Every action in support of the poor and the deprived to get them justice and health and housing and food and work, and every action, be it individual or collective, to protect the environment and every action in support of peace, is Eucharist. It is religion as much as a prayer or a retreat or taking part in the liturgy. That has to be the Church of the twenty-first century.

That is what today's man and woman, young, middle-aged and old, will identify with and can do, and should do. Every one of us in the name of what our Christianity is should do. That is a moral action just like donating towards a charity.

It's got be local as well as worldwide. For instance, to have taken part in the Great Winter Nurdle Hunt (plastic pellets found on 73 per cent of the UK shoreline) on Newquay beach, launched by local environmentalists a couple of years ago, is doing good for humanity and for all that lives in the sea. It is not a religious activity which commences with the Sign of the Cross or is interspersed with prayers, but it is religious, because it is doing good, just like Jesus did. "A truckload of plastic waste enters our oceans every minute, much of it packaging, and it poses a threat to everything from the smallest plankton to the biggest whale. It breaks down into microplastics which like a million tiny sponges collect the toxic chemicals they encounter, concentrating them up through the food train to big predator species, including most of the food we eat."[35] To stand outside a supermarket and call on people to object to the use of plastics is "going about doing good". Demanding a living wage for every worker is "going about doing good"; so is campaigning against the sale of weapons to countries which in their own interests inflict them on whole populations. "Doing good" out of love of our neighbour, local and worldwide, is prayer.

Bland prayers for peace in the world are worthless without specifying the places where cease-fires are urgently needed and cruel immoral acts of violence are being committed. Bidding prayers should name names. At the time this was being written, there was a campaign going on, with a strike a possibility, among cleaners in certain London hospitals, nearly all of whom are from Africa and South Asia, nearly every one of them being paid well below the living wage, and being forced to work awful hours by a private company which is being paid millions out of NHS funds. Bidding prayers in their support, naming the hospitals and the private company, from every Christian pulpit or lectern in London at all Sunday services would be "doing good". This is what modern culture enables Christians to do, it was not available to Jesus nor to the early church members. This is what modern cultures demand of us. This is what today's church members must do as Christians. Salvation should happen here and now, not just in our afterlife.

> See, I will make of you a sharp threshing sledge, new and studded with teeth; and you shall thresh the mountains and crush them and reduce the hills to chaff. You shall winnow them, the wind shall carry them away, and a great gale will scatter them. Then shall you rejoice in the Lord and glory in the Holy One of Israel. I have formed you and appointed you to be the light to all peoples, a beacon for the nations, to open eyes that are blind, to bring captives out of prison, and out of the dungeons where they lie in darkness. I am the Lord; the Lord is my name. (from Isaiah 41–42)

"The Roman Catholic Church is the largest organization in the world—a global faith indeed."[36] That fact alone places on it an immense international humanitarian responsibility openly to oppose economic and political evil at an international level, be it modern slavery and women and child trafficking, low wages, absence of basic employment legislation, workshops operating dangerous and unhealthy practices, the denial of women's equality and rights, denial of climate change which is at this very moment driving the world towards catastrophe, the oppression of homosexuals, the exploitation of ill-health by the private medical industry, the denial of democratic and religious freedom, the destruction of the environment, the destructive abilities of modern weaponry and much more besides. These things, giving concrete local and national instances, and asking for action, can be said from pulpits and in all Christian schools with the same frequency and earnestness as when at bidding prayers we pray, as we do, abstractly for peace in the world.

If the largest organization in the world in every diocese and every parish were to encourage its 1.3 billion membership, across every continent and in every country, to "go about doing good" in such ways and on such issues, it would then become what Jesus called on his disciples to be: "the salt of the earth" and "the light of the world" (Matthew 5:13f.). That would really be letting the light of our faith "shine out before people". For the Church from its pulpits and its school and college classrooms to call upon its membership to join in all campaigns and movements and lend full support is going about doing good as much as Peter working a miracle on behalf of a man "who had been a cripple from birth". That is religion. Christianity should be a byword for social equality, for social justice, for equality, and that most of all in its own ranks, for the defence of the environment, for progress in all spheres of life. That is our baptismal identity. That is what youth will identify with and then carry on through life, and do it with a growing enlightenment.

There is another realm of human action, however, where morality can be difficult and complex. The normal approach of the Church is caution in the very difficult matter of changes in medical practice and the ethical issues that arise out of them. It is wise to be cautious, because it is territory where one walks on eggshells, and the cautions the Church raises and the questions it poses are generally sound and necessary. However, it must never just be negative but positive and supportive wherever it can, showing, just for example, a full understanding and genuine empathy for the anxiety of couples who want inheritable genetic defects eradicated. Such developments as gene editing, mitochondrial transfer and other ways of germline therapy definitely present problems, moral as well as medical, and most thinking people understand the need for caution in these matters; but the issues should be met with warmth and goodwill, not with negativity. No Christian couple wants to pass on an inherited illness or disability to their children. That is instinctive and right; and a cleric, if married, male or female, would feel the same if, and when, they had children. The Church should not accept, for example, that the danger of designer babies is reason to stop medical scientists researching progress in preventing the inheritance of malevolent genes.

Modern science and medicine have achieved incredible progress and liberation. Does the Church resonate with it? Or does it meet everything with suspicion? Is distrust its default position? Does it greet the medical advances that have been made, which have done wonderful things for people, with the amount of support, enthusiasm and gratitude they deserve? There is no question that the Christian moral theologian has an immense responsibility, that there are issues which are very difficult and stands have to taken, but for every gesture of caution, even opposition where the Church so judges, the Church should give many more genuine gestures of enthusiasm and appreciation for every individual good advance the medical profession, modern science, modern technology and today's social and humanistic life achieve. They deserve it, and if they get it, they will listen more to what the Church has to say. So will the members of the Church too. Every medical and scientific breakthrough which helps humanity should receive a message of thanks and appreciation. There should be no negativity; the Church is not responsible for the world. It shouldn't be dour and guilt-giving; it should do its best, difficult though that can be, to be a bright light, a blazing beacon on a hilltop, a free soul fully in support of people's best efforts, attracting people by its warmth and happiness and a driving desire for progress and improvement in people's lives. That would be the spirit of the Council of Jerusalem alive this very day.

And then there is the matter of education in the Christian faith. If ever an adequate education in the Christian faith mattered, it most certainly does in this day and age. Today's world in all sorts of ways is a world in which education matters. The forces lined up and active against religion are immense. In the West there is opposition to ethical and religious teaching such as never before experienced. In science dismissal of it as myth is widespread and in much of the entertainment community and the media religion is frequently treated with scorn. I entertain no doubt that if things continue as they are, the existing membership will continue to fall away, especially the younger generation, and there is no way the faith can be preached with any hope of numerical success among the non-Christian population of the Western world by the Church as it is today. For the Catholic Church to continue to be sexist and authoritarian, regimental and centralist, is not at all acceptable in today's Western world.

First and foremost, in schools and from the pulpit, there has to be conveyed, firmly, clearly and repeatedly, with no watering-down, an understanding of what God is, what the Trinity is, what the Father, the Son and the Holy Spirit are, what creation is, why science and evolution are totally compatible with creation, what it means to be a creature of God, what the Incarnation is, what Christ is, what Christ did for us, what he did in his life, what his sufferings, death and resurrection were for, what salvation is and why, what our relationship to God and his Christ is, what all human beings in the sight of God are, what they became in

Christ and what baptism does to us, what the Church is, why it exists, what its life, sacraments and holy days of celebration are, what it has to contribute to the lives of everyone around it, what this life is for, how we should live it, what death is and what the eternal life that follows it is, as best we know it.

Christian education in schools should not just be anti-sexism, anti-racism, appreciation and tolerance of other ways of life and supporting charities and overseas aid. All that should just flow from the basic Christian belief that every single person is beyond price, because every one of them has been made by God in his own image and likeness, has been redeemed by the Son of God and is open to the infusion of the Holy Spirit of God and is entitled to live in a just and peaceful society. No pupil should emerge from a Catholic education without a word by word, line by line, explanation of the Apostles' Creed; and every one of them should be helped to understand the proofs for the existence of God. As Thomas Aquinas says in the very first section of the *Summa Theologica*: "That there is a God needs proof", and of his five proofs his fifth is the easiest to understand and at the same time the one that captures mind and imagination most readily, namely "the design or guidedness of nature". All of that is the level of Christian education our Catholic and Church of England schools should be aiming at.

It is impossible to put too much stress on the necessity for Christians to read the Bible daily, for example one chapter per day from the Old and the New Testaments and one of the Psalms. The New Testament is special: it should be the principal text in the education of the clergy; they should be taught to understand it in Greek, the language it was written in, and in the Vulgate translation. Biblical theology should be principal in their theological education. The New Testament is the first and the foremost statement of the faith of the Church; it and the Church are indissolubly linked, they are as one. The Bible is both the receptacle and the proclamation of the faith which the Church preaches. It has flow and dynamism. "The word of God is living and active. It is sharper than any two-edged sword, it penetrates even to dividing soul and spirit, joints and marrow, it judges the thoughts and attitudes of the heart" (Hebrews 4:12).

Every church should have copies of the Bible in the pews all the time, with people repeatedly being invited and encouraged to read them. However, in the sharpest contrast to Anglican churches and nonconformist chapels, I have yet to come across a Catholic church which has copies of the Bible put there for people to read. I have gone into church after church and found none there at all. A great lot can be, and should be, read into that. It tells us that the Catholic Church, and doubtless the Orthodox churches, still have not learnt from the churches of the Reformation. Our churches should be places of reflection and meditation as well as where a priest says Mass. Our churches shouldn't be priest-orientated; they should be people-orientated. They should be the place where people gather. They should be where the Christian faith isn't just preached but also shared through reading and discussion. There should be a monthly, maybe in Advent and Lent a weekly, Bible reading session. Every Christian household should be encouraged to keep a copy of the Bible.

What's more, every youngster at their confirmation could be given an edited version containing just the most pertinent writings in the Bible, with a space for a handwritten personalized dedication to him or her. The Old and New Testaments make up a magnificent narrative; they contain the really great stories, hymns and prayers which are part and parcel of salvation history and our Christian culture; but they also contain a large amount of material which need not be read, not least because it is very repetitious and even turgid. This edited Bible need not contain everything. Not at all. I would suggest just the key sections of Genesis, Exodus and Deuteronomy, the story of Ruth, an edited Job, the story of David, no more than a dozen or so psalms, which are prayers beyond price, just the section of Kings that deals with David, a little of Isaiah and selections from Amos. That is enough from the Old Testament. As for the New Testament I would suggest a compilation of the four gospels into one story without any repetition of material with sources being indicated, a little of the Acts, careful selections from the letters to the Romans, the Galatians, the Corinthians, the Philippians, Ephesians and the Colossians and both one and two of the letters of John. No one in this day and age wants a book of 1,300 pages, close print, to carry about, and anyone wanting more will know where to find it. It's better something rather than nothing is read. I am aware that this proposal will create shudders stretching to the ends of the earth, but if one thinks about it, it is after all only an extension of how the Church organizes its presentation of the Bible to its people in the liturgy of the Mass. Nothing could be more selective and piecemeal than that. The Bible is the Word of God because it is the word of the people of God recounting salvation history. Getting that story across is what matters.

What I have proposed in this final chapter is what I believe to be some, just some, of the main and most urgent changes the Church must make if it is to take Jesus Christ and his gospel successfully to the people of the twenty-first century. I believe it has the Apostolic Church meeting in Jerusalem in the year 49 as its guide, example and inspiration, and that with the direction in sermons and encyclicals that Pope Francis is giving it, it is beginning to take the path to the renewal and the reform of itself that is needed. In every way the Church in doing this will meet with opposition, both from within the Curia and College of Cardinals, and from many members of the clergy and laity across the world. However, as Jesus promised, the Spirit of Truth will guide it. But for that certain things are necessary. First, it must be open to the Spirit if it is to walk with the Spirit. That means opening its mind to the reforms that are needed and getting on with doing them; and secondly it must have confidence and hope. God is with it.

> Have no fear for I am with you.
> I will bring your children from the east and I
>     will gather you all from the west.
> I will say to the north: Give them up, and to
>     the south: Do not hold them back.
> Bring my sons and daughters from afar.
> Bring them from the ends of the earth
> Bring everyone who is called by my name,
> all whom I have created, whom I have formed,
> all whom I have made for my glory. (Isaiah 43)

It is a nigh-on incredible statement that every single person has been created, each and every one of us, for God's glory. Every single person is important. God glorifies himself in us. God the Father, God the Son and God the Holy Spirit, is with us. God is with his Church, we need not fear.

Despite all the difficulties the Church is facing, if it changes itself where change is needed, with the same courage and insight that the apostles and elders showed at the Council of Jerusalem, it can then go out to take the Christian faith to all the nations in all cultures and circumstances with confidence and power.

> Do not fear for I am with you.
> Do not be dismayed for I am your God.
> I will strengthen you and help you.
> I will uphold you with my righteous right hand.
> Do not be afraid, it is I who helps you,
> says the Lord, your ransomer,
> the Holy One of Israel. (Isaiah 41:14)

# Bibliography

## Versions of the Bible

Ἡ Καινὴ Διαθήκη, second edition, 1958, The British and Foreign Bible Society.

Biblia Sacra Vulgata, Latin Vulgate Bible, optimized for Kindle.

The English and Original Parallel New Testament, Westcott Hort (1881), American Standard Version (1991).

The New English Bible, the delegates of the Oxford University Press, the syndics of the Cambridge University Press, New Testament 1961 and Old Testament 1970.

The Holy Bible, The New International Version, New York International Bible Society 1978.

Revised New Jerusalem Bible, New Testament and Psalms, Darton, Longman and Todd Ltd 2018, translated by Dom Henry Wansbrough OSB.

The New Testament, translated by Nicholas King, published by Kevin Mayhew 2004.

King James Revised Version, 1881.

## Other sources

Catechism of the Catholic Church (London: Geoffrey Chapman, 1995).

Brown, Raymond E., An Introduction to the New Testament, The Anchor Bible Reference Library (New York: Doubleday, 1997).

Cupitt, Don, The Sea of Faith (London: BBC, 1984).

Duffy, Eamon, *Saints and Sinners: A History of the Popes*, 3rd edn (London: Yale University Press).

Fredricksen, Paula, *Paul The Pagans' Apostle* (New Haven: Yale University Press, 2017).

Fredricksen, Paula, *When Christians were Jews* (New Haven: Yale University Press, 2018).

Lumby, J. Rawson, *Acts of the Apostles*, Cambridge Greek Testament for Schools and Colleges (Cambridge: Cambridge University Press, 1904).

Scott Jr, J. Julius, Wheaton College Graduate School, *The Church's Progress to the Council of Jerusalem according to the Books of Acts, Bulletin for Biblical Research* 7 (1997) 204–25 (© 1997 Institute for Biblical Research).

Stourton, Edward, *In the Footsteps of Paul* (London: Hodder & Stoughton, 2005).

# Notes

[1]  Raymond E. Brown, *An Introduction to the New Testament*. The Anchor Bible Reference Library (New York: Doubleday, 1997), p. 306.

[2]  J. Rawson Lumby, *Acts of the Apostles, Cambridge Greek Testament for Schools and Colleges* (Cambridge: Cambridge University Press, 1904), p. 105.

[3]  *The Apostolic Fathers Part II S. Ignatius, S. Polycarp* by J. Lightfoot, Bishop of Durham, Vol. II, Sect. I, Macmillan and Co., London 1885, Letter to the Ephesians para 7, pp. 48f and para 18, pp. 74f.

[4]  Lumby, *Acts*, p. 83.

[5]  Lumby, *Acts*, p. 239.

[6]  Lumby, *Acts*, p. 93.

[7]  Lumby, *Acts*, p. 283.

[8]  One cannot but speculate whether the apostles, through their spokesman Peter, actually made the reference to the Holy Spirit, namely "We are witnesses to all this, and so is the holy spirit given by God to those who are obedient to him." We instinctively read it in a trinitarian way, indeed as my use of capitals indicates. But that was hardly the theology of the members of the Jewish Council. Peter was speaking to them as a first-century Jew to Jew. How did he mean it at such an early moment in his, and his fellow apostles', understanding of God? And how would they have understood it?

[9]  Brown, *Introduction*, p. 294.

[10]  See p. 250. "Imaginable" should be placed after "country".

[11]  Cf. the remark of Fr Scott Brodeur, Professor of Pauline Theology at the Gregorian University in Rome: "I hold the chair of Pauline theology; there is no chair of Petrine theology." Quoted in Edward Stourton, *In the Footsteps of Paul* (London: Hodder & Stoughton, 2005), p. 83.

[12]  Lumby, *Acts*, p. 224f..

[13]  Josephus, *Antiquities of the Jews* XIX, 7:3..

[14]  Don Cupitt, *The Sea of Faith* (London: BBC, 1984), p. 164.

[15]  Brown, *Introduction*, p. 304, fn. 66.

[16]  Lumby, *Acts*, p. 273.

[17]  King, *New Testament*, p. 307.

[18]  See Stourton, *In the Footsteps of St Paul*, p. 80.

[19]  St Augustine was very aware of this short psalm; and from verse 3 he very likely took the title of his book *The City of God*, a book which has exercised influence on Western Christianity, indeed on Western civilization, like few others.

[20]  Lumby, *Acts*, p. 281.

[21]  Brown, *Introduction*, p. 469 (and in other places in its chapter on Galatians) seeks to show that the "gospel" (his word) preached by the members of the faction to Paul's converts in Galatia "sounded plausible"; and on p. 470 he makes a scathing attack on Paul's preaching to his converts. However, his opinion on this issue is not just irreconcilable with the judgement which the Council in its letter to the churches of Antioch, Cilicia and Syria pronounced on the matter but also quite plainly contradicts it. In Acts 15:24 the Council describes what the faction preached as a "hollowing out and plundering of the gospel from the minds" of the Galatian Christians, and Paul, also in a canonical text, describes it as a "perversion of the gospel of Christ".

[22]  Lumby, *Acts*, p. 283.

[23]  Lumby, *Acts*, p. 280.

[24]  Human language to the extent that I know it can only use one or other of the pronouns he, she and it when speaking of God. "It" of course is non-sexist but, in my opinion, it is unacceptable. "He/she" is not suitable either here, so, with nowhere else to go, I am using just "he" because it is commonplace.

[25]  Cf. my "Sex, Death and Religion in Philip Pullman's Trilogy 'His Dark Materials' A Critique", available on Kindle.

[26]  By reason of its understanding of divine revelation Islam has to be reactionary. It believes that God himself composed every word of the Qur'an and having that source it is unchangeable and infallible in what it teaches. In reality, however, in very many aspects, in particular its moral teaching, it gives expression to the mentality and mores of the sixth- and seventh-century Arab tribes to which Mohammad belonged. For example its endorsement of polygamy and slavery. One need only read Surah 4 "Women" as an illustration. Unless it repudiates, for example, such practices as polygamy and slavery and accepts gender equality in all aspects, Islam in the person of its principal spiritual leadership in whichever countries or societies where it has political

control will always be incompatible with modern civilization. However, in countries where Islam does not have this degree of control, its members on the whole will adapt to their cultural surroundings, either ignoring or even defying their own local and private sharia courts.

[27] Andrew Brown, *Guardian*, 28 October 2017.

[28] *Guardian*, 28 October 2017.

[29] *The Tablet*, 21 October 2017.

[30] Andrew Brown, *Guardian*, 28 October 2017.

[31] *Catechism of the Catholic Church* 1268.

[32] *Catechism of the Catholic Church* 1216.

[33] Eamon Duffy, *Saints and Sinners: A History of the Popes*, 3rd edn (London: Yale University Press), p. 325.

[34] *Catechism of the Catholic Church* 1216, quoting Gregory of Nazianzus, *Oratio* 40, 3–4.

[35] Hugh Fearnley-Whittingstall, *Guardian*, 22 January 2018.

[36] Jason Berry, *Tablet*, 8 July 2017.